Track List
(Table of Contents)

Side A — **The Foundation**

Track List

Table of Contents (cont.)

Side B **The Takeover**

Knock The Hustle.

How to Save Your Job and Your Life from Corporate America.

ProdigalPen • Chicago, Illinois
www.prodigalpen.com

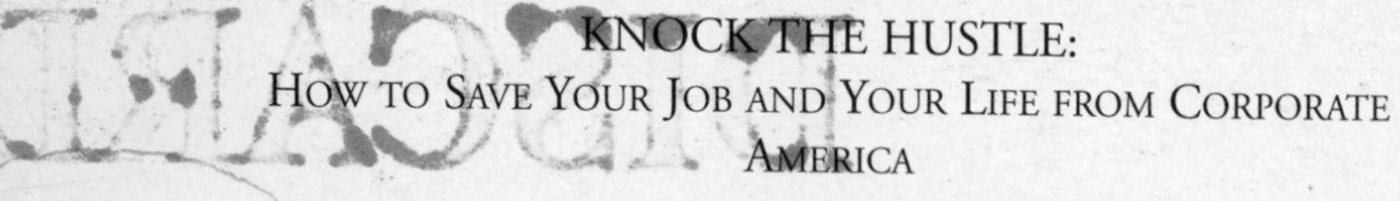

KNOCK THE HUSTLE:
How to Save Your Job and Your Life from Corporate America

PRODIGALPEN, INC.

ProdigalPen, Inc.
PO Box 236
3023 North Clark Street
Chicago, IL 60657
info@prodigalpen.com // info@knockthehustle.com

Cover Design: Hadji Williams
Executive Producer (Editor): Hadji Williams
Editors: "SG" and "Big Momma"
Typesetting/Proofing: Janice Phelps & Joan Phelps (www.janicephelps.com)

ISBN-10: 1-932523-00-6
ISBN-13: 978-1-932523-00-3

First Edition.

For what shall it profit a man, if he shall gain
the whole world, and lose his own soul?

—St. Mark 8:36

The Streets to The Suites...
(A Dedication)

To my Lord and Savior Jesus Christ
for keeping me on Your path
and out the dirt and grime
that swallows up so many.

To my parents
and my gramma,
who sacrificed to make
my life easier than theirs.

To my brothers, sisters, nieces, and nephews
and every Black child in America:
We are not what they say we are—
It's all part of The Hustle. Knock it.

To The Streets:
For showing me the good,
the bad, and the ugly.
And for teaching me
that those who win
are those who don't play.

To anyone who has ever
pimped, hoed, hustled, sweated,
or drowned in elbow grease for a living:
You are more than bricks in the wall.
The wall was built to brick you in and keep you under.
May you rise up and break free.

Side A

The Foundation

Play this book as frequently as possible.
Then, as it becomes easier for you,
play it once a day or as needed.

HUSTLE *(huh-sél) n.* 1. Any job or endeavor driven by money and/or power. *v.* 1. To earn by any means necessary—legal, socially acceptable, or otherwise. 2. To work hard or apply extreme effort. (One must *hustle* in order to succeed.)

The Hustle *(the huh-sèl)* n. 1. The paradigm(s) and constructs of systemic oppression, suppression, and manipulation of the masses in order to enrich the few. 2. The Business World a/k/a Corporate America. 3. The Material World.

KNOCK THE HUSTLE *(philosophy)* 1. To put God, humanity, family, and self above business, money, or power. 2. To be truthful, honorable, humane, and just in all endeavors, even at the expense of profit. (v) 1. To get out from under. 2. To break free from The Hustle.

Mic Check: One two, one two . . .

(The Introduction)

You're about to witness something
you've never witnessed before...
—Slick Rick

Old school, new school, even B-school need to know this: Corporate America is a hustle. Just as the drug game, the music game, and the political game are hustles, so too is the corporate world. Worldwide companies have become income-agnostics: They believe all money is good money and it's only wrong if it fails or you get caught. The only god most of 'em trust is on the dollar bill. The Dow Jones is Christ and capitalism is its Holy Spirit. Everything and everyone is a potential commodity and a means to making ends. And The Hustle's core principle: *The world's a zero-sum game—so before you get yours, I'll get mine.*

You can't knock The Hustle—at least, not while you're blind to it. It's like Spacey said back in *Usual Suspects*: "The greatest trick the devil ever pulled was convincing the world he didn't exist." That's how The Hustle gets most. Its first mission is to keep you in the dark. Why? Because you can't hit what you can't see.

But *Knock The Hustle* is going to help you see what you've been missing. *Knock The Hustle* combines the most powerful insights of the streets and the office suites with hiphop's noblest self and a mustard seed's worth of faith to create a one-of-a-kind movement that will change the business world and society at large for the better.

Knock The Hustle is all about businesses run right, businesses run wrong, and businesses run right into the ground. It's a collection of cautionary tales about employees and CEOs. Consumers versus Fortune 500 brands. Crooks and coworkers. Stupid people and smart leaders. Commodity versus Culture. Companies versus communities. Pimps and hustlers versus professionals. People versus profits. Street knowledge versus conventional wisdom. Common sense versus stale paradigms. Denial and complacency versus potential and change. *Knock The Hustle* is also about finding your way home long after you've lost your way.

The writing style of *Knock The Hustle* is Black ink meets Wall Street. It flows like a classic hiphop album: track lists, vivid imagery and lyrical flavor, hot quotables...and of course, there's absolutely no filler. It's a delicious gumbo of the practical, the biblical, plus straight-ahead, everyday-people speak guaranteed to enrich the mind, body and soul.

But most importantly, *Knock The Hustle* is 100% fact. Every word is true. Real companies and real case studies. Real people with real struggles. Real actions and real consequences. Real insights and real truths. And I'm sharing it all as it was, still is, and as it could be. (Only certain names have been changed.) *Knock The Hustle* is southern-girl thick, but reads easy, goes down smooth, and will stick to your ribs like an old soul record.

Knock The Hustle breaks down into 2 sides, like an LP or cassette tape. "Side A: The Foundation" focuses on workplace dynamics. Each chapter is packed with easy-to-follow strategies that will empower you to see thru corrupt bosses, coworkers, and clients. It'll help you dodge daily BS, think sharper, move smarter, and get more out of work than ever before. You'll also learn how to redefine your job and change the very soul of your company and how it functions for the better, regardless of your position on the flowchart.

"Side B: The Takeover" is about evolutionizing business and society on a macro level. (And by *evolutionize* I mean making fundamental positive change and laying the groundwork for real growth.) It'll change the way you understand marketing and branding, entrepreneurialism, consumers, consumption, culture, and mostly importantly, people. Side B will open eyes, minds, and hopefully more than a few hearts. It may even help open a few doors. (There are also a couple *bonus tracks* at the end; so don't stop until you hit the back cover.)

With all this said, let's turn the page and get free.

Waaaaake up!
—DJ Señor Love Daddy[1]

Killing Me Softly

Our growing softness,
our increasing lack of physical fitness,
is a menace to our security.
—John F. Kennedy

As much as we complain about our "tough" days and our "brutal" meetings and "vicious" clients, the truth is there is really no such thing as "hard work" in Corporate America. Think I'm wrong? Ask your IT crew if they want to join Special Ops and get shot at in some war-torn village on their next vacation. Ask the VP suffering from "hurried woman's syndrome" or some other narcissistic mainstream pseudo-malady if she'd rather work a construction site lugging 50-lb sacks of SAKRETE in 85-degree heat on her next day off. Ask the 30-something middle manager who keeps whining about no one "being on board" with her if she'd rather wait tables at $4.50 an hour plus tips. Ask your CEO who swears they're a bargain at six figures 'n' change to trade their power suit for a Wal-Mart greeter's vest at 9 bones an hour with suspect benefits.

Don't sleep: The toughest corporate gig around is sponge cake compared to sweeping floors or being a trash man. Or driving a cab. Or being a cop. Or driving trains like my pops did for 33 years. Shuffling papers in a cubicle for 20G a year is better than being in the projects or a trailer park. The most stressful job on Madison Ave is a thousand times easier than working in Haiti, Iraq, Mexico, or just surviving the 'hood like I did for 25 years. But Corporate America has us all convinced that our shirt-'n'-tie lives constitute hard work and real drama. They've got us sheltered, pampered, and shook. Consequently, we've gone soft. And like Mickey D's, the business world has softened us from the inside out.

To tha' tick-tock, ya' don't stop...

I did the math one day: The 40-hour workweek is a lie; nobody gets in at exactly 9, leaves at exactly 5. Most come in early, like 8 or 8:30 A.M. and don't head home 'til 6 or 7 P.M. The average corporate workweek is really closer to 50, more depending on your job and industry. For me, even with my ad copywriter's "Roll-in-near-10A.M.-'cuz-things-are-slow" days, 55-hour weeks were normal. Plus, I stacked more 70-hour weeks than Madonna and J-Lo have done bad movies. (And like most corporate types, I never made a lick of overtime.)

So if you break it down for the average office type, we're looking at 10-hour days, minimum. That's 10 hours a day of sitting. Sitting in meetings. Sitting on the phone. Sitting punching keyboards until the carpal tunnel sets in. Sitting and reading memos, emails, project briefs, and client files as your eyes cross. Sitting. Ten hours a day. Five days a week. Every week. Tack on a couple more hours of sitting on buses, sitting on trains, or sitting in traffic for your daily commute. Add the all-too-typical "working late/working weekends" and your butt cheeks are kissing seats for 60–70 hours each week, 52 weeks a year (minus holidays and vacations).

Now, let's go home...

And sit: Sit to eat dinner. Sit on the toilet. Sit 'n' watch TV. Sit with your PS2/X-Box. Sit on the Internet... Clock another 3 hours of glute-flattening for all of the above. Toss in a night's sleep—figure another 6 hours or so. Tally it all up and you're pushing 22 hours day of sitting down and lying down. Twenty-two hours—that's nearly 92% of your day. The other 2 hours? Well if it's Thursday or Friday, you're probably out sitting in a bar, a restaurant, or a movie theater just to break the monotony of sitting at work or at home. Otherwise, those hours vanish into the ether.

All that sitting and lying down... It just makes people soft. And once you get soft everything around you gets hard. The office vending machine gets hard. The clogged copier gets hard. The coffee kid screwing up your latte gets hard. Your $2500 company-leased desktop with the Intel processor choking on your MP3s and emails gets hard. Office politics gets hard. Your flimsy cube walls with the soft, lacquered desk gets hard. The office with the soft cream-coated halls and soft abstract art gets hard. The stale bagels and catered meeting food gets hard. Traffic gets hard. The fall TV line-up gets hard. Eventually the happy-hour scene gets hard. Slowly but surely, every little, soft, easy thing becomes hardcore drama.

Next thing you know, your mind's so soft that you're wasting meaningful words like "survivor" on songs and TV shows, or celebrities who've accomplished little more than marry well, divorce better and weigh under 180 lbs into their 40s. You start using "marathon" to describe any activity lasting longer than 30 minutes while "crucify" now equals negative criticism or bad PR. You also start believing that being a rebel or a revolutionary is about wearing thrift-store clothes, playing three chords, and acting too hip for the room.

Corporate America makes you so soft that "war" becomes a legit metaphor for everything besides actual wars. It makes you soft enough to apply "brave" to guests on Dr. Phil or folks who take fashion risks or raise their kids with just one nanny. Corporate America softens you to the point that you believe most anyone with dark skin has a violent streak and any neighborhood filled with dark-skinned people is ghetto or unsafe, while most any foreigner just might be a terrorist. Corporate America turns your vision pillow-soft.

So to toughen up, you seek strength and comfort—in purchases. You hit Wal-Mart instead of Nordstrom's. Target over Neiman Marcus. You buy Starbucks in the grocery store instead of at a Starbucks. It's two credit cards instead of four. You get cultured—by listening to world music and alternative bands. You pepper your speech with references from obscure writers and foreign flicks. You stuff your gut with fusion cuisine from tragically hip restaurants. You train for one of those *WALK/BIKE FOR THE TRAGEDY/DISEASE OF THE MONTH-ers*. You cop a Bally's membership to build some soft workout muscle hoping people softer than you will say, "Hey have you been working out?"

And to feel like even less of a cog in the machine, you periodically shoot at clay pigeons: Fast food, Reality TV, pop divas, conservatives, and gentrification—all while living in soft, conservative neighborhoods with nice (white) people while smoking, eating French fries, and sub-referencing your life away. You front like your job doesn't matter, knowing full well the main reason your timesheets look like a NASDAQ chart is because your job is the only thing that matters.

Corporate America makes people soft.

In fact, the only truly hard things in Corporate America are the buildings: Sun-blocking, shadow-casting, stoic, cold, hard buildings. They're usually leased to these hard-hearted LLCs, parent companies, multinationals, or whatever bit of corporate slang you're partial to. They're mostly all the same: androgynous, amorphous, gluttonous behemoths all doped-up on cash flow and quarterly projections. And they all eat the same meal: *daily human sacrifice.*

Corporations need bodies to perpetuate their own existence, coal for the furnace. So each day, the masses sacrifice a little more of their souls, a little more of their talents, a little more of their perspective, and a little more of their humanity. They're farm-raised on a steady diet of BS, brass rings, and carrots dangled on strings until their brains, personalities, and abilities are squeezed dry like used condiment packets. And if they behave themselves long enough, the volcano gods reward them with a plaque or a watch plus just enough money so they can sit down in retirement and grow softer until they lie down and die.

Unfortunately, by the time I realized this I had gone soft myself. By 17, I could identify a gun's caliber by the sound of the shot alone. Growing up, guns were everywhere. Just about everyone I knew under 30 who wasn't dead or in jail had *heat*: gangs, dealers, storeowners, kids, nervous neighbors. The cops didn't come around to protect and serve as much as they came to search and seize. We didn't have hospitals we had *clinics*. We had 5 liquor stores for every grocery store and at least one trash-filled vacant lot for every 3 houses or apartment buildings. Everyone was getting shot up, locked up, caught up, and if you were a girl, knocked up. Weed 'n' crack were (and still are) easier and cheaper to get than cigarettes or fresh milk. But again I'd become too soft to care. Why? Because Corporate America gave me a door.

I was 21 years old and they gave me my own door. Granted it was a small door to a just-cleaned-out janitor's closet-turned-office. But it was my door. It was a door to my little desk with my little beige Mac Classic and my little manila folders. It was a door I could slam. I was so broke at 21 I was still living at home with my folks; even at 21 I couldn't slam home doors without catching leather to the backside. (My parents were not soft.) But no matter. I could go to work, make 300 bucks a week and slam my own door whenever I felt like it.

Plus, I had a window: an 8-story view of Michigan Ave just off the Chicago River. When I got bored I could stare out my window and watch cops on horseback, movie crews filming stuff, parades, tourists and suburbanites, luxury cars stuck in traffic, sightseeing boats floating up and down the river, pretty corporate women strutting up and down the street, fancy storefronts with overpriced merchandise in the window displays... Man, I had a view.

At home, I had a view: Graffiti'd-up walls, streets Swiss-cheesed with potholes, broken liquor bottles, rolling papers, used condoms. Schools that resembled warehouses and functioned like temporary storage facilities. Mini-Tupacs, pseudo-Goodfellas and bad cops, junkies and alcoholics. Pushers and hustlers, apostolic churches and liquor stores, chicken 'n' fish and gyro shacks. Plus lots of hardworking black folks raising families in brick bungalows and aluminum-sided apartments trying to get by. But in Corporate America, even when the weather sucked, even when the hours sucked, even when the pay sucked, I still had my own door and my own view.

I'm telling ya', these walls are funny.
First you hate 'em, then you get used to 'em.
Enough time passes you get so you depend on 'em...
That's "institutionalized."
—Red, Shawshank Redemption[1]

Charmins, Potatoes, Tofu's, and Alternicans

I worked all over, from Chi to Manhattan to Cali; met folks from pretty much everywhere else. Now I'll be the first to admit that it's wrong to say "all" about any group—everyone's an individual and people are different, good and bad; but I will say this: Socially speaking, Corporate America can be a lot like high school—lots of little cliques and clubs, which a good three-quarters of the businessfolks I've met belong to. Near as I can tell (besides the geeks, ex-jocks, etc.), there are four major cliques:

Charmins.

White, squeezably soft, and often full of crap. Charmins will rock V-necks and khakis; wrap blouses, capri pants, chunky heels, cargo pants, and hip-huggers... Mini-skirts, collegiate sweats, and cheerleader-style shorts with their school/sorority on the butt... STEVE MADDEN, KENNETH COLE, and NINE WEST shoes... or whatever soulless uniform *Details/Cosmo/Elle* declares fashionable that year.

Charmins usually come from Big Ten schools or places where most of the minorities they knew were athletes. Many join frats, golf, play fantasy leagues, fawn over nondescript, anglofied hotties and throw keggers until age 30. They tend to have most every SNL skit-turned-movie on DVD.

In their world, the Beatles are God, Kurt Cobain is Jesus Christ and techno is the Holy Spirit. Eating ethnic cuisine makes them experts on ethnic people. (See: alpha males, frat boys, and Jimmy Kimmel.)

Charminas (female Charmins) join sororities, pull *Girls Gone Wild* stunts, and plot to become desperate housewives by 28. Many talk in raspy college-girl voices and rock ponytails pulled thru baseball caps well past 30. (See: Soccermoms, suburbanites, MILFs, etc.)

Charminas, along with their potato counterparts (see next group) have a uniformed walk: Shoulders slightly hunched, arms folded like some kind of yuppie force field that can only be breached by other Charminas. This walk often comes with a broomstick-up-the-butt posture, I'm-about-to-whine facial expressions, minimal awareness of immediate surroundings and extreme indifference to anyone not exactly like them.

Potatoes.

They're basically Charmins with melanin—if you peeled off their skin, they'd have no ethnic flavor at all. They often struggle with self-hate and detachment from their heritage and community. Potatoes go tanning, view dating within their race/ethnicity as interracial and miss the irony in both. They're often the lone minority in their group and insult other minorities in order to help maintain their "Charmin's mascot" status.

Tofu's.

Charmins and Potatoes whose flavor comes from other cultures' seasonings. They're culture vultures. They've been known to rock knit hats, ball caps, and brims cocked over one eye...hip-huggers/low-rider jeans with exposed thong straps, pricey bohemian pseudo-hippie gear...have tribal tattoos but zero interest in tribal people... Some have dreadlocks, cornrows, etc., and adopt ethnic vernacular and mannerisms. Others brag about their interracial sexcapades or their def poetry skills. Besides fueling gentrification, Tofu's along with Potatoes make up many companies' diversity initiatives. (Think: MTV's core audience and 99% of Hollywood.)

Alternicans.

In lieu of genuine individuality, Alternicans are just different for difference's sake. They isolate themselves from mainstreamers by wearing thrift-store gear, rehashing grunge/punk/industrial trends, and going out of their way to embrace all things artsy or alternative. (See: most punk/alt. underground types, etc.)

No matter which group I hung with, it was one skull-softening convo after another: Random SNL skit reenactments. Must See TV, David E. Kelley, and Larry David show recaps. *Sex and The City/Bridget Jones's Diary*-style relationship rants. Guys whining that their weekend was one big sausage-fest/swordfight. Endless *Entertainment Weekly* and *People* synopses. Grown, college-educated women referring to men as *boys*, *hotties*, and *hookups*. Random *Glamour* and *Marie Claire* surveys and dating tips. Debates over who invented the blues—The Rolling Stones, Led Zeppelin, Janis Joplin, or Eric Clapton. Constant Howard Stern worship. Random *Seinfeld*-isms. Debates over who's more beautiful: Tom Cruise, Brad Pitt or Colin Farrell? Rampant fawning over the latest *Playboy/Maxim/Fhm* "it" girl. People saying: "quirky," "happy camper," "zeitgeist," "post-modern," "kitschy," "campy," and "cheesy" 15 times a day. And endless statements made in soft noncommittal inflections and followed by pauses...like they're questions even when, like, you know they're not? (*Know what I mean?*)

James Baldwin once said, "The American ideal, after all, is that everyone should be as much alike as possible." The Hustle leverages this truth to create constructs; not in the name of organization or efficiency or unity, but constructs in the name of control. The first step of control is division. Once you divide a person from all that gives them identity, independence, and community, they'll look to you for those things. And if you can front like you're a good substitute for those things, they'll happily control themselves for you. That's why these goofy cliques and mindsets exist in business and society—people have been hustled into believing they're necessary for acceptance and success.

Everywhere I worked people bought into theses and similar social circles hook, line, and sinker; and God help those who didn't. One minute they're smiling in your face, working with you, partying with you, even having sex with you. Next thing you know, they're circling the wagons and putting you in your place. Sometimes it was subtle: an off-color remark, an insensitive underestimation or omission. Usually it was blunt—slurs, blatant discrimination, etc. But regardless of the method, the message was always clear: *You are not one of us.*

Still, I felt sorry for them. It seemed like they were always chasing something, buying something, or trying to maintain and protect some weird standard of humanity. But it didn't stop me from being a potato: I played the game—kept my eyes closed and rationalized everything I saw while they were open. I tweaked my speech, tailored my dress, flipped my attitude and even my ideals just to be down. I did everything I could to buy into it, to fit in, to accept and be accepted. Why? Because like every human being, I wanted to be a part of something bigger than myself. Also, the last thing I wanted was to lose out and go back home. (Again, work was play; home was work.)

> *It is a peculiar sensation, this double-consciousness,*
> *this sense of always looking at oneself through the eyes*
> *of others, of measuring one's soul by the tape of*
> *a world that looks on in amused contempt and pity.*
> *—W.E.B. Dubois*[2]

Don't Get High Off Your Own Supply

Generations of street pharmacists warned against it. O'Shea's "Dopeman" took the proclamation global. Chris Wallace revived it as a commandment. *Don't get high off your own supply.* Translation: don't believe the hype—especially when you're part of the hype machine. As a marketing insider, I knew better. And when you know better you should do better. But I didn't. I fell for the hype. We all did.

I gained 75 pounds in 8 years, mostly from sitting and scarfing fast food, candy, and soda—made by many of the clients I served. I knew it was all bags of fat wrapped in pretty pictures. I knew about the hormones and preservatives. I knew the truth. Still I ate. Most of my colleagues were suckers, too. We knew how the stuff was made. We knew it was all sugar-water, empty calories, and smoke 'n' mirrors. The ridiculous body images and ideals, the addictive slogans...We knew most of what we pushed was worthless. We knew it was mostly a bunch of cruel jokes and consumers were the unsuspecting punchlines. We knew it was all mental poison. Still, we bought into it just like the fiends we sold to.

Like Hollywood (or would they not), the marketing industry publicly prides itself on being liberal, inclusive, and open-minded risk-takers. Truth is, on the whole, we're anything but. When it comes to setting trends, spotting opportunities, etc., we're usually bringing up the rear like a thong. And that's mainly because the ad/marketing industry (like much of the corporate world) is still flooded with Charmins and such, who are followers by nature. So much of the work we create is about preying on the same anxieties, paranoia, desires, myths and prejudices that we ourselves have bought into.

Many of the images and messages you see in marketing are intentionally based on people's worst ideas of themselves and each other. It's no accident that ethnic minorities are marginalized to look and behave in the same commoditized ways in commercials, movies, and music. It's no accident that women, particularly women of color, come off as accessories or get pigeonholed into degrading constructs. It's no accident that certain products are pushed on certain communities but not others. (And believe me, it goes deeper than simple supply and demand.)

Marketers play these trips because they work. Clients like 'em. Consumers accept 'em. And most businessfolks were raised believing in them, too. In the end, we're all just people. And people buy what they trust. They trust what they're comfortable with, and they're comfortable with what they accept, and they accept what they're familiar with, and they're familiar with what they've been taught and fed repeatedly. Business does nothing to break this cycle—we just ride it until the wheels fall off; we profit from it until it stops being profitable, then we move onto the next thing.

But the funny part was working with all the college-educated, intellectual types who bought into it, too. At some point they'd make the same disclaimers about how their families raised them not to be prejudiced, homophobic, or misogynistic. They'd brag about how they, too were the outsider in whatever so-called narrow-minded town or suburb they proudly escaped from; yet their words and actions always revealed otherwise.

Still, and I hate to say it, I never expected any less from my male peers. As a guy, I know how we do—we're selfish and hardheaded about most social ills. Our catchall philosophy is "Stuff happens, walk it off." However, I always expected better from the women. I just assumed they'd be more open-minded, more aware. (Stereotypes, I guess.) But my female colleagues were the same, only slicker, more passive-aggressive with theirs, and quicker to deny all. They believed in and promoted just about every stereotype you can imagine. They bought into every diet craze and fashion trend. They cried because they too believed women should be size-3 blondes even though most of them weren't. They believed all men should be like the ones in the movies and commercials and magazines... Overall, we weren't just getting high, we were full-blown junkies.

So what was my pet addiction? *Shopping.* Soon as I got me some money I spent, I think mostly out of self-hate. Maybe I was giving back the money I felt I was making by ripping people off, I guess. The Bible says, "A fool and his money shall soon be parted." Once I hit 26, I had nothing but one-night stands with my paychecks, serial monogamy at best. (I swear somebody at Visa put a kid thru college off of me.)

Clothes were my big sin. As a kid it was JC Penny's and Sears. Everyday it was TOUGHSKINS and WRANGLERS plus WINNERS—Sears' Nike knockoffs. Nike had THE SWOOSH. Winners had THE SWOOSHIFIED ARROW. And throughout college it was Army surplus and bargain stores. But soon as I could afford to I changed clothes.

I started off low-key: Akademiks, Triple 5 Soul, FUBU, and a nice shiny pair of the ever-ubiquitous Timbs at work. Then after 5 and weekends I was outta control: Mitchell & Ness throwbacks. Sean John. Rocawear. Iceberg. Silk. Linens. Suede...I probably could've bought a car with all the money I wasted on clothes. And if it wasn't clothes, it was trendy clubs and restaurants. Or $18 CDs and high-tech gadgets...anything to ignore my own ever-increasing softness.

The Hustle teaches us to measure ourselves by money and possessions. So we shop to self-medicate. We shop to elevate. We consume to validate. We've been raised (especially as blacks) not to feel whole unless we have (or front like we have) a lot of stuff. And like a sucker, I bought into it. Ah, a fool and his money...

Don't believe the hype.
—Harry Allen, media assassin[3]

By my 12th year in the league I was completely twisted. I had been in the rat race so long I thought I'd contracted SARS or something. I didn't know where I was, had no idea how I got there, and I'd forgotten what folks where I'm from were still going through. I was starting to get sick of watching folks around me get reduced to drones and reflections of their possessions. But my bosses didn't care because I was good and always produced. And in the end, that's all business truly cares about—work. Produce for us. Make money for us.

I knew there had to be a better way than this. I had to re-examine things: myself, business, society, everything. By then it was 2003, and I was 31—a little too late for a *Logan's Run* but still young enough to *Shawshank* my way out.

I have seen the writing on the wall...
—Pink Floyd[4]

(You Can't) Knock The Hustle

A realist is always hated in a society of sanctimonious hustlers, which is what America is.
—Gore Vidal

My hustle of choice: the advertising and marketing industry. Been in it for almost 15 years. Now the best way to explain marketing is this: Hold up your hand, either one: Go 'head, get it up—I'll wait... Now think of your hand as the marketplace. Look at your fingers—they're products within the marketplace; or better yet, consider them as competing products within the same category (i.e., cars, airlines, restaurants, etc.) Now answer these questions: Which finger do you use to point? Which finger do you use to flip someone off? Without thinking, I bet you said the index finger and the middle finger, respectively. Why? Because those are the tasks we've all been conditioned to identify those fingers with. Whether we like those fingers or not is secondary. What matters most is that those fingers have a purpose, an identity, aka a brand. And that folks, is marketing.

On an execution level, marketing is like baseball—even topnotch all-stars only hit a little over .350. For every successful catchphrase-inducing, sales-spiking marketing campaign, 20 fail, while another 5 or 6 more not only fail but also get someone fired. For every successful product or brand, hundreds more fall off. Why? Because consumers are just people and sometimes people are just straight up flaky. Consequently, great marketing is like great hitting or great comedy—it's mostly timing. The rest is art, educated guesses, and whose guesses and art you're willing to ride with. Any CEO, researcher, or guru who claims otherwise is just hustling you. (And themselves.)

But the ad game's biggest enemy is corporate denial. Most advertising agencies just can't accept the fact that building brands and advertising isn't the same thing. Usually the best ROI (return on investment) isn't a print ad or a TV commercial. Sometimes it's street teams and sampling. Sometimes it's a sponsorship angle or a product placement in movies or videogames. Sometimes it's getting an emcee to name-check you. Sometimes it's an online promotion or a ring-tone or an IM campaign. Sometimes it's a mixture of all these things. Sometimes it's just good old fashioned word-of-mouth... But whatever the solution, ad agencies will admit this much: If it isn't advertising, we probably can't bill for it; and if we can't bill for it, it's competition, a threat to our bottom line and the client doesn't need to know about it. After all, they're called *advertising* agencies and not *branding* agencies for a reason. Speaking of which...

Marketing has changed. Target audiences are about as stable as an Israel-Palestine peace treaty. Consequently the traditionally billable and lucrative marketing mix of TV/Radio/Print with the occasional sponsorship has become less and less effective and the ad world knows it. That's why most ad agencies are doing all they can to get while the getting is still good in addition to buying up and boxing out competition wherever they can. But it won't last much longer. Seasons change and spring's right around the corner. (We'll discuss the future of marketing in "Tribes, Merchantnaries and Warlords.")

*It's worth noting that an earlier use of the term "branding"—
as in burning a symbol of a rancher's identity into the
hide of cattle—is the forbearer of the logo.*[1]

Frozen Frogs & Cooked Books

The first time I caught a glimpse of The Hustle was probably back in '96. It was just a glitch, but that's how it always starts. (Any hustle worth running is worth disguising.) Anyway, my firm had a client—the big aquarium in

Chicago. They had a new exhibit—exotic frogs from all over the world. Our mission was to get butts thru the door even though the exhibit was debuting in the dead of winter. As a pro bono account, the client never spent much—I think they had less than $50G for this deal—peanuts by industry standards. But they were open to creative uses of their dough, so we eagerly took the job.

My partner and I had an idea: *Frogs On The Block.* It was similar to Chicago's popular "Cows on Parade" from a while back. Our deal was to plant ice sculptures of these crazy frogs on random street corners with some "You're-just-a-hop-skip-and-a-jump-away" messaging. It was focused, cheaper than an ad and would've gotten tons of free PR. In short, major bang for the buck.

Stupid us.

We take our idea to our boss who says, "Nice idea but we can't make any money on it." We look at him all confused. That's when he proceeds to spit game:

Basically, ad agencies and marketing firms are glorified salesmen and middlemen—they get paid mainly off of markups and commissions. If you check industry pubs like *Adweek, Advertising Age, Brandweek,* etc., accounts are listed by annual "billings." Billings are how much a client spends on media each year. When an agency or firm takes on a client, they usually agree to do creative (i.e., create TV commercials, print ads, radio, etc.), handle media placement, do consumer research, etc. For doing so, agencies mark everything up, especially the media placement—usually by about 17.65%, give or take. Why 17.65? Dunno. My guess is it's the biggest number agencies think they can get away with before anyone starts asking to see the books. Actually, it's been that way since the early 1900s when the great J. Walter Thompson was selling ad space in newspapers and designing the ads for clients as a freebie. Now, if my history is correct, Thompson took a 15% cut for his troubles. Over the years, somebody threw in another 2.65% or so to cover God-knows-what. I say God-knows-what because I'd like to think that creative, research, account services, etc., is worth a little more than 2.65 cents on a dollar. Anyway...

Say Client X wants Agency Y develop a TV spot. Well, once Client X settles on one of Agency Y's TV ideas, the agency bids everything out—hires the director/production company, does the casting, buys the airtime, etc. Along the way Client X is getting invoices and bills, all of which have been marked up: A 17% (or more) stick here, a 17% (or more) jab there... Before you know it, a $100,000 job (which probably only cost about 90K) tops out around 120K, 140K if the client ain't careful.

But whether the take is 17.65% or as high as 25% as I've heard over the years, it's still peanuts compared to how much some clients have actually grabbed ankles on for some jobs. And because so many people are marking stuff up along the way, it's almost impossible for the client to get a straight answer on actual cost from anyone. And since clients still can't write ads, build brands, etc., without us, they keep getting fleeced. (Nothin' like a good hustle.)

Now here's the funny part:

The one thing that ad agencies should actually bill clients for, the one thing that clients can't do themselves work a lick is creative—the ideas. The brilliant tagline. The award-winning commercial. The iconic logo and/or brand identity. But nope, agencies make enough money hustling markups that many would rather treat the creative product like cheese in a mousetrap. Creatives like myself come up with brand-building ideas—catchphrases that become part of the lexicon, pop culture changing moments, imagery that gives a faceless corporation a personality people can relate to... And for our troubles? We get an annual salary, maybe a little bit of change per day or per project as freelancers.

You see, creatives don't get a cut of the markups or a percentage of the sales or anything like that. We lose ownership of our work soon as our bosses see it. We sign contracts (even as freelancers) making our agency/firm the sole owners of the concepts and campaigns we develop, whether they use our work or not. The agency then signs agreements with its clients making them sole owners of all creative work developed during the relationship whether the client uses it or not. So the client really is getting its creative ideas for next to nothing. So why do things this way? Because it's a hustle; and in a hustle you're a hustler, an angle to be worked, or overhead to be used and tossed when the time comes.

Every client and ad agency has one thing in common: they're businesses. And businesses only understand one thing: *formulas.* And because every client is different, and every idea should vary by need, budget, target audience, etc., there's no formula for determining the true value of marketing ideas and creative concepts. I mean, how do you bill *JUST DO IT?* How do you bill *WHERE'S THE BEEF?* How do you bill *JARED, THE SUBWAY GUY?* In other words: How do you bill clients for tailor-made disposable intellectual property, which is what advertising and marketing is?

As a copywriter and brand consultant, I say it's simple: Like athletes and actors, creatives should be free agents and negotiate contracts for their services based on their track record, portfolio and potential, and let them get whatever the market bares. Specifically, a creative would get an upfront fee for time and energy spent on developing creative ideas plus some type of usage royalty, licensing fee, plus a cut of the client's sales over a specified time frame. Or better yet, since building a brand is literally about adding equity to a company, creatives who produce top work might earn stock options. After all, in most all cases, a company's image is just as important to its success as the product/services it actually provides.

But it'll never happen. Why? One: Because it's a fundamental paradigm shift, and unless they cause it, change scares the snot out of most businesspeople. Plus, most agencies are still so big and/or inefficient that they can't afford to do anything but maintain the status quo. Two: Just like every kid thinks he can rap, every brand manager, account exec, CEO, etc., thinks they can write a great tagline, a hot commercial or design a lasting logo.

When push comes to shove, many businesses believe the only reason they've hired an ad agency or a marketing firm is because they're too busy to do the creative and media buys themselves. And that's why many clients still treat marketing as overhead in their business plan. That's why when business goes bad the first thing to get cut is the ad budget. This is also why agencies treat creative work like door prizes and party favors. And that's why ad agencies and marketing firms run the hustle that they run.

Suckers.

Anyway, with the sculpture idea, the client could've just hired sculptors, told them what to carve, where to carve it, and been done. It would've been neat, quick, and effective. And our company wouldn't have made squat. Oh, we might've gotten a small creative fee, but that's about it. And of course, that was unacceptable. So like good little kids, we did our ads, our bosses sold the client on 'em, and we promptly out-spent the statue idea—by a lot. And the client paid us. (Ta-da!)

Whether it's a blue-chip brand with a multi-million dollar budget or a mom-'n'-pop shop with baby bucks, the marketing hustle's the same:

budgets. Get the budget up, spend the budget up, and then get the client to re-up the budget. The golden rule on budgets: Use it or lose it. (Ask any politician or CEO and they'll tell you the same.) It's hard to justify needing more later when you didn't spend all now. So if the client wants to go right send them left because left is more profitable for you. I saw it with almost every client almost everywhere I worked.

This thing is bigger than mean and you.
This is big business. This is the American way.
—Nino Brown[2]

Once again,marketers really can't guarantee much of anything. Maybe consumers will like my product, maybe they won't. Maybe they'll respond to an ad campaign, maybe they won't. Maybe they'll pay $10 for this movie and $20 for that CD, maybe not. But maybe don't pay salaries. Maybe doesn't land new accounts or get budgets approved. Banks don't do loans for maybe. Shareholders don't buy stock in maybe. I need guarantees. The only guarantees are budgets and BS. So, out comes The Hustle: Inflate the overhead. Wag the dog. Flex the formulas. Get those budgets as fat as possible. Right or wrong, it's consistent income and businessfolks love consistency. Sure, clients could revolt, but then who'd do their work? As it stands, most companies still don't know how to market what they make and they know it. But more importantly, *we* know it.

Still, most marketers work hard to do right by clients. But the revenue must flow in order to keep The Beast fed. So at some point the artificial markups and blown budgets come. And as they come, the markups get passed on to the client who then passes them on to you, the consumer. Now if everything works out and the consumer bites (and buys), then everyone's coffee gets cream. But if it doesn't, if sales slump and we all just take the L while our accountants, comptrollers, and CFOs duke it out with the taxmen and shareholders. Meanwhile, it's back to the drawing board.

I know half my advertising budget is wasted
every year, I just don't know which half.
—William Wrigley, Sr.[3]

Game Recognize Game

Ever seen one of those $100 million blockbusters and thought, "Where'd the money go?" Well it went to The Hustle: Producers skim off the top. Studios deal from the bottom of the deck. Everyone in-between overcharges for this; overpays friends for that. Pre-sell the foreign plus rentals and syndication rights. Then hype it all up to sucker the masses. Next thing you know, it's $9.50 per tix, $4 per bottled tap water, and $6 for candy and popcorn to watch a gassed-up B-movie. It's all a balancing act and Hollywood's been spinning plates ever since vaudeville. Their main goal is to get paid, quality flick or not. (Laugh at those B.O. bombs and wack sequels all you want but know this: Every high-level hustler involved usually gets paid long before those ships sink.)

The record biz loves budgets, too. The Warner Bros., IDJ-Universal's, EMI's, Interscope's, PolyGram's, Virgin's, and Sony-BMG's of the world lock down the distribution, retail, radio stations, and video channels ensuring their status as the gatekeepers every artist must go thru in order to shine. Next, they leverage their power in order to stick artists with pimp/ho record deals that force them to re-up, recoup, and reimburse everything before they see a nickel. After the budget gets bled dry, consumers have to grab ankles on $18 CDs that might've cost $4 per unit. The artists goes platinum but only gets around $.80, maybe $2 if they write their own songs, and that's before taxes and expenses, while the label and distributor (usually the same company) and retailer get fat off the rest.

But you know who the true OG hustlers are? *Governments:* Monarchies. Dictatorships. Democracies. Communist regimes. Regardless of country or era, at some point they all hustle. In the West, the ruling classes and politicians wrote the book on hustling. Just look at the local, state, and federal budgets and the election processes. Ask yourselves why the deck stays stacked against the little guy generation after generation. Ask yourselves why the same groups keep benefiting. Ask yourself why, despite all the outrage and reforms, the corruption continues.

Newsflash: Despite the McCain-Feingold Bill, campaign finance reform married "Never-gon'-happen" and it's 'til death do they part. Big businesses and rich folks will always have more clout than regular voters. Kin, cronies, and insiders will keep snagging the cush jobs, fat contracts, pork projects, and preferred treatment while the masses will go on ignored and reaping the results of stupid, mismanaged government projects that will eventually need to be scrapped or overhauled then refunded by taxpayer loot and re-implemented all over again. It's all 100% USDA Grade-A-Certified Hustle.

The Hustle is soylent green—it's made of people. This is why nobody trusts anyone anymore. Most everyone's scheming and most everyone else knows it. Some hustles are legal and ethical, others aren't. When it comes to endeavors for income, I've done everything from selling jewelry to cleaning toilets... Worked fast-food in bars, about 13 years in corporate, plus a few unmentionables on the side. And make no mistake: all that ever separated one hustle from the next was semantics and the slippery slopes of rationalization and social acceptance. Regardless of the fancy titles, regardless of the industry, a hustle is a hustle is a hustle. And every hustle is, on one level or another, all about getting paid.

(But again, The Hustle is made of people and people can change, if they want to.)

My father always told me that all
businessmen were sons of bitches,
but I never believed it till now.
—John F. Kennedy[4]

Corporate America:
Ground Zero of The Hustle

It's like a jungle sometimes it makes me wonder
how I keep from going under.
—Melle Mel

Part of knocking the hustle is knowing your environment. My mom called it street smarts—made sure all her kids and grandkids had it. We learned the potholes: Pushers. Bullies. Gangs. Bad cops. Fatmouths... We learned the good book, plus the good neighbors and bad ones. We learned to handle just about any situation. "Book smarts can get you a job," she once said, "but street smarts can save your life."

Knowing my environment was the difference between beef and peace, jail and not, and on a couple occasions, life and death. If you don't learn who's who and what's what, sooner or later you'll have problems. Business is no different.

Where I'm from...

Chi-town. Before my "Have-torch-will-travel" act, I spent 10 years on Chicago's then-C.I.V.L. (Cicero Insane Vice Lords) infested Westside, plus another 15 on the Southside (aka Folksville). Overall, we're talking struggling black neighborhoods (an annoying redundancy for many): Currency exchanges and corner stores that overcharged and underserved, foreign-owned gas stations, vacant lots, liquor stores sandwiched between ragged

Baptist and apostolic churches every couple blocks. And of course, drugs. On the Southside I lived near Gage Park, just a puff and a snort from what was once known as "Crack Alley." If you wanted crack, straight 'caine, dro', heroin, 8-balls, or just cheap weed with the occasional sticks 'n' seeds, my section was the place to shop. Also, there were no black-owned businesses to speak of—minus the occasional Harold's Chicken, J&J Fish, carwash, or lounge. (Even today, non-blacks own most of the businesses in black communities.)

But again, despite the dysfunction, my neighborhoods had lots of good people trying to make better lives for themselves. But being good people doesn't always bring jobs, good schools, or opportunities, so out comes The Hustle. For many, The Hustle meant hoop dreams, spitting 16s, or some other scheme. Most chose to grind it out blue-collar style and praying our weekly investment in lottery tickets would pay off.

I didn't have a car, which meant taking the green limousine or the Redline train—it was one big third-rail caravan: On one car you had kids selling candy for their "basketball team." The next car had self-styled preachers and beggars working the "God-loves-you-gimme-a-dollar" angle. Other cars had deaf mutes selling knickknacks and bric-a-brac with Xeroxed sign-language guides... Emcees and Boys II Men-wannabes riffin' for demo money... Grifters running 3-card monty and shell games... Street comics trading punchlines for spare change... Pickpockets and snatch 'n' grab artists... But the best were the street vendors who went car-to-car with sacks of 'hood staples:

Gym socks (usually 6 pr. for $5). Cigarette lighters, Phillies and rolling papers for a buck or two. Incense (something like 10 sticks for a buck). Scented African oils, 25 ft. & 50 ft. phone chords (those were always popular, never knew why), bootleg movies, CDs, and porn tapes. And winter specials: $3 knit skullcaps and $5 scarf-'n'-gloves sets; during spring and summer it was $5 umbrellas, plus bootleg designer gear... Wal-Mart had nothing on the Redline.

My commute was also a constant reminder of our entrenched racial divide. The Redline bisects Chicago from 95th (south) all the way up to about Evanston (around 8000 north). Blacks and Hispanics mainly live on the south and west sides of Chicago from about 35th on. Save for a couple select areas, they're considered the bad and unsafe parts of town. Whites mainly live on the north side and east sides—from about Roosevelt up thru Morse or so, plus along the Lakefront—Old Town, Lincoln Park, Wrigleyville, etc. They're considered the good or safe spots. As the old joke goes, "If white folks go past Cermak (22nd/Chinatown) it's because there's a Sox game or they're students." (Comiskey Park was/U.S. Cellular Field is right off 35th, while U. of Chicago is in Hyde Park, just east of 55th/Garfield.) But the best part was that no matter which route I took, I always passed at least one CHA complex.

The Chicago Housing Authority, probably the worst collection of housing projects in America: Henry Horner Homes. Ida B. Wells. Stateway Gardens. Robert Taylor Homes. They were scattered all over town, but they all looked basically the same: Big, dehumanizing brick structures—not unlike prisons. Or factories. Or warehouses: Overcrowded. Overrun with crime, frustration, and despair. But above all else, they were filled with regular folks just trying to make it. It was a social experiment that fell quicker than a cheap facelift. (The local and federal powers that be ran those places in to the ground—usually at a profit.) I had a couple friends around there. Visiting them was usually depressing.

The worst part was that all of our projects were just a short cab or bus ride from the Sears Tower, the financial district, and world-class retailers and 5-star restaurants, not to mention clients and companies that I'd later worked for. In fact, Magnificent Mile—one of the richest areas per square foot in the whole country—was shouting distance from Cabrini Green, one of the worst projects in America—until they tore most of it down and shipped the people out. (Progress, I guess.) And that's how it goes down nationwide: poor folks and minorities isolated a hop and a skip from wealth, commerce, and to be blunt, white people. One planet, different worlds, just blocks apart.

But this projects/land-grab hustle is global. Every society warehouses and marginalizes its undesirables. Australians do it with the slums and reservations for their Aborigines. Rich Middle Easterners get over on the poor ones. New Zealanders get over on the Maoris. Indigenous Hawaiians are stuck in slums way-the-hell-away from the fancy beaches and hotels and tourists... Black Brazilians are stuck in favelas while the fair-skinned elites and tourists live it up on the beaches... Plus, you've got slums all throughout

India, Ireland, the UK, Indonesia, etc. Again: One planet, different worlds, just blocks apart.

But in the last few years, gentrification's set in. The projects are being torn down nationwide. The poor neighborhoods are being overhauled. The people—mostly blacks and Hispanics and poor immigrants—are being shipped off to suburbs like Harvey and Calumet City, while the well-healed offspring of the 1980s yuppies are swooping in to reclaim the cities. Basically, it's reversed white flight. (Apparently, the land's quite nice once you remove all the minorities and poor whites.) Gentrification, or socio-ethnic cleansing, as I call it, is ravaging minority communities worse than crack in the 1980s. Anyway...

Before I got in, I thought Corporate America was some sort of mecca. I started reading *Forbes* and *Fortune* in college—they always felt like glossy tour guides to fancy vacation spots I could only hope to visit someday. Every issue was packed with shiny skyscrapers and fat salaries... Blue-chip companies and economy-driving industries... Global brands that raised people's quality of life... Upwardly mobile, stylish folks who looked nothing like my neighbors... Artsy offices with open-air workspaces and plush carpeting... Free long-distance and Internet access... Cool bosses and hot secretaries... Happy hours just like the ones in those old *Ally McBeal* and *thirtysomething* reruns... And soon as you're hired, the Wizard of Biz magically transforms you into an upwardly mobile citizen with benefits and a purpose.

But after a while, I turned off that hazy Barbara Streisand halo lighting, blocked out the PR spin, and spit out the Kool-Aid. That's when I was able to see the good stuff—starting with drugs.

Chicago is one of the biggest illegal drug hubs in America. Coming up, I knew a dealer or two, mostly small-time. Chicago was home to infamous pushers like Flukey Stokes and Willie the Wimp. I'm talking about coffins made from Cadillacs—spiral-cut rims and all. Their funeral processions filled entire streets and made the evening news for days. They were treated like ghetto pharaohs sailing off into the afterlife. Still, I met more pushers and hypes on Madison Ave and Michigan Ave than I ever saw on any block in any 'hood.

At one company, I knew this kid who sold E from his cubicle: $25 a pop. He had clientele in every department on every floor. We all knew. The bosses right down to the mailroom guys knew. And nobody cared. He was a productive worker and basically a nice guy. He had pockets stretched with product every day. And why not? Who'd think of searching a white guy, especially one in an office building, for narcotics?

I also worked with a VP (one of many such execs I knew) who was a huge cokehead. He often came out of the restroom with blow residue on his upper lip. He was sort of a running punchline in the office. But he did his job, always performed. Plus he was well liked, so everyone let it slide. Still, he was as big a hype as any of the junkies from around the way.

At other companies, psychedelics were more common—people always seemed to be looking for something new. We'd regularly talk about weekenders with GHB. LSD. Speed. 'Shrooms. Something called "K"... And everyone had different connects. If my supplier was out or locked up, I could just email "Bob in accounting" and get with his source. It was casual like that. And if you had a 3-day weekend coming up, it was nothing to go "rolling" (do E for a couple days) and club-hop with friends. I even knew a couple of media execs that messed with peyote. (Don't ask.)

It was also common to see people loan out prescription meds: Prozac and Valium to ease stress. Vicodin and Percodin for weekend-warrior injuries. OxyContin to catch a nice buzz, often with a beer chaser. Some swapped Ritalin, others shared the occasional methadone just, because, well...because it's methadone. And happy hour has been nonstop hilarious ever since Viagra and Cialis. But the most popular illegal drug in the office: (surprise, surprise) *weed.*

Weed is the new beer. For every excuse most businessfolks once used to drink, nowadays, they're just as liable to blaze up. Helped land a new client? Puff-puff-pass. New guy on the job? Welcome aboard, wanna smoke? Helped somebody move or land a hot date? You might get a nickel bag out of it. Party on the weekend? Blunts for everyone. Boss giving you a hard time? Let's smoke it off on our cigarette break. Working late? Let's puff while we burn the midnight oil... Hallmark should be so opportunistic. But usually, the occasions for weed were (and are) even more innocuous.

I saw people smoke on lunch breaks, just 'cuz. Others smoked after work, just 'cuz. We'd go out for happy hour and blaze up in parking lots or behind a bar, just 'cuz. One-hitters and rolling papers were as common as Marlboros and cellphones. Speaking of one-hitters, most corporate folks I knew treated their one-hitters like pets or a favorite pair of jeans—they took care of 'em, kept 'em clean...some even had special carrying cases for theirs. Plus they had cool stories about how they got their hitter or some adventures they had with it. They came in all shapes, sizes, and colors. Some looked like cigarettes—those came out during lunch and coffee breaks. Others resembled pipes, kazoos, lanterns, etc.—those were for parties and nightlife. The diversity just proved that regardless of age, race, or class, weedheads are a creative lot—at least when it comes to getting high. (I might write a book about corporate folks and one-hitters someday... Working title: *It's the Joint.*)

Point is, if you think the corporate world's got PR issues now, just be glad the DEA and ATF haven't come knocking. Speaking of which:

The Memo.

Rewind to 1996: Jordan's still flying. Clinton's busy juggling Lewinsky and White Water. *Baywatch* and *Melrose Place* are top shows. Eric Rudolph bombs the Atlanta Olympics and the FBI responds by arresting Richard Jewel who's more Barney Fife than bin Laden. I'm still bumping some New Jack Swing at work, which I just couldn't let die. Plus I'm one of a handful of black folks at a large Chicago ad firm.

One afternoon I get an email from "Chris," one of our media planners. (Chris looks like a Details model, acts like Ashton Kutcher, and is easily the world's biggest Morris Day fan. He was also one of those really smart, hard-working types that you could see retiring rich by 55 or dropping from an ulcer by 39.):

Chris: "You in tomorrow?"

Me: "Yeah."

Chris: "Good. Come in early."

Me: "Why?"

Chris: "Just do it."

Tomorrow comes and I show up early and clueless. I walk to my desk only to find an official memo from the CEO. It states that as of today, the company is instituting random drug testing on all employees, absolutely no exceptions. Failure to comply would be grounds for immediate termination. As people file in, Starbucks and bagels in hand and begin checking their in-boxes, things... Start. Popping. Off:

"Oh my God, did you see this?! Is this real?" Up 'n' down the hallways the news flies. Every department. Every floor. *Random. Drug. Testing.* The empire was finally striking back. I was clean, so peeing in a cup didn't bother me one way or the other. But for the other 160 plus employees, most of whom were under 40 and known to "party," it was code red. The natives were shook.

After a couple hours Chris calls: "Happy April Fools, dude!" I checked my calendar. It was indeed April 1st; I'd totally forgot. A bogus memo. (Crazy white boys.) So I wiped the smirk off my face and walked the halls to see if anyone else had figured it out. Near as I could tell, none had. A few seemed skeptical, but not enough to challenge the memo, which was a pretty good fraud job I have to say. "Didn't they say something about this on *Dateline?*" Speculation reigned.

For the rest of that morning, bullets were being sweated up and down the flow chart. I overheard people talking about getting lawyers and suing over invasion of privacy. I saw people reading company rulebooks to see if random testing was mentioned in there. But me and Chris? We just kicked back and enjoyed the show. *Punk'd* would've been proud.

By early afternoon a second memo came out—from the real CEO. It stated that the first memo was a joke courtesy of an unknown source that had better stay unknown and silent if they knew what was good for them. There would be no random drug testing. The only other time I saw white folks so relieved was when *Friends* came back for its 10th season.

It was once said by a man who couldn't quit,
"Dopeman, please can I have anotha hit?"
—Ice Cube[1]

But without a doubt, the corporate world's legal drug of choice is booze. And I'm not talking the occasional Heineken or Chardonnay with lunch. I'm talking about liquid lunches that go for hours. Office parties with open bars and employees throwing 'em back until their faces turn red. Happy hours that run 'til dawn. Friday nights that run thru Sunday afternoon. I swear, some weeks the only thing missing was "I-love-you-Mom-send-beer-money" signage.

Like free high-speed Internet access and long-distance calls, alcohol is just another job perk. I'd say 3 out of every 5 nights that we worked past 7 somebody made a beer run; and it wasn't uncommon for that somebody to be a boss. (Short of pink slips, ice-cold 6-packs are great motivation.) And it wasn't always cheap stuff. It wasn't uncommon to pop bottles of good wine, whiskey, vodka, bourbon, rum, imported beers, even champagne on occasion. And whenever possible, we'd bill it to a client or wrote it off as expenses. As long as it didn't interfere with work, nobody cared.

So that was the deal at pretty much every company I was at from the early 1990s right thru 2005. Widespread drug use of all kinds. The only difference between work and home was color and class. The users and pushers at work were a little more educated and a lot whole lot whiter, therefore a whole lot more innocent. No matter were I worked, I spent my nights and weekends watching and dodging cops as they rolled thru snatching up black, brown, and occasionally poor whites for doing the exact same stuff my corporate brethren did almost day and night. The hypocrisy always broke my heart. Still does.

The funny thing was I didn't drink or do drugs until I got into the business world. Where I lived all I saw were the addicts, the prison records, the ruined lives, and the violence that came with narcotics. It was a big turn-off. But at work, all I saw was the fun, the camaraderie, the innocence and silliness of it all. No one ever got arrested. No one ever OD'd. And only the most extreme abusers ever got fired or hurt. There was no difference between cigarettes, hard drugs, and liquor—it was all part of the same buffet and you ate according to appetite. Now, of course, you make your own choices regardless of environment, but one thing was for sure: The business world's indifference and mainstream society's denial are at the core of America's current drug epidemic.

America racializes its social problems—we rank their importance/urgency according to who's helped or hurt by them the most. And overall, most every societal ill goes ignored until white America and/or the most powerful among us decides it's worth addressing. (That's where the phrase, "How could it happen here?!" which is often code for "We're white; this shouldn't happen to white people!" comes from. And by then, the problem's usually so out of hand that it's too late to fix.)

In fact, my gramma used to say, "It ain't an epidemic until white folks get it." She said white people don't see problems as problems until the repercussions hit their communities. I didn't get her at first. But after a decade-plus in business and in mainstream neighborhoods, gramma makes sense now more than ever. Just consider:

While they've been ravaging black communities for generations, obesity, failing schools, and a lack of health insurance didn't become epidemics until they hit Middle America. Teen violence wasn't an epidemic until Paducah, Columbine, et al. Drugs didn't reach epidemic proportions until suburbanites and heartlanders started OD'ing. And from Baby Jessica, Adam Walsh, Polly Klass, and Samantha Runnion to JonBenet Ramsey, Danielle Van Dam, Elizabeth Smart, Chandra Levy, and Laci Peterson to Dru Sjodin, Audrey Seiler, Brooke Wilberger, Lori Hacking, Jessica Lunsford, Jennifer "Runaway Bride" Wilbanks, Natalee Holloway and countless others, we're constantly reminded that missing women and children only matter when their skin is white. (After all, they're called "Megan's Law," the "Jessica Lunsford Act" and Amber Alerts versus "Jamal's Law" or "Tawanna Alerts" for a reason.)

Anyway, drugs weren't the only parallel between the 'hood and business.

A street kid gets arrested, gonna do some time.
He's out in 3 years, just to commit more crime.
A businessman is caught with 24 kilos—
He's out on bail and out of jail and that's the just way it goes.
—Melle Mel & Grandmaster Flash[2]

Welcome to Crooklyn

Airports warn you to keep your eyes on your luggage. Restaurants and nightclubs tell you to watch your personal belongings. But for my money, every corporate joint ought to post signs right in the lobby reading, "Not responsible for lost or stolen items," because there are thieves in the temple. And I'm not just talking about 401(k) raiders and corporate book-cookers; I'm talking about actual pickpockets, larcenists, burglars, grifters, and plain ol' crooks.

I've seen people get ripped off at every company I've ever worked. I'm talking about stolen cellphones, PDAs, jewelry, CDs, CD players, watches, purses, wallets, credit cards, payroll checks, software, laptops and computer equipment, loose change, petty cash, office supplies... And don't even think about leaving your food lying around—that's community property. But you name it, and as sure as I'm breathing, corporate crooks have stolen it, are currently stealing it, and will steal it again.

And what's worse is many of 'em are just stupid. They'll steal something from work then bring it back to work like it's theirs and be all shocked when they get caught. Or they'll steal stuff that's monogrammed, tailored or something they couldn't possibly afford on their own, which prompts anyone who sees them with it to think, "So who'd you steal that from?"

But the worst part of it all is there's no retribution. On the block when people steal, you find them and you beat them. If you catch them in the act, you shoot them. If you're nice you call the cops so they can shoot 'em...but not in the business world. Nope. Steal in Corporate America and you might catch a minimum-security bid—that's if they're really mad at you. Steal enough, and you can become a Jay Leno punchline. But touched? Un-uh. You can't go beating up execs; besides getting hemmed up for assault, you might get sued. Nope, when you get ripped off at the office, you pretty much have to take it.

When I was a teenager my pops said, "Son, the worst thing a man can be is a liar and a thief." He wasn't a businessman but he definitely knew business. But truthfully, I can't be mad. Complaining about greed and thievery in business is like complaining about herpes outbreaks on Spring Break. Anyway, if you're in business watch your stuff—things have a habit of walking away out there.

Scheming on taking what your brother has?
You little sucker—you talkin' all that jazz!
—Daddy-O & Wise[3]

Wanna Bet?

Like it or not, corporate gambling is as rampant as memos and suits. Nationwide, companies have office pools for everything: Fantasy Leagues. Boxing. The NFL. The Final Four. The NBA. BCS games. The Stanley Cup. The World Series. The Olympics. NASCAR. Horseracing. Elections. Award shows... Looking back, I can't remember a month where someone wasn't taking or placing bets on something.

And the best part? It's usually done out in the open. We had brackets and squares posted on office bulletin boards. We sent out reminder emails and interoffice memos. If you had time, you threw up a makeshift website and took bets online. And when the time came, you went around collecting cash/paying off the winner(s). It was mostly nickel-'n'-dime stuff—$5 or $10 bets here 'n' there among colleagues. But for more than a few I knew it became a nice sideline business. Let me explain:

Take an average company with let's say, 50–100 employees. Figure half go in at 5 or 10 bucks a pop on their alma mater's college hoops game—that's $200–$500, easy. (I've seen some March Madness pools pull thousands.) Now consider all those sporting events I mentioned earlier: multiple opportunities every month for 12 months with repeat customers betting a day or two's lunch money just for kicks.

Now figure some enterprising lads decide that coworkers aren't enough; so they start taking action from other companies. Maybe they just focus on companies where their friends work, or local companies within their industry. Now, we're talking hundreds, even thousands of people betting those $5 to $20 clips. Next, they throw up a website with passwords and an out-of-state ISP to keep the law off their tails... Next thing you know, you're pulling thousands of dollars per event, easy. Shave 10% or 15% off the top for your troubles and watch out.

Now figure this is all real and it's going on in every big city across the country. Hundreds, make that thousands, of inconspicuous corporate folks *gambling*. Offshore casinos. Online and over-the-phone betting... And believe me, it's even more rampant on college campuses. (But hey, in the end, it's all just a couple extra bucks between friends, right?)

And like I said about the drugs and drinking, as long as it didn't interfere with company business, I had coworkers who were and still are full-blown bookies on company time. And since the higher-ups were often betting right along with us, they usually let it slide. But hey, whaddya expect when the world's biggest casino is in downtown Manhattan?

Don't sleep: Wall Street is one big "My-company's-better-than-yours" roll of the dice. Most stockbrokers are just puffed-up bookies. It's no coincidence some in the trading pits are called *runners*. And if you've ever been on the floor of the NYSE, the CBOT, or the NIKKEI, you've seen the pit bosses and security guards. You've seen the whales and the sharks gawking at the boards like they're slot machines or blackjack tables. You've seen the suckers and the little fish ready to slit their wrists because they just lost everything on a tip. It's all gambling. The only difference between The Strip and The Exchange is Wall Street handles more action and attracts uglier women. Oh yeah, Vegas might have better drugs and I do mean *might*.

Personally, I trust the faceless mob families in the gaming industry way more than I trust that book-cooking-backroom-deal-cutting Federal Reserve/SEC/FCC/FTC/FDA syndicate in DC. And long as the powers-that-be are running things the odds will never be in your favor, not without inside info. At least in Vegas, Atlantic City, etc., they tell you going in: The House always wins in the end.

The Numbers Racket

And how could I forget about the granddaddy of all gambling hustles: *lotteries*. The similarities between the lottery and old-school numbers runners and policy bankers always surprised me—that is, until I did some research:

From the 1900s until the early 1960s folks like Dutch Schultz, Newsboy Moriarty, Lucky Luciano, Casper Holstein, and other mob families made tens of millions annually from numbers racketeering. They bought off cops. Officials. *Everybody*. Even when Adam Clayton Powell, Jr. and the Feds went after 'em in the 1950s, they still couldn't stop it. So, just like with alcohol and prohibition, Uncle Sam got in on the action. Enter: *state lotteries*.

Invented around 1963, America's state lotteries currently make an estimated $40 billion a year (that we know of). Most states run numbers—make that hold drawings—2–3 times a day: Lotto. Super Lotto. Pick 3. Pick 4. PowerBall. MegaBucks... And recognize: Scratch 'n' Win's are just slot machines on paper. The rest is pure racketeering. Daily lottery tickets are just like the numbers only now your state is your bookie and you pay upfront. And if you think some of this loot isn't getting skimmed and funneled by God-knows-who for God-knows-what just like in the old days then you probably believe that it's a complete accident that players in our poorest and darkest communities seldom if ever win more than a few bucks or free tickets.

And besides easy money, marketing types like me are a big reason folks accept numbers-running as legit. We launch slick, feel-good ad campaigns. Endless PR-spin about how lottery revenues fund education and public works, which is obvious, based on the condition of our schools and streets. Plus, warmhearted profiles of select big winners... Let's face it: Most state lottery officials are just glorified pit bosses.

But with that said, do we view gambling as negative? For the most part: nope. Do the cops or the Feds ever conduct raids or stings in the business world? Rarely. Why? (1) Too much power. Remember: For the most part, Congress calls Corporate America when *they* need favors. Besides, how would you like to have the ATF or DEA busting down your cubicle every basketball season? (2) Money. Sometimes, sin is so profitable you just have to look the other way.

Ain't nuthin' but crooks in here,
gettin' mad money off the books this year...
—The Beatnuts, Big Pun, & Cuban Linx[4]

It's the first of tha month...

Say "welfare" and most envision minority women towing a bunch of babies and spending up food stamps. But truth be told, most welfare recipients are poor whites; in addition, since the 1920s corporations have gotten more tax breaks than anyone. We pay farmers not to grow certain crops. We give guaranteed loans and bailouts to certain industries. Congress packs pork and set-asides into just about every bill it passes. And you could do a Million Workers' March with the beneficiaries of corporate and political nepotism alone.

Then there are those company loans: High-level executives borrow from their companies all the time—usually with ridiculously lax deadlines and wafer-thin interest rates. At best it's an elitist credit union; at worst, it's worker-subsidized welfare. And if it's not shiesty loans, it's suspect stock option packages, many of which are little more than off-the-books cake shoved through SEC loopholes. But of course these cookie jars are only open to your company's highest-level execs—the ones you only see on the business shows or in your company's annual report.

And don't sleep on petty cash and company credit cards. Petty cash gets abused regularly at larger companies. As for company credit cards: Here's a monthly credit line—give us the receipts and we'll foot the bill. They're no different from *WIC cards.* And they might as well call expense accounts by their real name: *Food stamps.*

Still, for all the parallels, folks in the projects would much rather sit in big ugly office buildings making 100K, or even 30K a year while most businessfolks wouldn't switch places with them for anything.

It was important to share all of this because once I saw the parallels between where I was from and where I was at, The Hustle got a whole lot easier to knock. And once you do the same, the game will get easier for you, too.

Don't get me wrong; America's a great place to live
just listen to the knowledge I give.
—KRS-One[5]

Pimps, Hustlers 'n' Hoes... Oh, my!

You are now about to witness
the strength of street knowledge.
—NWA

In 1952's *Black Skin, White Masks,* Frantz Fanon wrote about the masks people oftentimes wear in order to survive and excel. Most days, the business world is just one big costume party. This chapter is about 7 of the most common masks I saw (and wore).

The Pimp

Pimps done left the streets, climbed the ivory tower suites,
now they runnin' hoes in corporate track meets.[1]

Chicago has three great industries: Politics, Hustling, and Pimping. In the political arena, Chi-town's main mottos are still "Vote early, vote often" and "Jobs—that's what family's for." Chicago's got the best government money can buy. We'll discuss hustling and politics in a bit, but for now, let's talk *pimps.*

First off: Chicago didn't invent pimping. Black people didn't even invent pimping. From ancient China's concubine system to the Greek and Roman empires to Europe's medieval feudal system to the transatlantic slave trade to sharecropping, pimping has a storied past. America was practically built on pimping. We pimped the Native Americans right out of their land;

we pimped Chinese immigrants into building railroads. And of course we pimped blacks into slavery and then some. Today, America pimps immigrants into cheap labor on the home front while our multinationals pimp workers abroad. So if you ever see a street pimp and think, *Oh, how sad,* know that he's just carrying on our founding fathers' legacy.

Next: Pimping has little to do with sex or gender; and not as much to do with race as it used to. The business world has female as well as male pimps. Some pimps have MBAs; others barely finish high school. Some pimps got started with family connections while others came up the hard way. Some pimps are entrepreneurs; others are CEOs and execs. But all good pimps have one thing in common: *pimpnosis.* Pimpnosis is the street art of mind-games. And make no mistake: The business world is the major leagues of pimping—a sprawling maze of mind-games for power, profit, and position.

Growing up, pimps were as common as potholes and corner liquor-stores. Chicago birthed legends like Pimpin' Ken...Don Juan...Robert Maupin Beck (Iceberg Slim)... If these names sound foreign, just imagine Larry Flint or Hugh Hefner on a smaller, more urban scale and you'll get the idea. (In fact, Hef was actually born in Chicago and Playboy was of course based in Chi for decades.) Ignore the movies, and the hiphop bravado—they're mostly fables and frauds. The truth on pimps (and hustling for that matter) starts with this:

More than money, more than sex even, what people really want is power over another person.
—Gore Vidal[2]

The street pimp convinces you that the best thing you can do is make them happy. They convince you—usually thru words, sometimes actions, that their happiness is your happiness; and their success is your success. And before you know it, you'll do anything for your pimp. The Jedi mindtricks get so deep that when you screw up (i.e., come up short on money), you feel bad believing that your failure has hurt your pimp. And once your pimp sees that level of control in your eyes they know they've got you.

Corporate pimps run the same game. Your job isn't to achieve specific goals for the company. Your job isn't to win clients or complete your workload for the good of the company; your job is to make your pimp's life easier.

Your job is to make them look good in front of *their* boss, *their* clients, etc. Your biggest reward is having your pimp give you the ball so you can run with it. You become the workhorse while the pimp sits tall in the saddle cracking the whip. They go home at 5 or 6; you work 'til 10 P.M. Why? *Gotta keep your pimp happy*. Everything else is just window dressing and semantics.

The biggest mind-game pimps play is "To do for me is to do for us." Everything you do isn't for me, but for us. The pimp also reminds you that everyone except them is out to get you. It's "us against the world." In the workplace, the pimp talks about "being on board," "being a team player," or taking one for the team in order to get you to do what's in their best interest, not yours. Check this jewel from Dr. Carter G. Woodson—it's a nice bookend to Vidal's:

> When you control a man's thinking, you do not have to worry about his actions. You do not have to tell him to stand here or to go yonder, he will find his proper place and stay in it. You do not need to send him to the back door; he will go without being told. In fact, if there is no back door, he will cut one for his special benefit.[3]

Here's a fun example for all the makeover show fans out there:

By the time she's 4 years old the average black woman has had her hair straightened. It's a long, often painful process that can involve lye, perms, relaxer kits, hotcombs, etc. Since the late 1800s, black women across the world have straightened their hair—and these days, gone blonde—for the same reason many black men got Jheri curls, waves or shaved heads: black hair is ugly.

We've convinced people, women in particular, that black hair in its natural state is ugly while straight hair, particularly straight blonde hair, is the pinnacle of beauty. In fact, words like "nappy" and "kinky" are often code for "ugly" or "unkempt," while afros have become somewhat of a joke. As a result, black women voluntarily spend millions of dollars every year mimicking the Anglo hairstyles they've been force-fed as the standard of beauty their entire lives. And when the time comes, they pass those standards on to their daughters who see it reinforced by marketers, media and the larger society. (Now how's that for mind control and staying in your proper place?)

Anyway... How do you spot an office pimp? Well, here are some clues:

Corporate Pimp Rule #1: Every boss is not a pimp.

Good bosses are hard to find, but of course they are out there. But being a bad boss, even being a terrible boss still doesn't make you a pimp. There is nothing wrong with bosses trying to get the most out of their employees. Part of being in charge is delegating and making sure jobs get done. Too many employees play the "my boss is a jerk" angle to excuse being a bad employee. (Grow up and recognize that your boss is just that—your boss. If you want your boss to be your friend, go work for one of your friends.)

Now, one of the worst bosses I ever had was actually a pretty good pimp...

"Motown Philly"

As executive VP, Chief Creative Officer, Motown Philly ran our creative department. Mo' P wore designer suits everyday. He drove a Range Rover. He played golf. Had a big house in a nice Chicago suburb. Had a pretty wife and cute kids. His lunch and bar tabs were bigger than my salary. He flew across the country and around the world wining and dining clients. I looked up to him a lot. Mo' P was probably the first black male I personally knew who was living the so-called American dream—not as an athlete or an entertainer, but as a legit businessman. He was cool—for a pimp.

As I quickly learned, Philly's style was to kill you with common interests. If you liked baseball, he talked Cubs or Yankees. If you partied, he talked up the hottest nightspots and liquors. Whatever your special interest was, he convinced you he was connected to it. But it was all a front, cheese for the rat-race trap. He wanted you to like him just enough so that you'd work way too hard for him.

Now don't get me wrong; P wasn't a bad guy or even a mean guy. He was just a pimp. His main concern was keeping his crown, maintaining his position. He was a high-profile dude at a Fortune 500 company, maybe about three heart attacks from the CEO spot. Doing his job came second to protecting all of that.

P was East Coast—spitting image of the late-great Gregory Hines but always reminded me of Laurence Fishburne in *Deep Cover*. You just knew he started out good, but it was clear The Hustle had eaten him up over the years. He had a gang of talent back in the day and was once a hot industry commodity. But by the time I met him he was wearing golden handcuffs and was pimping to get paid. He had this huge poster on his wall of an old, old quote from one of the shop's founders. It went something like this:

> *"The businessman has gone soft. He has put on a shirt and tie, which has strangled his thinking. He has bought a house in the suburbs and with a boat in the driveway, which he is always careful not to rock."*

The simplicity of it: big, bold black type on a stark white background. You knew he spit it out as some raging act of defiance or in a moment of enlightenment, probably after a night of scotch or after one of those team-building retreats. First time I saw that quote was during my first interview with him. He was so proud of it. He said it reminded him and anyone who entered his office of everything he hated and refused to become. But after a while, the poster became an office-wide joke with him as its walking punchline.

After a year or so I realized that Philly was only nice when he thought you were helping him. When I was new and cheap he was cracking jokes, telling me about restaurants, small-talking me up and down in the hallway... But the older I got, the more money I wanted, the less cool he was with me. We talked less. He smiled less. His door was open less. A lot less. Near the end, I literally had to make appointments with his secretary just to talk to him even though our offices were only feet part. I'd been reduced to a number... Just another ho.

Come to think of it, he was pretty blatant about it. He'd periodically walk down the halls and stick his head into the younger folks' *officles* (offices smaller than cubicles) and say, "You makin' me any money today?"

"You makin' me any money today?" He always said it with a smile and a wink, but it was never a joke. Pimps are funny like that; they always coat the poison with honey. Your job is to produce for them. *Betta have my money.* And when Philly felt folks weren't producing or were in the way of him getting his, regardless of the validity of his suspicions, they were g-o-n-e. He'd either leave you hanging until you got frustrated enough to quit or he'd make it known to the HR sharks and other higher-ups that he wouldn't mind if you got clipped. Then he'd miraculously disappear just long enough for one of them to take you out. You see, for all of his juice, Philly wasn't much for direct confrontations. (Most pimps don't like to get their hands dirty—unless it's from counting old money.)

Corporate Pimp Rule #2: We don't love these hoes.

Corporate pimps view employees as hoes and a ho's job is to make money and do as they're told. Haven't seen your kids all week? The pimp doesn't care; you're working this weekend anyway. Haven't missed a day of work in months or years, even? Pimps don't care. No vacation for you, your pimp "needs you here." Want a raise? Pimp can't afford to give anyone raises but themselves. Pimps don't care about your personal life. They don't care about your career goals. All they care about is keeping you working and under their control.

Corporate Pimp Rule #3: No shame in a pimp's game.

Pimps have egos and need to show off. Street pimps flash their pimp hand—the quantity and quality of their hoes and their control over them. When they go out, they'll bring a couple into the club just for show. After all, what's the point of being king if you have to hide your crown?

Office pimps are no different. They want everyone to see their power; so they'll flex in meetings or thru CC'd emails and memos. They'll ask you to do tasks that aren't in your job description or your responsibility. But they'll couch it as doing them a favor or taking the initiative. They'll have you putting in extra hours, multitasking like there's no tomorrow, and making countless revisions for their benefit. The point is they want people to know that when they say "Jump," you'll ask, "How high?" (Sound familiar?)

(Remember Heidi Fleiss? A first-rate pimp. She got rich and famous pimping other women out to Hollywood's elite. She wrote a book. Did press junkets. Never apologized; never shed a tear. Zero shame in her game.)

Corporate Pimp Rule #4: Your pimp isn't always your boss.

Sometimes your pimp is just a coworker. You know the one: They always need your help. They always want you to cover for them. "Have my back on this and I'll have yours later," they'll say. But quiet as kept, they won't—unless it's in their best interest to do so. And once it's clear they can get you to put in work for them, they will. And before you know it, your coworker is pimping you.

Corporate Pimp Rule #5: Choose me.

Funny thing about pimps, they never really choose hoes. Pushers let their dope sell itself; pimps let prospective hoes do the same. Potential street hoes give off signals: Low self-esteem. Hunger for companionship. No concrete goals. No father figure. Material greed... Corporate hoes give off similar signals: Hunger for the spotlight. The need to impress. Craves companionship/role model. Low self-esteem. Material greed...

Pimps are good at reading signals. Once a pimp spots a problem, they step in and offer themselves as the solution. Again, the pimp may not be your boss but you'll treat them as if they are. You'd rather work for them than your actual boss. In short, you choose them.

Once the choice is made, you're put on the track. The track is where hoes earn money: Select streets, hotels, clubs, tourist spots, etc. (In Chicago, a certain stretch of Madison Ave near where I grew up was once a very popular track—prostitutes everywhere.) In business the track can be a salesperson's territory, the boardroom...any environment you're sent to make money for your pimp. (It's all a matter of perspective and recognition.)

Corporate Pimp Rule #6: Pimps will pimp until you fight back.

It's been said that power is taken, never given. When someone has power over you, they won't give it up without a fight. Pimps are no different. Usually, getting out from under is as simple as a polite conversation. A stern "Do it yourself " or, "Sorry, I'm too busy." Whatever nice way you want to use, fight back. Other times, getting free takes a little more...

"TJ"

First time I got pimped was back in 1995 when I got my first big ad agency gig in Chicago. It usually goes like this: Copywriters work with Art Directors to develop ad campaigns. Campaigns are multiple ads with a unified theme across disciplines (TV commercials, print ads, radio, billboards, Internet, sponsorships, etc.). Campaigns are presented to a creative director for input, revisions, etc., before going to account execs and to the client. "TJ" was my Creative Director; everything I did went thru him.

He was as straight as they came: starched-up buttoned-down shirts usually buttoned up to his Adam's apple, plus Dockers or straight-legged Lees. He'd throw on Keds, boat shoes, and golf shirts on Casual Fridays. He was tall, lanky, and pale with dark curly hair that wasn't too long but generally had a mind of its own. (Huggy Bear, he was not.) Plus, he thought SCTV was the greatest show ever. He was an industry vet, way older than me, with a big office and title. I was new to the game and saw him as a mentor as much as a boss.

TJ was slick, I never even saw him coming. He started off by reminding me of how young and inexperienced I was—first occasionally, then almost daily. He always offered to present my work for me—so I could learn "without screwing up," as he often put it. When assignments came, we worked on things together in order to "compare notes." Whenever I messed up, he'd sigh and say, "Man, if we can't figure this out, they'll get someone in here who can." And he always made it clear who "we" was.

For my first 4 months, TJ had me believing every day was my last. Whenever I went in his office to present work or review assignments, he'd show me portfolios and resumés of candidates to replace me. "Man, these kids are really good. Too bad we don't have any openings—*yet.*" He had me busting butt—working 'til 10 P.M., coming in early, working thru lunch... And whenever he called me into his office, he made me feel like it was to fire me. It was like Kevin Spacey in *Swimming with Sharks*, but with less yelling and cheaper clothes.

Several months later, the agency pitched a pharmaceutical account—about $40 million in billings that could grow to $100 million down the road. Serious cake was at stake. We were showing 5 different spec campaigns. (*Spec*: Speculative creative campaigns for promoting a client if awarded the account.) This time TJ wasn't my boss; it was a gang-bang—everyone worked on it independently and presented their own work directly to the head honchos, who then pitched the cream of the crop to the client. Everyone had to show 'n' prove on this one.

The entire department worked from sun to moon for weeks. They sifted thru all the work on Sunday, made their selects and flew out at the crack-of-dawn on Monday. It's been said that sleep is the cousin of death; and by Monday morning, I was a zombie. With my eyelids weighing a ton, I pass TJ in the hallway.

"Hey, man. S'up?"

"That's bull@#%!" He's fuming. At me.

"Huh—?" I'm all confused and nervous by now.

"That's bull@#%!" he rages "...that they picked your work over mine!"

It's 10 A.M. I have no idea if I even have a job from day to day, the copier looks like it might make for a good pillow if I catch it at the right angle and *this* is my morning greeting. After a few seconds of looking stupid I turn around and follow TJ into his office for an explanation.

"Man, I can't believe they picked your stuff. I mean, your stuff wasn't that good." And the whole time he's directing this heat at me like it's my fault. He then spends the next 10 minutes ranting about how none of his ideas were going to be presented and how "conservative" the client was and how "political" the process was. Blah, blah, blah... Typical creative whining; I knew the routine. Still, I left his office stunned.

My first thought was, *Yes! Of the five campaigns going to the client, two were mine.* But then I thought, *That @%&*! Just cursed me out! I oughta...* But instead...

Maybe he was having a bad day. I knew he had a sick relative and was also having girlfriend drama. Maybe he was just blowing off steam. Maybe he was having problems with his boss. (After all, crap does flow downhill.) So I checked with the secretaries, asked them if he was okay; if he had any personal drama. Nope. Next I combed the halls asking everyone who knew him what his deal was. No one knew.

I walked back in my hole in the wall to calm down. *This %$#@! Just cursed me out,* I was heated. Boss or no boss, you don't treat people like that. I've seen folks beaten for less. That was it. I marched down to his office...

"Hey TJ... About what you just said a few minutes ago—"

"Yeah, I'm sorry dude..." *Was this an apology? Nope. He was just in between clips:* "...but your work just wasn't that good. I mean you and I both know it wasn't on strategy. I don't know why they'd pick stuff like that."

Okay that's the third time he's trashed me for no good reason—three times in the last 20 minutes. Now it's about to go down.

"Look TJ, I didn't have to run anything by you on this. If you have a problem with what they picked, tell them. Don't yell at me."

"Look yourself, Hadji. This is business. You need to have a tough skin—"

We had these computers, *MAC CLASSICS*—little beige and gray portable TV-looking things with keyboards. Slower than a sundial. (They actually made noise when they were "thinking.") Weighed maybe 10 lbs. TJ was working on his when I walked in. Thru our whole back 'n' forth I kept having flashes of smacking him upside the head with his.

"I don't care! There's way you talk to people and a way you don't. Don't ever talk to me like that again!" By now, I'm yelling and pointing at him like a hoodlum.

"Hey pal, you need to grow up!"

Pal? Grow up? From the look on his face and his tone of voice, he wasn't the least bit fazed. He thought he was talking to a child or something.

"Don't you ever f**kin' talk to me like that again!"

Now it's serious; I, the new guy, destined to be replaced any day now, am cursing at my boss. Loudly. Don't you ever f**kin' talk to me like that again!

His face flushes red, he butches up and yells: "Get out of my office!"

I take 3 steps back, which puts me inches outside his doorway. I look him dead in the face and shout, "Don't you ever f**kin' talk to me like that again!" Then I mean-mug him like *what?!* before casually walking away.

As I walked back to my office you could see all these heads sticking out of offices and from around corners trying to figure out what just happened. Half the faces looked confused; the rest seemed near mortified. Everyone heard me but I was too heated to care.

I sat back in my chair and stared at the phone. Any second now TJ, his boss, or someone from HR would be coming for my key-card and name-plate. I just knew I'd be on the corner with all my crap in a box by noon. I was so completely fired and I knew it. As I stared at the phone I could hear my mother telling me, *You know you can't talk to white folks like that and expect 'em to keep giving you a check!* Yep, I was sooo fired.

Actually I was kinda hoping TJ would call me back so I could—well...let's just say that I was still upset. But he didn't. In fact, he didn't do anything. No one did. My phone never rang. That's when I realized that I'd just fired my pimp.

Some pimps get you working out of love; others get you working out of fear. I never knew TJ well enough to like him. But he knew my fear: being broke. When TJ hired me, like many companies do, he underbid me. The job actually started at 25K to 26K, but he only offered 21K and claimed it was the company's final offer. "Dana," my headhunter at the time couldn't believe I took it.

"Never take a first offer; always negotiate!" She was right. Always negotiate. But I was just too broke to play poker, so I folded and took a bad deal.

After taxes, that 21K worked out to a little over $650 and change every two weeks or $325 a week or $65 a day for 12-hour workdays spent growing multimillion-dollar accounts with no overtime and not knowing if I had a job from day to day.

Still it was worth it. I hadn't worked in months and I was 21. Everyone my age was dead, locked up, hustling, or working minimum-wage gigs, usually to support a kid. I just didn't want to go out like that. My 21K seemed like a good start. I think TJ sensed some of that and used it against me. But after our little chat, we both knew I didn't care anymore.

Also, since all my work up to that point went thru him, I had no idea what anyone else thought of me. I just figured all his talk of replacing me came from on high. Turns out, most everyone from clients to the higher-ups was impressed with my work—almost from jump. (Go figure.)

We hardly spoke after that morning. I eventually got another creative director and TJ left the company a few months later. But it was all luv. Besides realizing that I was good at my job, I also realized that I wasn't going to let anyone—especially not someone in Dockers and Hushpuppies—push me around, even if it meant getting fired.

(By the way, cursing out your boss: bad idea.)

Garrett's Bluff

Shortly after my little run-in, one of my friends at a rival ad firm told me about "Garrett." Garrett was a young writer like myself; "Lori," his boss was this big old brunette (think: Camryn Manheim circa *The Practice*) and a top VP creative director.

Garrett worked non-stop—not out of fear, but out of like. He admired Lori's track record, wanted to learn from her and wanted her approval. She milked all of that to work him like a dog, jumping thru hoops whenever. He was clocking crazy hours just to impress but nothing ever seemed to be good enough. Then one day he found out she'd been taking his work and passing it off as her own. Garrett got heated. But rather than knuckle up he fought with his mouth.

He handed in his resignation—to Lori's boss. Dude went over her head to quit. Of course, Lori's boss promptly asked why he wanted out. Once he ran it all down, the skeletons tumbled out of Lori's closet like a clown-car. Turns out, Garrett wasn't the first to want out from under her. Lori had racked up bunches of complaints over the years. But she'd been profitable in the past, so the problems were overlooked. But for whatever reason, this time they underlooked and decided that Garrett was the last straw. Garrett stayed; Lori got fired.

(Remember: Pimps will pimp until you fight back. How you fight is up to you.)

Pimp Rule #7: Pimps can't run the point.

A point guard's job is to make everyone around them better. They know everyone's strengths and weaknesses, and they do what it takes to keep those weaknesses from hurting the team. A great boss is also a great point guard.

Your boss should always make you a better employee. Next to a fat paycheck, professional growth and acquiring new skills are the most valuable things a company can give you. You should always feel like you're growing and learning under your boss. If you don't, something's wrong. Maybe it's their fault. Maybe it's yours, so check the mirror first. (Remember Rule #1: Every boss is not a pimp.)

Why managers pimp:

While some make it to the top, most pimps never get past middle-management. Why? For starters most managers and supervisors are neurotic and paranoid as hell. They believe they're overlooked and underpaid. So they try to protect what little they have by pimping. It's a great way to control your enemies—specifically younger, hungrier (and sometimes smarter) workers who might be able to do your job for less someday. When folks don't get the raise or promotion they want, they might pimp to make up for it. (Again for some, pimping is a job perk.)

Big Pimpin'

Pimping isn't restricted to individuals. In fact, every archetype in this chapter has a collective counterpart. There are more than a few pimps on the Fortune 1000 list. Just study how companies behave and treat their employees and you'll be able to see who's who. My advice: Recognize the pimps in your industry ASAP. Otherwise if you don't, you'll end up as one of their hoes.

Pimpin' is death.
—Fillmore Slim, legendary San Francisco pimp

The Ho

Next up to bat: *Hoes,* or if you prefer the grammatically correct, whores. Note: *Ho* is singular form of whore while *hoe* is a garden tool. Grammatically speaking, the proper contraction of whore is "h-o"; plural and possessive forms further complicate this. So for simplicity's sake, we'll use ho for the singular and hoes for the plural. Now for the good stuff:

> A rich man meets a woman in an upscale nightclub. After some dancing, drinking, and a little charm he asks her, "Would you sleep with me for $100,000?" She sizes him up. "Well, maybe; let's relax and see where the night takes us." A few drinks later he offers, "So would you sleep with me for $100 instead?" She snaps, "What kinda woman d'you think I am?!" He observes, "Baby, we've already established what kind of woman you are—we're just negotiating price."

If you sell yourself, you're a ho. If you charge a high price, you're a high-priced ho. If you do it for crumbs, you're a dumb ho. Hoeing is the world's oldest profession with pimping holding down second place. Street whores sell their bodies. Corporate whores sell their souls, their talents, their integrity, and yes, even their bodies. (You'd be surprised how many folks—male and female—still use sex to succeed in business.) No matter how tight you spin it, a ho is a ho is a ho. But don't confuse a whore with a hard worker. The line between the two, while thinner than ever, is still pretty clear.

One of the biggest corporate concubines I can think of was actually the first major company I worked for. We were considered a "sweatshop" which means you bust your butt nonstop doing anything, for more or less, anyone, integrity be damned. If you had the money, we had the time.

For years we were the butts of tons of industry jokes. Our mocked acronym/motto was, *Bring Back Do Over* because that's what our clients always made us do; and again, as long as the checks cleared, *the client was always right.* We did what we were told, no matter what we were told. We got yelled at. Talked down to. Pushed around. And we always came back for more. Why? Because a good ho always sticks by their pimp. But we weren't alone. The business world is filled with companies that'll whore themselves out to the highest bidder.

In the midst of my own hoishness, another business truth became apparent: Just as many companies and businessfolks are hoes, *most clients are tricks.* They're tricks in the same way a man who visits a prostitute or a stripper is a trick. They go to be served how they want to be served. You're not human to them; you have no real value to them. You are simply a *thing*, a tool to be used. Your job is to shut up and give 'em what they want, like a good ho should. And in return, you reciprocate that callousness and ride with the program. Long as the checks clear, you do whatever they want, no matter how wrong or stupid it may be.

As a marketer, a businessman, or even as a lawyer or doctor, you want partnerships. You want to use your perspective and expertise to help people who respect what you bring to the table. The last thing you want is servitude and someone holding money over your head and acting like, *When I want your opinion, I'll give you one.* But unfortunately, that's how too many companies, especially those in the marketing, ad, and PR industries get down.

Business is about money and wherever there's money to be made, hoes are never far behind. The business world loves a ho. Hoes are predictable, easy to control, and easier to replace. Hoes are a commodity; no matter what you're offering, somewhere there's a ho who's good for it. Again, hoes are easy to control because they're greedy, shortsighted, insecure, or some combination thereof. As a pimp you just have to pull the right strings and you'll have 'em wrapped around your finger as long as you need 'em.

There's some hoes in this house...

The biggest pimps are in the business world; but without a doubt the biggest hoes in the world are in government. The first thing I learned when I began following politics is that "politician" is actually Latin for "Ho for sale." Capitol Hill might be the biggest whorehouse in the country. Now I'm not saying every politician is a ho, but I'm guessing that most every successful politician has a little ho in them; and most folks in Congress will hit their knees and grab ankles for enough votes. And if you listen closely, you'll hear them admit as much.

Just peep C-SPAN, ABC, FOX, and the rest for the sanitized sound bites and voter-friendly phrases. Watch their faces. Watch the alliances. Do your research. Once you sift thru the "bringing home the bacon/pork barrel spending" comments and the "concessions," "my constituents" and "special interests/lobbyists" euphemisms, you'll realize that it's all about some hoes making sure they don't go back to their pimps empty-handed. And the classic "politics makes strange bedfellows" bit is just white folks' way of saying, "there's some hoes in this house so check your neck and guard your grill."

The one thing a ho hates and will not tolerate is a weak pimp. Once a ho realizes a pimp can't check 'em, they'll walk all over them. And most politicians, knowing that they're hoes simply walk all over voters. Voters are lousy pimps. In fact, voters aren't pimps at all. Truth be told, voters are just tricks—we mindlessly pick from a menu of somebody else's hoes to see who we want to get screwed by. That's why politicians only listen to the real pimps: rich folks, businesses, the RNC and DNC powerbrokers and shot-callers, etc.

I got hoes (in different area codes...)

The saddest thing is hoes are people, too. Make no mistake: You can be a kind, wonderful, and loving person but still be a ho. You can be smart and articulate and hardworking. You can be supportive of others and a good human being but still be a Grade A 100% all-world *ho*. Most hoes I worked with over the years were perfectly nice, intelligent, and decent people. But they were still hoes.

In fact, America loves hoes so much that we broadcast our ho fairytales: *Pretty Woman. Barbie. Cinderella.* Great American ho tales, all. In fact, you can make a case that just about everyone on Reality TV from *The Bachelor/Bachelorette* and *Who Wants to Marry a Millionaire?* to *Fear Factor*, those makeover shows, etc., is whoring themselves out to one degree or another. And we've been feeding this stuff to women for years, rewarding this behavior, pamper them on talk shows and in the media, then we have the nerve to wonder why all of a sudden America is being overrun with neurotic, materialistic, scheming hoes.

The Turn Out

We all complain about work. But at some point, you choose to be complicit, compliant, or a full-on willing accomplice. At some point, every ho decides that as much as they hate being a ho, they hate not being a ho even more. At some point you embrace the bad parts of business and internalize 'em to the point that you can't imagine working any other way. We call this mindstate being "turned-out."

I've worked with hundreds of people over the years who clearly hated their jobs but they kept coming back over and over again because they just couldn't imagine doing anything else. The job sucked but they'd put their life on hold for it. Worked weekends, postponed vacations, blew off dates, you name it. And they'd talk about their job 24/7 like it was a cheating boyfriend they just couldn't leave or a drug habit they just couldn't shake. Some call 'em workaholics; I just say they've been turned-out.

In the end, being a ho is about low self-esteem and consistently making exceptionally bad choices regarding what's important and what's the best way to get it. Being a ho is about the selling the priceless and profiting off of vices. And there's nothing business loves more than a good bargain.

There's no business like "ho business"!
—Denis Hof, owner Nevada Bunny Ranch

The Hustler

On the street, a hustler is income agnostic. The hustler has no loyalty to what pays, only that it does. Drugs. Stealing. Gambling. Pimping. Odd jobs. Bootleg merchandise. Legal or otherwise, it's whatever works. And if/when one hustle fails, it's on to the next.

I think Chicago invented hustling, that "survive by any means" street-economics mentality. (We even had a women's pro basketball team in the 1970s called the Chicago Hustle.) Growing up, I knew a few hustlers, most were harmless neighborhood fixtures: One week it was phone cords and incense on the CTA, the next week it was bootleg music and nicklebags.

Similarly, the Corporate Hustler is a nomad. They'll hop job to job, company to company, industry to industry, whatever works. And they do so without any real loyalty to where they're going or where they've been. I had a friend who transferred from Chicago all the way out to her company's Japan office just to get a raise and pay some bills. It's all about the agenda and usually the agenda is money: Make X salary by Y age. Buy this; flip this into that... Meet the agenda.

So what's wrong with agendas or having goals? Nothing. But to a hustler, the agenda is king; and the agenda is always a selfish one. Hustlers are never out for the good of the company or the client or their co-workers. The Hustler works angles only for themselves. If it doesn't satisfy their agenda first and foremost, they're out. They'll quit. Switch departments. Pass the work onto someone else. Hustlers never see the big picture as it relates to the whole. Nobody wants a selfish colleague or boss. But selfishness is a hustler's greatest asset—it's a survival instinct.

On the come-up.

Somewhere between whore and professional, I hustled. I grew up around folks who pitched weed 'n' rock on the block and sold whatever else was sellable. I learned a lot about salesmanship from watching them. They sold dreams; I sold dreams. They sold solutions to people's problems; I did the same. They built identities, so did I. But while they were hustling on the streets, I was up in the suites serving fiends a different kind of dope: *Marketing.*

I chopped and bagged consumers into little demographics. Fed 'em 30- and 60- second samples of how good my product could make them feel. And once they got hooked, I reeled 'em in and took their money. And when they came back, I re-upped with more addictive dreams and cooked up more product. My friends had hundreds of customers, but my clientele was in the hundreds of thousands. Now, was the product I pushed dangerous? Sometimes. Did I corrupt people? More than a few. Did I have loyalty to anything other than money? After a while, no.

In the end, it's all hustling. It's all sugar water, dirty money, and serving dreams to fiends. It sucks. And what's worse is that it can't... won't...don't...stop. (Unless we want it to.)

The Divine Miss M

I met "Miss M" in the mid '90s. I call her that because that's exactly what she had on her office door: Miss M. She'd been in the business world since the 1960s, an era when people in the workplace addressed each by last name only. Whether boss or coworker, everyone's first name was Mister, Miss, Misses, and in some cases Madame. When she explained that to me, I thought it was crazy. But after thinking about it for a while, I decided it was actually kinda cool.

One reason people go soft in business is that the corporate world breeds a false sense of intimacy. In business we swap first names and nicknames like we really know each other, like we really care. Then those same people will call you by your first name while they're firing you or stealing clients and money from you. Truth is nobody really knows each other, not in business, nor in life. Sometimes it takes years to get to know someone well enough to consider them a true friend. M's crazy nameplate was a reminder that this is always business, never personal.

Miss M's agenda was simple: Don't get laid off. She started out as a secretary. In order to dodge cutbacks, she did what all hustlers do: made herself as valuable as possible. She didn't just do her job; she did all the jobs that no one else would do. She learned the advertising business mainly by watching everyone around her do their thing and reading everything they asked her to type or file. Then she looked for opportunities to exploit. Her goal was to become so valuable they couldn't afford to let her go. (Hustlers are scavengers.)

By the time I met her, she was in her late-50s and had clawed her way up to a VP slot. She ran her own department—I guess you'd call it Billing & Account Receivables. She handled invoices, made sure clients were properly billed, stuff like that. She also negotiated fees and contracts with vendors (i.e., freelancers, commercial directors, photographers, actors, etc.) But like I said, hustlers are scavengers. So she did what every good scavenger does—find more ways to eat.

Now the one thing every company worries about, especially nowadays, is getting sued. In marketing the only thing worse than getting yourself sued is getting a client sued. Sued for making false claims. Sued for using unlicensed music or unauthorized celebrity likenesses. Sued for marketing adult products (cigarettes/liquor) to minors. Sued for breach of contract or breaking confidentiality agreements. But my favorites are the "Contributing-to-the-delinquency-of-a-minor" suits. Besides aping movies, videogames, wrestling, and old MTV staples, kids copy what they see in commercials. (Remember that Reebok "Pump" commercial with the bungee jumpers? Reebok had to yank it because some kid actually tried it at home.)

So to protect our clients (and ourselves) out come the lawyers. Corporate lawyers are hilarious. They live to beat lawsuits. They know they've got more money than you and more time to sit in court than you do. More manpower than you. More connections than you, no matter who you are... They're built for this.

Anyway, we were in Chicago; our lawyer was in our home office in New York. It was simple: If you had a legal question, call the lawyer. Got a great idea for a commercial, but not sure if it's misleading, call the lawyer. When in doubt, call the lawyer. Now if you used common sense, you hardly ever had to call him. But this is Corporate America—land where, as Will Rogers once noted, "Common sense ain't common."

So to keep a lid on the calls, our account execs and creative directors were selected to be the liaisons. One problem: They didn't want to do it. The account execs just wanted to schmooze clients and tell creatives how to do their jobs. Creatives just wanted to do ads and push the envelope. But seriously, most were just too busy to sit on the phone talking legalese. Plus there's nothing fun about sitting through, "I don't care what you told the client; legally, we cannot say/show this," on 9 out of 10 calls. You'd much rather pull an "Okay, here's what we did/said. Now how do we get away with it?"

This is where Miss M came in. She did what we wouldn't. Whenever there were legal questions, *she* called the lawyer. The more she talked to the lawyer, the more she learned about law. It got to a point where she became the agency's unofficial official legal counsel. After a while, she stopped calling the lawyer and began making calls as the lawyer. She started judging what we could and couldn't do, based on her understanding of the law. She threw around phrases like "damages," "negative press," and "settlements." Scared the crap out of folks. (We often joked that with her, every silver lining had a cloud.) But that was just the beginning.

The way our department ran, the higher-up creatives also dealt with creative budgets. Let's say you had an idea that required illustration or photography. First step would be to find out the budget from the account exec. With a budget in mind, you search out illustrators, etc., then start taking bids. Next you negotiate rates and do the work. Well, most creatives hate doing budgets and bids. (It's that whole "artist" thing, I guess.) So Miss M scooped up a lot of those responsibilities as well. She began dictating the flow of all sorts of things like a dam. Good thing too, because she had serious management issues.

Miss M had a Lily Tomlin, circa *9 to 5,* vibe going—tall, dark-haired, glasses, very straight-laced and serious. But to hear her staff tell it, she was more like Dabney Coleman. She actually had a nice smile, but when you saw it, you often wondered if any blood had been shed within the last 30 minutes. She went thru staffers like frat boys thru kegs. Percentage-wise, she had the highest turnover rate in the company next to the media department. (Traditionally, media folks—the planners and buyers that keep us all in the black, get low-balled, especially in Chicago.) I don't know what Miss M paid her folks but according to them it was never enough.

Our departments were on the same floor but at opposite ends. Still it was regular to hear her chewing people out all the way down the hall. Everybody I knew in her department was either constantly looking for a new job or drinking to deal with this one. And she couldn't keep a secretary or personal assistant for squat. Looking back, I remember one secretary who stood up to her. Miss M promptly fired that person in front of everyone

But when it was all said and done Miss M fulfilled her agenda. She never got cut—she had too much juice and too many aces in too many holes. She'd stepped on all sorts of folks along the way. Consistently made people's jobs harder than necessary. And they couldn't do a thing about it.

I remember being in a big department meeting where everyone whined about some of Miss M's antics. Philly (yeah, him), being the pimp he was, stood up and calmly said, "It's your fault—she's just doing what you won't." He knew a hustler when he saw one. Game always recognizes game. I think that's why those two actually got along.

Don't mind me, I'm just grindin', Jack.
—The Clipse[4]

O.G. Hustlers.

When it comes to business, department stores are the biggest legal hustlers I know. Think about it: You can walk into a Wal-Mart and buy baby food in one aisle, tires in another and a pair of jeans in aisle #8. That's not business, that's hustling. They're no different from the guys I saw on the trains pushing phone chords and incense. They're income agnostic—no loyalty to anything but the almighty dollar. Whatever you want, they'll get it. Just like they say on the block, I got what you need.

But many of us don't consider any of this hustling. We'd rather categorize it as diversification, reinventing yourself, or changing with the times. Those phrases are nice and tidy. For many, hustling (like much of this book) may be too urban to describe something as noble and American as business. But hey, that's part of The Hustle, too. (Besides, if Gore Vidal can cop to it, what's everyone else's excuse?)

I sell ice in the winter, I sell fire in hell—
I am a hustla baby, I'll sell water to a well!
—Jay-Z[5]

The Bridge

Now batting cleanup: The Bridge. Every company has one; most have more. I call 'em bridges because all they do is get over. They do just enough to not get fired. They're seldom if ever motivated unless they believe their job is on the line. The bridge lives from paycheck to paycheck, by choice. Folks used to call 'em slackers.

Bridges are pretty easy to spot. They're usually stuck in entry-level positions for way too long. Every now and then one slides up to a supervisory role, but it's rare—too much work and responsibility. Funny thing about bridges is, by and large, they're smart and talented folks. They have potential. But quite often potential is just a fancy word for "not yet."

Most bridges get jobs thru nepotism and networking. (In Chicago, half the city workers are somebody's cousin or nephew.) You know the types: Daddy's the boss, or they're the client's daughter or son. Or they went to the right college, joined the right frat or sorority. Somebody owes somebody a favor and *they're* the favor...

L-Boogie.

One classic bridge I knew was "Laurie." Laurie was a party girl, straight out of college. Kind of an Abercrombie & Fitch type: Tall, dark-hair...real girl-next-door looks, but with a better body. She went to a Big Ten school, probably would've pledged if she wasn't so busy laughing at 'em. Laurie's old man was a shot-caller for our biggest client. If I remember correctly: Pops worked a lot. When she was 16 he got her a Porsche. At 18 he sent her to Europe. When she graduated from college, he got her this job.

Near as I could tell Laurie was cool people. She was easy to talk to, mainly because she was hardly ever working. She came in hung over sometimes. Spent most mornings drinking Starbucks and reading magazines. Spent afternoons on the phone with friends planning happy hour. Occasionally, someone yelled at her and she'd do some work. Sad thing was, like most bridges, Laurie wasn't stupid or terribly lazy. Actually, she was smart. She could've been good if she wanted to but she didn't have to. And that's the way of The Bridge: Don't just cross the bridge, become the bridge. (It was some sort of Zen/*Dharma & Greg* thing.) Anyway, after a while, Laurie quit. I think Daddy got her a better job somewhere else.

The thing is, most bridges learn their behavior early. I see lots of 'em when I speak at colleges. They're kids whose parents let them coast their whole lives. Momma never tells them "No." Daddy gives 'em everything. The notion of working and being grateful for opportunities is foreign to them.

Burning Bridges

As for the collective bridges, you have a few contractors, vendors, and firms in every industry whose sole purpose is to get over—to do as little as possible for as much as possible. Just look around, you'll find them. For my money insurance companies are classic bridges... Their whole goal is to get as much out of you in premiums and deductibles while paying for as little of your medical bills as possible. (Now if that's not a bridge, then tell me what is.)

The bridge is ova, the bridge is over.
—KRS-ONE[6]

Bad Cop

One of the biggest hazards where I'm from is the Bad Cop. Not crooked cops but bad cops. Lemme just say that cops have the worst job in the country. It's the only private-sector gig I know where getting shot at is part of the deal. It's an ugly job and thank God somebody's doing it. Still, bad cops suck.

The bad cop has one major motto: Better them than me. Their agenda is self-preservation at all costs. They overreact to most everything and most everyone most every time. They're so paranoid that every teenager of color becomes a suspect in their eyes. Every traffic violation is the result of an armed felon that's on the run. Any group of minorities must be a gang. On the inside they're just a bundle of nerves *this close* to unraveling.

The workplace has its bad cops, too. I've known so many that it's better to just give a composite sketch:

For starters, the corporate bad cop is usually in the lower-end of middle management. Bad cop works hard, but is more concerned with the 401(k) than the promotion. Bad cop's fairly anonymous, a good worker who could be great if they weren't so terrified of failing or taking chances. Bad cop is always convinced their job is in jeopardy, no matter what.

So bad cop avoids risks. Always trusts formulas over instincts. Follows trends instead of setting them. Avoids confrontations with anyone who seems to have juice or be on the fast track. Bad cop seldom, if ever, agrees with the higher-ups but always makes sure they know that he's on board and in the loop. When in doubt, bad cop passes the buck. Never makes any decision without CC'ing others. Bad cop is never the first person to suggest anything but usually the third or fourth to agree with it. In short, Bad cop plays not to lose. Bad cop is the consummate moderate.

Most importantly, just like the bad cop on the street, this character manages to handcuff everyone under them. They stifle growth, not out of jealousy or envy but out of fear and self-preservation. They're content to fall in line, do what they're told and keep cashing that check.

Note: Bad cop is not a bridge. Unlike the bridge, the bad cop knows exactly what they're doing and why they're doing it—and that's what makes them bad. They're deliberate. Bad cops won't kill a company, but if you get enough of them, they'll stunt a company's growth.

Yeah, "officer" from "overseer"...
You need a little clarity? Check the similarity.
—KRS-ONE[7]

The LaMotta

Every 'hood has at least one "LaMotta"—that one cat with a world of talent: The honey with the golden voice. The young gun with the 4.25 speed or the 44-inch vert. The studious kid that's been pulling straight A's since pre-school. But for some reason—bad friends, bad choices, bad breaks—Local Kid never quite makes good, never fulfills their promise. They're like pimps or hustlers except the only people they ever misuse are themselves. They become walking cautionary tales of what not to do or what not to take for granted.

The business world is no different. Every company with over 25 employees has at least one LaMotta—the staffer with corner office talent but is still in a cubicle... The CEO who should be on the cover of *Forbes* but just can't get right... You know the type. My favorite one was "Frank."

Met him back when I was about 22. Frank was about 45 and comfortable; not CEO-comfortable, but more like country-club-pro comfortable:

He had a nice office, nice salary, nice clothes, stable predictable clients, and a nice 401(k) stashed away. He was VP Creative Director at a place where being a Creative Director didn't mean much and being a VP meant even less. But if you asked anyone in town (and I asked plenty), Frank was easily one of the best ad minds in the business.

When it came to writing ads and developing marketing campaigns, Frank was nice. He could write an ad as long as a feature-length magazine article and have you read every word. He could do sharp, smart headlines plus pithy copy. TV, radio, print, outdoor... You name it; Frank was surgical with a pen. If you wanted reach any segment of mainstream America, 8–80, rich or poor, Frank could bring it, regardless of client. Plus he was a decent teacher—younger creatives always learned from him. Frank could've been a Chief Creative Officer, a group creative director at a top shop at least.

But again, he never quite made it off the block, so to speak, and everyone knew it. Like most LaMottas, Frank had a tragic flaw (or maybe it was a tragic choice—that one mistake that you'll never make twice, but God knows that once is all it ever takes): Frank fell in love with the game.

More than being an adman, Frank loved the trappings of being in the ad industry: He loved the client-schmoozing, the high-powered boardroom meetings, the Reality TV-style alliances, the reps and vendors taking you out to lunch and dinner, the big-budget commercial shoots, the industry parties, and the politics... Frank could politik like an old Roman senator. He loved all that stuff. But as KRS said, "Love is gonna get you."

Regardless of industry or endeavor The Hustle wants you to fall for the shine—the periphery, the perks, the parties... And once you're hooked, The Hustle slaps the golden handcuffs on you. And next thing you know, you're a jaded lawyer who'd rather maker partner than make justice...or a doctor who'd rather *Nip/Tuck* a few than give quality healthcare to all...or a bloated one-hit wonder doing Vegas who should've been a great musician instead. And now, you're too old, have too many bills, are too entrenched in a certain lifestyle or are just too scared to do anything but keep playing the game.

That's when you do what a lotta LaMottas do: embrace your role. Remember the Frozen Frogs project? Frank was my Creative Director on that one. He didn't have to explain the billing hustle, but he did. He wanted us to understand what we were getting into. Over the years, he dropped lots of jewels to work by: *Work in New York before you turn 30—it'll add 0's to your salary everywhere else... Don't take a VP title too soon—nowhere to go but sideways and down... Get in good with the account execs—the suits know stuff you don't... Every contact now is a potential job later... Don't stay at one place too long...Writing is a craft—never stop working...*

Don't get me wrong. Frank was no failure. But he could've been so much more than he was. He was twice the writer that I'll ever be. He shoulda been a contenda.

The Professional

And your MVP: The *Professional*. I love professionals...they're kryptonite to the other five. Pimps can't intimidate professionals because they have strong minds. Professionals don't become hoes because they have integrity and standards they won't comprise for a paycheck or someone else's approval. Professionals aren't hustlers or bad cops—they understand that the best way to achieve any personal agenda is to do the job they got hired to do as best as they can. As for bridges: Professionals are too busy working to become bridges, which leaves bridges out in the open and easy to spot.

So no matter how profitable it looks to be a pimp, be a professional. No matter how much job security the hustler or ho seem to have, be a professional. No matter how much the bridge coasts and you sweat it out be a professional. Professionals always win in the end. When in doubt, be a professional.

Mom & Dad.

The best professionals I ever knew were my parents. They worked hard all their lives. Pop's grind was working for the city. He only used sick days when he was truly and genuinely sick. "That's why they're called 'sick days,' " he'd say. He only took on extra shifts when he needed money for his family. That's work ethic. Maybe it's a southern black man thing, maybe not. But the hardest working folks I've ever seen in my life have been southern black folks. (Just my opinion.)

But Pops was the man I respected most. He was cool. The dealers and hustlers often had more money or fancier stuff, but they were as temporary as a Chicago summer. Dad was consistent like Karl Malone—he just worked for his, day in, day out, year in, year out. Weathered all sorts of drama and stood up for himself and his coworkers when necessary and always did his job. He was a man first. People respected that. Besides, I never really trusted the hustlers and dealers because I realized that they always had an agenda. But Pops was a professional—professionals don't have agendas, they just are.

Mom was a professional, too. She worked non-stop her whole life. She worked in a hospital, was a switchboard operator, a pricing analyst, a secretary, she had all kinds of jobs. Plus she raised 6 kids, helped raise grandkids, too. She worked a few 9-to-5 gigs. She kept God and family first. Bosses tried to get her to do all sorts of crazy things—snitch on coworkers, play office politics, sacrifice her home life, etc. But she wouldn't play the game. She just made sure she did her job well and was home everyday by 6:30 P.M.

My folks never made huge dough. Never had big fancy titles. Never had golden parachutes or big stock options. But they never lost sight of their humanity or priorities. In short, they were professionals.

Monty.

Monty was another good professional I knew. By the time I met him, I was an in-demand freelancer, turning down more gigs than I accepted. I made my own schedule, set my own fees, and had no shortage of companies willing to pay. Plus I was teaching part-time at my alma mater. I was having fun. Monty screwed all of that.

I wish every interview I had went like ours: I told Monty I wouldn't quit teaching; he said that as long as I did my job he'd work around my schedule. He asked me what title I wanted; I told him I didn't care. I asked him what was the most important thing to him; he said, "Catching the 6:20 train." (He had a couple kids and wanted to get home to his family everyday, ASAP.) It was hard to turn him down.

Like my folks, Monty had working-class roots—he'd been a carpenter or something before going corporate. He came off like a woodsier David Letterman: Glasses, thick mousy hair. Rarely dressed up. Professional, but never took things too seriously. Had an everyman demeanor and told cool stories about all sorts of regular things. He seemed to have a good sense of humor and perspective about people. Plus, clients dug him.

As a boss Monty didn't put his thumbprint on everything, which ultimately became his thumbprint. He hired people then got out of their way and let them work. You presented your own work. He let you live and die with your own ideas. He gave input, made cuts where he saw fit, but your work was your work and the spotlight was yours to shine or fail in. If you could do the job in 2 hours, fine. If it took longer, that was fine, too. And where most bosses got hung up on timesheets and agendas, Monty couldn't have cared less. Ideas and results impressed him most. I don't think I ever worked late or worked a weekend under him that wasn't truly necessary or at least not his fault. In the end, I can't really say that Monty was my friend. We got along and he was good people, but he was just my boss. He kept the job fun; you really can't ask for much more than that.

Pause the ho processionals;
save the hustler confessionals;
learn the professional lessons, y'all.[8]

So how do we get rid of 'em?

As you may have noticed, pimps, hoes, etc. have one thing in common: *Selfishness*. Selfishness and self-preservation blurs their vision until they only see what is of obvious benefit to them. Sure the professional is selfish, but the professional tempers their selfishness with perspective and respect for themselves and their environment.

As for the rest, they're all reactionaries; they do what their environment allows and rewards. If your company rewards selfishness, mind games, and taking shorts then that's what you'll attract. (Birds of a feather...) But once you lay down the law and walk the walk, people will follow. And the non-professionals, seeing the writing on the wall, will quit. But if they don't, fire them. Getting rid of professionals is even easier—just keep the others around. The professional, having a sense of self-worth, will happily quit.

And those are the masks I've seen people wear. At some point you'll probably wear one yourself. Which one you wear is up to you. (Just remember: The goal is to become a professional as quickly as possible and stay one until the end. If your company or industry doesn't respect, encourage, and reward professionals, watch out; because you're in a situation that's either destined to fail or sure to swallow you up in its success.)

Career Opportunities!
—The Clash[9]

Less Bosses, More Leaders

Slow down, let the leader lead.
—Rakim

Corporate America has too many bosses and not enough leaders. Being a boss is easy; all you need is a title and big mouth; and if there are 2 things business is full of, it's titles and bigmouths. But *leaders*? Not enough of 'em. In fact, I've only known a few genuine leaders myself; the rest were just bosses with big offices and matching egos.

Whether you're talking sports, military, or business, people want to be led. What people don't want is to be bossed around. Bosses simply boss folks around. But leaders lead. That may sound simple, even trite, but it's the truth. Leaders lead. Let's break down the differences:

While the boss says, "My door is always open," the leader comes out from behind the desk, gets out of the office and stops you with a "How's everything going? You need any help?" Leaders engage. Whether their workforce is 50, 500, or 5, a leader gets involved and stays involved. Leaders understand that they're as important to their workers' productivity as the workers themselves. (By the way: saying, "My door is always open," is like saying, "I'm in the Mafia." If you really are, you don't have to say it. People know if your door is open based on how you run things.)

I'm stone-cold runnin' thangs.
—Busy Bee[1]

Serve

"And whosoever of you will be the chiefest, shall be servant of all." (St. Mark 10:44) All bad bosses have one thing in common: they are lousy servants. Leadership is about service. Leaders are servants to the people they lead. Leaders are servants to the cause, to their mission, to their responsibilities, to the greater message. You don't measure a leader by who serves them; you measure a leader by who *they* serve and by how willing they are to serve others. The most important thing you can do in this world is serve. Service teaches leadership more than any MBA program.

So if you really want to be a leader, learn to serve.

Be Humble

Arrogance is a sure-shot path to failure. Arrogance blinds vision and impairs judgment. No one wants to follow or work hard for an arrogant boss. No one wants to support an arrogant person, even when that arrogant person is right. You need humility. Humility works wonders. Humility makes people want to help you. Humility helps you see the bigger picture. Humility helps you spot flaws and opportunities. Always be humble.

Care

You can't lead if you don't care. There's nothing worse than working for someone who doesn't care. In high school we had teachers who didn't care. We were kids but we weren't blind. As students, they were our leaders and we followed them. When they didn't care about teaching, we didn't care about learning, at least not from them. Work is no different. If you're in charge, it starts and ends with you. If you don't care, why should your employees?

Now don't mistake caring for passion. The only thing worse than not caring is having passion for business. Passion is for people. No one, I repeat, no one should have passion for business. It's just a job. We're not curing cancer or saving the world. We're just supplying products, services, and getting paid to do so. It's all simple, replaceable stuff. Save the passion for living. Life is special, business ain't.

So then what is caring? Well it's not rah-rah speeches or 18-hour days. And I don't mean, whatever-it-takes zealotry, either. Caring means being a professional and encouraging others to be professionals. Caring means doing your job well and helping those around you do theirs better. Caring is about putting people first. All the speeches and passion in the world won't help a company that's more concerned with numbers and things than with human beings.

Make Believers

Great leaders always have a message or a mission that's bigger than them. Why? If people only believe in the leader, they'll only work as long as they believe in the leader. But once that leader is gone or becomes disliked, the people stop working. People can hate a leader, a leader can die, retire, or whatever, but if the people believe in the leader's message they'll keep working and fighting for it no matter what.

The most successful companies are filled with people who believe in their company, who share its vision. Great movements, be they social, political, religious, or economic, are always filled with people who believe in the bigger picture, not just in the artist who painted the picture. So remember: Don't make them believe in you, get people believe in what you're doing. That way, they'll work just as hard at achieving your goals as you.

They're Investments, Not Overhead

I was watching *60 Minutes*—I think it was late 2002. They were interviewing Dr. Jim Goodnight, CEO/president and co-founder of SAS Institute, one of the largest privately held software companies in America. Based in North Carolina, SAS was making money hand over fist regardless of the economy and their turnover rate was lower than Allen Iverson's body fat. *Working Mohers* named 'em one of the *100 Best Companies for Working Mothers* 13 times.[2] *Fortune* named SAS one of its *100 Best Companies to Work for in America* 6 years running.[3]

So as I'm watching, Dr. Jim says: "Ninety-five percent of my investment drives out the door every day; my job is to keep it coming back." He doesn't hire employees; he invests in employees. They're not overhead to him, they're partners. And based on SAS's high performance and the fact that there's a crack-line wanting in each year (nearly 1,000 applicants for every position) I'd say Doc is on to something.

Truth be told, what a business makes or provides is secondary to how it connects with people. Once you connect with your people, you've won over half the battle. The rest is connecting with the people you want to buy whatever you're selling. And if you have nothing to sell or are trying to figure out what else to sell, just listen to people—they'll tell you what they want to buy. (I didn't write this book just because I had something to say, I wrote this book because businesspeople told me what they felt was missing and what problems they needed help solving.)

From a hustler's angle, employees are overhead and consumers are commodities. But leaders aren't hustlers. Leaders understand that people are your most valuable investment. But above all else, leaders understand that people are human beings, not just tools to be used or resources to be drained. So whether it's business, government, etc., great leaders understand that it's all about people.

Labor is prior to, and independent of, capital. Capital is only the fruit of the labor, and could have never existed if the labor had not existed first. Labor is the superior of capital and deserves much the higher consideration.
—*Abraham Lincoln*[4]

Quit Being So Selfish

Over the years, I've worked with and heard about tons of selfish bosses, but I've never heard of a selfish leader. Why? Because there's no such thing as a selfish leader. You can't be selfish and lead. People just won't trust you enough to follow you for very long. And more importantly, selfishness blinds—if all you see is yourself, you'll miss the bigger picture. Leadership is about sacrifice and balance. If you're out for self, fine. But the last thing you should be is responsible for other people's livelihoods.

Find "the Whole"

Bosses see the parts; leaders see the engine. Great leaders recognize that everything is connected and everyone feeds off of each other. They understand workers are only as good as their bosses empower them to be. As a result, leaders are constantly listening, learning, talking, and adjusting. And where bosses and supervisors simply delegate and pass the buck, leaders find their role in the big picture and help everyone else do the same. That's how great companies keep it moving.

There are No Grassroots Movements in Corporate America

Nothing gets done in Corporate America from the bottom up. Companies don't fail from the bottom up. They don't succeed from the bottom up. Every movement, strategy, or paradigm starts with the top dogs or requires their open support early on. Just look at every major change the business world has undergone: Malfeasance, dress codes, new product launches, new business models, restructuring, pay scales... Good or bad, at some point, those in charge either start it or co-sign it.

Change comes from the top. If you want certain dress codes, don't wait for employees to show up in khakis or suits hoping it spreads thru osmosis or consensus—get up and lead. And don't lead by example—that only works in sports and this is not a game. Go speak it. Explain it. Let people know that whatever the idea, movement, or initiative is, it came from you. Be a catalyst for change. Then reinforce it, reward it, and live it yourself.

Get Dirty

I've worked with some lazy bosses in my life—people who, once they got their title, went soft. They got selfish. They forgot how hard it was to reach the top and started resting on their laurels. If you want to be a real leader, you'd better work; in fact, you better work harder than everyone under you. People will never work hard for someone who won't even work hard for him or herself.

When it comes to getting things done,
we need fewer architects and more bricklayers.
—Colleen C. Barrett, president/COO Southwest Airlines

15 Steps Every Leader Should Take:

1. Follow.

Show me a stupid person and I'll show you somebody who probably thinks they know everything. No matter who you are, no matter what you know, someone else is smarter than you. Somebody knows more than you. Go find 'em and listen to 'em. Nobody knows everything about anything. Real leaders are smart enough to know that learning never ends. They're also humble enough to follow when the time comes.

2. Listen.

Listeners learn more than talkers. Leaders who listen become great leaders. So listen to your employees, your coworkers, and your environment. You'll learn a lot more a lot faster.

Leadership and learning are indispensable to each other.
—John F. Kennedy

3. Accept blame when something goes wrong.

Everyone screws up sometimes. Leaders take the heat when they do.

4. Share credit when something goes right.

Nobody wins alone. I don't care how big or small the achievement is, when something goes right, share the glory with those who helped you get it right. Few things anger people more than having their contributions and sacrifices ignored.

5. Share information.

This isn't the CIA; it's okay to share info. Keep employees informed whether the news is good or bad. ("Because I said so" or, "Don't worry about it" only works on children.) Secret meetings and ignored questions make people suspicious; and no one works hard for people they don't trust.

6. Hire people better than you.

There should be people under you who can step into your shoes and keep it moving when the time comes. You want people who every few years you have to ask, "How much will it take to keep you here?" You need thoroughbreds. Thoroughbreds grow companies.

Challenge: Right now you should be able to call your competitors and say, "I've got 3 people under me who are as good if not better than you." If you can't say that now or won't be able say it soon, then you're in trouble. And if you're currently leading the pack, trust me, the comp is gaining on you, you just don't know it yet. If you want the sky to be the limit for your department or company, you cannot be the ceiling.

Everybody around me is smarter than me.
—Russell Simmons[5]

7. Get out the way.

Why hire someone then waste your time and theirs by hawking (standing over their shoulders)? You hired them, now get out of their way and let 'em work. Give them room to grow, succeed, and fail. Also, be understanding when they do fail. *Notice*: I didn't say "if" I said "when," because everybody fails. Every person in every company in every industry will fail more than they succeed; the key is knowing someone's got your back when you slip.

8. Don't reel people in.

You see this one a lot in the marketing and ad worlds—companies hire someone with a really left-field perspective, someone whose ideas seem original and risky. Then, they "reel them in"—tone them down. Make them conform to company culture or client standards and expectations. This is beyond stupid, not to mention a waste of talent and opportunity.

Creativity is uncomfortable. Breakthrough ideas don't come in nice predictable boxes with pretty bows—they come from strange places and strange people. Remember, it's called, "status quo" for a reason.

9. Hire some "No" people.

A real leader understands the value of "No." A real leader knows they're not always right and that they need at least one person in their camp who'll tell them so. Don't confuse no with disloyalty or disrespect. Quite often no is just healthy criticism, a chance to reexamine a situation or a decision with a fresh set of eyes. Skeptics can be a good thing.

Egomaniacal celebrities, out-of-control athletes, and bad bosses tend to have one thing in common: Not one person in their camp ever told them no. Not family, not friends, not an agent, not an adviser... Not one person said, "No, this is a bad idea." They were surrounded by folks who were too afraid, too indifferent, or too greedy to say anything but yes.

So hire a couple no people. And when they tell you no, *listen*.

10. Lose the attitude.

Leave the drill sergeant bit at home. You're not Donald Trump. You're not Bobby Knight. You're a human being and this is just business.

If you have to yell or intimidate to motivate, then you don't know how to lead. If you equate threats with power, you have no real power. Power is what people will do because they believe in you, not because they're afraid of you. (And again, if you yell at the wrong person on the wrong day, boss or no boss, you just might "catch one.")

11. No superstar rules.

One team, one set of rules. If the grunts have to be in by 9 A.M., so should the execs. No double standards. Employees need to see parity. They need to know that as a leader, you're looking out for everyone, not just a select few. Parity reflects equality. Equality reflects quality leadership. Quality leadership creates unity; unity breeds success.

12. Don't make them ask for what they've earned.

A big reason many employees enter salary negotiations with chips on their shoulder or come out frustrated is because they feel like they're asking for what they've already earned. There's nothing worse than working hard to help grow a company only to have to beg for a bigger piece of the pie. It makes people feel disrespected and undervalued. (And we all know how hard folks work when they feel like that.)

So don't make employees beg for rewards and raises. As a leader, you should already know who's producing, who's earned what, etc., and just give it to them. Don't make them come to you; go to them.

13. Leave your drama at home.

Sorry the wife is mad at you. Sorry your hubby/boyfriend cheated on you. Sorry you're in debt, too. But recognize: your drama has nothing to do with your employees, so don't bring it to work. That's soft.

If you're having personal problems, take time off and work it out. Or pull your employees aside, tell them what's up and ask them to be patient. But boss or no boss, leave them out of it. Employees are not punching bags.

14. Promote from within.

Too many companies choose outsiders over homegrown talent. Too many employees spend years slugging it out in the trenches only to watch outsiders reap the rewards of plum positions. Sure you want the best person for the job, but sometimes the best fit is already right under your nose. So give your own employees a chance before looking elsewhere. After all, why should anyone work hard for you knowing there's a permanent glass ceiling over their head?

15. Go to the bottom.

If you want to see how good or bad things really are in your company, go to the bottom of the food chain. Why? Because crap flows downhill. People at the bottom are the ones who see the results of policy more so than anyone else. They have to; they have no choice but to.

So if you have stores, go to the stores. And don't talk to the manager, talk to the lowest kid on the totem pole. Talk to the stock boys, the secretaries, and the folks who get paid the least. Find out how your policies and strategies are affecting their ability to do their jobs. You need that frontline perspective in order to find the holes and the opportunities. (And don't just do it once; make it a routine, monthly, if possible.)

And that's that. Regardless of company or industry, these tips are sure to turn any boss into a leader and any good leader into a great leader.

Leadership is not just a position...
Leadership is the capacity and the willingness to respond
to what is needed in a situation.
—Dr. Dorothy I. Height, President Emerita
National Council of Negro Women

Role Call!

For as we have many members in one body,
and all members have not the same office.
—Romans 12:4

Now that we've talked leadership, let's talk about the people you're leading. Grab your flowchart and repeat after me: "At least 20% of my employees are playing out of position."

Regardless of industry or company a good fifth of staffers aren't working efficiently. From New York to New Deli to New Zealand too many people, based on what they're good at, are in the wrong department, have the wrong title, the wrong responsibilities, are way too busy, or aren't busy enough. I've watched this problem go from bad to worse every year with more and more employees complaining about it. And for the most part, it's not their fault; a lot of companies just aren't doing very good jobs of putting people where they can do the most good. In fact, I'm starting to think that some bosses are shifting bodies around to hide the fact that the only thing they're really good at is shifting bodies around.

Screw the Pay Scales

Many companies work under the theory that non-execs shouldn't make as much as executives. So once an employee reaches a certain salary, they're pressured into taking promotions and responsibilities they don't want or aren't good at in order to justify a salary they've already earned; or they get passed over for someone who's more "promotion-ready."

This is asinine.

Employees are common; talented, productive ones aren't. All-pro talent deserves all-pro salaries. If your "I-can't-function-without-you" assistant wants 75K and she's performing, pay her the 75K. Don't be cheap. Likewise, if you have a VP who's only giving you a 40K effort, then cut their salary to 40K. People should get paid by their value, not their title.

A downward move up...

Not long ago I worked with "George," a hot graphic designer and commercial artist. He always came through with quality work. As a reward, our company gave him a raise—with one condition: George had to take a promotion. They made him a Creative Director which meant supervising people, making client presentations, handling budgets, etc...all the stuff George hated doing, didn't want to do, and really wasn't good at. Supposedly, George's boss couldn't justify paying a non-supervisor what George wanted, so he had to take the new position. The result? George spent more time creative directing and managing and less time designing.

Not only that, but instead of doing one job extremely well, George was now doing lots of jobs not so well. And on top of all of that, he hated it. In the name of policy and protocol, we turned George, a long-time asset, into a potential liability.

One Job Per Person

Bosses:

I understand restructuring on the fly and filling gaps. I even understand wanting the biggest bang for your buck. But I'd rather pay a lot for one employee to do one thing well than force a bargain by overloading said employee and hoping their quality doesn't slide or they don't screw something up all together. (You don't tell Donovan McNabb, for example, to add linebacker to his QB duties because you need extra speed and athleticism on defense. You simply get yourself a good linebacker.)

This is why they invented temps. Temps are built for getting stuff done without overloading permanent staffers. If things get hectic, bring in a temp or two—they're worth the extra loot. Or just suck it up and staff up.

And lastly, beware of maniac multi-taskers. They're talented folks who, for whatever reason, get hell-bent on doing everyone else's job in addition to theirs. Let those folks know that it's best for them and the company if they just focus on their assigned responsibilities.

Remember: Value isn't one person doing a lot for one wage; value is the right people in the right position doing the right job well.

Employees:

Play your position; don't let bosses play you. You're only getting paid one salary so only do the job you got hired to do. If you're being underused or intentionally overloaded, talk to your boss. Let 'em know there's a problem.

I've seen as many people fail from attempting
too many things as from attempting too few.
—J. Paul Getty, billionaire businessman

Role-players Win Championships

Some employees are just natural-born role players. They don't want to be superstars; they don't want the pressure that comes with the big office and big title. Some employees just want their check and their benefits plus a little respect. Well, you need those people as much as you need the big shots. The Chicago Bulls won 6 rings with MJ, Pip, and a mob of role-players. Six-time Tour de France champ Lance Armstrong's cycling team is him and, um...you get the point.

Superstar execs are nice, brilliant charismatic CEOs are cool. But your company will fail without quality role-players. So love your role-players as much as you love your high-priced talent. Pay them well and respect them always. Because when that superstar exec or flashy supervisor slips, goes on vacation, or quits, it'll be the role-players that hold it down and keep it moving.

Remember: Talent out of position is talent wasted. When you put talent in the right position, you'll save on costly mistakes and increase production. Plus you'll keep talented employees from quitting for better-defined roles elsewhere. As a leader, your job is to find out who's good at what, put them where they belong, and pay them fairly. If your company has holes, it's not your employees' fault nor is it their responsibility to fill them. That's your role. So stay in your lane, play your position, and get it done.

...yea, thou shalt diligently consider his place...
—Psalms 37:10

Support Your Support Staff

I love my posse and it ain't no joke!
—Disco Dave

The most undervalued and overworked people in business are support staffers: IT workers, secretaries, administrative assistants, executive assistants, receptionists, and mailroomers. In over 12 years, everywhere I went the support staff was the backbone of the company. But more often than not, they were treated like the tailbone.

Again, I didn't grow up around CEOs or execs; support staffers were my first exposure to the corporate world, so I never looked down on those jobs. But once I got into business I saw lots of folks do just that.

I watched execs consistently dump work on secretaries at the last minute while yelling at them over every little thing. I saw assistants insult support staffers just because a presentation went bad. I watched people tee off on mailroom workers and receptionists just because. I saw IT folks get yelled at because execs couldn't follow basic computer instructions. I saw folks fresh out of school roll into companies treating secretaries and mailroomers like crap and get away with it. It's like they saw support staffers as office furniture, only easier to replace.

On the whole, support staffers were my favorite people wherever I worked. From "Joyce," "Connie," and "Tommy" to "Cindy," "Alex," and "Odie" they're the ones I miss most. We'd hang out in the mailroom. Goof off at lunch. Hit the bars, etc. We didn't always have stuff in common, but we got along. They had perspective. Work was just a job to them. Plus they were smart—they knew how things ran and how to get things done. Speaking of which:

On a slightly selfish tip: support staffers are incredible sources of insider info. Secretaries know all the gossip: Who's doing who... Who's on drugs... Who's on thin ice... Mailroom folks see everyone's mail before they do. And whenever someone gets let go, some type of support staffer is in on it.

I'm not much of a gambler, but for my money the smartest person at any company is that one old secretary who's been there for like 15 years. She's probably got enough dirt to raise 8 kinds of hell, but she's smart enough to keep quiet and stay above it all. She just does her job, goes home and keeps her benefits.

And let's not forget IT. (*Fred?! Fred?! Fred?!*) Ever seen a company when the servers crash? Or when its ISP/office email system goes down? There's nothing like watching adults panic because "the 'thingy' just froze again." In between catastrophes, it's the IT folks who're debugging viruses from the spam they warned you 25 times not to open. They're upgrading networks and firewalls, and of course recovering the crucial files you deleted because you didn't pay attention when they showed you how to back stuff up. Plus they're monitoring emails so the execs know who's downloading porn and trashing the company online. And when the pink-slips start flying, it's IT that shuts down your computer while you're getting your walking papers.

So whether you're an exec or an entry-level type, recognize the truth: *Support staffers run things.* You'd be stuck with notepads, pencils, rotary phones, typewriters, and getting about half as much work done with out 'em. Peace and blessings to support staffers everywhere. Without you, we'd all be charities.

Worse comes to worse my peoples come first.
—Dilated Peoples[1]

No More CYA!

Funny, how things change:
A "stand up" brotha, now you sit down to aim.
Used to have a firm grip, now you droppin' names...
—Jay-Z & Too Short

The above is from *A Week Ago*, a near-classic Carter 'n' Shaw collabo and great example of the CYA mentality that's infected the business world. The song tells of a partnership done in when one of the men becomes a snitch—CYA in its basest form. At work, CYA is about making sure you never get blamed for failures and can at least share in successes, deserved or not. It's about never being seen as a liability, even if you're the biggest one around. CYA is about job security for people who arguably shouldn't have been hired in the first place.

Here's a few common CYA tactics:

Office Politics

It's Corporate America's favorite pastime. Conniving, spreading rumors, backstabbing, hording information, secret alliances and agendas... It all goes back to the notion that doing the job right just isn't enough. But truth is, if you need to scheme and politick to succeed, either you suck at your job or your job sucks. If you're not good at your job, get better. If your job encourages and rewards office politics, get out. Otherwise, that garbage will eat you up. It always does.

Paper Trails

In business, nothing drives over-documentation like CYA. *SIGN THIS, CC SO-'N'-SO, BCC THAT*, back-ups of back-up files, saved emails, phone call transcripts... I can't tell you the number of meetings I sat thru where whole chunks were spent making sure our bases were in rows and our ducks were covered or whatever. And I can't tell you the number of Friday nights we drank away rationalizing it.

The best protection in business is to do your job and be honest and upfront about your capabilities every step of the way. If people were more focused on that and said "No" every once in a while, businesses would save hundreds of trees, cut carpal tunnel cases by 35%, and recover millions in wasted time. (Might even have fewer alcoholics, too.)

Brownnosers

Brownnosing sucks—it's a demeaning waste of time and energy. Be professional enough to work with people who are not your friends. Have enough dignity to not jock anyone with a little bit of power just because. And save your compliments and friendship for folks who actually deserve them.

Liars

Lying might be the most popular form of CYA around. Want to land that new client? Lie about your capabilities. Need to keep your boss happy? Lie about the status of a project. Want people on board with your agenda? Lie about how well it's going to work. When in doubt, lie.

But lying has one huge flaw: Most lies can't stand up without the support of other lies. Once you start lying, you have to keep lying and hope no one catches on.

"I was in the room . . ."

Think about all the great success stories in business. Think about the great accomplishments in your company's history. Few were actually the result of across-the-board teamwork and great minds thinking alike. Most came from one person or a small group who believed and pushed while many were against them. But fortunately, those against ultimately got out of the way or looked the other way while those few "This-is-crazy-enough-to-work" types did their thing.

Next thing you know, a monster success is born: A simple commercial turns all-time catchphrase (*CAN YOU HEAR ME NOW? WHAASSUP?*). An upstart suddenly dominates (KRISPY KREME). An obscure flick or trend turns global phenomenon (*The Passion of the Christ*, *The Sopranos*, *hiphop*)...

Suddenly all those soft doubters, haters, and under-estimators come out of the woodwork to tell anyone who'll listen that they were *in the room* when it happened just to share that spotlight and CYA. Why? Because the only thing worse than being seen as a screw-up is being seen as too stupid to tell a good idea from a bad one.

I told you so...

The flipside of "...in the room," *"I told you so"* occurs when something fails or goes wrong and all involved suddenly swear that they'd been warning against it from jump, which of course is usually a lie. (Think: *9/11 Commission* hearings.)

Rationales

When abused, it's the greatest CYA tool in the marketing game. A rationale is a document that explains why certain creative directions are being explored and why certain ideas are being executed. Rationales are written up for client approval *before* any actual work gets done.

Why?

Because if the work doesn't come out the way the client wants the agency can hold up a sheet of paper with the client's signature and say, "See this? This was your idea, too." In fact, in all my years, rationales rarely lead to better work or better thinking. They often lead to over-thinking, over-analyzing, and supreme confidence in the fact that somebody besides you will get screwed if it fails.

Focus Groups

I've been involved in over a hundred focus groups for a variety of clients and projects, great and small. They all had one thing in common: *Somebody had to CYA*: A client. An agency. A brand manager. An account exec. A studio exec. A film director. A creative director... Someone who's forever scared of being wrong about anything got to thinking, "If this fails, I'll need a scapegoat. I know, let's 'focus-group' it. That way, if it bombs, we can blame 'them'."

So month after month, year after year Corporate America and Hollywood round up their built-in excuses: Groups of random people—most of whom would never voluntarily associate with each other under any other circumstances...place them in sterile rooms, usually with two-way mirrors like they're lab rats or suspects in police line-ups. Next, they're shown storyboards. Concept boards. Unfinished movies. TV pilots. Product samples and prototypes. Then soft, by-the-book execs base anywhere from 5–7 figures worth of manpower, ideas, and strategies on the opinions of people who usually have no idea what they're talking about because they've been shown things they've never seen before in conditions they'll never see again while being asked a bunch of stupid questions under an even stupider set of circumstances.

Why?

Well, besides being an added source of revenue, focus groups imply research and research implies formulas. Formulas imply predictability and predictability implies certainty. And business loves certainty. It's all about comfort. And as stressed as most businesspeople pretend to get over focus group results, the fact is, they love them. Focus groups help businessfolks CYA. If the focus groups agree with you it's because you're brilliant and they "get it". When they don't or want something that turns out to be a world-class disaster (*New Coke, Yugo*, the *Arch Deluxe*) it's <u>their</u> fault and you were simply giving consumers what they said they wanted. Either way, you're covered.

"It's okay; you've been wrong before,
you'll be wrong again."
—Arnold Drummond

There are two certainties in business: (1) Each day, something will go right; (2) Each day something will go wrong. Now it may not be big either way, but it will happen. The question is, "How will you react?" Will you CYA? Or will you handle it like a professional? Choose the latter and remember: We all fall short and it's okay. Just learn from your mistakes, congratulate those who're right, and keep it moving.

And don't worry about the person who screws up, worry about the person who swears they never have or never will. That person is either lying, unwilling to take risks for what they believe in or just stupid. Either way, they're CYA'ing, which means they're liable to dead a business faster than most of the mistakes and bad ideas combined.

In order to kiss someone's butt
you have to let them turn their back on you.[1]

Shook Ones

Scared to death, scared to look, they shook.
—Mobb Deep

Blame the economy. Blame global geopolitics and terrorism. But whatever the cause, a lot of folks are shook. Workers are afraid to speak against company policy or do anything not preordained from on high. Bosses are afraid to take risks and innovate. Companies are so afraid of losing market share and shareholders that they won't do anything that might alienate anyone. In short, businesses and even consumers are stuck playing not to lose.

But what amazes me more than all the fear is the number of people in power still pretending that this is good for business. Whoever convinced bosses that fear is a great motivator lied. On-the-block fear can get you killed or arrested. In sports, fear leads to injuries and losses. In business, fear creates complacency, stifles creativity, and stunts growth. And as with most business ills, fear starts and ends at the top.

Tanya the Tyrant

I once worked for "Tanya Patten," a brilliant big agency CEO. She was a trade press darling—usually made those "most powerful women" and "Top 40 Under 40" lists, and rightfully so. She had skills; knew her industry inside and out, knew her company top to bottom. She was good, real good. But she had a major flaw: People were afraid of her. I'm talking, "Yes-m'am-no-m'am" shook. There were endless stories and rumors floating about her rise to power: Backstabbing... Firing anyone she deemed a threat... Secret alliances... Sexual liaisons with colleagues... To hear most tell it, she was the original pit bull in a skirt.

Not surprisingly, company morale sucked. People at the bottom felt ignored. They felt most of the higher-ups were impatient, incompetent, or some combo thereof. Many felt they were forced to grind late-nights and weekends without cause or rewards. And of course every other person, especially the media department, felt they were underpaid. But because everyone was afraid of Tanya, no one ever griped out loud.

But like I said, she was smart; and it didn't take a genius to see that things were bad. So Tanya Patten started something called, *Dear Boss*: She had IT set up an open computer in with a generic email address. Anyone could send anonymous complaints and suggestions about the company or any exec's performance—only she would read the emails. And unless you signed your name, she'd never know who wrote what. The problem? Folks thought the computer was bugged. Turns out we weren't totally wrong. Using a few IT tricks and some deductive reasoning, anyone could figure out who wrote what. So that idea went bust after about a month of "I-love-my-job/Tanya-Rules!" notes.

Next came, *Let's Do Lunch*: She divided the company into groups of 10 or 15 and took each group to lunch every week. Over a few drinks and some good food, you could tell her, face-to-face, whatever you wanted with her promise that nothing you said would be held against you. You could snitch, criticize, praise, or just shut up and enjoy a free meal. But since no one wanted to talk themselves out of a job, it went about as well as Bush's search for WMDs in Iraq.

But again, Tanya already knew folks were too afraid for any of this to work. I think this was just her way of sizing up the fear factor and CYA'ing herself against our board of directors. (Rumor had it they'd been unhappy with our office's performance ever since she took over.)

Looking back, I actually do remember a couple folks standing up to her at various points. I can also remember those same folks having a rough time there afterwards. In fact, one or two ended up "quitting." And of course, nothing improved until Tanya dropped the bully tactics.

Neva scared...

Once again, fear is a fake motivator. You can't turn a company around or drive a company forward out of fear. You can't encourage brilliant work, creativity, or increase productivity out of fear. The last thing you want is people coming to work every day afraid. Fear breeds stress, aggravation, and stagnation. Another thing about fear: It only works for so long. At some point people stop being afraid of you. That's when they start undermining your authority or quit on you all together. Or worse.

Fear makes the person who's afraid of you feel weak and helpless and nobody wants to feel like that. Another thing about fear is that it's a vampire—it sucks the other emotions right out of you. So even if you like the person or respect that boss or colleague, your fear bleeds those good feelings dry until all that's left is resentment and anger.

I knew this kid that everyone was afraid of. (On the streets you seldom admit to being afraid of someone, you say, "He/She's crazy!" which basically means that person might do what you're afraid to. If you stepped on his shoe he'd swing. If you swung, he'd grab a gun. "That's the Chicago way," as Connery told Costner in *The Untouchables*.) So people stayed scared and he ran wild. But one day something happened: Some kid—a younger kid—got tired of being afraid and shot him. Dead. No more fear.

So lead thru respect. Lead thru encouragement. Lead thru understanding and professionalism. To lead any other way just isn't leadership.

What're they gonna do, fire me?

Every company has at least one problem or person that if openly challenged, will get someone fired. Every industry has at least one practice that if exposed would get someone blackballed. The saddest part about writing this book was the realization that most ad agencies won't want me around once this book gets popular. It raises too many questions, exposes too many practices, and challenges too many people. My pops once told me that a man should never burn his bridges. I'm fully aware that this book is one big canister of napalm on most every bridge I've ever crossed. But you know what? It was necessary.

Knock The Hustle raises issues that need to be openly addressed once and for all. But more importantly, much of this book is the voice of thousands upon thousands of business professionals I've met over the years, all of whom were afraid to speak the truth themselves for fear of retaliation. So when it comes to shook ones and denial, know that *Knock The Hustle* is the child of those parents.

The fear of man bringeth a snare...
—Proverbs 29:25

Word Is Bond

There is no "maybe" in their language—
you're either going to do something or you're not.
—Amistad

Word is bond—Black wisdom from hiphop's golden era. Word is bond. From Africa to now, our word has always been our most powerful and connective tool. We used to conduct business, build governments, and pass on entire histories and cultures based solely on the spoken word.

Word is bond. My word matters. When I'm not there, my word is. Just as a dollar bill once represented a dollar's worth of gold, my word represents me. I say what I mean; I mean what I say. If I say I'll pay you back tomorrow, you'll get paid back tomorrow. Regardless of the stakes, my word will always be as good as the action it's meant to represent. Or, to break it down to its last compound:

Trust

Next to talking, trust is the biggest thing missing in business today. No one trusts their boss. Bosses don't trust employees. Clients don't trust agencies. Consumers don't trust marketers. Voters don't trust politicians or governments. Nobody trusts the average lawyer, stock analyst, or accountant. Some days in business aren't much different from a typical drug deal: watch the money and watch your back.

But more so than mutual trust, most folks don't trust themselves. People are afraid to trust their own instincts and talents. Some people don't trust themselves even when everyone else says they're right. Lack of trust is often inbred into a company's culture from the top down. Many companies teach employees to be drones: follow protocol, stick to the script, and make the boss/client/consumer happy. It's pretty sad.

Roach.

We didn't work together much but "Roach" probably taught me as much about trust as anyone I ever met. Whenever we hit our usual spot: Billy Goat's Tavern on lower Michigan Ave, he drank Schlitz. On tap. In a glass mug—the grimier the mug, the happier he was. He was an Irishman. Played rugby—which was a riot considering he wasn't more than 5'7" and a buck forty soaking wet. (He always came to work with something broken or bruised.) He was good people. Real smart, too.

Now when it comes to account execs, most tell you what the client wants followed by what they think their bosses want. Then, at some point, usually right after you've shown them some work, they'll tell you the client won't like it even though the client hasn't seen a thing.

But the first time I worked with Roach he looked at my work and said, "I don't really understand what you're showing me, but explain it to me so I can sell it." Explain it so I can sell it. No second-guesses. No "Lemme-tell-you-how-to-do-your-job" ramblings. Just, "Explain it so I can sell it." In short: I trust you.

It wasn't that Roach was soft, some sort of creative groupie, or just didn't care one way or the other. He was quite the opposite. If he thought something was wrong, he said so to whoever needed to hear it. Roach just trusted you to carry your weight the same way he knew he had to carry his. If you told him the client should go left, he'd tell the client to go left. And if you were wrong, then you were wrong. But Roach gave you the chance to be wrong, which ultimately gave you more chances to be right. (It's amazing how hard you'll work when people trust your talents and your judgment.)

I probably worked harder with Roach because I knew my opinion mattered more. In fact, everyone stepped up their game when they worked with him. He made work fun. I just wish I had met him later in my career—I was 24 when I worked with him and wasn't polished yet. I made some mistakes on his clients but I also learned a lot. Most importantly, I learned to trust.

It is better to trust in the Lord
than to put confidence in man.
—Psalms 118:8

Honesty

You can't have trust without honesty. And to be honest, Corporate America still breeds way too many liars. Businesspeople lie about everything. Our resumés. Our profits. Our past. We lie about what our products can actually do. We lie to clients about our capabilities. We lie to coworkers. Corporate America just loves to lie. Why? Because most businessfolks can't handle the truth. The truth isn't always "on strategy." The truth isn't always a formula. (Remember, business lives for formulas.) The truth doesn't care about image or PR spin. And let's face it: the truth isn't always profitable.

Plus, honesty is hard. It doesn't care about your brand or your shareholders. Honesty isn't interested in your career or your agenda. Honesty is glue—once you use it, you're stuck with it, profitable or not. Once you say it, you have to do it. Honesty can expose a company or an employee's weakness. Honesty challenges you to back it each time it shows up. Honesty is hard, especially when money's involved.

But what makes honesty so hard? Fear of failing, mostly. Or, to be more precise: fear that failure won't be forgiven. The main reason I saw people lie and use dishonest tactics was because they were terrified of failing. And again, bosses, clients, shareholders, and flaky consumers have everyone shook—scared to take chances of any kind unless success can be guaranteed. Everyone's afraid that failing will get them fired, embarrassed, or bankrupt.

But I can't front. Not everyone dodges honesty out of fear of failure. Some businesspeople are dishonest because they're just flat shiesty, greedy, lazy, or some combination thereof. But if you don't have the common sense to fire those people or cut ties with them, then you get what you deserve.

Now with all that said, how do we bring back trust and honesty?

Satisfaction Not Guaranteed

Part of increasing trust in business is being honest about expectations. Bosses and stockholders need to accept the fact that success is a process and failing is part of that process. I'm not talking about lowering standards; I'm talking about raising patience and understanding. I'm talking about creating environments where honest bad news is as welcomed as dishonest good news.

We need to be supportive when employees make mistakes. Most successful entrepreneurs don't succeed until their second or third business venture. Again, I'm not trying to encourage or excuse failure. But mistakes are part of growth. Until we accept this, dishonesty will continue.

Provide things honest in the sight of all men.
—Romans 12:17

N-O

Remember the "*no people*" from "Less Bosses...?" Well here's why you need them: Corporate America hates "No." ("No" is so strong that hearing it makes you wonder if before God said, "Let there be light," maybe He was thinking, *No more darkness.*)

But I like "No" because "No" is usually the truth; and most businesspeople would rather have certainty than truth. When you say "No" (or even "maybe") to a businessperson, they usually have to pass it onto someone higher up the food chain. And no one wants to tell their boss, client, or shareholders "No." On the flipside, people like "Yes"—it makes 'em feel good, like chicken soup or ice cream. Even when it's wrong or a lie, "Yes" usually sounds pretty good.

Businesspeople need to hear "No" like children need vegetables—it's good for 'em. "No" forces people to justify what they believe and explain it rather than just hope momentum pushes it thru. "No" can save money. "No" can overcome "Yes" mistakes. "No" can kill bad ideas and revive brands. When used properly, "No" can be an important business tool.

My advice: Do at least 25 "no" reps a day. Get those "no" muscles strong enough so you can use 'em when the time comes. (And again, hire some "no people.")

Documentation: What's Your Word Worth?

We touched on paper trails in the last chapter, but lemme add these:

1. Don't equate having it in writing with trust or honesty.

A paper trail is nice, but if someone will lie to your face, they'll probably lie to you in print. And if you're documenting things because you don't trust the folks you're dealing with, then you've got problems that no memo, contract, or paper trail will ever solve.

2. Treat verbal agreements like written contracts.

Pop a cork. Swap spit. Take a blood oath. Hug. I don't care how you consummate it; just give promises and agreements the same weight you give the printed word. Let folks know that you expect their word to mean something and it will, or at least it'll remind them that it should.

That's it. Live by your word; make your word matter. Business will be better for it.

Let us walk honestly; as in the day...
—Romans 13:13

Less Communicating, More Talking

Seeing then that we have such hope,
we use great plainness of speech.
—II Corinthians 3:12

Once upon a time, communication was a good thing; that is, until businesspeople got hold of it. Now it's a steaming pile of nonsense in a neatly pressed power suit. Business communication is the foolishness of people trying to impress, intimidate, and sometimes exclude thru fancy jargon and industry terminology. Just as knucklehead emcees spit clichéd verses trying to prove their realness, too many corporate folks waste their breath "communicating" instead of just talking to each other like intelligent human beings.

I have a confession to make: I never touched anyone's bases. I've never put any ducks in any rows. I never took any balls and ran with them. I never interfaced or delivered synergy. I never wrote a living document. I was never on board, though I was occasionally bored to tears. I was never in the loop, unless you count downtown Chicago. My plate was never full. I was never on the same page with anyone else. I never preached to a choir. I was not an alpha male. And I never thought about boxes long enough to care about how to think outside of one.

Dumb words reflect and encourage dumb thinking. You know what? If businessfolks communicated less we'd talk our way into better ideas a lot more often. After all, how can you avoid clichéd ideas if you can't even avoid clichés in conversation?

And for the record: "*Soup to nuts*" is the dumbest business phrase I ever heard for describing a company's capabilities. Why soup to nuts? I've never been in a restaurant or over someone's house and started with soup and ended with nuts. I've had salad and ended with chocolate cake or ice cream... I've started with beer and ended with, um, beer. But no soup, no nuts. Ever. (How about, "Kool-Aid to freeze pops"? That's something I've actually done.)

One nice thing about street life: we don't communicate we *talk*. And by talk I mean keep it simple. State your business. Make your point. Make sure people understand your purpose and your perspective and keep it moving. Even the most insider-ish phrases are fairly blunt and direct. And just as importantly, we listen. To do less creates unnecessary drama.

"For his letters," they say, "are weighty and powerful;
but his bodily presence is weak and his speech is contemptible."
—II Corinthians 10:10

Nine Keys to Better Talking:

1. Say what you mean, mean what you say.

'Nuf sed.

2. Speak plain English.

Simple words clearly spoken work wonders. Just say, "From start to finish" and actually mean it. No, you won't be as hip as the cool kids, but at least people will understand you and that's what matters most. Polish your ideas, not your jargon.

3. Shut up and listen.

Nothing good happens in a vacuum. The more you listen, the more you learn; and the more you listen to others, the more they'll want to listen to you when you need them to.

4. All meetings: 30 minutes, max.

We can get a pizza in 30 minutes but not a clear set of instructions or coherent client feedback? C'mon, y'all. If you speak plainly, honestly and listen, you should be in and out of most any meeting in half an hour.

5. One meeting per week, max.

When you're meeting, you're not working. People should work more than they sit around and talk about work. If you need multiple meetings every week just to function, something's seriously wrong.

6. Learn to write.

Unless your name is Shawn Carter you'd better learn how to properly put pen to paper. I'm still amazed by the number of businesspeople who can't write a decent document. (I swear I've gotten memos and white papers that read like Aramaic in Braille.) Writing is talking in print. If you can't write, you have no voice.

Also, writing is a muscle—work out often and yours'll get stronger. Read more, too. Strong writers tend to be strong readers. If your employees are poor writers, help them improve.

7. Technology is a talking crutch.

We're emailing, faxing, paging, IM'ing, PDA'ing, 2-waying, and bluetoothing each other to death. We're spellchecking without learning how to spell. I think we expect all this stuff to do our talking for us.

Technology is just a tool. Technology can't talk. Technology can't listen. Technology can't understand. Technology doesn't have common sense, instincts, or insights. So less tech, more talk.

8. More face-offs.

Business needs more face-to-face discussions. It's like the first marathon: The word came from a soldier who ran 26 miles to Marathon, Greece so he could personally relay an important message to his captain. Why? Because if he'd given it to someone else, they would've screwed it up.

But seriously, we need to lose the middlemen and messaging and talk to each other. Make time for personal conversations. It may seem inconvenient at times, but it'll definitely build trust and cut down on mix-ups—both of which are priceless.

9. Share info.

Hording info doesn't make your words more powerful; it just makes you stupid and selfish. The more you share, the more people will listen to you and the more they'll be able to understand what you're talking about.

Excellent speech becometh not a fool:
much less do lying lips a prince.
—Proverbs 17:7

Get yourself a...mouthpiece

Mouthpiece is about articulation. Eloquence. Flow. Mouthpiece is talking that sells. A strong mouthpiece can convince a woman to sell her body and give a man the money. A strong mouthpiece can put mediocrity in the White House and innocent people in prison. When I say mouthpiece, I'm talking about talking at its highest level.

Ever worked with a totally brilliant person who couldn't talk their way out of a paper bag? Me too. (Sorta felt sorry for 'em, didn't you?) Nothing's sadder than watching intelligence and truth smothered by the inability to relay it. Conversely, I've witnessed countless mediocre ideas and bad products, dumb strategies, and incompetent people succeed by virtue of strong mouthpieces.

So, how does one go about developing a mouthpiece? Well I'm glad you asked...

5 Steps to a Better Business Mouthpiece:

1. Be humble.

Humility sells. When you speak, people should feel like you're an extremely grateful representative of a great idea. Humility creates comfort and support. Once people are comfort with you, they'll pull for you and whatever you're selling. Success is never a solo act. It requires help; and in this case, the help is your audience. So again, be humble.

2. Be clear.

Answer questions don't create them. If I have 3 questions before you open your mouth and 4 after you close it then you weren't clear. Before I can judge what you're saying, I need to understand what you've said.

3. Believe in what you're saying.

If you don't, why should anyone else? Don't be conceited just be convinced.

4. Care about the people you're talking to.

If you think you're better than your audience, it'll show. If you see people as nothing more than an opportunity to enrich yourself, it'll show. No matter how great your idea is, no matter how good you are, if people sense that you don't care, they'll tune you out. The best way to get people listening is to show 'em you care.

5. Manifest.
Talk is only about 70% of the battle. If you want people to do business with you, at some point your words must manifest. Action gives words weight and nothing solidifies an idea or a promise like results. The more people see your words come to life, the more they'll listen to you and the easier it'll be to talk to them.

These are the words that I manifest... I manifest!
—Gang Starr[1]

And that's that. Communicate less, talk more; back it up with honesty and action and you're in there.

My doctrine shall drop as the rain,
my speech shall distill as the dew,
as the small rain on the tender herb,
and as showers upon the grass...
—Deuteronomy 32:2

Do You:
What are you selling?

I'mo do me, you gots to do you.
—Heather B.

Dre and D.O.C. said it best: It's *the formula.* Business loves a sure thing; and nothing's surer than what's already been done. Most every client wants the predictable, stable formula. And if that means biting everyone else's formula then so be it. Long as it sells, ride the formula. And should it fail, CYA—blame the formula.

That's why so many emcees are still trying to out-jigga Jay-Z, out-TRL Em, Nelly or Usher, out-crunk the Dirty South, or out-thug Fiddy, who's trying to out-thug Tupac's ghost. Every singer is trying to out-pop the latest prepackaged MTV princess. And the fashion industry is so homogenized that you can't tell OLD NAVY from GAP from AMERICAN EAGLE from BANANA REPUBLIC from ABERCROMBIE & FITCH from J. CREW from POLO from CALVIN KLEIN from SEAN JOHN from PHAT FARM from ROCAWEAR... No matter what restaurant you go to all the food tastes the same... Every sitcom has the same 20 jokes per 22-minute episode. Every movie is a sequel, a remake, a cartoon, a comic book, a kitschy TV show, or some "high-concept" that's been done to death. It's raining commodities and cookie cutters and consumers are getting soaked.

But clones don't last. At some point formulas get stale and people get wise. At some point you have to look in a mirror and ask, *What am I?* At some point you have to stand on that foundation and stand up for it. At some point, you have to let people see your truth as an individual and as a company and let it ride. At some point you just have to do you.

Do You. It's not a question or a fragment; it's the complete solution for the business world's lack of innovation and integrity. For example:

Unlike Any Other (Sorta)

From about 2001 to early 2005 I worked on a leading luxury European car account. Once, they were jewel of the Nile, the industry standard. They were the ultimate "I-got-it-made" mobile. Everyone wanted one. When you saw one parked, you'd stop, stare, and wonder how much the owner was worth. In fact, black folks used to joke that if you were truly successful, you had three things: (1) A house in the 'burbs. (2) A white girl. (3) One of these stupid cars. (Yes, they were truly that serious.)

But times change. Between a few generations of competition, slip-'n'-slide economies and evolving tastes the company struggled. Sales dropped. The brand weakened. And with the exception of their highest-end models, they really weren't moving units. So as part of their comeback tour they decided to get all multicultural, which meant reaching out to black, Hispanic, and Asian car buyers—folks they traditionally ignored.

This is where I came in. My job was to help them become more "relevant." *Translation:* Work some blackness into their brand. Get a few dark faces and urban slang into their ads. Give them some soul. Help them "be down."

Anyway, before I did any ads, I analyzed their brand, the marketplace, trends, etc. and discovered that they had three serious problems.

Strike One: Attack of the clones.

Over the last 15 years the auto industry has become one big strip mall. With few exceptions, all the cars now look alike. There was a time, as recent as the late 1980s, when a Jaguar looked like a Jaguar and nothing else. A Porsche was a Porsche. And you could spot a Mercedes doing 85 mph in dense fog at night from 10 miles out and still know that you just got lapped by a Benz.

But today, if you line up most cars and strip the off logos, a BMW looks like an Acura looks like a Lexus looks like an Infiniti looks like a Honda looks like a Chrysler looks like a Nissan. Even most SUVs and minivans look alike. Besides the Hummer and maybe the Beetle, you could probably get hit head-on by a car doing 5 mph in broad daylight under the California sun and still not be sure of exactly what hit you. Blame CAFTA/NAFTA, blame globalization, blame scared money, but whatever the cause carmakers have *me-too*'d themselves into a milquetoast traffic jam.

For decades, our client's logo—a silver, encircled three-point star—always sat up on the 'hood like a middle finger to the whole world. Well they changed it. On some models they slanted it back; on other models they pulled it completely off the hood and recessed it into the grille like an insincere apology. Every model used to have these stiff, upright, purposeful curves and uppity lines, even on their convertibles. But they changed those, too. They went sportier, more laid back, more "whatever, guy," more like everyone else. Next thing you know, they're asking folks to drop 45Gs on soupped-up Camry clones.

Strike Two: Ballin' out of control.

Funny thing about the whole "affordable luxury" movement...it's an oxymoron. Luxury and access don't mix. If everyone can afford it, it's not luxury; it's *standard.* Luxury is about being better than standard and being too unique to be average. When you're pushing a luxury brand, the last thing you want to do is franchise it. You want to be in the *Robb Report,* not Wal-Mart. Luxury is the velvet rope outside the club: your brand becomes exclusive because you exclude, luxurious because you brand it as such. You get hot by trading volume for a sky-high price-per-unit and elitist cache. And if you're patient, selective, and focused you'll become a luxury brand for decades, generations even.

For the longest time, my client was a master at this. But then all of a sudden, they got dumb or arrogant or greedy or all of the above; and somewhere around the mid-1990s, they jumped on the affordable luxury bandwagon along with ARMANI EXCHANGE, LADY GODIVA, STARBUCKS, gold/platinum cards, cellphones, etc. They started rolling out entry-level models for around 40Gs. (Today some of their models start as low as 29-and-change.) They also started pushing fleets of pre-owned models to attract even more working-class folks... Almost over night they drove 100 years of luxurious elitism and exclusivity right off a cliff.

Sure, they started pulling in drivers who couldn't afford their cars before; but now they were alienating their core upscale consumers, many of who now felt like they needed to upgrade to a more luxurious status symbol to further differentiate themselves once again. And that's another problem with affordable luxury: people love to exclude. As much as people want to belong to something that's bigger than them, they also want some control over just how big that 'something' gets.

If you sell me a product on the premise that it's tailor-made just for me, and I buy it looking to feel special and stand out from the crowd, and then I turn around and see 500 other folks with it, eventually I'm gonna feel like I just got hustled; and to a certain degree, I'll be correct. And of course, you'll make money short term, but long term, that affordable-luxury angle really hustles all involved. It artificially expands the status quo and cuts the legs right out from under luxury.

(This is largely why our client regularly spends tens of millions of extra dollars developing additional higher-end models in hopes of winning back some of their original core consumers.)

Strike Three: Minority drivers wanted.

Even with its cheaper entry models our client had never really targeted people of color to any degree before. They didn't want to. They didn't need to. Intentional or not, there has always been a seldom-spoken but always-understood position of "This car isn't meant for minorities." In fact, when older folks discussed racial profiling and *Driving While Black,* they were often referring to blacks that drove our client's car. But now that they were out for dolo all bets were off; minorities were now welcomed.

But their brand image was actually their biggest obstacle. Like I said earlier, they were the quintessential elitist brand, especially among minorities. Consequently, owning one was almost an act of defiance or selling out, depending on your view. But a funny thing happened on the way to the rainbow coalition: Some minority consumers grew suspicious of the brand's newfound inclusion. It was a, "You-ignored-us for-years-now-you-want-to-be-our-friend...what's-up-with-that?" vibe. Also, many minority consumers were still having issues with negative and even discriminatory treatment from some of our client's dealerships.

Still, I took their money and pimped their ride. First off, I paired them up with Jay-Z. They were a *Robb Report* staple while Hov' was the $300 million man from Marcy who brought the suburbs to the hood. It was a perfect fit. I convinced them to license select Jay-Z lyrics that were brand-centric enough to build a print campaign around. Next we ran the print work in top urban pubs including: *Vibe, XXL*, and *Black Enterprise*. The next move was to build momentum by promoting his upcoming tour and designing a signature edition Jay-Z/ROCAWEAR vehicle. It was almost brilliant.

Notice, I said *almost*.

For starters, the client was a pain. They insisted on toning down every print ad, radio script, and storyboard that came their way. They were trying to go urban, but not "too urban." They were hell-bent on maintaining a look and feel that when combined with everything else, had zero relevance to this new audience. This meant that every ad had to fit into their stupid, old, stodgy template (which hadn't worked since Clinton was in office) and maintain a vocabulary that didn't alienate their core base (which they'd alienated years ago without me).

The most obvious and funniest example of this came when the client who, after forking over money to license Jay-Z's lyrics, complained that they weren't grammatically correct and needed to be fixed. So they started correcting the grammar in the lyrics in every print ad. It was insane. They paid God-knows-what for street flavor only to Pat Boone it to death. Look, I'm not on the dude's jock or anything, but you don't tug on Superman's cape; you don't spit into the wind, and you don't take a red pen to the work of one of the nicest lyricists in the last 50 years of music.

Plus, the client wasn't the target audience; and as I've told dozens of clients over the years that aren't part of the demo that they're trying to reach: "You don't need to 'get it.' Your target gets it and that's what matters most."

Also, like most mainstream brands that target minority consumers, they skimped on media and production budgets. We had to piggyback off the mainstream agency's budget, which meant we couldn't shoot any of the fresh car shots we needed to. It was so insulting to hear them say they didn't have money for us but then watch them shell-out for fresh mainstream work with good production values then back it up with quality media buys. (We'll get more into this in the "Universal Hustle" chapter.)

And to make things worse, S-Dot's now multi-platinum classic *Black Album* dropped right around the time our campaign launched. Had they listened, they could've had exclusive sponsorship of his farewell tour and really made some inroads. We also had plans to cut a deal with his girlfriend, then "the hottest chick in the game," which would've given the brand even more relevance with an even wider consumer base. (Think: "His- & Hercedes.")

But no. All of that would've required taking multicultural, specifically young black car buyers (along with black marketing professionals) seriously—something they weren't ready to do yet. It was a total blown opportunity. Still, my work made some buzz, and actually moved a couple extra cars off the lot. And as a reward, they bailed on the Jay-Z campaign after just a handful of executions.

They asked for a new round of creative work that was less street. So I went back to the drawing board and developed some safer, more conventional approaches. First up: A profiles campaign featuring universally upscale figures (minorities that don't offend white people) like the top pediatric surgeon on the planet, along with other blacks that everyone was comfortable with. It was your standard "We-salute-these-'credit-to-their-race'-folks-now-buy-our-product" advertising.(Every mainstream client does it at least once a year, usually in February.) The client bought it and gave us a slightly bigger budget, but still not what was needed or deserved. Anyway, the campaign launched to decent reviews and positive consumer feedback. That was back in June 2004.

But today, they've still got serious issues—the biggest being that they're obviously still not being true to themselves. They took a perfectly unique brand, let it get stale then almost trend-hopped it to death. (Currently, they're struggling to balance their newfound urban sensibilities with their traditional roots; it's been a rough road, to put it mildly. They're also juggling perception with reality— in terms of style and innovation, many of their cars are pretty average now and no brand campaign can hide that.

Anyway, to my former client, if you're reading this: *Do You*. Be the elitist snobs you were born and bred to be; go back to the pristine style that the top 10% love to love and everyone else loves to hate but loves to chase after anyway. And please, get back to making high-performance luxury cars that truly look and ride unlike any other. Or, be the car of semi-upscale masses and make the systemic changes necessary to do that right. Just make up your mind, one way or the other and do it.

And to everyone else: Don't sleep, there are literally hundreds of brands and companies in every category running this exact same playbook, to varying degrees. Some get away with it, most don't. But make no mistake: things won't improve for any of them until they respect the game and change.

(And yes indeed, the client was Mercedes Benz.)

Be your own guy; follow your own movement.
Heavy D.[1]

Still tippin'...

In late 2000, prior to MB and before *Fast and the Furious* hit and car shows were on every cable channel, I worked on another major car account—one of the Big Three. But with all the parity, calling 'em the Big Three is like Americans calling our sports teams world champions—it's true provided you ignore the rest of the world, which, ironically, is precisely why the Big Three's biggest problem. (It's no wonder S&P dropped GM and Ford stock to junk-bond status in May '05, while foreign carmakers held strong-arm steady.) Anyway...

To prop up eroding market share, Mr. Big Three wants in on the then-emerging street car culture. They wanted all those 16–29 year-olds who were spending millions of dollars by industry estimates customizing their buckets, heaps, and factory-issued cherries with custom kits, nitrous tanks, monster engines, fancy rims, next-level sound systems, etc.

Their angle: An official Big Three Branded Accessories store. Our mission was to create a store—something hip, edgy yet inviting where said car enthusiast would find everything they needed under one roof. We were to name the place, give it a look and recommend inventory.

It was a nasty pile-up. For starters, against our advice the client picked the most middle-of-the-road name possible. They followed that up by requesting store designs that were more CRATE & BARREL than AMERICAN CHOPPER. Then, there was the inventory. We made a list of items based on what the culture was doing and where we thought it was headed. For example, not only did the client not like the idea of doing branded dubs, they couldn't understand why anyone would want rims larger than the factory-issue on any car.

Our client wasted tons of money plus some really great work from some of the best designers I've ever seen. And to this day, they're still spinning their wheels trying to compete with foreign carmakers, urban car culture, etc. Why? Two reasons. *One:* Biting is a no-no. The client wasn't part of the culture and they bit off more than they wanted to chew trying to co-opt it. *Reason Two:* Ain't no half-steppin'. I'm against trend-hopping, but if you're going do it, check your ego at the door and go all out. Fully embrace whatever it is you're trying to link yourself to. And contribute something to the culture you're jocking; otherwise you're just a fifth wheel.

(By the way: This client was Ford Motors.)

You're a beat biter, dope style taker
tell you to face you ain't nuthin' but a faker!
—MC Lyte[2]

5 More Tips for Doing You:

1. Know you.

Whether you're a brand, a business, or a person, you can't be yourself unless you know yourself. You'd be amazed by the number of companies and professionals who really don't know who they are or what they're about. The biggest marketing hurdles I faced were clients who didn't understand their own brand/company well enough to decide how they should be marketed. You'd also be surprised by the number of consumers who get hustled into buying things they don't need because they don't know themselves well enough to know what they really want.

When you have knowledge of self, business (especially marketing) gets a whole lot simpler and easier. So in all things, know you.

1a. Know your character

Part of know you is knowing your character. Personality is what you are around other people; character is what you are regardless of who's around. Whether you're a company or an individual, ask yourself one simple question: What am I truly about? What am I will to ride or die for, popular/profitable or not? *That's* character. When you can answer that, you're half-way home. (The other half is knowing people—we'll get to that in the "People Trying To Give You Their Money"chapter.)

2. Don't reinvent, retool.

Reinvention ranks among the most overused business phrases ever. Companies, celebrities, and regular folks who reinvent themselves often end up worse off than before. Why? Because *reinvention* is about starting over, but *retooling* is about improving while remaining true to you. Sometimes, wholesale change is the only way to improve; but usually a smart tweak here 'n' there is really all it takes. So think and retool before you reinvent.

3. Don't trend-hop.

The saddest thing about modern hiphop is watching companies who spent years avoiding minority consumers suddenly become "urban brands"...It's trend-hopping at its worst. Once *APPLE, GATEWAY,* and *DELL* blew up the home computer market, *IBM,* who'd ignored that market for years and actually rejected the Apple guys when they first started up, decided to trend-hop itself into the home computer arena. They sucked at it. Fortunately, *IBM* remembered why they're called International Business Machines and went back to what they did best—themselves—and they've lived happily ever after since. Sorta. (On Demand solutions—treating business-computing like a utility; i.e., electricity or water? You can't be serious. Louis Gerstner, where are you?)

Anyway, don't do what's hot, do what's you. (After all, individuality is always "in.")

4. Don't be greedy.

Most businesses lose their identity (or can't stick to one) because they get greedy. They chase untapped consumer groups or certain trends just because there's money to be made. And once it fails they realize that every mistake they made was a by-product of them not being themselves. Line-extensions are also a sign of greed.

Remember: Greedy people are never true to themselves because greed never lets you see yourself; it only lets you see what you're chasing.

5. Focus.

Most actor/singer/restaurateur/fashion designers suck. They could be good or great at one or two things, but they're usually spread way too thin to be good at anything. Same goes for most brands stretched across multiple product lines. In an attempt to cash in, they start slapping their name on too much stuff, most of which is either inferior or runs counter to whatever made their brand great in the first place.

I say focus on one thing and do it great. The marketplace needs more "great at one thing" and less "sorta good at a lot of things." You can't Do You if you're trying to do everything at once.

That's it. *To recap:* whether it's business or personal, *Do You.* Copycats create clutter; individuals innovate and rise above. Do You. Clones create noise; individuals make music. Do You. Don't counterpunch the competition; don't do the kid next door; don't do last summer's blockbuster or pop hit. Do You. In the end, who you followed, who you copied, and who's formula you bit won't matter. What will matter is what you became; so you better become true to yourself. Do You.

Oh, one more thing: You are not a brand; you are not a product; you are a human being. Lemme say that again: People are not brands. People have personalities and souls. Brands, even the strongest, most powerful brands in the world on their best day are nothing more than Pinocchio—commercial puppets on marketing strings that can only dream of someday becoming real little boys. Brands are illusions; people are real. Period.

And be not conformed to this world: but be ye transformed by the renewing of your mind, that ye may prove what is that good, and acceptable, and perfect, will of God.
—Romans 12:2

Kill The Dogs 'n' Ponies

You know you got me working,
day and night; got me working...
—Michael Jackson

Every businessperson has witnessed or participated in at least one dog 'n' pony show. Dog 'n' Pony shows are part CYA, part "More is better," which goes like this: "Eighty hours on my timesheet makes me more dedicated than someone with 45 on theirs. Offering 5 solutions to a problem means I care more than someone who only offers 3, even if 4 of mine are wrong or stupid. If I compliment you twice, I'm more sincere than someone who only compliments you once. Dog 'n' pony shows, all.

Well guess what? The dog 'n' pony shows have got to go.

Keep It on the One

This just in: Size doesn't always matter, quantity isn't quality, and activity doesn't equal achievement. If the food is nasty, bigger portions won't help. If the schools ain't teaching, a longer school year won't help. Whether we're talking clients, bosses, or average folks, focus on providing them one great idea. One. One effective executable solution. One intelligent answer. One is usually all it takes. If you can do more afterwards, great. But focus on getting one right first. I'll take a drop of right over a bucket full of almost any day of the week.

Now I bet I know what some of you are thinking, *Hadji, my boss/client won't accept "just one." They'll accuse me of not working hard or not perform-*

ing." To that I say, "You might be right." And if you have a boss, a client, or work for a company like that, get out now. Run. Because (1) They're stupid and stupid people always make life harder than necessary. (2) Their stupidity will ultimately lower your quality of work and brainwash you into confusing quantity with quality. And (3) Once your quality drops (and eventually it will) the stupid people will blame you instead of their stupid standards, which drove down the caliber of your work in the first place.

Don't confuse activity with accomplishment.
—Mark Grace[1]

No More Timesheets

Corporate timesheets are among the stupidest advents to come out of the business world in years. Now there's nothing wrong with tracking man-hours and employee performance, but for too many companies, timesheets have been reduced to *Scantron* tests for adults—we use 'em to measure success and work ethic, yet they prove little, and all you end up doing is scribbling patterns out of little boxes and numbers and hoping you don't get sued or indicted. You know why most of us fill out timesheets? Because we broke Hustler Rule #5: *DON'T GET HIGH OFF YOUR OWN SUPPLY.* We've spent so many years convincing consumers and clients that quantity equals quality that we've bought into it ourselves.

I don't care what CFOs, comptrollers, or HR-types say about timesheets; no company makes long-term loot by billing lots of hours unless those hours translate into results. Companies make money by generating results and getting people to pay for the time it took to generate those results. Think about it: When's the last time you heard any businessperson say, "This a great idea/solution, but it only took us 25 hours to create it. So let's go with the other one that's not as good but took us took us 45 hours to develop." Never happens. Results. Solutions. Great ideas. *That's* what people care about. At least, that's what they *should* care about.

If most businesses had any *real* hustle in 'em, they'd get a college kid or a secretary to fill out everyone's timesheets for them. That way, the bean-counters and pencil-pushers can get the numbers they want every week and the workers can focus on working and not wasting time trying to account for every hour they work.

C'mon folks, let's be real: Companies have been cooking books for decades but until now it's been about leeching off clients and overworking employees. (In fact, screwing clients is precisely what got those geniuses at O&M convicted in early 2005.[2]) Now I'm not suggesting either one. My approach simply relegates timesheets to the side-dish position where they belong and makes performance, relationships, and results the main course. With my approach, clients will get the caliber of work they want at the price they agreed to and the agency will get the necessary numbers they're looking for.

Clients and consumers care about one thing: the end result. More and more these days, people don't care how you got there or what you went thru to make it, just so long as you get the job done. If it's good and ready when they want it, people will pay your price if they can afford it.

Then again, we could just abolish timesheets altogether except where they're absolutely necessary, stop being clock-watchers and just focus on rewarding people for good work. And while we're at it, let's start being upfront with clients and consumers about how marketing really works as well as how products are made. (Nah, that almost makes sense.)

I work, I work, baby. I get the job done.
—Big Daddy Kane[3]

Dress Codes

One of the most common dog 'n' pony shows going is businesswear. We put on suits and fancy clothes for client meetings and presentations...new business pitches...interviews... We're always dressing up for some occasion or another. But uniforms aside, I've never understood the value of corporate dress codes. My clothes have never written a single ad or built a brand. I've never seen a suit of clothes solve a problem or run a department. I've never seen a tie or nice pair of heels improve any company's bottom line. It seems like the only reason we dress up in business is to impress people who either don't have the good sense to measure people by their character and results or who've been hustled into embracing that tired old "Image-is-everything" paradigm.

And no, I don't buy the "Look-like-a-professional" argument because the most professional person I ever knew was my dad and the only time he wore a suit is when someone jumped the broom or passed away; plus, some of the most corrupt and unprofessional folks I've ever dealt with wore suits and nice clothes every day. As I've said before, professionalism is a matter of behavior and work ethic, not wardrobe.

Dress up your ideas and your performance, not your bodies.

Ain't no future in your fronting

Fronting—pretending to be something you're not. It's huge in the corporate arena, especially in marketing. People front on their resumés and in job interviews. We front for bosses and colleagues. We front for shareholders and consumers. No matter how you slice it or rationalize it, it's all part of the great dog 'n' pony show.

The worst cases of fronting I saw and continue to see come in new business pitches. In the ad world, Chicago's still known as a "packaged goods' town." Lots of old-school, tangible goods, brick and mortar companies like WRIGLEY'S GUM, KRAFT, SARA LEE, QUAKER, etc. As clients, they tend to be very conservative—"Show the product, explain its attributes, show happy people using the product. Repeat if possible." Not the most cutting-edge stuff. Contrast this with the typical ad agency that brags about their "edgy, cut-through-the-clutter" work—the commercial that makes bar patrons do spit-takes and gets on-air personalities small-talking it up throughout the week or the campaign that wins industry awards and scores cool points with trendsetters and pop culture critics.

So how do agencies like this win clients like that? Usually by fronting. Rather than be upfront, said agency often puts on their "Strategy-first-it's-all -about-sales-spikes" outfits and courts the prospective client with the kind of conservative work that makes them comfortable. Then they bring out all kinds of research data and case studies that demonstrate their core philosophy of moving the needle. The client bites and offers them the account.

Some months later the client starts complaining about the work being off strategy while the agency, specifically the creatives complain that the strategy sucks and all the cool work is getting killed in favor of safe stuff. Meanwhile, the account folks are doing all they can to hold the client's hand and hope the account doesn't go back up for review.

It's like any bad relationship—everybody fronted during the courtship, and now that you've shacked up together, gotten hitched, or gone into business together, everyone's true colors are showing and you're ready to choke the snot out of each other.

The solution here is simple: *Stop fronting.*

Let people see the true you as often as possible. Let clients, colleagues, consumers, potential bosses, dates, etc., know what you're really about from jump. Sure it's potentially embarrassing. Sure it might make you a little vulnerable. But in the end, you'll have a lot more birds of a feather and a lot less cockfights.

Perp-walks

Oh, before we proceed, I need to speak on our white-collar arrests: For the most part, they're a joke. Breads 'n' circuses. Dogs 'n' ponies. First off, no matter who gets pinched, no one's getting any part of their money back. Ever. The pension loot is still gone. Most of those affected stocks are still toast. And none of those lost jobs are ever coming back.

Secondly, insider trading might be the biggest dog 'n' pony show in the history of corporate governance. My pops once gave me a little bit of advice that was given to him by a "connected" guy. He said, "The only people who win at the racetrack are those lucky enough to bet with the gangsters—they're the only ones with the inside information." Business is no different. Wall Street is 40% who you know and 40% what you do about who you know (the other 20% is what you know). And the average investor—the one who's trying to flip their tax return into a college/retirement fund—doesn't know anybody with inside info, so they get up every day and hope they're putting money on the same horses that Warren Buffet and the rest are.

Thirdly, whether we're talking about Bernie Ebbers, the Fastows, the Rigases, etc., those goofs got pinched for breaking the golden rule: *DON'T FLOSS YOUR HAUL.* Showoffs are always the first to go. That's how they got Gotti in the 1990s. It's how Boesky, Milken, and Keating got pinched for the S&L scandals in the 1980s. Had they stayed humble and simply lived off their legal, declared salaries until they retired they would've never been touched. But no, they had to floss: Multimillion dollar homes in multiple states and countries. Six-figure parties. Five-figure toys. Ten figure art collections. Private planes. Fleets of cars and yachts... They might as well have worn sandwich boards reading, "Hello, I'm a crook. Ask me how much I took."

But even with these motley fools in the clink, there're hundreds, probably thousands of corporate snakes that'll never get caught. Why? Because The Hustle needs 'em like strippers need poles. The Hustle is all about harnessing and channeling greed—been that way ever since the Captains of

Industry were privates. (Back in the day it was called, trickle down economics—the elites drop trousers and trickled down on everyone else's head and told 'em it was raining prosperity and equity.)

Also keep in mind: Most of the hustlers that're still on the loose ran companies that ran our economy. Enron and Halliburton execs helped write America's energy policy. WorldCom execs helped shape FCC policy. Arthur Andersen was a standard-bearer in accounting practices. Their brands were leading market indicators. They ran lobbying groups that have and continue to influence various levels of government. They put politicians in office. Whole cities and industries spun on their axis. Now when that many people are eating off of you, don't be shocked if they look the other way when you get greedy enough to scrape the plate. And yes, I know they caught Ken Lay. But so what? You could open a MEN'S WAREHOUSE with all the other suits that've gotten free passes.

As a man once said, *Greed works*. The SEC and the FTC know this. Wall Street knows this. The White House knows this, too. And once again, they also know that as long as the masses get the occasional sacrificial lamb (thank you, Elliott Spitzer), we'll accept getting fleeced by The Hustle's army of wolves in sheeps' clothing.

Do what you do playa—
juss keep that money on your mind.
—E-40, Automatic[4]

People Trying To Give You Their Money
(Consumers and Customers)

Until you do right by me,
everything you even think gon' fail!
—Cellie, Color Purple

Whoopi was as right as she was homely in that movie. If you don't do right by people, you will fail. But I don't think most businesses really understand people these days. Just check how we talk: *Consumer. Customer. Demographics. Viewer. VIP. Subscriber. Target Audience...* Heartless, mechanical words, all. We measure our relationships with people with phrases like market share, trends, box office, tipping point, saturation, ratings, market penetration, retention, and brand loyalty. We talk about winning customers like they're trophies or purses and wallets waiting to be pried open. It's more of that communication nonsense. And besides getting in the way of people talking openly and honestly, it's gotten in the way of the one truth most businesses fail to recognize:

CONSUMERS ARE JUST PEOPLE TRYING TO GIVE YOU THEIR MONEY.

Consumers are just people with money looking to give it away. And they'll give it to anyone who gives them a good enough reason to do so. Once the mood strikes and depending on what's going on in their lives, they'll even give it up for a bad reason. The only difference between a consumer and a customer is the consumer is trying to give their money to *someone* while the customer is trying to give their money to *you*. And the more reasons you give us, the more of our money we'll give you.

Consider: People already have bottles and fresh running water at home, yet they'll pay up to $2 for bottled tap water. We stock our fridges and cabinets with groceries and then order out. We buy clothes based on changing trends. We'll buy place settings and silverware then get paper plates and plastic forks because we don't want to waste the silverware. We buy disposable contact lenses and disposable cameras. Why? Because America is a consumer culture and consumers are just people trying to give away their money.

I shop therefore I am.
—Popular 1980s slogan

Not too long ago I worked on a project for Absolut vodka. Now I'm not much of a vodka drinker, so I hit the bars to see what people were into. It took a minute but in the midst of my field research, I realized that I wasn't interested in the people at all. All I cared about was Absolut and how to get these 20-somethings to drink more of it. I forgot about the people inside the consumers—they were just codes to be cracked.

I felt like the bad cops I had run-ins with growing up. Most cops don't live in the neighborhoods they patrol; so many cops only see people, particularly minorities, when they're investigating a crime. Now if you only see the worst in people as a career, at some point you detach from them. Business is the same way: If you only see people as demographics, target audiences, and marketing opportunities, eventually you start treating them that way. After a few years, that's exactly what I did.

With each passing assignment, I could feel myself getting a little more heartless and callous. It got harder and harder to do everyday activities without wondering if there's an angle I could flip for one of my client's brands. Everything and everyone became an angle to hustle. People became numbers and target audiences. Parties and events became sponsorship opportunities. Art and music became trends and untapped resources... And though I was getting good at my job, I also felt myself getting uglier and a little more inhumane with each passing year.

We have to remind ourselves that business, when done right, is just people and money hooking up. No more, no less. Give folks a good product and they'll pay. Make that good product or service affordable and accessible, and they'll pay more. Wrap it in an honest and compelling message and you've got a great, profitable brand. But many businesses have lost sight of the "people" in the consumers. Today everything is just bait for the catch. And if the catch is too small they throw it back and fish for something bigger. Consider this from William S. Burroughs' classic *The Naked Lunch*:

> *"The junk merchant does not sell his product to the consumer; he sells the consumer to the product. He does not improve and simplify his merchandise he degrades and simplifies the client."*

Like I said earlier, we use fancy, oftentimes non-human phrases like "consumer" and "viewer" because we don't see people as human anymore. I think that's why so many marketing campaigns have no heart. It's why so many of the products that come out have no real relevance or use. People just don't care enough to connect with each other anymore. Businesses just think they can monopolize and bully their way into market share. I think most corporations care more about their revenues than their employees, and their competition more than their customers.

We've got to remember that everything you do as a business is about understanding that consumers and customers are just people with money. Your marketing campaign: That's talking to people with money. Your sales force: That's meeting and engaging people with money. Your retail and distribution: That's getting your product to people with money. The quality of your products and services: It's all a reflection of how much you respect and care about people with money. In business absolutely everything you do is about people and whether or not you care about them.

Here are 7 things to remember about people with money:

1. Profit is a privilege

I've read the Constitution front to back; I've studied the Declaration of Independence from preamble thru John Hancock's signature. And you know what? "*The right to make a profit*" isn't in there. It's not in the Pledge of Allegiance. It's not in the Star Spangled Banner. *Thou shalt make a profit* isn't one of the Ten Commandments. It's not even on the dollar bill. But too many corporations act like making a profit is some sort of inalienable right guaranteed to every "inc." But they're wrong. Profit is not a civil right.

No business is owed success. Nobody owes you a Fortune 500 slot. Nobody owes you consecutive quarters of growth. Profit is a privilege that you earn. Profit is a reward for well-made products and services fairly priced. It's a reward for treating people like human beings. And the best way to do this is to understand people with money and give them a good reason to give you their money.

So how do you find good reasons? Start by caring about people. "People over profits" must be your ends, your means and your everything-in-between. You have to care about people as communities and as individuals. You have to care about their wants, needs, and desires. Businesses should make every effort to tell consumers and employees, "Hey, I care about you and I know that your support is my reward for doing so."

Again, business is an opportunity and profit is a privilege.

2. Don't equate "fixing mistakes" with "not making mistakes"

People equate poor service, poor quality, and bad attitudes with not caring. While fixing it or replacing it is good, the fact is, people go in with the very reasonable expectation that *it* shouldn't be broke in the first place. People forgive but people with money rarely forget. They remember the bad meal, the button that fell off, the new car that broke down, the overcharge for the under-service. What you sell and how you sell it reflects how you see people. So get it right the first time.

3. Get your butt off your shoulders

Got this one from my gramma. It means, don't act like you're better than everyone else. Don't treat customers like you're doing them a favor just by being in business. Large companies do this a lot. I don't care how prestigious your brand is. I don't care what your track record is. People are human beings and you'd better treat them as such every step of the way.

Also, "attitude" is not a unique selling proposition. Bring something to the game besides ego or "style." Have a better product, a better way of delivering it, or something tangible that people want or need. If you don't you'll go broke the second the attitude wears off.

4. Don't abuse your employees

Retailers in particular would do well to learn this one. When you treat your employees like dirt, they pass that energy on to whomever they have to deal with. Ever seen a crabby cashier, waitress, or salesperson? Chances are, they've been beefing with a coworker or boss and now that customer is about to become collateral damage.

Again, crap may flow downhill, but so do kindness and respect. Treat the people who work for you well and chances are they'll treat the people they deal with well, too.

5. Put people before policy

Whether it's billing, product availability, or warranties, too many companies use "Sorry, it's company policy" to excuse not fixing screw-ups. Knock it off. I'm not saying the customer is always right but no company policy is perfect.

Company policy doesn't boost sales, happy paying consumers boost sales. So when choosing between policy and consumers, ride with the person trying to give you their money.

6. If you're too busy to help customers, you're too busy to have customers

In late 2003 an assistant manager at a Bank One branch decided she was too busy to help me. (She actually said those exact words to me.) I needed help and she was too busy. I promptly withdrew my money from the bank. Her behavior was just inexcusable. But unfortunately she's not alone.

Modern business is bloated with folks who're too busy to help coworkers, clients, consumers, or anyone who can't obviously or immediately benefit them. Remember: The only reason your doors open each day is to help people give you their money. Whether you're a waitress, a financial analyst, or a CEO, your job is to help people. Customer service means "I got your back from start to finish." Help people get what they want then help them get the most out of if it once they have it. If you can't or won't do that, you might as well close up shop.

7. Build with your consumers

Brands are based on relationships; relationships are the only way you learn what someone really wants, what really moves and inspires them. And guess what? Relationships don't start with marketing; they start with building and they continue long after the purchase.

As marketers, you can't just reach out to consumers when you have something to sell. It's not enough to do an ad campaign or donate to a charity. You have to become part of people's lives. You have to become a presence in their communities. You have to be an advocate for their lifestyles and wants. They have to see that you're in it for the long haul. In short, you have to build.

All I'm askin' for is a little respect!
—Otis Redding[1]

Company Cancers

Everybody has a job with somebody
*that's this close to you whoopin' they a**!*
—DL Hughley

In sports, they're called "cancers"—athletes whose mere presence consistently makes life miserable for everyone around them. When they're not whining about salary or playing time, they're fighting with teammates or the press. At some point their behavior eats away at everything around them leaving you no choice but to cut 'em loose.

Well, companies have cancers, too. There are three types; and if you let 'em take root, they'll shatter your dreams and assault and batter your team. Here's a little recon on each:

Self-made Messiahs

Ever see *Backdraft*? It's an old Kurt Russell and Robert DeNiro flick. The gist: A fireman secretly sets fires then plays hero by putting 'em out later. That's a Self-made Messiah; they're fire-starters. They create all kinds of drama just to make themselves the solution. They'll make mountains out of molehills then charge up those hills blowing their own horn of self-adulation.

Brand Leslie

On my first day at one of my last full-time gigs a vice-president warned me to "Beware of 'Brand Leslie'." Leslie was my new boss and a vice-president creative director. Real good at her job; but after a few weeks, it became clear why they called her Brand Leslie: she made sure it was always all about her. Any opportunity that came up for her look good she took—even when it wasn't good for those around her or under her. Whenever someone else's screw-ups created more work for her team Leslie countered with, "Here's a chance for us to 'score points.' " When bosses or clients imposed ridiculous demands and deadlines, she'd say, "Let's 'make good' on this one." She was like a coked-up gymnast—always jumping through hoops and bending butt-over backwards just because someone somewhere might be keeping score.

Leslie was classic, but over the years, I worked with others. Here's a 5-point profile:

1. *Self-made Messiahs hoard information.*
   In business, information is power. Usually the Self-made Messiah feels vulnerable without it so they hide info from others. If it's a file, the file never leaves their office. If it's a presentation, they have to make it. Whenever possible, no one talks to the client but them. In their mind, the more information they share, the less valuable they are. Conversely, they always want to "be in the loop" on every little thing.

2. *Self-made Messiahs won't teach.*
   Good businessfolks are willing teachers. Whenever possible, they teach those around them how to work better. They understand that the stronger the squad, the easier everyone's job. But SMs hate teaching—it's like sharing information. It's hard to be a 'savior' if everyone around you already knows how to save themselves.

3. *Self-made Messiahs never shut up.*
   Self-made Messiahs are glory hounds. And if there's no glory to be had, they'll make some up. They'll work all weekend then come in on Monday and tell everyone how they worked all weekend, even if it wasn't totally necessary. For SMs, every accomplishment—no matter how small—comes with an email, a memo, or some random self-congratulatory comment. No matter what they do, Self-made Messiahs make sure everyone knows about it.

4. *Self-made Messiahs love bridges.*
   Self-made Messiahs like mediocre colleagues. Why? Because 'medi-

ILDS COL

ROUTE ITEM

Title: Knock the hustle : how to save your job and your life from corporate America / Hadji Jon Steven Williams.

Author: Williams, Hadji J. S.

Enum:

Chron:

Copy: 1

Item: 32711001182231

Route To: CIRCULATION DESK
Columbia College Chicago Library
ILDS: COL
624 S. Michigan Avenue

Chicago
IL
60605
USA

ocrity' means more opportunities to play 'savior'. I've seen some SM bosses intentionally put under-trained or unequipped employees in positions knowing they were in over their heads, just so the SM could step in and save the day later.

5. *Environment kills SMs.*
   Why do Self-made Messiahs exist? Mostly out of fear. Again, many employees believe that simply producing isn't enough to make it, so they look for any opportunity (legit or not) to say, "See how valuable I am?" It becomes a self-fulfilling prophecy: "If I don't make noise, my work goes unnoticed, therefore I make noise in order to keep my work from going unnoticed." (Think Munchausen's by proxy, only the child is their work environment.)

In the end, people will adapt to their environment. Surround a child with negativity and the child adapts. But put that same kid in an environment that rewards discipline, self-worth, and hard work, and the child excels. If employees believe hard work matters most, that's what you'll get. Create a healthy performance-driven environment and your employees will adapt and the Self-made Messiahs will change, quit, or be easier to fire.

...Yea, all of you be subject to one another,
and be clothed with humility...
—I Peter 5:5

A#*@%?!'s

Some people are A#*@%?!'s—just thinking about them makes you curse a blue streak. And some days, it takes everything inside you not to beat them into a coma.

"Carter"

While at BBDO Chicago, I worked with a guy named "Carter." He was your classic office *A#*@%?!* He wasn't in management; he was just from New York. Even though he was in Chicago and had been for some 5 years, Carter constantly justified his *A#*@%?!*-ish behavior with a dismissive "I'm a-New-Yorker-so-get-over-it." In his world, being an *A#*@%?!* was a sign of inner-strength and self-confidence. Carter was your classic late '90s Gen-X copywriter: Long hair, pale, fancy coffee sipping, obnoxious, judgmental, narrow-minded, Howard Stern loving, obscure indie-flick referencing, *Village Voice*-quoting punk. Basically, he was a slightly taller, louder David Spade, only with talent.

Carter regularly insulted female coworkers about their weight. He insulted colleagues' wardrobes. He insulted people's taste in music. Knowing that she'd just returned from her beauty salon appointment, he told a secretary she that needed to dye her hair again because her roots were showing and she looked old. When an account exec died in a horrible skiing accident, Carter spent days trashing the guy and his girlfriend, also a fellow coworker. Carter once got himself banned from his own commercial shoot because he bugged the director and the crew to the point that they refused to continue working until Carter was sent home and not allowed to come back. The entire accounting department wanted to kick him in the nuts—once a day. And while he never took aim at me, after seeing some of his handiwork, I confronted him one day. He told me that everyone else, not him, should just lighten up.

But the most amazing thing about Carter was how asexual he was about criticism. People would curse him out, call him every name in the book and it would go thru one ear right and out the other. He wouldn't even acknowledge what you said, which made arguing impossible. People usually argue for three reasons: (1) They're stubbornly passionate about their beliefs. (2) You hurt their feelings and they want to make sure you know it. (3) They don't like you and will stand against you on anything, no matter what. But none of this applied to Carter because he truly didn't care what anyone else thought. He just didn't care. He was unreal.

Nobody liked Carter. Not women. Not men. Not nuns. Not priests. Nobody. Even if you started out liking him, as I did, eventually he made you want to beat him until all his meals had to be eaten thru a straw. No one liked Carter. Actually, I take that back—there was this one guy "Kurt" who liked Carter. But Kurt was such a high-strung neurotic goof that his sense of judgment was often suspect.

Nearly every week a different person walked into our boss's office demanding that Carter be fired. But there was a problem: Carter was good at his job. Dude cranked out quality ads by the pound. Plus, a couple clients actually liked him—the ones that didn't hate his guts, that is. Carter was profitable. And for our company that meant he stayed no matter who wanted him gone. And of course, Carter was smart enough to never insult anyone who could fire him—not to their face anyway.

The only guy that could handle Carter was his partner, "Mac." Mac was a senior art director who'd been in the game for years and was liked by everyone from secretaries to clients to CEOs. He was just a good guy who worked hard and stayed loose. He was the consummate professional. So no matter what Carter said or did, Mac always brushed it off. One day I asked him how he managed.

"Pages and pages of ideas," he'd say.

Like I said, dude was talented. And when money was on the line, Carter usually came thru with the goods, which made Mac's job easier. But one day Mac quit—bounced to another agency. The money and responsibilities seemed so comparable that it came off as a lateral move, even a step down. On his last day I asked him why he was really leaving. He said he'd had enough. Among other things, Carter had worn him out to the point that he needed a change of scenery.

After Mac left, Carter went thru several art directors, one after another with none ever lasting longer than a few weeks. The only one that ever measured up to Carter's standards was "Deek," an award-winning freelance art director. Deek had an ego too, but show me a creative who doesn't. Anyway, after a few months, even he wouldn't work with Carter no matter how much loot they threw his way. Deek bounced to Wyoming. A few months later, Carter got bored or frustrated or something and quit himself. Some celebrated his last day; just about everyone else celebrated every day afterwards.

You drive a brotha to drink!
—Robin Harris[1]

Stoopid People

Stoopid People are so stupid that you have to spell it with two O's because one U just isn't stupid enough. However, stoopid people are not ignorant. Ignorance is simply a lack of knowledge—everyone's ignorant about something; some are ignorant about a lot of something. Stoopid people aren't in over their heads, either. Again, everyone's like that sometimes. No, stoopid people are a very specific lot.

Stoopid people are that rare combination of shortsightedness, misguided stubbornness, laziness, and selfishness. Given the chance, they'll make easy jobs hard and hard jobs near impossible. Stoopid people are the type of employees you just want to give a crash helmet, some milk 'n' cookies and sit 'em in a corner away from sharp objects until the yellow short bus that dropped their detrimental butts off that morning comes back to pick 'em up. (My apologies to anyone who's ever ridden in a yellow short bus.)

There is more stupidity than hydrogen in the universe,
and it has a longer shelf life.
—Frank Zappa

"Janet"

It's summer of 2000 and "Janet" joins UPSHOT Chicago as our new senior account director, just a notch below VP. She comes in with a good reputation from the client side with a couple Fortune 500 companies on her resumé. She's given a couple clients (Mello Yello, Sprite, etc.) to run plus a handful of account execs to supervise. On first impression, she shows herself to be a perfect fit—she's charming, knows all the business jargon, echoes all the same goals, yak-yak-yak... Fools the whole joint cold.

My first clue that Janet is stoopid comes when she starts bringing back assignments from our clients without creative briefs. Written by the lead AE, creative briefs are instructions explaining how a client wants a project executed. The brief tells what's due, when it's due, budget, etc. An account director who can't do a brief is like a doctor that can't write a diagnosis.

Instead of writing a creative brief, Janet would come into meetings with a legal pad fulla chicken-scratch and soundbites of what she thought the client said. Next she'd tell everyone how she promised the client that we'd deliver everything ASAP. Then we'd waste a half-hour on basic questions like: "Do they want a print ad or an FSI? What exactly does the product do? Who's the target audience? What is our budget?" It was Account Service 101 and any entry-level AE could've and would've done it. But not Janet—she was from the stoopid people tribe, which meant she only knew how to do one thing well: Make everyone else's job harder.

Janet also had a wonderful habit of ignoring advice. Whenever she screwed something up (which was early and often), people would stop and explain to her how to do it right. But Janet would just give 'em that vacuous Paris Hilton stare and then run off and do the exact same stoopid thing all over again. Why? Because:

Stoopid people are hardheaded.

They don't listen. In their minds they're smarter than you. Some actually think they're doing you a favor by letting you talk to them.

When in doubt/danger, stoopid people lie.

Janet's favorite lie was, "[Someone Powerful] wants you to do this." People were usually too busy not to take her at her word so they just did whatever she said believing she had backup. Sometimes it got out that she was a lying name-dropper, but it didn't matter. See, Janet had an ace in the hole:

By mid-2001 the economy was crashing. Budgets were getting slashed and accounts were going up for review all over the country. And while she was stoopid, Janet had some big-time industry connects. She knew people—people who managed brands with big budgets often up for review. We laid-off some 60 people that year, but not Janet. Her Fortune 500 connects made her a potential cash cow so they kept her around.

Stoopid people are like roaches—where there's one more will come.

As I said earlier, Janet had several AE's under her. A couple were fresh out of school, the rest were older but still somewhat raw. Part of Janet's deal was training them to be good account execs. But she was too stoopid to do her job right, never mind teaching others how to do theirs.

So Janet's bad habits became theirs. She didn't write briefs; they didn't write briefs. She misunderstood clients; they misunderstood clients. She was disorganized; they were disorganized... Instead of having one bad account exec, we ended up with *six*. Actually they really weren't bad account execs, they just made mistakes that were the direct result of having a genuinely stoopid boss.

Stoopid people fail upward.

In business, people tend to rise to their level of incompetence. But every now and then some get just dumb enough to go a little further. Sometimes stoopid people get on winning teams and reap the same rewards as everyone else, like when a company has a banner year and everyone, including the stoopid ones get fat bonuses or promotions. That's *failing upward.*

Self-made messiahs love stoopid people.

Stoopid People create drama and Self-made Messiahs are drama queens. Our company's SMs loved Janet. They followed her like dogs after fat people knowing sooner or later they'd eat. And Janet rarely disappointed. Whenever they caught her slipping they'd slide right in with, "Janet screwed up but I fixed it..." But after a while some of them got sick of her. There's stupid and there's crazy. Janet was stoopid—working with her was just plain crazy.

Stoopid is as stoopid listens to.

You can't reason with stoopid. You can't discuss with stoopid. You can't counsel or reassign stoopid. Stoopid people only understand other stoopid people. Truly stoopid people only understand one thing: *ultimatums.*

Understanding is a wellspring of life unto him that hath it:
but the instruction of fools is folly.
—Proverbs 16:22

Change or Pack

As a boss, no matter which Company Cancer you've got, the solution is simple: They have to change or they have to go. If you let them stay, you're cosigning their behavior. And once they make life miserable for everyone else, which they will, good people will quit. Professionals will leave. Money will be lost. Company cancers are never good for business so get them before they get you.

Also, if you're an employee who works with a company cancer, I recommend two things. One: Confrontation. No violence; just let them know that you won't tolerate their attitude, incompetence, stubbornness, etc., anymore. Make it simple and plain that as long as you're colleagues, you will not allow them to make your job or your life difficult.

And while you're at it, go to the higher-ups and let them know the deal. Let them know that if they don't step in and help resolve this, then they're part of the problem and you'll walk before you stay at a place that encourages this type of behavior.

I know all of this sounds tough, but it's been my experience that the only thing company cancers understand and respond to is tough love.

I see dumb people—
some of them are just walking around dumb
and don't even know it.
—Sixth Sense Spoof

Caste Warfare

For the love of money,
some people will kill their own brother.
For the love of money,
some people will rob their own mother.
—The O'Jays

People love to separate; we love to pick sides. We'll group up by race, religion, gender, income, age; you name it...anything to feel part of something greater than ourselves. Anything for a sense of purpose or meaning.

But I've seen a type of division in business that goes way beyond "who likes who" and who fits in where. I'm talking about *caste warfare*. It's about white-collar vs. blue-collar. Management vs. Employees. Offices vs. Cubicles. Them vs. Us. And no matter who them is, no matter who us is, the rule's the same:

THEY'RE THE ENEMY AND WE BETTER GET "THEM" BEFORE THEY GET US.

It's the cold war gone corporate.

For example: Back in 2003, Don Carty, then CEO of AMR (American Airlines' parent company) tried to snake some $41 million in salaries and golden parachutes for himself and some high-level execs while asking American Airline's unknowing mechanics, pilots, and flight attendants to take pay cuts in order to keep the company out of bankruptcy. Once the loot made the press all hell broke loose and Don resigned. (He still got paid, though.) All Don & Co. saw was "us." Had they seen "we," things would've gone down a lot differently.

I meet folks in different industries from all over and to hear them tell it, lots of workers are suffering from caste warfare. The secretaries and IT folks have one set of rules; the managers and supervisors have another. The MBAs get more respect than those with just BAs or high-school diplomas. Depending on what group you're in, somebody in another group is either screwing you or benefiting at your expense.

Jay, Crew

Jay was among the coolest managers I've known. He ran our super-duper new media department. (I forgot their official title.) They developed websites, interactive media...whatever high-tech stuff clients wanted, they did.

Jay's team was small, maybe 6 deep, but they worked like demons knocking out job after job. You should've seen their timesheets—100-hour weeks were common. I mean, legit Sunday-to-Sunday, 100-hour workweeks. They'd go 12 hours straight; play *Wolfenstein* or something to break up the monotony; nap in a conference room, wake up and order a pizza, then go back to work for another 6 or 7 hours. They were highly gifted, highly disturbed individuals.

And once more, no matter how much work came their way, no matter how much everyone else took them for granted, as long as Jay was there, they were just fine. You see, it's like this: Some folks work *at* companies; some folks work *for* companies... But these guys: They worked for Jay. I figured out why the first time I met him.

One day I'm in this meeting with a bunch of account execs, creative folks, promotion folks, etc. We're all going over this big assignment. The lead AE says the client wants a high-end website with all sorts of bells and whistles up in something like 3 weeks. She adds that she's already told the client that we'd do it and do it cheap. The purpose of this meeting was to make good on her promise. So she looks at Jay and says, "So when can we see something?"

"You can't. No." He says.

"What do you mean 'no'?"

"I said 'no'... What you're asking for, in the timeframe you want is not possible."

"But I told the client— "

"I didn't tell the client anything."

Everyone gets quiet, except the AE—she blows a fuse and gets all loud, but not Jay. Jay stays calm and cool. He leans back in his chair, never raises his voice above a one-on-one tone and just explains. He starts by highlighting the sheer stupidity of promising to do something without knowing if it's even doable. Next he lays out realistic costs based on reasonable man-hours and a logical timetable for meeting the client's needs. He goes on about how this project will require dedicated servers, passwords, splash pages, extra bandwidth, running test pages and all kinds of web stuff that was over my head. And once Jay finished and made sure everyone knew what was really good, he politely smiles, stands up and says, "Lemme know if you need anything else." and walks out leaving the AE looking like the unprepared fool that she was. It was beautiful.

Near as I could see, Jay's goal on every project was to do it right. That meant getting proper instructions, planning, timelines, etc. He didn't care about brown-nosing or CYA'ing. And whenever possible, he never let anyone push him or his guys around. And that's why they worked for him. That's also what got him screwed.

Several months later, the company went thru an internal re-org and a fresh VP slot was created—*VP of Hi-Tech Cyber Stuff.* (You get the idea.) This slot had Jay's name written all over it. He was a vet. Had leadership skills. Got results. And when they were smart enough (or desperate enough) to listen to him, the company made money. That fresh IKEAfied office was his, right?

Wrong.

They gave it to an outsider—some Banana Republic-looking marketing geek who happened to be tight with one of the *higher* higher-ups. He was awful. And though he was their boss, that guy still saw Jay's crew as "them." He helped the company milk those boys dry. He had 'em chasing their tails and jumping thru hoops whenever the phone rang. They started working harder, longer, and under tighter deadlines than ever before. And when their quality of work started to suffer, everyone simply blamed them. It was Caste Warfare 101.

When it first happened I told a couple VPs I felt Jay got screwed and we'd all suffer for it. I was basically told to mind my own business. But "Terri," one of the VPs who'd recently quit to make a life change (blew town to get married) let me in on a little secret:

They screwed Jay on purpose.

Over a few beers during her send-off party, Terri said the reason Jay lost the VP gig was because he wasn't one of "them." Sure Jay was qualified and deserving, everyone knew that. But some of the higher ups didn't like Jay personally. (Execs can be a little clique-ish.) But more importantly, they didn't trust Jay to keep his mouth shut about impending layoffs and budget cuts. In the end, Jay was one of them and the execs wanted one of us. So Jay lost out.

Sad part is, Jay got off easy. For years I've witnessed or heard about too many people's careers getting hurt over this crap. It's straight childish, not to mention bad business.

Bosses, listen up:

All the divisiveness, backstabbing, and secret alliances...knock that crap off. Just because you're older, more expensive, or have a bigger title doesn't make you better than those people under you. And if you think you are better than them or your consumers, then you're a fool. And I already explained fools and money.

(For more ammo, review the "Less Bosses, More Leaders" chapter.)

Employees:

If you have this nonsense in your company, polish up that resumé and run. If your bosses won't clean up this mess, then it won't get cleaned up at all, which means it's just a matter of time before caste warfare ruins their company and/or your career.

...For we are members one of another.
—Ephesians 4:25

A Quick Ode:

For the record I have to say I love working-class people now more than ever. I'm talking about farmers—not those greedy agribusinesses and biotech conglomerates like ADM, Conagra, or Monsanto, but regular ol' family farmers. Truckers. Nurses. Mechanics. Machinists. People who get paid by the hour and work in shifts. Hotel workers, janitors, and valets. Fishermen—not *fisheries*, but small "If-we-don't-catch-we-don't-eat" fishermen. Bartenders and waitresses. Dishwashers and cooks—not chefs, but cooks. Folks with nametags on their shirts. Cashiers and cabbies. Construction workers and secretaries. Bus drivers and train conductors. City workers. Teachers. Union folks. Cops. (Yeah, I actually like cops—go figure.) Working-class folk just seem to get it.

Working-class folk don't have country club memberships. They don't have clients or agendas. They drink beer, whiskey, and Kool-Aid. They don't do lunch; they shoot pool and go hang out. They smoke cigarettes instead of cigars. They don't Botox and they don't do therapy. They drive pickups and big heavy old cars with actual bumpers. They wear comfortable shoes until they wear 'em out. They buy the stuff most folks think they're too good for and shop in stores most folks wouldn't be caught dead in. And when the old white folks declare war from on high, working-class people bury their sons and daughters. They can't afford to go to fundraisers; they just go to the polls hoping their votes count as much those $1,000-a-plate dinner eaters do. Every day, they roll up their sleeves and bust their backs until they get tired, then they bust their backs some more...

I love working-class people. They get it. They have no choice but to get it. And I'll tell you another thing: We all better get it and bust up this caste system and soon. Because if we don't, as a man once said, "You ain't seen trouble yet, but it's coming."

Behold how good and how pleasant
it is for brethren to dwell together in unity!
—Psalms 133:1

Equally Yoked

Be ye not unequally yoked
together with unbelievers.
—II Corinthians 6:14

This one was among the simplest yet hardest lessons The Hustle ever taught me. In business, you have to be equally yoked. You can't work for a company whose practices or ideologies aren't inline with yours. You can't go into business with people if you don't have the same goals and beliefs about how to achieve those goals. You just can't ride with people if you're not all on the same level. It's just that simple.

I also learned that being Equally Yoked doesn't mean being clones, suffering from codependency, or being mutual sycophants. It doesn't mean rolling lockstep just to avoid friction or conflict, either. Equally Yoked means that you have enough common ground that your differences become assets and strengths, not liabilities or barriers. Equally Yoked means that you both recognize the same starting point and destination and realize that if you don't get there together you won't get there at all.

You see this a lot in bad relationships: A woman gets down with a man who's totally not on her level but all she sees is what she might be able to turn him into or the one or two things she really likes about him. Next thing you know, after a few months (or years) of *back 'n' forth* he's still not where she's at, she can't bring herself to go where he is, and now they want to kill each other.

Vibe

Partnerships, alliances, boss-employee or even brand-endorser relationships have to be built on more than just, "Hey, I think we can make a lot of money together," or "We've both got mutually beneficial talents." There has to be a real connection, a *vibe*.

You don't need to be friends; you don't need to finish each other's sentences; you just need to vibe. *Vibing* is when all involved share an almost unspoken bond that makes success feel predestined because everything feels connected. You feel like the soil has been already prepared, the seed has been planted, and all that's left to do is sow it and grow.

When you're vibing with the right woman, you can just relax with each other and let things unfold because you know that everything's in place. When you're vibing with a business partner, you just know that *this thing*, whatever it may be, is going to work because you two are right for each other. When you're vibing with the company you work for, you're fully aware that you could probably make more money or get more perks somewhere else, but *this place and time* is the perfect fit.

But when you're not vibing, when you're not Equally Yoked, it's like pulling teeth to get anything done. Every discussion feels like a debate, every little task seems like a big project, and every disagreement is *thisclose* to an argument. And even if it actually works, all involved know they don't ever want to do it again. When there's no vibe, the successes don't feel as good and the failures hurt worse than they should.

StocktontoMalone...

On paper that's what we were: Two really talented individuals who should've complimented each other like two sides of the same coin. At least, that's what our bosses thought when they paired me with "Luke."

As people went, Luke was a really nice guy. As art directors went, he was really good. We were both young, seemed to like the same stuff. Seemed to have the same philosophy about work and business, even faith. We shot the breeze in each other's office most every day, hung out during lunch, etc. I thought we had a vibe...the operative word here being, "thought."

But when it came to work, all we did was fuss and fight. He didn't like any of my ideas; I didn't like any of his. With the exception of a couple good-to-great projects we pulled off, we got virtually no work done for about 6 months. We were like two eighth graders. We went to our bosses on several occasions and actually said the words: "We don't like each other, please separate us." It was sad... God was it sad.

To this day, Luke's my guy and all is forgiven. But I swear, for those 6 months I wanted to stab him in the tongue with a SHARPIE. He felt the same way.

Just goes to show you that birds of a feather may flock, but if they ain't equally yoked they'll peck each other to death.

Moonlighting.

While doing some boring packaged goods stuff by day, I once had the chance to do some hot creative after-hours, so I approached a former coworker—an art director—to help out. It was a great chance to do some award-winning work and make a little loot to boot. Now we had our differences at work, but she was talented and hungry; and when you confuse having business opportunities with having a vibe, valleys can seem like ditches. So we hooked up.

It was a disaster almost from jump. We didn't share the same goals; her views on creative and day-to-day stuff were totally different from mine. We weren't equally yoked, but I felt that the chance to do some great creative, build our reps and make some extra loot was enough to keep pushing. Man, was I wrong.

Not only did things not go as we'd hoped, but our lack of vibe drove us to part ways. Some nasty paperwork changed hands, some insults flew, and we never worked together on the side again. It also made our daytime gig a little awkward, to say the least. And what's worse is we're still not friends, not even to this day. Haven't spoken in years, in fact.

Hopefully, I've laid out the importance of being equally yoked in business. We'll get deeper into building business relationships in the "Let's Build" chapter. Until then, lemme leave you with the following:

4 Keys to Getting Equally Yoked:

1. Be honest.

You can't vibe with folks if folks don't know what you're truly about. (Do you?)

2. Be patient.

Sometimes you'll vibe slow, sometimes you'll vibe quick. Just be patient.

3. Don't settle.

Go for what you know and keep working 'til it comes.

4. Pray.

God's the best matchmaker in the game. Period.

...like peas 'n' carrots.
—Forrest Gump[1]

Friends vs. Coworkers

Friends, how many of us have them?
"Friends"—those you can depend on. Friends...
—Whodini

Friends are rare. Pops worked with thousands of men over the years. Maybe a dozen of 'em ever set foot in our house; few of them were ever considered true friends. "You may have 3 or 4 real friends your entire life," he told me when I was about 10. I thought he was crazy then. Looking back, he was right.

Sometimes Corporate America weakens our ability to make friends. Business can stifle our ability to connect with people on humane and intimate levels. Business trivializes the whole idea of friendships. You start believing that because you're around someone a few hours a day or making money with them that they're your friend. Business likes that mindset because it tricks employees into pledging allegiances and energies that much quicker.

Whenever I'm around businesspeople, I always hear stuff like, "I've got friends at Company X," or "Tell 'em I sent you—we're friends from way back." But once the smoke clears all many of those folks really know about each other is their name, title, and maybe their favorite drink. Most met at some conference, went out a few times, or closed a deal or two. That's not a friendship. There's nothing wrong with those kinds of alliances or connections, but they are not friendships. Friendships are like sex: if somebody's giving it up that quick *just because*, it's probably not worth having, at least not without protection.

The main reason business friendships fail: Most everyone in business has a price. I've seen childhood friends go to war over drug money and gang ties once they hit their teens. In business, I've seen college buddies sell each other out for a fatter paycheck. I've seen scheming to win accounts and clients or reach sales goals. For the right money or opportunity, some businessfolks will sell secrets, organs, and family members, and not always in that order. Money is divisive and business can be the Great Wall of China.

Look, there's nothing wrong with liking your colleagues. But every coworker isn't your friend; and unless it's family-owned, no company should ever be considered "family." Calling someone a friend should go deeper than "we work together." You can be human, humane, cordial, and even friendly without pretending everyone is your friend. You can be a great employee, a great boss, a great coworker, even a great business partner, and still not have a single friend at work. It's called *professionalism.* (Again, when in doubt, be a professional.)

A real friend and a mentor is not on your payroll.
—Prince, at his 2004 Rock & Roll Hall of Fame induction speech

This brings me to another bit of advice: Never take a job because of "the people." I've heard many say, "I love the people I work with." That's great but do you like your job? Do you like what your company stands for? Do you like the opportunities your company provides you? Does your company respect you as a human being? Does your company understand your desire to have a life outside of work? Those are the reasons you stay at a company for 20 years, not the people. Why? Because people get fired. People get laid off. People quit. People change.

Once I was at a company for three and a half years—which was, looking back, about 18 months too long. Every few months I got offers to go elsewhere, always for more money. But I always stayed put because I liked the people. They were cool—around my age, fun to be around, etc. But then the company went thru layoffs: 10 people here, 15 there, another dozen or so later... After while, I was working with complete strangers or people whom I just flat didn't like. They weren't bad folks; I just didn't fit in with them. It was like being the new guy all over again. My job had become work and work just wasn't fun anymore.

My mistake was putting my social calendar ahead of my work environment. I could've switched companies and remained friends with those folks.

But hey, you live and learn. Jobs are first and foremost about work. Now does this mean you shouldn't be friends with your coworkers? Of course not. Just remember who's who and which one is truly important.

Wealth maketh many friends,
but the poor is separated from his neighbour.
—Proverbs 19:4

For My Seeds...

Be a father to your child...
—Edo G. & Bulldogs

I've met plenty of working parents over the years—women, men, single, divorced, execs, secretaries and such, all in the same struggle. And by and large, they always tried to put their families first. But I knew (and still know) entirely too many who are out there stacking 80-hour work weeks trying to make partner, get the corner office, the bigger title, etc. all in the name of "for the kids." To all of them (and all of you) I say:

QUIT USING YOUR KIDS AS AN EXCUSE FOR YOUR CAREER CHOICES.

You want the big-time career? Fine. You want all the perks that come with being the CEO? Good for you. You want a secure future? Who doesn't? Climb that ladder and go as high as it'll take you. But don't ever get it twisted: Your kids would rather see you than see what you've accomplished in their name.

Besides working parents, I also met plenty of kids in college and at work who were children of extremely successful, career-driven parents. And you know what? As God sits on the throne, the vast majority was among the most over-privileged, under-worked, and under-raised folks you'd ever want to meet. I'm talking about: Jerks. Morons. Spoiled brats. First class head-cases. No perspective at all. Their egos, sense of entitlement, and pent-up issues hit the room two steps before they did. And it was all because mommy and daddy were too busy closing deals to be loving parents and occasionally knock some sense into 'em.

(And I'll tell you another thing: Most were also more than a little bit bitter. They were on the receiving end of the fact that money can't buy lost years.)

Sarah Bernsen

During a 6-month stretch when I was was punching out every night between 10 P.M. and 11P.M., I got to know "Sarah Bernsen." She was this big-time executive VP, about a couple heart attacks away from running the agency. I guess she was around 45 or so. Every night we'd see each other in the elevators, or signing out in the lobby. She always looked exhausted, irritated, or both. She was usually carrying files home or laptops or something. She always struck me as a nice lady; no matter how many power suits she rocked, she came off like a suburban schoolteacher or a CPA, old-school Sally Jesse Raphael glasses and all.

The more we chatted, the more I learned. She was one half of your classic late-'80s power couple. Hubby was a big shooter for some Fortune 500 shop. She had 2 daughters and, between her work and their teenage lives, seldom spent more than a few hours a week with them.

When Sarah told me all of that, I just shook my head in confusion. I mean my folks weren't execs, but they worked just as hard and still made time for us. I always thought the whole point of being a boss was, in part, to have enough juice to delegate and enjoy your success. But Sarah didn't see it that way. She hustled 24/7, year in, year out. "I'm doing it for my kids," she'd say. Then one night she dropped a bomb:

"I'm leaving."

Her kids were growing up without her, as she put it. They were a couple years away from college and she wanted to enjoy what was left of their teens at home. She decided to start by taking the summer off to hang out with them. Shop with them. Meet their friends. Do girl stuff. Be a mom again. It was one of the coolest things I'd heard in a minute. But eventually it became little more than best-laid plans...

Sarah came back about 3 months later and went back to her old ways. Back to the 80-hour workweeks. Back to the grind. Back to wondering what her kids looked like. Back to chasing God-knows-what for God-knows-why... But Sarah wasn't alone.

Over the years I met hundreds of white-collar women and men on the same trip. The guys seemed worse because they seemed willing to sacrifice even more. (As a male, it's expected I guess.) They'd miss school plays and soccer games then buy the kid a bunch of crap to make up for it. They'd blow off dinner with the wife and buy her jewelry or something later. And they always swore that the main reason they worked so hard was so their kids could have everything they never had and be financially set. But somehow, their new suits, cars, condos, and fancy vacations made that hard to believe.

Poppa was a rolling stone...
and when he died all he left us was 'alone'...
—The Temptations[1]

Choices...

Pops took a different route. He gave 33 years to the CTA—lots of graveyard shifts: 10 P.M. till 6 A.M. He did it so he could be home when we got up for school and in the evenings to help us with homework, etc. He'd tuck us in around 9:30 P.M. then go earn his cream. He probably could've gotten more shine by switching up, but no dice. Family first. He didn't take day shifts until we were old enough to understand "working for a living." He never made big dough. Never got an office. Never rocked a business suit. He did what he had to and put his family first.

Among other gigs, mom worked for Santa Fe Railroad after doing time at Michael Reese hospital and answering phones for Coca-Cola. She put family first as well. She never worked weekends or clocked long hours chasing a corner office. She worked to live, never lived to work. No 6-figure income or fancy house in the 'burbs. She made her peace with being a mom and played her position to the fullest.

I'm glad she made that choice. I'm glad they both did. Next to God, my parents are the reason I didn't end up dead or in jail like so many I came up with. And again, we weren't rich by anyone's standards. And I wouldn't change a thing about any of it.

Most of folks I grew up around didn't have a choice in how long they worked. Overtime and extra shifts were the difference between making car payments, maintaining 3 squares a day and not. They had to punch clocks for 30 years if they wanted to keep a house and put kids thru college. But when stakes is high, you do what you gotta do.

But again, I believe that many businessfolks have a choice. And I believe too many are choosing the wrong things. Don't get me wrong; I'm not saying career success and family are mutually exclusive because they're not. But what I am saying is (1) Don't measure your worth by your title. (2) Don't lie to yourself about why you're making the choices you're making. And (3) Don't lie to your kids about it because they know the real deal even if you don't.

Help the grown folks...
they need more help than their children do.
—Raphael Saadiq[2]

Do The Knowledge:
Schooling Business on Education

Teacher, teacher, tell me how to do it—
it looks so easy like there was nothing to it.
—Slick Rick

One of the most important things my parents ever gave me was the opportunity to get a college education. My life would've been very different, probably a lot worse, if it weren't for their sacrifice. I thank them for that every day of my life.

And now that we've gotten that out of the way:

I spent over 12 years working with MBAs and college grads, many from the finest institutions America has to offer. Some were colleagues and bosses, others were clients, some were subordinates; and a stunning majority were flat-out clueless. Sure, they were well-read, articulate, etc., but they were clueless. They had no real sense of how their industries worked or what was expected of them. All they knew was wrote theory and textbook learning. I call it the *The Apprentice* Syndrome—get the fancy business suit, have the polished resumé, learn the buzzwords and protocol, show up with ego and attitude, and wait for your bosses and coworkers to fill in the blanks. I tell you, there's nothing sadder than having a 20-something who, after a few months on the job, comes to you saying, "We didn't learn any of this stuff in school." Actually there is something sadder: A 30- or 40-something who's been in the business even longer and still doesn't get it and refuses to get it. (I've met more than a few of them.)

Education is among the most necessary and profitable investments there is; yet one of the business world's biggest shortcomings is its inability to properly educate workers and future leaders. One of the reasons America is lagging in so many industries is because other countries are killing us when it comes to pertinent education and job-relevant training.

Too many of our colleges and grad schools are run by academics who've either never done it and can't do it or those who've been out the game so long that they've forgotten how to do it, much less teach it. Furthermore, too many companies in too many industries are more interested in hiring and promoting finished products than grooming diamonds in the rough. Consequently, they put almost no pressure on schools to do better thus leaving the schools to do the work in the dark.

We've got to do better than this. We've got to do a better job of equipping high-school and college grads with smart learning not just book learning. It's just not fair to ask a kid to pay 70K for a BA or an MBA then give that kid an education that's so irrelevant that they end up making lattes or stacking pillows and candles just to get by. It's not fair to ask homegrowns to compete with kids in India and Asia for jobs when American schools are giving them inferior educations and most American companies are too greedy and/or shortsighted to help out. A mind is a terrible thing to waste and we're blowing thru ours like Hummers thru 20 bucks at the local Amoco.

Some ideas on education reform:

1. Teach.

Business pros need to go back to school and teach. The only way your future workforce will get better is if business experts get involved. So go back and teach. You don't have to quit your job. You can take a sabbatical or teach a night or two at a local college or high school even. Just make time and teach. Your company's future depends on it.

Businesses are also consumers and schools are just businesses that provide a more sophisticated product—your workforce. You know what you need more than they do, so tell 'em—they'll listen. (Supply and

Demand, aka "*B-School 101.*") And if you don't have time to teach at least make time to help a school develop proper business curriculum.

Remember: Knowledge in the hands of selfish people is worthless. It only accrues interest and value when you pass it on.

If corporations demanded more, B-schools would be forced to respond.
—Luke Visconti, co-founder, Diversity, Inc.,
on getting more qualified black business candidates[1]

2. Internships/apprenticeships.

Nothing teaches like experience and nothing teaches experience like internships and apprenticeships. They're cheap, easy to run, and if you do them properly, you'll develop a mob of qualified talent from all backgrounds. Here's a quick internship story for you:

I got my DDB Needham internship after interviewing with "Jeanne Clemson," then their VP creative recruiter. I still had 2 years of college to go but I needed full-time job money bad. I was thinking like a high-school baller: *If I've got pro potential, draft me now.*

So Jeanne checks my portfolio and tells me I'm good but "not good enough for a job—yet." She mentions a minority internship program she's running. "I'm tired of walking down the halls and seeing the same people generating the same ideas from the same perspective," she adds. She figured an internship would get me the seasoning I needed, so I took her up on it.

This was back in 1993. It was a lot easier to discriminate and probably easier to be inclusive, too. If she pulls this today, she probably gets sued for reverse discrimination. She might've been on some sort of Angelina Jolie kick—she'd adopted an ethnic kid a while back and it's possible she saw me as another pet project. Still, she was cool people. I just chalk it up to God's grace. Still, there's no reason why more companies don't do the same thing.

Some saw Jeanne as flaky, but she was a top-flight judge of talent and the whole industry knew it. She wasn't much for handouts, either. You don't get to her level by giving opportunities to folks who can't cut it. In fact, of all the interns she recruited that summer, I'm the only one to my knowledge to leave the business and it took me 13 years to do it.

Point is, business needs more internship programs. We need more apprenticeship programs, too. It's just smart business. Don't say there's a lack of diverse talent then do nothing to train and nurture diverse talent.

Each one teach one.

3. Mentor.

In business, quality mentorship is the difference between rookies and veterans, good players and all-stars, dynasties and the LA Clippers. The best way to maximize talent is to take it under your wing and nurture it. Mentorship is investment, pure and simple. Here are a few examples of different types of mentors and how they helped me:

Lynette

I had three great mentors in my career; my first was "Lynette." Lynette was one of very few black ad women in the '70s and '80s. She worked at places like Leo Burnett, had great success as a marketing consultant before becoming a professor at my alma mater.

First time I met her was a Monday morning, 9 A.M. freshman Intro to Advertising. After an hour of no teacher and 65 students chirping about walking out, Lynette walks in, slams some books on a desk and yells, "Hey! Anybody got a cigarette?!" It was classic.

We all hit the hallway for a smoking break—indoor smoking on campus was still legal in the early 1990s. (We didn't have many ashtrays so we just used the carpeting—it looked like rotted Swiss cheese. The only place you really couldn't smoke was in the classrooms, but the cigarette butts under the partially melted plastic seats told otherwise.) Over a few Marlboros she told me about her days in the ad industry. And after weeks of "Here's-a-product-make-up-an-ad" assignments, she says, "You can do this for a living you know..."

"Do what?"

"Advertising. You can do advertising for living."

Besides her, I didn't really think black people did advertising; like most aspects of business, it just seemed like something only that whites were allowed to do. I hadn't heard of Tom Burrell, Jo Muse, Carol H. Williams or anyone like that. I knew Spike Lee's Mars Blackmon commercials but that was about it. "People make money in marketing, lots of money," she noted. And since I was black, she said I could bring a perspective that most weren't used to. (I think I was the only black student in the class so she took an interest in me.) "You're good enough to do this. You should try it," she'd say. My parents, God love 'em, always told me I could be anything I wanted. But Lynette told me I could be something specific.

So I hit the campus library and loaded up on every business publication from *Advertising Age* and *Brandweek* to the *Wall Street Journal*. She started schooling me on all things "business," including race-and-gender politics. She figured I'd have it easer than her, partly because times change, partly because I was male, mostly because she thought I could be really good. Anyway, Lynette's a big reason why you're reading this book.

(Thank you, Lynette.)

Word to Hal...

Professor "Hal Rallen" ran my college's advertising curriculum. He eventually replaced Lynette as my mentor-figure as she got busier and I got older. He schooled me a lot on being a black male in business. He was a big reason I stayed with copywriting as opposed to going account-side or client-side. Where Lynette was very strategic and product attribute-driven, Hal was more creative—he'd been a commercial producer for years. He liked the eye-catching, entertainment approach to selling, which kept me interested. He also hooked me up with "Brenda," my very first headhunter and got me my first big agency job. (She saw my race as an asset when most didn't.)

"Crazy Eddie"

I met "Eddie" back in '93 back while interning at DDB Needham. Ed was this crazy copywriter who was always on "something else." Not something else as in, "Where's happy hour?" but something else as in, "What's next?"

One day Ed sits me down and tells about me about something else called "the Internet" and how everyone will have it someday and no business or consumer would be able to function without it. It was in cyberspace (wherever that was). He said that in 20 years the post office would go belly-up because something else called "email" would replace letters, postcards, stamps, and most paper communications. And if the USPS didn't collapse completely, it would be streamlined to compete with FedEx, UPS, and Airborne Express for freight customers.

Now you have to keep in mind that it's 1993: Cellphones are the size of water bottles and beepers are still cool. Almost no one in my neighborhood owns a computer and I have no clue what cyberspace is. Plus, stamps were still 29 cents. Ed was coming off like some burnt-out yuppie that did too much blow in the '80s. So I just nodded my head and hoped I'd be off the day he shows up armed and in fatigues.

Later he adds that maybe a couple generations from now, circa 1993, America will become a 4-class society: (1) Those who provide product, content and information for the multinationals that will control technology, the Internet, and by default, most of society; (2) Those who can repair, program, and operate computers along with our hi-tech world's infrastructure; (3) Manual laborers (truck drivers, service and hospitality workers, etc.); and (4) Poor people. In Ed's world, the poor and manual laborers are permanently at the bottom because information and training will be too valuable or expensive for the "analogued masses." (Like I said, he was always on *something else*.)

So it's been 12 years since that conversation and let's see how crazy Ed did: The post office has been losing money since about '98 and a book of first-class stamps now costs more than a music CD. Information and Internet-related technology have spread faster than AIDS in Africa. And these days, if you're not computer-literate/tech-savvy, you're lucky if you can work your home appliances let alone get a decent job. That leaves poor folks and manual laborers. Well, college tuition and quality job training's skyrocketed; plus corporations have manipulated globalism and outsourcing to the point that all the good blue-collar jobs are going oversees thus creating a mob of working poor from coast to coast. And of course poverty is on the rise. (Okay, so his predictions need some tweaking, but he's closer than Cleo and Dionne's Psychic Friends.)

And where's Ed now? He's either working for the Trilateral Commission or sitting in a Utah cave fortified with strippers waiting for Armageddon. But whatever he's doing, I'm sure he's thinking about something else.

HERE'S ANOTHER REASON WHY HE BECAME MY MENTOR:
During my internship, I put together a portfolio and showed it to Ed. (Again, copywriters are hired by their portfolio or "book"—ads they've done throughout their career. My portfolio was mostly "spec"—speculative ideas I was capable of developing, given the chance to work on more real clients.)

So I hand him my book thinking, *Soon as he sees my brilliance I'm hired.* But once he cracked it open, Ed's head went down and he blew through it like a coked-up accountant at 11:30 P.M. on April 14th. All he did for 5 minutes straight was shake his head disagreeably and mumble, "No" as he flipped thru pages. "No." Page flip. "No . . ." Page flip. "Nope, nope, nope . . ." Flip, flip, flip.

Now I'm sitting there completely dejected. This new-world-order geek has just ruined my career before it's even started. He looks up and asks, "What do you want to do?"

"Huh?"

"Do you want to do ads or do you want to build brands?"

Next, he sits me down and spits game:

"Look, if you want to make $800 a week cranking ads for soap and gym shoes, you can. You're good enough that you'll figure out what you don't already know and you can make a nice living on cute puns and clever taglines. But can you build a brand? That's where the money and power is."

"Brands? What's a 'brand'?"

Almost every week for the rest of my internship Ed taught me about brands and marketing. (Lynette taught me about branding but I was more interested in doing cool ads so I just snoozed thru her brand lecture.) He also taught me about budgets. Strategy. Manipulation... He was on some Machiavelli/Sun Tzu trip, but as I quickly learned, so was everyone else; he was just more honest about it. He got me thinking and scheming. And on one level or another, I've been scheming ever since.

And that's why he became my mentor.

There's "good crazy" and there's "bad crazy." Ed was good crazy. Good crazy people can teach you a lot. They tend to see things differently and take chances others won't. Plus, they tend to ignore constructs, and are seldom afraid to tell the truth (or at least their version of it), which means they're liable to help people that others won't.

So, if you're good crazy, go mentor or start a mentorship program. (And if you're bad crazy, go seek help.)

MBAs are Stoopid People, too

Mark Twain once said, "I have never let my schooling interfere with my education." A big reason so many MBA/Ph.D.-types get stupid is because they think they already know everything. Now of course, MBAs have their place, but don't sleep: Anyone can get an MBA—a good MBA from a great school—with enough student loans and free time on their hands.

Every truly successful person I ever met, admired, or worked with had one thing going: *they understood people*. They understood the people they did business with plus the people they were trying to do business with. And while getting the extra sheepskin will do mom and dad proud, you don't learn about people by sitting in classrooms memorizing B-school jargon at $1,900 a credit hour.

These days, I am an adjunct instructor at my alma mater. Each semester students ask me what's the one thing they can do to succeed in business. I always tell them the same thing: People. Talk to people you wouldn't normally talk to: Old people. Young people. Foreign people. Rich people. Poor people. Business will always be about understanding people—usually people who are way, way different from you. Understand people and what makes them tick. Understand what they want, why they want it and how you get it to them.

Business will always be more about people than degrees.

Right vs. Liberty

Lastly, let me add that in my opinion many of the flaws in our schools go back to the fact that we've never honestly figured out as a nation what education is about or who's entitled to it. Up until the mid-1950s, whether it was college or K–12, the only Americans guaranteed access to a quality education were English-speaking whites; everyone has had to march, sue or fight their way into school to one degree or another. So in order to improve our education system we need to ask ourselves a question: *Is education a civil right or a liberty?*

Is being educated so crucial to being a productive American citizen that it should be guaranteed and protected like we do the right to vote, free speech, or anything else in the Constitution? Or is education just a liberty—an enriching and empowering part of American life, but something that should be left up to the individual/private sector to provide?

If education's a civil right, then we should run our schools like social services or public works' programs and ensure that absolutely everyone regardless of race, class, or need gets an education that's sufficient enough to make them to be employable and productive members of society. On the other hand, if education is (just a liberty or "Everyone for themselves, lucky sperm unite,") then schools should just follow a capitalist's model where an education is simply a product in a marketplace and we would allow free market dynamics to determine who gets an education and what form a quality education takes and how much one costs. In other words, education becomes no different from a car or a pair of shoes—you buy whichever one you want or can afford (if any at all) and the entire school system from K–12 thru college and universities becomes privatized, for-profit businesses that make their learning product as they see fit.

But whatever the case, we need to start being honest about it one way or the other. Otherwise American education, be it K–12 or beyond, will simply become about constructs, smokescreens, haves vs. have-nots, profits-over-people...aka just another part of The Hustle. (And depending on who you are, that's what it's become already.)

So you're a philosopher?
Yes, yes, I think very deeply...
—KRS-One[2]

And that's my take on modern education. Once again, I'm not knocking higher education; I just want to make sure people get the right kind of education. We need to arm our future with the ability to think, flow and innovate, not just memorize, duplicate and follow orders. If we don't, as an economy and as a society, we'll get exactly what we deserve: *Hustled.*

Teach the children, save the nation.
—*Rakim*[3]

Movin' On...

Gotta go, gotta go, gotta go!
—Robin Harris

Sometimes, as Achebe once wrote, things fall apart and heads have to roll. I'm talking *layoffs*. Downsizing. Outsourcing. No matter what you call it, the result's the same: unsuspecting hardworking people losing their jobs. Now, as adults we all know that nothing is forever and layoffs are part of life. But there has got to be a better way to do this.

As it stands now, pretty much every layoff goes down the same: The company waits until about 4:30 P.M., maybe 4 P.M. if they're feeling generous. They call the victim(s) into an office. If it's a blood bath, folks get herded into a conference room. Once the cattle have been rounded up, the slaughter begins. Someone with a little juice stands up and says, "As you know we've had a tough quarter... We've done everything possible to avoid this situation, but..."

Then they tell you your job is gone and you have until 6 P.M. to pack up your cubicle and go home. But don't worry, you'll get a severance package: a day for every month you've worked, give or take. They're really sorry to let you go, as they'll reiterate, but times are tough and the company is just trying to stay afloat. And depending on the joint, the layoffs may go on for months. And those left are usually stuck with twice as much work, which reminds them just how inefficient things were beforehand, which sinks morale even lower. But what's worse is that no matter how ugly it gets, the execs are usually spared.

When you treat people inhumanely, don't expect them to respond humanely. If you leave your wife of 20 years for a nice firm coed, don't be shocked if her lawyers flip you over and shake you like a baby's rattle until the alimony comes out. It's not that your now-ex-wife is vindictive, it's that you screwed her over and karma sucks. Business is no different. You can't take employees who've given you 15 years of their lives and kick 'em to the curb on an hour's notice like used crack whores.

My biggest fear with all of these layoffs is that someone's going to snap—*bad*. To me, the fact that folks like Kenneth Lay and Jeff Skilling are still breathing is an act of God. I can't believe that not one high-ranking corporate crook hasn't met at least one Louisville-slugger-wielding ex-employee screaming, "Severance this package!"

Corporate America is due for a real live *Burning Bed* party. Remember *Burning Bed,* that old made-for-TV Farah Fawcett flick? Every week her drunkard husband would come home from work, ball up his fists and pound the snot out of her until he passed out. Well one night he gets drunk and beats her like Lewis beat Tyson. But this time, as soon as he passes out in bed, she grabs the kids, packs up the car, douses the homestead with a few jugs of gasoline, drops a match, and rides off into the night. She's arrested for murder and arson but gets acquitted on temporary insanity.

Now here's the fun part: For about 6 months afterwards, real women all over America started torching their abusive husbands and boyfriends—maybe half a dozen cases total. Some got off, some didn't.

Picture This:

Meet "Edna," a loyal 58-year-old grandma and secretary who's been with The Company for 35 years. One Friday afternoon the CEO lays off poor Edna along with maybe 50 others—the stock was bloated, the books were cooked and the execs bounced to France. Left with no pension, no new job skills, and maybe a few months' cash reserves, Edna snaps. She follows Mr. CEO down to his executive parking spot and bladow! Caves his skull in with a bolt of Xerox paper.

Now tell me, who'd lock Edna up knowing the only reason she did it was because they stole the rest of her life? The day this happens for real and hits the press, it's open season on crooked execs worldwide. As for Edna, prison or not, she's getting a parade, a book deal, plus guest spots on *The View*. (Hey, it could happen. In some 'hoods when you steal, the cops are the least of your worries.)

Again, it's not the layoffs, it's how and why they're being done that's bound to backfire. If your company is struggling and cuts are necessary, I totally understand that and so can most everyone else. But if you're laying people off to cover greed or stupidity, then I might side with the overworked grunt in the cube that goes upside your head.

But seriously, if you've got cuts to make here's a few tips on severing ties the right way:

1. (At least) two weeks' notice.

If employees are expected to give two weeks' notice before quitting, employers should give two weeks' (or more) notice when laying them off. There's no reason you can't sit an employee down and say, "Look, we have to make some cuts and you're on the list. But they won't go into affect for a couple more weeks, so can you stick around and help us out until then?"

Now I know what some of you are thinking, "If we say that, our lame-ducks will put viruses on our computers, call the trades, slack off..." All I can say is if you don't trust the people you hire to be professionals until the end, you shouldn't have hired them in the first place. (If you believe your fiancé might kill you in your sleep, you don't jump the broom anyway, do you?)

2. Be upfront and honest.

Don't lie about layoffs. Lying only makes it worse. I once knew a guy, "Stan." His company's revenues were directly in line with his job. The better the company did, the busier Stan was. Well, during a few months' stretch, things slowed down. Then they got slower. And slower. Stan got nervous and went to his boss with, "Are we in trouble? Is everything okay?"

His boss, a VP, assured him he had nothing to worry about and things would pick up soon. So Stan went out and bought a car. A few weeks later, Stan got laid off along with 20 others. Turns out, the company was bleeding red ink and the layoffs had been in the works for weeks. Stan was stuck with a fat new-car note and no way to pay it. It wasn't a fancy car, just something to get to and from work. Still, Stan snapped and rightly so, he'd been lied to. They had to bring in extra security just to deal with him.

They also axed "Ted," a graphic designer who had a similar deal going: Also working under the assumption his job was safe, Ted went and bought a house for his wife and newborn daughter. Locked up all his money in escrow and everything. Ted got canned about a month after he moved in. (Try paying house notes on SSI.)

So if you know for sure that you have to lay people off, warn them. Tell the truth. Tell folks that cuts may be coming so they can prepare, too. The only thing worse than losing your job is being lied to about it. That's when people snap.

3. Fire some coaches.

Of all the layoffs I've witnessed and been told about—less than a handful ever involved execs. It's the equivalent of cutting all your players after a bad season but keeping the coaching staff and front office in tact.

If things have gone so bad that you need to lay off 20 folks in a department, maybe it's not the 20 that need to go but the one or two bosses that helped run things into the ground. Look, if a company is struggling, why layoff 10 fish at 30K per when that whale in the corner-office raking in 250K a year isn't helping either? Just as we need fair and balanced hiring, we need fair and balanced firing.

Ask yourself: *How hard will any employee work knowing they'll always be the first to go no matter what?* And when your company recovers, what professional will come work for you once they find out that this is you how do business? So let's have some parity. When the time comes, cut some execs.

4. Post-layoff support.

Where's the luv once you're gone? When you're done with a hooker or a stripper, at least she gets a kiss if she wants one. But what do we give the people we lay off, besides a couple weeks' severance? Not much else. I say if you're laying folks off and it's truly not their fault, give support. Make a phone call to see how they're doing. If I give 10 or 15 years to a place, can't I get a follow-up call?

I say help the fresh cuts out. Let them use company facilities so they can revise and update their resumés. Or letters of recommendations or job leads. If you can't directly help them move on, at least cheer them on. Just as you don't burn bridges as an employee, you shouldn't do it as an employer.

You're Fired!

Firings are like divorces—you're splitting up for a reason. But you can still part ways respectfully. Make sure the firing is justified and fair and that employee will go away quietly and possibly respecting you (and less likely to return armed).

And if you get fired, don't hate. Just be mature and go. Before you blame "them," check yourself. Maybe the place was a bad fit. Maybe you screwed up. Maybe you just needed to grow up. Whatever the case, just learn from it and move on.

I Quit.

At some point, you get sick of the same faces, the same tasks, and the same place. At some point, it's just time to go. But even under the best circumstances, quitting can suck. Still, there's a right way and a wrong way to blow town.

I think I've seen 'em all: The "Face-to-face-curse-out-then-bounce." The "Sneaky two-word-email" getaway. The surprise "Screw-this-job" voicemail. And the classic "Two-weeks'-notice-ride-off-into-the-sunset" special. Pops loved that one most. To him, taking any other route was blasphemy. "You give your *two weeks* like a man," he'd say.

But the best one I ever heard came from "Joey," our senior VP's 21-year-old son who worked in the mailroom. One day he says, "Wait until there's one of those big executive meetings—the monthly ones with all the bosses... Walk in. Don't say a word. Just turn your back to 'em, drop your pants and bend over. Have, *I QUIT* written on your cheeks in big letters. Then pull up your pants and walk out." Classic.

But me? I never did any of those. I just wrote a resignation letter that ended up all over the Internet plus in a major industry trade. I even got a few job offers out of it. (Scout's honor.) But when I wrote mine, my escape was all planned out. I'd saved some money, cut expenses, paid bills... I was ready. Or so I thought.

Truth be told, I wasn't. I ended up on unemployment for a while, maybe 6 months. I ended up freelancing to make rent. Looking back, I should've planned better. Those "Me-against-the-world" manifestos only worked for Tupac and Jerry Maguire. So plan before you quit. Think things thru. Save some money. Lots of money. And to paraphrase Pops: don't burn bridges. Split on good terms. Don't quit out of anger; quit out of focus, planning, and greener pastures. (By the way, they're rarely greener.)

I'm walkin' thru the door—
ain't comin' back no more.
—Mya[1]

Well that's it for this one. Break-ups suck. But just because money and careers are involved doesn't mean people can't or shouldn't part ways with humanity and respect.

Now, let's get ready for the B-side...

Darling you got to let me know,
Should I stay or should I go?
—The Clash[2]

Side B

The Takeover
(Power to the People)

Get Free or die trying!
—Dead Prez

Honor Among Thieves?
(Ethics vs. Morals)

Better is a little with righteousness
than great revenues without right.
—Proverbs 16:8

Ethics. Some got 'em, some don't. Me? No ethics at all. I don't have any ethics and I don't want any ethics. Thanks to my business and life experiences, I finally figured out the difference between the two; and the day I did, I tossed my code of ethics out the window. Life's been pretty good ever since. I'm not preaching here, I'm just going to offer a few angles up for consideration. So keep an open mind and ride with me for a bit, okay? Cool.

Little Ms. Can't Be Wrong

About nine years ago I had a crush on this girl, actually this *woman* named "Kara." I met her during one of my copywriting gigs. She was a commercial director's assistant. Gorgeous girl. Long, curly dark hair, smoky gray eyes, sexy smile, tall... Plus she was one of those women who didn't really know she was attractive. She never had that "I-know-you-want-me" attitude or style of dress that a lot of women have, which made her even hotter. (Guys feel me on that one.) And to top it all off, she was smart.

Her pops was a well-respected professor at Northwestern University—he taught Business Ethics. So one day we're in a car, don't remember where we were going, and she asks, "Which would you rather be: ethical or moral?" She asked every guy that question because it usually made for a good debate and she was turned on by intelligence. (Like I said, she was smart.)

Well, at the time I didn't really know what ethics were. I'd never really heard the term before—at least not enough to bother looking it up. (Hey, I went to publik skool; sue me.) I just figured it was similar to moral, and I knew moral from church. So I said, "Gimme morals... Besides, ethics and morals—same difference, right?"

"No," she said, "I'd rather be ethical."

According to Kara, morals were the product of close-minded perspectives and rigid dogma seldom pertinent to changing times and real world needs. (Say that 10 times fast.) In short, morality is like beauty—a matter of taste. But ethics? To Kara (and her pops), ethics are code of conduct that everyone agrees to abide by—a common denominator if you will. Ethics are consistent. But religion is morality and morality can be flimsy depending on who's defining it. Morals were based on seemingly arbitrary restrictions, often better in theory than in practice. Ethics were about intelligence, democracy, critical thinking, and open-mindedness.

At the time, that was a little over my head so to illustrate, she said selling cigarettes was ethical. That's when the light went on and I realized I didn't like Kara anymore—at least not like *that*. Something about being ethical suddenly wasn't all that sexy.

As I said earlier, I once knew a few dope dealers. Looking back, many of them had ethics: They didn't sell to children or around schools. They never knowingly cut their product with poisons, etc. They didn't snitch. They sold mainly to support their families and swore they'd stop first legal chance they got. Within the realm of their occupation, there were rules to the game and they followed those rules. They had ethics.

It's really juss like sellin' smoke...

Contrary to most of America's know-nothing pundits, most my friends weren't corrupted by over-enabling white liberal guilt or victimization-peddling black leadership. (Though they haven't helped by any stretch.) Nope. Most every criminal enterprise we embarked on and every twisted social value we embraced came from Corporate America and Hollywood.

As children we watched Wal-Mart, Nike, and other crews roll into town and take no prisoners. We watched Trump and Gates. We watched Gotti and the immigrant mob families. We watched Boesky, Neil Bush, and the corporate raiders of the 1980s. We memorized *The Sopranos, Gangs of New York, The Godfather, Scarface, Wall Street, King of New York, White Heat,* etc. We watched every pale-faced, manifest-destiny-touting hustler before and since. We watched, took notes, and learned from the best. Then we took our turn.

Narcotics, as I learned growing up, is America's greatest commodity hustle, no different from pork bellies, orange juice, or anything at the CBOT. Weed, crack, Meth, LSD, and E are commodities—basically the same in every city and every state. The cut and quality varies some, but it's all sugar-water, just like soda. And like any commodity, the only serious money to be made in narcotics is by moving weight—importing and exporting mass quantities of dope in its raw form. You push it wholesale or do consignment and get your cake upfront while the retailers *OK-Corral* it on the block for table scraps. Otherwise you end up playing the grocery-store model: *NOW ON SALE, BUY ONE GET ONE FREE*...and all of that.

Once someone perfects a formula or finds a great new supply, the marketplace follows suit. If you're getting quality weed from Canada, I'm getting a Canadian connect, too. If you're soaking your weed in codeine and it's selling, I'll do the same. It's all about commoditization. In business, when your product/service becomes a commodity, there's only four ways to win: Price wars, mergers 'n' acquisitions, strategic alliances, or added value.

Since there's a dope dealer on every corner, you can discount your product until a dime sack or a nickel bag is $1.99. Or you can consolidate/form alliances with the competition. But if the competition isn't down for joining forces, then you're forced into goh-rilla tactics: Out come the knuckles and nines. You drive your comp out of business by any means necessary—just like Wal-Mart and Starbucks have done to mom-'n'-pop ops for decades. And if a few bodies have to pile up, then so be it—such is the cost of doing business.

As for added-value, with the advent of the Internet and cellphones, the kids are coming off the corners and running operations out of apartments, cubicles, dorms, or wherever. But of course there's the (slowly shrinking) digital divide—while most of the white drug dealers run their ops from behind closed doors, the black and brown pushers are left out on the streets, which means more minorities still disproportionately get locked up.

Now the pimps I saw were a little different; theirs was also commodity hustle but it had a nice direct-marketing wrinkle to it. The marketplace's tastes and trends dictated the pimp's inventory. When enough guys wanted blondes, the pimp stocked blondes or women who looked good in blonde wigs. When enough customers express racial preferences, the pimp adjusts his stable accordingly. Some guys, often businessmen, would rather have their merchandise delivered to discreet locations (hotels, motels, etc.) versus picking up women on street-corners. So the pimp alters his channels of distribution and fulfillment.

Also, with so many niches to satisfy, there really hasn't been much need for violence among pimps. After all, when's the last time you heard about pimps killing each over territory? Over the years the pimp's biggest problem hasn't been other pimps so much as his product. It's hard to convince a woman to do what amounts to white slavery when even the multi-billion adult-entertainment industry offers her more equitable opportunities.

Plus, pimps usually have an extra angle that keeps the dough flowing rain or shine: *Shame.* Besides the fact that everyone loves sex, most people still don't want their sexual appetites and escapades made public. So whether it's cops, politicians, married men, etc., blackmail, while dangerous, is almost a de facto ancillary revenue stream. As a result, pimping is a safer, more lucrative business model than the drug game. Come to think of it, pimps and whores were probably the first marketers to leverage and refine niche marketing, market research, and targeted distribution and fulfillment.

(By the way: over the years, I met lots of businessfolks with timeshares. I never quite understood timeshares until I saw an interview with Dennis Hof, pimp/owner of the Moonlight Bunny Ranch in Nevada. He started out as a real estate broker. But one day, he realized that a woman's body was the most valuable real estate around. So, he started "selling 'timeshares' in women," as he put it. It was then that I understood timeshares and why so many folks had 'em... And why many folks have headaches trying to unload 'em.)

But again, all of this is straight-up business formulas and corporate philosophy I'm relaying—that's why it probably seems familiar. The only real difference is street kids and criminals are tailoring these principles to fit our environment, circumstances, and resources. The products and consumers may be different, the distribution channels are a little unorthodox, but the principles and strategies are comparable to anything that's ever come out of Harvard, Kellogg, or Wharton; and truthfully, they may be better because they were developed and tested under much harsher conditions with by folks with less resources than 99.5% of the folks in Corporate America. Conversely, I challenge you to show me one MBA grad, Wall Street CEO or Madison Ave professional that can thrive in the 'hood. I dare you to show me just one.

Anyway, it was my home life that got me revisiting Kara's cigarette argument: Cigarettes are toxic; contain poisons and carcinogens. And when used as intended, they're addictive and deadly over time. So are cigarette manufacturers and marketers ethical? Of course—just ask the FDA. Cigarettes are perfectly legal long as they stick to the script: Warning labels. Don't market to minors, etc. Plus just about all cigarette companies fund antismoking campaigns, *We Card* programs, and cancer research. Yes Virginia, cigarettes are as ethical a hustle as there is.

But are cigarettes moral? Is it moral to sell a product that you know is harmful by the very nature of its design, legal or not? No. The only difference between cigarettes and street drugs is legality; and laws are amended and rewritten daily. Remember: In the early 1900s, alcohol was illegal while cocaine, heroin, and opium were not only legal but sold over-the-counter and in some instances available to children. Bayer Co. and Martin H. Smith sold heroin everywhere thru the early 1900s. Coca-Cola was made with a cocaine derivative; so were famous wines of the day such as *Vin Mariani* and *Maltine.* And besides heroine, Sigmund Freud also prescribed cocaine and opium for everything from asthma to hot flashes to full-on psychosis. In fact, a big reason those drugs were eventually outlawed was due to the myth that cocaine and heroin made black men more prone to rape white women and more resilient to small-arms fire.[1]

So in a debate of ethics vs. morals, legality is, as Basia once sang, *time 'n' tide.* It just depends on the era, who's in charge, and who stands to profit most. And if you follow their rules, they'll deem you ethical. In the end, ethics is just honor among thieves. Morals say, "Don't be a thief." To this day, Robin Hood is the quintessential folk hero. Why? Because he stole from the corrupted rich then gave it to the poor. He had wonderful ethics—for a crook.

Also, don't sleep: the day marijuana becomes legal is the day your friendly neighborhood weed pusher becomes at least as ethical as *PHILLIP-MORRIS*, *ANHEUSER-BUSCH* or *GNC*.

> *Murder and Insanity Increasing Among Lower Class Blacks Because They Have Taken to Sniffing since deprived of whisky by prohibition!*
>
> —New York Times[2]

Dopeman, Dopeman...

Viral infections are approaching epidemic proportions in America. The two biggest problems in fighting them are that many of the new viruses (most notably MRSA, AIDS, and new strains of STDs and flu) are becoming increasingly resistant to current treatment options. And believe it or not, the drug industry is doing less and less R&D on stronger antibiotics and vaccines.

You see, taking a drug from R&D, to FDA approval, to market can cost tens of millions of dollars while antibiotics usually have higher success rates with lower R&D costs, not to mention a built-in consumer base. In other words, most antibiotics and vaccines don't have the profit margins or ROI that Wall Street and shareholders want. So many pharmaceuticals are instead pouring their R&D budgets into drugs with longer-term usage prospects like LIPITOR or VALTREX which must be taken for months and in some cases years, and drugs with more mass appeal like ALLEGRA, which is used by tons of people, not to mention the forever-lucrative OTC (over-the-counter) cold medicines and pain reliever segments.

Also, despite the constant threat of bioterrorism, many pharmaceuticals won't properly fund counter-bioterrorism R&D. Their position is: Why spend money developing drugs that may never get used? Consequently we don't have enough of the necessary drugs on hand to protect against a bioterrorism attack. And if it weren't for Bush's 2004 BioShield Bill, which subsidizes participating drug makers at a profit, some pharmaceuticals probably wouldn't work on bioterrorism vaccines and cures at all.

Now sure, being thin, having great sex, and low cholesterol are all important, but immune systems are struggling; bioterrorism is *thisclose* to *everywhere* and in too many cases, the folks best equipped to help are putting profits over people. But hey, at least they're being ethical.

(Oh by the way: That big flu vaccine shortage of 2004 was just the beginning. Thanks to all these pharmaceutical hustlers, the masses will be coming up short on all kinds of essentials for years to come. Just you watch.)

Pushing Rhymes Like Weight

As I've said before, marketers are the world's best psychiatrists—we identify consumers' wants, needs, and desires. We probe until we discover insecurities and phobias. Then we convince you that the best way to fix your insides is to buy our clients' stuff. It's called "problem-solution" marketing, the oldest trick in the book.

My SOFTSHEEN and ALBERTO CULVER ads never told 13-year-old girls their hair or bodies were okay as-is. My Mercedes ads never told guys that most cars are the same and prestige was all in their head. I never wrote a SPRITE ad that said, "It's just sugar-water and food coloring." Nope. My job was to convince you that somehow, my sugar-water would make you cool. And that this 6-piece or 9-piece chicken wings pack is really the perfect in-between meal snack. And that having this logo on your butt, in your mouth, or in your house would make you a better, happier person.

As a mental dope pusher, if I sell my product straight (with no psychological additives) you may or may not buy it. But again, business loves formulas. So I tilt the odds in my favor by cutting my product with additives: *Sex. Cool. Soul. Youth. Power. One-upmanship. Self-empowerment...* Whatever dreams you're chasing, whatever images you're craving is what I'll cut my cars, my fast food, my soda, my beer, or my overpriced sneakers with. It's all about finding that special recipe for addiction. And when marketers like myself get that cut right, we have brand loyalty—and your money.

(Ever seen holiday mobs chasing after the toy-of-the-moment? It's like watching a bunch of crackheads; and as a dealer, I just sit back and smile all the way to the bank.)

Food, Folks, & Fun

I want to discuss obesity and business because I also worked on a couple fast food and soda clients. First off, I think it's funny in a sick sort of way that half the world is near starving yet two-thirds of America is literally eating and sitting itself to death. In 2003 obesity was declared the top killer and cause of disease in America. And our solution? Make fast food the new tobacco. Sue the hell out of the sugar and grease pushers. But believe it or not, I have a few problems with that, too. As a former Illadelphian prince once said: "Drums, please."

Problem 1: Fast food is retail and retail is about moving weight. The only way you can move mass quantities at a profit is thru low overhead, low cost-per-unit, and lots of outlets. How do you keep overhead down? Cheap labor and materials. Next, expand: You can't push weight from just one or two spots; you need territories. Fast food is in the business of locking down as many locales as possible. Weight plus expansion equals empires.

Next, you can use fresh-baked breads, organically grown vegetables, and 95%-lean ground beef cooked in little or no oil. You can have free-range chicken or turkey with no hormones. Customers can have baked potatoes with the skins on, veggie sticks, and all that good stuff. You can use pure cane sugar and honey instead of artificial sweeteners. You can lose the sodas, the corn syrups, etc., for water and natural juices. You can dump the preservatives in favor of making everything fresh each day and tossing the leftovers every other night. But then you, as a fast-food business, will only have maybe a few hundred outlets, tops, catering to only the top 20% or so of the population that can afford $10 lunches and $20 dinners on a regular basis. Because believe me, none of those changes are cheap.

Like the drug game, fast food's also a commodity hustle—quality goes out the window when it comes to commodities. It's about value meals, over a bazillion served, and convenience. If you want cheap food for the masses it'll be made cheap, sold cheap, and probably taste cheap. When you consider Pizza Hut, Outback, TGI Fridays, KFC, Taco Bell, BK, Wendy's, and the rest, you're talking about thousands of outlets serving hundreds of millions of customers worldwide each day. The price-points, competition, and barriers of entry alone force them to use cheaper (and consequently less healthy) ingredients just to compete and grow.

Conversely, people can't afford not to go along with it. Sure, everyone wants 3 meals a day that'll make Jenny Craig proud and Wolfgang Puck jealous. But that's 1,095 meals a year (assuming 3 a day, 365 days a year), not counting snacks and desserts. You know how often I heard coworkers complain about their lunch options over the years? *Let's see, do I have the chicken wrap or the tuna salad? The bagel or the rice cakes and yogurt? The fruit salad or the grainy cereal bars? Pasta or steamed veggies?* The healthier they tried to eat, the more they spent.

On average, they forked over $8–$10 a day for lunch, 5 days a week. And that was in addition to their grocery shopping and other meals. Even for some white-collar types with good salaries it was tight. So as long as "healthy" is more expensive and less accessible than unhealthy, most folks will consciously sacrifice health for value.

Consider: A dozen KRISPY KREMES are way cheaper than a dozen servings of fresh fruit. WHITE CASTLE burgers are cheaper than rice cakes or pretzels. A Popeye's 2-piece is cheaper than a fresh deli sandwich. A 40 oz. beer is cheaper than the same amount of 100% pure fruit juice, while 10% fruit juice is cheaper than 100% juice. KOOL-AID's cheaper than distilled water. A bottle of water is more expensive than a bottle of pop. An order of French fries is cheaper than a baked potato. A fried fish sandwich is cheaper than a baked salmon filet. White rice, which is bleached and processed with God-knows-what is cheaper than brown rice. On average, you can get 2, maybe 3 big, chocolatey, goo-filled candy bars for the cost of one PowerBar. A month's worth of salty, fattening, starchy Ramen noodles is cheaper and more filling than a week's worth of yogurt. And pound for pound, once you factor in groceries, time, and labor, buying a cooked meal from most joints is still cheaper than cooking the same meal yourself.

In Chi's urban communities, there's some type of heart attack-to-go joint on every corner—Harold's Chicken, J&J Fish, Gyro and BBQ joints—that's in addition to all the fast-food chains, corner stores and liquor stores. No Whole Foods. No Trader Joe's. No health-food stores or farmers' markets. Why? Too expensive. Plus many of the "better" stores don't serve certain neighborhoods until they get gentrified. (Then they come out like roaches at night.)

But at least the stuff we do have is affordable. It's clogging our arteries, raising our blood pressure and weight, but at least we can afford to eat actual food more than once a day. Otherwise most of us would probably eat soul food every other night. (And we know how healthy soul food is.) As consumers within certain tax-brackets and demographics, your menu is partially chosen for you.

The only people that can really afford to eat good on a regular basis are upper-middle class and rich people, which excludes a good three-fourths of the country, mostly minorities at that. (And before you say the V-word, the vast majority of America's vegetarians are those who can afford to be so.)

Bad Tech Support

Another issue: *Technology*. Technology is great for lowering fast food's cost-per-unit but it's forced our digestive systems to process additives, preservatives, and hormones that no other generation of human beings have ever had to process before. We're growing tomatoes the size of babies' heads. Melons as big as medicine balls. Cucumbers are looking like Louisville Sluggers. I swear I've eaten foods with colors that don't occur anywhere in nature or outer space. And forget the natural stuff; thanks to folks like Kraft, Ocean Spray, General Mills, Nabisco, etc, we've got packaged goods with expiration dates measured in dog years. It's no wonder we've got 12-year-old boys that're 6 ft., 200 lbs and teen girls with 34Cs. You show me a typical American teen and I'll show you internal organs that have been terrorized by bioengineering since birth.

By the way: When's the last time you saw an actual chicken? I mean a living, breathing, clucking chicken? I don't think I've seen one since I visited some of my kinfolks down South as a teen. But you look around today and chicken is everywhere. Chicken tenders. Chicken wings. Chicken nuggets. Chicken salads. Chicken wraps. Chicken parts. Sports bars have chicken. Liquor stores sell chicken. Gas stations have chicken. Vending machines have chicken. Joints that don't serve any kind of food at all can still whip up a plate of Buffalo wings for you. Chicken is the new potato chip. I've seen everything but chocolate-covered chicken. (And don't think some R&D guy hasn't at least tried it.) Now I'm not saying the chickens are juiced, but if it ever comes down to a chicken versus a baseball player for passing a drug test, the only bird I'm betting on is a St. Louis Cardinal.

Also, our love of technology has made most traditional fat-burning activities obsolete. We have remote controls because we don't want to get up to change a channel or turn a radio dial. Catalogue orders have replaced shopping trips. Dishwashers have replaced standing up and washing dishes. Videogames and the Internet have replaced playing outside. All our hand tools are now "power tools." Then we developed diet pills because we don't want to workout to compensate for poor eating. We're always making and buying things to make life easier, cheaper, and cooler. But in the end, everything's gotten harder because we've made ourselves softer. Only market shares are getting stronger and healthier. (God bless The Hustle.)

It's good for you

No marketing scheme can make people fly someplace within driving distance. Same with food. People only eat when they're hungry. People have a built-in mindset about when, why, and how much they'll consume. Since you can't always trick people into being hungry, you have to give them other reasons to eat. Marketers call it Creating Consumption Opportunities.

Consumption Opportunities are how you get flatlanders to buy mountain bikes. Consumption Opportunities is how you get people who don't know a dirt road from a dirty road to buy an SUV even when gas is $3 a gallon. Consumption Opportunities sell disposable contact lenses and bottled water. They sell tanning beds and suntan lotion to minorities and bigoted whites. Consumption Opportunities sell high-priced athletic gear to non-athletes and couch potatoes. Consumption Opportunities sell reruns of marginal TV shows on DVD. Consumption Opportunities can sell a swimming pool to a cat.

Before McDonald's jumped off in the mid-1960s there was really no such thing as "casual dining." Average folks ate at home, while the notion of eating out as entertainment was reserved for wealthy types, lowlifes, or special occasions. And hamburgers weren't snacks; they were dinner food. Just ask anyone over 45 or 50 hamburgers were a sit-down, when-you-could-afford-beef dinner food.

Back in the day, most people couldn't afford to eat beef more than once or twice a week. In fact, livestock, along with whiskey (see *The Whiskey Rebellion of 1794*), was among the first forms of currency in America. Wealth was often measured by the amount of land and livestock one had. And since most minorities were on the outside looking in, beef was rare. This left pork and chicken (much cheaper meats) more commonplace in minority communities, even to this day.

But times change. The cattle industry figures out how to grow bigger cows and steer. Beef slowly gets cheaper. And along comes the McDonald's brothers with their hamburgers—no crime there. After all, they weren't the first or the cheapest, or even the tastiest. But once Ray Kroc got involved, more consumption opportunities were needed in order to grow business, which brings us to:

"I'm lovin' it."

Remember Mickey D's "You deserve a break today"? That line transformed McDonald's from a restaurant to a stress-relief zone. Burger King's "Have it your way" was about empowerment as much as it was about food. "Everybody needs a little KFC" was a well-orchestrated spin on TLC (tender loving care). Who doesn't want a little more of that in their life? "We love to see you smile!" wasn't about food; it was about feeling good. Who wouldn't go to a place where everyone wants to make you smile? Isn't feeling good worth a few extra empty calories a day?

These days, McDonald's brain-numbing, but effective "I'm lovin' it" has increased consumption opportunities by playing up an artificial post-modern nostalgia. Everything about it is so pseudo-retro that "I'm lovin' it" could've easily been, "Eat a good memory." It also creates consumption opportunities by riding the "universalism" movement—homogenizing ever-popular urban imagery and music for mainstream consumption. (Hence their initial use of Justin Timberlake and their failed attempts to court emcees to rap about Big Macs, and get urban fashion designers to redesign McD's uniforms in 2005.)

Stackin' chips...

In 2003, I caught a *60 Minutes* segment on Frito-Lay. Like most U.S. conglomerates, they're working their hustle overseas. And they'd found an untapped market in of all places, The Netherlands. Guess what the biggest barrier to entry is? For the most part, Netherlanders see snack chips the same way our parents and grandparents once saw burgers—as a specialty item. To most Netherlanders, potato chips are a sit-down, after-dinner, every-now-'n'-then type of thing. They really don't buy 'em much. But they have a ton of young people with lots of disposable income. *Ah, if we could only convince them that they can't eat just one...*

So Frito-Lay is spending millions on Consumption Opportunities—convincing these folks that potato chips should be eaten way more often for reasons other than just hunger and dessert. It may take a few years, possibly a generation, but once they come around, Lays will start stacking chips like a casino. And once that happens, the floodgates will be opened on all sorts of other processed foods and fast food ventures. Before you know it those Netherlanders will be built like snowmen. And it's just the beginning.

As other countries become more Americanized, our multinational food hustlers are moving in for the kill. In January 2004, KFC opened its 1,000th outlet in China with hundreds more expected to come.[3] In the same month Pizza Hut opened its 300th restaurant in South Korea.[4] And in 2005, McDonald's added an estimated 100 new stores to its former total of 560 Chinese locales.[5] And besides China's billion plus mouths, India, with nearly 1 billion folks of its own has also become a hotbed for America's fast food and sugar hustlers. So don't be surprised if obesity and diet-related illnesses eventually become problems in these parts of the world, too. And if all goes according to plan in the Middle East you'll see *Oil for Oreos* programs within a couple generations.

But this is nothing new. American businesses have done this at home for decades. Besides hamburgers, pasta used to be strictly a dinner dish. Now pasta is lunch, a side dish, an in-between-meals snack for kids, fuel for a workout. We've flipped most of our favorite candies and candy bars into breakfast cereals. Tacos and quesadillas have become the new chicken—folks have begun inhaling 'em like popcorn shrimp. (By the way, how much of IHOP, Taco Bell and Denny's revenue comes from drunken bar patrons binging at 3 A.M.?) God bless Consumption Opportunities.

Soul food?

Another consumption opportunity is borne of Americans' need to consume other cultures. Traditionally, food was a form of cultural expression. Food marketers have tapped into that by positioning ethnic cuisine as tourist attractions for folks looking to explore.

The result has made tortillas the domain of Doritos and Tostitos while burritos have been reduced to "wraps" leaving actual burritos to be sold in gas stations. Taco Bell owns tacos. And whether it's Japanese, Vietnamese, Korean, etc., *all* Asian cuisine has been reduced to Chinese Food/Take-Out, Sushi, or Ramen Noodles. We've reduced Italian cuisine to pizza, pasta, whatever's-on-*The-Sopranos,* and Spaghetti-Os. Indian cuisine is simply "curry." Irish cuisine is Guinness. Soul Food is now anything fried or dipped in hot sauce. Even most all so-called "fusion cuisine" is fused to appease mainstream taste buds.

Ethically, it's just supply meeting demand. But morally, one could argue that it's just another way in which business degrades and dismantles ethnic cultures and by extension ethnic people in the name of catering to a gluttonous consumer culture.

The Original Recipe

As I said earlier, marketing is all about *cut.* Cut is how drug dealers prepare and package their product for consumption. The goal is to stretch your supply while maintaining and, if possible, increasing your product's potency. For a while, a crowd favorite in my neck of the woods was "wet"—marijuana joints laced with dust or heroin then dipped in embalming fluid. So was "syrup" or "sizzurp"—cough medicine or codeine mixed with Hennessey or other types of hard liquor.) Coke dealers cut their raw with any number of additives, or they cook it up into crack to get more bang for the buck... (And to think, I only got a "C" in high-school chemistry.)

At some point all food brands resort to cutting their product with some type of marketing additive: Want to spend more time with your kids? Take 'em out to eat. Want to relax more? Eat meals prepared by someone else. Not good at one-on-one communication? Everyone's eloquent while talking over dinner! Want to show someone you care? Buy them some chocolates or a romantic dinner. Want to feel healthy? Eat Subway. Want to make sports more fun to watch? Order Pizza Hut. Feeling down? Eat Comfort Foods like Ben & Jerry's, Campbell's Soup, or Tollhouse Cookies. Want to feel more athletic? Eat a PowerBar, or better yet, try these diet pills... Whatever dream you're trying to make real, we'll cut our product with it. It's all about addiction. Why? Because when push comes to shove, people just aren't that hungry that often. There'd be half as many fast-food joints if people only ate when they were hungry. But business stays hungry for sales and profits, so we cut.

And of course, non-food brands cut, too: Hyper kid? Use Ritalin. Wanna get the party started right? Drink *MGD or Absolut.* Wanna be more masculine? Smoke Marlboros and visit GNC. Wanna feel sexy? Wear this cologne/perfume. Want to be patriotic? Buy *MADE IN USA.* Wanna be young? Try Botox... Pick a cut, any cut and we'll bleed you broke with it.

You know, I've actually seen pushers tell kids, even teenagers, "No, you don't want *this.*" But when's the last time AOL told kids to get off the 'net and read a book? And videogames didn't become an $11.4 billion a year industry[6] by telling everyone to drop the joysticks and go outside and play. I'll even do you one better: Dope dealers don't chase people down to sell drugs. But marketers? *We hunt you down.* If you don't watch TV, we'll show up in your favorite magazine. Don't read? We're on billboards when you're outside; we do pop-ups and email you when you're online. We'll sponsor your favorite team or sport. We'll product-place our way into your favorite movies and TV shows. We'll get your favorite artists to name-check us in song. And while we're hunting you down, we're going after your kids thru trumped-up cartoons and videogames, product-placement in schools, etc. We can't won't don't stop. We are relentless.

It's funny... Every addict I ever knew stayed chasing their first high—the one that made them feel like they could fly and anything was possible. I've seen people buy a new suit or a new car or a new pair of gym shoes and get that same look in their eyes, like it's a high. For a moment, a split-second, they believe the hype. For a day, maybe a week they actually feel better about themselves just because they're wearing that hot Sean John suit or driving a new Maybach or eating in that exclusive new restaurant. Whether they can afford the stuff or not is irrelevant; all that matters is that in that moment, in that space, at time they are feeling no pain.

So they become brand loyal, not so much because the product or service works or is affordable, but because they know how they feel when they have it. They're little boys who once jumped off their beds believing their Superman Underoos could help them fly or their Jordans could help them dunk. They're the adults who think they're important because they bought their way into VIP or the country club. They're just addicts, plain and simple. (And lemme tell you: As a pusher, there's nothing like hours of focus group footage of people talking about how they're hooked on your *cut*.)

All You Can Eat

Somewhere around the 1960s marketers began picking up on what's known as "impulse purchase decisions." They discovered that many shoppers were buying smaller ticket items not out of want or need, but out of impulse and convenience. The more opportunities shoppers had to indulge their impulses, the more they spent. So they began putting items near checkout registers where the opportunity for impulse purchase is highest. It worked like gangbusters. Today checkout lines are surrounded by racks and kiosks filled with nonessentials. And they never fail to move product. But it doesn't stop there.

Doctors say that more often than not when people feel hungry, their body is actually telling them to get water, not food. Unfortunately, water isn't what the food hustlers want you to buy most. That's why they've made sure some type of food is available everywhere you go: Laundromats. Toy stores. Coffee shops. Gas stations. Clothing stores. Music stores. Bookstores. Schools. Vending machines on every corner. Food is everywhere for a reason. As long as people see food, they'll think food. The more they think food, the more food they'll buy. Remember: Out of sight, out of mind; but top of mind, bottom of wallet.

It's just one more perfectly ethical part of The Hustle.

Super Size Me!

Been to a Pizza Hut, Applebee's, Panda Express, or a Chipotle lately? The portions are huge. No matter where you go, today's kiddie meal could've stuffed an adult 15 years ago. But now we've got burritos big as footballs... Steaks the size of Frisbees... Pasta dishes the size of LPs... Side dishes as big as entrees... 12-oz. and 16-oz. drinks have replaced 8 oz. as the norm... Pizzas are now as big as rims... It's outta control.

And what hasn't gone over-the-top huge has turned "mini-me": Bite-sized candy bars...mini-cookies...mini-snack cakes...mini-quesadillas and baby eggrolls...mini-burgers and baby chicken wings...Traditional sit-down fare is now on-the-go munchables. And since they're sold in quantity, that bang-for-the-buck angle sucks in cost-conscious consumers looking for savings (Sam's Club). Why?

Because marketers have also twisted folks into equating smaller portions with "healthier." Many health-conscious types roll with a couple small candy bars thinking it's healthier than eating one big one... Eight nuggets/wings/tenders are healthier than 4 big pieces of chicken and so on. But of course it's just as bad, only now we're eating more of 'em. And don't think McDonald's 2004 phase-out of their super-size portions won't wind up making them more money long term. It's all Drug Trafficking 101: Hook 'em with samples; reel 'em in on the comeback.

Why is size the great American USP? Well it's hard to compete on taste—everyone's picky, tastes change, and after a while everything tastes the same anyway. But size? Americans equate size with value. Ten pieces of chicken for 8 bucks is *value*. A 99-cent burger? Boring. A 99-cent burger bigger than your head? Value. And since companies buy ingredients in bulk and produce in volume, it's easier to compete on size than on just about any other attribute; regardless of language and culture, everyone understands "*Mine's bigger than yours*" or "*Ours is smaller, therefore more convenient than theirs.*"

And don't get me started on the multi-billion dollar diet industry. See how quick that Atkins' craze faded? The SNACKWELL'S madness lasted longer. (Marketers had the whole country inhaling those puppies by the bagful in the 1990s. People still got fat.) It's all a hustle, just like the notion that those $2.50 bottled waters actually came from some exotic spring in the French Alps. And while America diets and quick-fixes itself into more obesity and higher hospital bills, guess who's pocketbooks keep getting fatter?

Caveat Emptor:

Make no mistake, folks. The marketing hustle is no joke. This is how we do; this is how we breathe; this is how we live. Birds fly; cheetahs run fast; we sell. Period. We spend millions on research, scouting trends, analyzing who wants what and why. Marketing is an industry of art and science combined with greed and schemes. At its best it's a series of perfect storms. At its worst, it's *Jaws*. Like it or not, when it's time for us to eat, the average consumer is chum.

SELL ICE TO ESKIMOS AND CLOTHES TO NUDISTS—that's the mentality I had and the creed my industry lives by. We're professional pit bulls—your money is a major issue to us. Once we bite, we'll sink our teeth into you until we bleed you broke. Once we get you to buy one car, we're going to keep biting until we get you to buy the next model when the time comes. Once we get you to buy one pair of shoes, we go to work on making you buy a 2nd pair. (And if it means intentionally making shoes that wear out a little quicker to stretch our profits-per-unit while increasing our volume as you re-up, then so be it.) We're coming for your money and your minds. And you can't stop us.

So you still don't believe me? Think I'm full of crap or full of myself, even? Good. The blinder you stay, the easier you become prey. Keep denying. Keep pretending most of what you buy isn't programmed into you. Keep on thinking that you're not being manipulated. Keep believing this thing isn't deeper than it looks. Keep sleeping on The Hustle.

All around us there is a breakdown of values...
It is not just the overpowering greed that pervades our business life.
It is the fact that we are not willing to sacrifice for the values we profess.
—Jerome Kohlberg, Jr.[7]

Personal Responsibility?

I bet many of you are thinking, "Hey Hadji, what about personal responsibility? Nobody's making people buy that stuff or eat all that stuff! What about personal responsibility?" Yeah, so what about it? The only time Americans bring up personal responsibility is when we're talking about someone else's. I think, as human beings with any level of influence in any society, people, especially businessfolks, don't want to believe that any of us have any real power over each other. It's easier to sleep at night once you believe that no matter what you do it's always someone else's fault or choice.

When choosing between rights and doing what's right, we'll choose rights every time. Of course no one is physically forcing people to blow their paychecks or their waistlines. But we've spent trillions of dollars and generations conditioning people to believe that food and materialism are viable and necessary solutions to emotional, spiritual, and social ills. Now should people believe everything they see, hear, or read? No. But should we manipulate everything they see, hear, and read for profit then justify it with personal responsibility?

If consumers have personal responsibility, don't marketers and manufacturers have a personal responsibility not to manufacture, market, or sell harmful products? Isn't that why crack is illegal? Don't people have a personal responsibility to look out for their fellow human being—isn't that why we have laws? Or does the need to make money and fulfill personal agendas trump all that touchy-feely for-the-betterment-of-mankind crap?

After years of hearing the personal-responsibility defense, it always sounded like my pops' explaining defensive driving: "Once you hit the road assume everyone around you is careless or crazy and capable of wrecking your life at any time. So be on point 24/7." Personal responsibility is a wonderful ideal—when properly used and combined with the understanding that we're all connected and what we do affects each other. But as it stands now, personal responsibility is code for: "No matter what anyone does to you, it's always your fault in the end."

Am I my brother's keeper?
—Genesis 4:9

Just Desserts

Believe it or not, I'm not trashing my industry or business at large. I just know that there's a right way and a wrong way to get paid. I've met plenty of good moral people over the years. It was a struggle for them to market without manipulating, to brand without feeling like you're going to hell once you retire. Some chose to leave the game because the struggle was too much. Others stayed to fight the good fight. And more than a few developed drinking and drug habits to comfort the pain of contributing to a nation of soft-minded consumption addicts.

But again, we were always ethical. We did and continue to do exactly what the law allows and what our respective codes of ethics sanction. We do what society accepts, what our clients demand, and ultimately what turns a profit. That's business. And if you happen make a few generations soft in the mind, body, and soul along the way, then so be it, right? (Besides, where else but advertising and marketing can an expatriate of the streets make so much legal cream using these kinds of skills and schemes?)

And regardless of industry or product it all goes back to ethics versus morals. Ethics say do what's acceptable and tolerable. But morality demands you look into your heart, listen to that little voice inside you. Listen to God, even if you're getting rich doing the contrary. My morals may not be your morals. But as a leader, I shouldn't chuck my morals just to appease your ethics—even when money's on the line. It's a war of the heart, as Sade once sang. From now until you get toe-tagged, you fight to do what's right. That says "morals" to me.

And where do I net out on our sue-happy culture? Near as I can figure, suing isn't about right and wrong it's about legal loopholes, who has the best lawyers and which side blinks first. It's all relative. Besides, there's enough legitimate blame to go around and everyone knows it. But until everyone takes their share of blame, smoke 'em if you got 'em and eat up—*soup's on.* Also, in the immortal words of Doug Llewellyn: "If you think you've been unjustly wronged, don't take the law into your own hands; take 'em to court."

(And relax: in March 2004, the U.S. Supreme Court ruled you couldn't sue food companies for making you fat.)

It is truly enough said that a corporation has no conscience; but a corporation of conscientious men is a corporation with a conscience.
—Henry David Thoreau[8]

The Great American Paper Chase

All hail the almighty dollar.
Wherever there's money
you know power will follow.
—Queen Latifah

Let's face it: For all the talk of blazing trails and doing what you love most are just out for loot; everything else is just conversation. For a while I was no different. By age 27, I was neck-deep in The Hustle and focused on getting money. But as you get older you learn. One thing I learned is that the business world spins on 7 kinds of money. And before you start chasing, you'd better know which kind you want and more importantly, which kind you need.

Screw You Money

Back in college, "Vic," one of my favorite instructors, taught me about Screw You money. Besides teaching, he worked for a big Chicago firm. At one point, he wrote ads and brochures for target audiences of 8–20 people who were charged with spending billions of taxpayer dollars on fighter planes. (The client was McDonell Douglass.) He was a taller Danny Masterson-type (*That '70s Show*)—kickboxer build, thick curly brown hair, baby face and goatee. Couldn't have been more than 28. Most every coed wanted him. And as an alumnus, most of the department faculty dug him, too. Vic liked the business, but he saw The Hustle so we clicked like champagne and bubbles.

One day we're chopping it up over career stuff when he says, "I want Screw You money." I look confused so he explains. Screw you money is checking your bank statement then telling your clients/bosses, "Screw you, I don't hafta take this anymore." Screw you money burns bridges now but build new ones later. Screw you money doesn't necessarily mean you're rich; it just means you probably won't see poor unless you develop some really stupid habits or get robbed.

Here's what else I've learned: Screw You money doesn't rent or sublet. It doesn't have credit card debt. It definitely doesn't circle the last and the 15th on the calendar. If you want screw you money, you should (a) win the lottery, (b) marry well and divorce better, (c) go into business for yourself, or (d) change your priorities and your standard of living.

Now of those, the first one's a pipe dream, the second's a headache, but I've learned that a combo of the last two just might do the trick.

It gets dangerous/money 'n' power—
it's changing us/Now we're lethal, infected with d'evils.
—Jay-Z[1]

Quiet Money

While working in New York back in '99, I met this cat, an African art hustler. "Jamir" was 30ish, educated (master's in psychology), Brooklyn-bred. He'd go to Africa about 3 times a year to cop trinkets, masks, etc., in bulk from tribal artisans and make a killing pushing 'em in the States, the UK, and Canada. Much of what he sold wasn't really worth much, at least not to those who made it. Most of the artisans Jamir dealt with weren't stupid; they knew they'd been getting pimped since the trans-Atlantic slave trade. So much of the African art that comes West is mass-produced knock-offs made especially for us culture-vultures. The real stuff—what little that hasn't already been looted or lost, gets stashed away by locals.

Anyway, Jamir told me a story about his friend "Paul," a Jewish kid he met in college. Paul was cool people but he grew up in a sheltered, homogenous neighborhood—everything he knew about black folks came from MTV. He assumed all blacks were into money, cars, sex, clothes, and little else. Still, they became friends and broke down those barriers. Sorta.

During semester break, Jamir goes to hang out with Paul's family. One day while watching TV, a commercial comes on. Then out of nowhere, Paul tells Jamir, "Let's go shopping." They go to a fancy dealership where Paul buys what they just saw on TV—a brand-new Benz. It's 70-grand. Paul pays for it—in full; cuts a check on the spot, just like that. Jamir stands there shocked while Paul signs the papers and gets the keys. They spend the afternoon stunting and chasing girls. After a few hours they head back to Paul's.

The next day, Paul's uncle comes over to drop something off. He's this older, old-world orthodox kind of guy—Hasidic, I think. Soon as he spots the fresh Benz in the driveway, he questions Paul. While Paul nervously fills him in, the uncle notices Jamir in the living room watching TV. The uncle snaps:

"Take it back! We don't do things like this—that's what 'they' do! Take it back now!"

Paul had kept a small secret from Jamir: his family was rich. When some people write checks, the checks bounce; but when Paul's fam writes a check, the bank bounces. But you'd never know it. Their house was nice, clean, comfortable, but nothing fancy. The neighborhood was nice, but not conspicuous. But as it turned out, Paul's fam owned (among other things) bunches of gum and candy vending machines all up and down the East Coast. Innocuous, boring stuff...worth a grip and a half.

Paul's family was about Quiet Money. No big-ticket items. Very few brand names. No attention. Just quiet money. Stereotypes aside, Paul's family taught him not to waste loot like others do. And besides that Benz, Paul listened.

Over the years I learned that quiet money is all around you if you know where to look: Millionaires you can't pick out of a line-up. Awkward heiresses and geeky trust fund boys. High-powered yet introverted CEOs. Mob bosses who live in bungalows and wear old clothes. Companies in unglamorous industries who chug along, growing a couple percent annually rain or shine...quiet money. But every once in a great while quiet money pulls a Paul—builds a stadium or slaps their name on a BCS game or gets investigated by the feds.

Quiet money is cool if you do something with it like venture capitalism, charity, or community development. Otherwise, what's the point? No, you don't need 100Gs around your neck, a fleet of cars, or splashy ad campaigns. But are you working to live or living to work? If you don't want to live like a king, fine. But if you're not careful quiet money becomes just another volcano god that you're stuck sacrificing to. Money doesn't need to stay silent, it just needs to say something worth saying.

I'm out for presidents to represent me,
I'm out for dead presidents to represent me...
—Nas[2]

Scared Money

Scared Money collects dust more than interest. Scared money never gets turned into capital. Unfortunately, scared money is everywhere. Investors are playing with scared money. Businesses are trying to gain market share with scared money. Consumers are trying to shop with scared money. Employees are working for scared money. You have people out here trying to retire on scared money. Well in case you haven't heard, *scared money don't make money.*

Too many of us are working under "what if this fails" and still expecting to win. The farmer who's afraid to plant is a farmer guaranteed not to have crops. No matter who you are scared money will never prosper. As an employee you can't say, "I'm making 40K while everyone else is getting laid-off so I better not take any chances" at work. Market leaders don't counterpunch their way to the top. You can't be afraid to invest in growth strategies or to listen to the folks you've paid to help grow your business. Now I'm not saying be reckless and take crazy risks just so you can say, "At least I tried." All I'm saying is *YOU GOTTA BE IN IT TO WIN IT.*

Thy money perish with thee because
thou hast thought that the gift of God
may be purchased with money.
—Acts 8:20

Other People's Money

Credit cards. Loans. A business partner. Clients. Shareholders. Significant other. Parents. Angel investors... Regardless of the source, Other People's Money is a beautiful thing. But OPM can be tough to get, especially if you or your idea is unproven. Still if you get some, things can be pretty sweet. However, no matter what anyone says, OPM always comes with strings attached.

Over the years, every businessperson I ever met who used OPM eventually learned a painful lesson: You are beholden to whoever cut you that check.

America's funny with money—we equate cream with ownership. When you borrow money from someone, they treat you different, like they own a part of you. They want to give you their 2 cents on every little issue. They feel entitled to go too far; get personal, pry into stuff that has nothing to do with the money they loaned you. And depending on who loaned it to you, they're liable to get down right trifling with you. Why? Because your broke butt owes them money. So if you take OPM, watch for the strings.

Goodness gracious, where the cash at?!
Where the stash at?!
—Notorious BIG[3]

Capital

My younger brother once asked me what was the difference between money and capital. I didn't know the answer until I got deep into business. Then I learned. Man, did I ever learn...

Money votes, capital wins elections. Money buys brands; capital builds brands. Money gets you out of jail; capital built the prison and the system that hemmed you up in the first place. Capital funds wars. Capital gets buildings named after it. Capital doesn't even exist to the average person unless it wants to. You ever see names in your company's annual report with bunches of commas 'n' zeros behind 'em and think, *Who are they and why are we paying them so much?* Well, capital is <u>their</u> boss. And when you get a business loan, that's really not capital. That's just a bank letting you borrow some of <u>their</u> capital. Money is money; capital is money plus power.

Capital is the hardest to get because it's more about who you know than it is about what you know how to do. The best way to get capital, in lieu of banks, is to build and pool resources. Many immigrant communities are brilliant at this. They'll pool what they have and invest in each other. That's how they build businesses, schools, and entire communities so quickly.

Let me in now, let me in now.
Bill Gates, Donald Trump let me in now!
—Nelly[4]

Llama Money

Llama Money can do anything regardless of environment. Llama money goes where it wants, does what it wants, becomes what it wants. While the average joe can't tell a llama from a camel, Michael Jackson (a llama money pioneer), woke up one morning and said, "I think I'll have a couple llamas... And while I'm at it, throw in a zoo, a Ferris wheel, the Beatles' catalogue and about 2,600 acres—just 'cuz..." Next thing you know, he's got llamas with all the trimmings. *That's* llama money.

With the exception of Mustard Seed Money (which I'll get to in a sec) all the other kinds of money are reactionary—they're about compensating for existing circumstances and barriers. But llama money is answerable only to its own imagination—llama money wishes it and it comes true. Llama money is so powerful it's often clueless. (Which is usually where the trouble starts.)

As for how to get some... My guess is if your family's name isn't on par with Carnegie, Hilton, Kennedy, Bush, Heinz, Vanderbilt, or Hearst, you might have to marry someone who is.

For the love of money is the root of all evil:
which while some have coveted after, they have erred from the
faith and pierced themselves through many sorrows.
—1 Timothy 6:10

Mustard Seed Money

The best business decision I ever made was to realize that money and power can't free you. Only God's grace can. One reason it took me so long to finish this book and move on to the kind of writing I really believed I was meant to do was the fact that I didn't have screw you money. I kept putting things off until I had enough money to survive if this book failed. Then I remembered some things:

Abraham lived to be 175 years old. Adam got toe-tagged when he was 930 years old. Noah didn't keel over 'til he was 950. Methuselah held out longer than all of 'em—he didn't start his dirt-nap until he was 969. Point is: you can't live your life waiting and planning to live your life. Even the best laid plans of mice and men go...

Prodigy said it best: "Having cash is highly addictive." By 2003 I knew that no matter how much dough I got, it was never going to be enough. I'd have kept on hustling—one more check, one more fat client. But at some point you have to break the habit. At some point you gotta have faith and make moves based on that faith. I'm not talking about pie-in-the-sky faith or blind faith, but a little bit of that mustard-seed faith.

So that's what I did. I sucked it up, grabbed a pen and a pad and a little bit of mustard seed. It's not much but I'm willing to ride it and accept the results, good or bad. And far as I'm concerned, that's money in the bank.

Better is a poor and wise child than an old and foolish king.
—Ecclesiastes 4:13

It's been said that most people die with their music still inside them. So many people live this life scared and second-guessing. God trusts us; but because we don't trust Him we miss out on stuff. Don't be one of those people. Don't end up working someplace 20 years wondering if you should've been doing something else all along. Get yourself some mustard seed and live. Let faith fuel your finances. Live now.

For all these things do the nations of the world seek after:
and your Father knoweth that ye have need of these things.
But rather seek ye the kingdom of God;
and all these things shall be added unto you.
—St. Luke 12:30-31

Crop Circles and Alarm Clocks

Pride and Prejudice in Corporate America

There's still a lot of "nigger" callin'
in the corporate offices...
—Nas

Nas was right. There is still a lot of "nigger-calling" in Corporate America; only now it's mostly from hiphop, black comics, BET and Comedy Central. But in our daily lives and workplaces, we still discriminate and disenfranchise, only now we we've gotten slicker about it. And we protect ourselves by slinging political-incorrectness arrows and get-over-it stones at anyone who calls our bluff. We've still got some serious racial issues to deal with and we're going to discuss a few of them in this chapter.

What you're about to read is a collection of Crop Circles and Alarm Clocks—true stories illustrating the new face of workplace prejudice, discrimination, and disenfranchisement and its affects on business and people. This chapter is essentially a journal of 100% as-it-happened/as-it-is-still-happening true stories from 1990 to 2005. Only the names have been changed.

They're called crop circles because that's how the overwhelming majority of Corporate America still sees racism and discrimination—as random phenomena that fall out of the sky landing only in rural areas, small towns, myopic suburbs, or The South. At best they're isolated freaks of nature, at worst they're hoaxes made up by attention-starved minorities or sue-happy attorneys. In short, Corporate America, specifically *mainstream* Corporate America believes that it's too sophisticated, too evolved for prejudice to hit its neck of the woods, so it simply pretends it doesn't exist.

As for the Alarm Clock portion, most people of color fully recognize that thanks to the Civil Rights Movement, racism and discrimination isn't what it was in the 1950s or even in the 1980s. Instead the modern struggle for racial and social justice feels more like being in a world full of alarm clocks—random, often-heartbreaking reminders that injustice and struggle and bias are common and that there's still a lot of work left to be done.

So with all that said, *Once upon a time...*

Rob Lite

"Rob" was my boss back when I made $4.25 an hour at Pier One Imports, then on Wabash & Washington in downtown Chicago. This was 1990, so we're talking wall-to-wall chintz pillows in colors that defied nature and Crayola. We had futons, papasans, mamasans, babysans...plus every piece of overpriced, made-in-Manila wicker crap imaginable. We also had shelves packed with $15 candles plus more nasty brass than an HBCU marching band... It was a yuppie interior decorator's wet dream.

Anyway, as store manager, Rob's main goal was to make it to "corporate." With a then-200 stores nationwide, Pier One's best and brightest store managers were often promoted to corporate headquarters in Texas. Once you got down there, you were in The System: stock options, fancy titles, retire by 60 or springboard onto something bigger elsewhere... It was like going from triple A to the majors. Just one slight problem: Rob was Mexican.

At the time, Pier One had a horrendous track record on diversity. Everyone at corporate was either a *Charmin* or a *Potato*. At store-level, most all the managers and assistant managers were white. Only the most "presentable" minority employees were allowed to work the register. Most employees of color were relegated to stockroom duties. Black employees were often promised promotions only to be passed over in favor of white candidates who were often way under-qualified. And from what we heard from employees at other locales, this was the unofficial policy nationwide.

So in Rob's mind, success meant assimilation. It probably didn't help that his parents were darker and spoke more Spanish than English—he saw what they went thru growing up. And though he'd made store manager at a fairly young age, he was still an outsider, so he got with the program.

First, he changed his name. As we all found out later, Rob was actually *Roberto*—he'd gone by that since his college days where he was one of few Hispanics on his campus. He generally used "Robert" for formal occasions but he was "Rob" to everyone else. He also had one of those blatantly latino middle names, which he promptly dropped. Rumor had it, he even tried to change his very ethnic last name to something that was easier to pronounce, but his parents threw a fit, which partly explained why he and his parents didn't seem to get along. But that was just the beginning.

Rob kept his hair short and gelled-up, dressed preppy and avoided the sun, which kept him as pale as possible. He was fluent in Spanish, even had a slight accent, but he hid both by never speaking Spanish at work, always choosing his words carefully, speaking in low tones, and occasionally over-enunciating. And of course, he almost never talked about anything related to his heritage.

But one day, we caught Rob slipping. He was in his office on a phone call with a relative. They were arguing—in Spanish. He had his accent going and everything. If we hadn't have seen it we'd have never believed it. When he turned around and saw an employee staring at him, he seemed more embarrassed than anything.

For a while, our store, which was in the Loop and considered one of their flagship properties, was having a huge problem with loss prevention. No major stick-ups just 5-finger discounts, 8 days a week. Rob's solution: Watch and follow every black and Hispanic who came in the store. Good old-fashioned racial profiling. "They look suspicious," as he'd always say.

After working with a few off-duty cops and other area retailers, we were able to identify a large portion of the crooks. (Grifters and shoplifters tend to work the same area.) Turns out most of the culprits were white: fresh-faced kid-next-door types, lonely blue-hairs looking for attention, suburbanites out for a thrill... By the time Rob figured it all out, we had become a picnic for every delinquent ant in town.

But eventually Rob turned things around: got the thefts down and the revenues up. As a reward, they shipped him off to corporate headquarters trumpeting him as a rising star. He lived the classic hometown-boy-makes-good story. He also developed an ulcer by the time he was 35 and as far as I knew he never spoke Spanish in public.

Anyway, by the time Rob was done changing, he was about as ethnically Hispanic as Cameron Diaz or Martin Sheen. But truth be told, some days I was a little envious of Rob. Even if you're light-skinned, it's hard to hide being black. And I had more than a few times where, lets just say, being it wasn't an advantage.

Over the years I met tons of "Robertos" from just about every culture and community. In addition to self-hate and self-doubt, they battled crop circles and alarm clocks—people and practices that let them know that no matter how well they did their job they'd never be rewarded or accepted as they were. So they changed. As much as Rob changed, I'm sure he would've been happier being accepted for what he already was.

[By the way, according to the U.S. Census (see: uscensus.gov), 47.9% of Hispanics identified themselves as "white." This proves 3 things: (1) "Whiteness" is a stupid construct invented to unjustly marginalize people of color and ethnic immigrants in most every area of American society. (2) There are nowhere near as many so-called "white people" in America as the powers that be would like us to believe. (3) Pretty soon, somebody's gonna have some serious 'splaining to do.]

Another irony was seeing how this mental poison affected me. While Rob had me profiling blacks as an employee, I was being profiled in other stores when I shopped outside of work. In most every mainstream store I entered I was either followed around until I bought something, ignored when I wanted help buying something, or asked to leave unless I bought something immediately.

Once I turned pro the irony grew even thicker: On a macro level I was shaping marketing strategies and honing multimillion dollar brands, usually to drive traffic at the retail level, yet I was often profiled and discriminated against in stores. It got so bad that during much of my early 20s I shopped almost exclusively thru catalogues just so I wouldn't have to deal with it.

Funny, you don't "sound black."

I met "Madison" in February of 2000 thru "Gordon," another headhunter I knew thru "Will," one of the best art directors and VPs I ever worked with. (Six degrees is a beautiful thing.) One day Gordon calls all geeked about a job opening. "It's a great place with big-name clients and I've placed people there before," he tells me. "I already dropped your book off there, okay?" I was more bored than desperate for work then, but I trusted Gordon to rep me on this one.

"Man, they loved your portfolio!" It's Gordon calling me back a few hours later, now even more excited. "They really love your stuff. They really want to get you in there ASAP. I didn't mention salary. I figured I'd let you do that..."

About 20 minutes after he hangs up, Madison calls. She introduces herself and immediately compliments me on my work and resumé. Madison was the executive VP of "Frankel," a huge integrated-marketing department in a Chicago firm. National rep and blue-chip clients, just like Gordon said. She was looking to fill a senior-level position with some fresh talent. After a few boilerplate interview questions, an icebreaker comes in the form of a mutual connection: Madison's real name was so unique that I'd only heard it once before—from my then-best friend "Brady" who was also in the industry. He talked a lot about a "Madison" he worked with his at old company.

I asked her about Brady and once we realized we had a mutual connect the convo flowed from formal to friendly to chill. Next thing you know, a good 30 minutes plus have lapsed and things have gone so well that we've both agreed that I was the man for the job. We then agree on a ballpark salary, rough start dates, etc. This had gone from a tryout to a draft-pick inking a deal.

"You know, we've basically given you the job and we haven't even met yet," she notes. "So when do you want to come in and sew this thing up?" We pick a day for me to come in and make things official then hang up feeling real good about things.

My meet day comes—a Thursday, 3 P.M.; I show up about 10 minutes early. "Hi, I'm here to see Madison." The receptionist calls Madison's office and you can hear Madison gushing through the receiver, "Hey, cool! Send him back!"

The receptionist points the way—all of 2 doors south of her lobby desk. Soon as I hit Madison's door things fall apart. You know how you put your game face on and extend your hand to make a good strong first impression? Well Madison did just that. As I approached, she was already at her doorway hand extended flashing the textbook executive let's-do-business smile, pearly-whites and all. "*Heyyyy*—"

Then she sees my face.

Her smile quickly melts. Her lips drop over her teeth and purse up, almost frowning. The friendly eyes glaze into a straight-laced wide-eyed stare. It was like she stepped in a pile of dog crap. As I smiled and greeted her, she gave me a quick limp handshake. Madison quietly turned away and sat stoically behind her desk.

"I just want you to know that we are just beginning the interview process..." She barely looks me in the eye.

Beginning the interview process? I thought. That's classic HR slang for "If the other candidates turn up on a sex tape with R. Kelly and Michael Jackson, we might hire you."

Madison conducts the interview as if we've never talked before. She even asks to see my resumé—the one she's already seen and we've already discussed in-depth. She then rattles off a stream of standard HR questions, and she's not even in HR: Where do you see yourself in 5 years? What are your greatest strengths/weaknesses? Blah, blah, blah... We rehash everything we covered over the phone—minus the salary and start-dates and the Brady connection. It's clear something's wrong. I'm fairly sure what but maybe...

"By the way," I offer, "Brady says, 'hi'..."

"Brady? Oh, okay, well, um, I haven't really spoken to him in quite some time..."

Okay it's official. I'm screwed. Brady was an icebreaker days ago, now he's dirt on her shoulders. As we continue, I play back our phone conversation in my head: Madison assumed that "Hadji" was some sort of nickname and not my real name... Gordon's white... Brady's white... That's when it hit me: Madison must've assumed I was white, too. (Oh, in case you haven't guessed by now, I've been told most my life that I "sound white," which is a whole other book in itself.)

"Well, um, I think we have everything we need. Again, we're just beginning the interview process and..."

"If you have any questions, feel free to call me," I add. "I'm available."

"Right, well I'll just call Gordon and we can handle things that way—less confusion, you know."

Right. Confusion. Of course.

With that, we politely shake hands. "You can find the elevator, right?" Not even a cursory now-run-along escort. As I walk out, she goes back to the paperwork on her desk like I was a random interruption. I left feeling like the UPS guy.

By now, it's a little after 3—barely 20 minutes had passed. I head home; the weather's good and I want to enjoy what's left of my day. I was actually laughing on the inside because she was clearly more uncomfortable than I was. It was so surreal. Plus, by then, I'd been around for a while and seen it all or heard it all before: I had plenty of ethnic friends coast to coast with killer resumés, quality backgrounds, but at some point race got in the way. I'd also met plenty of older black professionals who'd experienced 10 times worse—this was a cakewalk compared to what they went thru. I guess I was grateful for not seeing a "Whites Only" sign there.

I got home just in time to catch my still-ringing phone. "What did you say to her?!" It was Gordon. "She said you didn't want the job." Madison called Gordon right after kicking me out to CYA. "She said you weren't interested." I told Gordon I'd stop by later to pick up my portfolio. When I showed up, he looked at me like he'd been thinking about it for a while. "Okay, what *really* happened in there?"

I told him to just let it go. It was either that or sue. About 6 weeks later and thru no fault of my own I got an offer from Frankel's biggest rival: 15G more in salary... Better clients... More flexible hours... More proof that no matter what, God is good all the time and all the time God is good.

Black Girls' Armpits

While in college "Griffith & Boyle," a small Chesterton, Indiana-based ad agency, offered me $5 an hour to be their creative department's intern/assistant. Since I never made more than $4.25 an hour I took it.

I was 19 and the only black person there. I remember being amped about the chance to learn advertising from real professionals. But like most bad internships, all I did was take lunch orders and send faxes and FedExes. (However, one of the art directors did teach me how to manually keyline ads—grease pencils, rub-on registration marks 'n' all.) But my biggest job was reminding my boss, "Matt" where he parked his Jeep everyday. Matt was our creative director and a raving bachelor who looked like a younger Magnum P.I. with longer hair and went thru women like Tampax. Matt was often too hung-over or scatter-brained to remember where he parked, so as low-man on totem pole, my job was to locate his car and tell him where he parked. (Don't ask.)

Shockingly, I didn't learn much my first few months. But then February came and they asked me to write one of those "We-love-black-people" billboard ads for Black History Month for a client. Sure it was a little condescending, but it was also a chance to do something besides memorize lunch orders and parking spots. So I eagerly wrote up a few ideas; and low and behold our client bought one. I was barely 19 and I had just produced my first real ad—for the *Chicago Tribune,* no less.

I remember seeing my billboard in of all places, my neighborhood—maybe 6 blocks from my house. It had my headline, my copy, and a picture of—you guessed it—MLK, Jr., plus the *Trib*'s big ugly logo. I remember feeling so "whatever" about it that I didn't even tell anyone I did it. I also remember that billboard being the only project I was ever seriously allowed to work on. Their other projects just weren't up my alley as it was explained to me.

A few weeks later, we're having lunch at the big conference table; there're maybe 8 of us—half men, half women. Since most of us were single, the conversation was often typical men vs. women stuff. Then out of left-field "Bertha," our chunky, loud, redheaded print production manager turns to me:

"Hadji, why don't black women shave their armpits?"

Just as I was about to mouth off, I noticed that everyone in the room was staring at me like it was one of Ari Fleischer's old press conferences. During that awkward pregnant pause a couple things dawned on me: Not only was I the only black person at work, I was probably the only black person most of 'em knew outside of Bertha's *Chewbacca*-armed sistahs. Secondly, Bertha was a lot of things; stupid wasn't one of them. She wasn't asking a question as much as she was making a statement. So to keep the peace, I just swallowed my food and bit my tongue.

"Uh, I dunno, Bertha."

Soon as I said that they all got the same deflated look on their faces, like this was Geraldo Rivera's infamous Capone's vault show from the 1980s. Here I was, surrounded by educated grown folks in a profession lauded for its open-mindedness and ability to connect with the masses, yet they all believed something this stupid. And worse yet, they believed black folks were so homogenous that any one of us could explain it. They just didn't know any better. At least, that's what I told myself.

I promptly went home and asked my sisters why black women don't shave their armpits. They looked at me like I was an idiot. Then when no one was looking, I shaved my armpits to just see what it felt like. Stupidest thing I ever did. I itched for weeks. (I'm still not even sure if armpit shaving is a good or a bad thing.)

Oreos

One day I was in a creative briefing with my two bosses, "Harvey" and "Jack." Both were VP/creative directors and a good 10–15 years older than me. At some point our conversation strayed from our client assignment to shooting the breeze. And I don't remember exactly what all started this... Maybe it was Harvey, who was black, trying to get me to go golfing with him. Then for some reason, out of nowhere, Jack, who was white, jumps in and says, "You are the two 'whitest' black guys I know."

Those words completely crushed the whole mood of the room. *You are the two whitest black guys I know.* Me and Harvey just stood frozen in our boots. It was like we were alone onstage naked in front of a packed theater. We never saw that one coming. On the other hand, Jack was as relaxed and nonchalant as could be. Then apparently just to break the awkwardness, he adds, "What? Don't act surprised. You know I'm right."

Jack, like many of my colleagues over the years lived in overwhelmingly white neighborhoods. And besides Harvey, his friends were all white. His judgment was based on the facts that both Harvey and I were college educated, lacked criminal backgrounds, and spoke proper English. And given our jobs as marketers we consistently displayed high levels of intelligence and professionalism. Plus we knew enough about golf to discuss it. So of course, this combination made us "white."

I felt completely insulted—again. Growing up, some black kids called me an "oreo" because on the outside I was black, but because I was chasing college degrees and swimming thru the mainstream, my mind and soul were white. I was also hurt because I never knew that Jack saw Harvey or me in that light. It never crossed my mind that he looked at us as black or that he saw black and white like that.

But as much as Jack's words hurt me, I remember feeling worse for Harvey. Not only were Harvey and Jack the same age but also as vice-presidents, they were on the same professional level. It's one thing to belittle an employee, but it's a whole other thing to belittle a coworker; especially once you reach the executive ranks.

Note: It's important to remember that the idea that whites as the standard-bearers for intelligence and education goes all the way back to the Black and Native American Holocausts: The Blacks and Native Americans who weren't killed off or shoved on reservations were put in schools and taught that only whiteness was good. They were forced to speak English and accept Anglo history and values as truth while having their native tongues and cultures classified as inferior before beaten out of them, literally and figuratively.

These days some have mistakenly thrown the baby out with the bathwater with sentiments of, "If being educated means being 'white' and forsaking my culture, then I'd rather stay dumb." Even some Native Americans have struggled with being called "apples"—red skin on the outside, white on the inside while blacks were (and still are) often labeled Oreos or Sellouts.

"Just Like the White Agencies Do..."

For years "DJ Rale" was a quality ad firm and a pioneer among black businesses; they also needed interns during my sophomore year of college. By then my resumé was mostly "*executed thousands of 1-on-1 cash register transactions.*" Still, I polished up my student portfolio, hit Kinko's and went for it.

I met with "Mary," a VP in client services—she was dressed to the nines, but ultra-conservative: All covered-up, no flossy jewels or gaudy fabrics. But there wasn't a stitch of TJ Maxx in her game—you could smell the mark-ups as she spoke. We sat in a conference room that cost more than my first apartment. First we talked a lot about the pride they took in being "a strong black company" doing first-rate work for major clients. Next we covered everything from my grades to my career goals. Mary was polite, but the whole time she just seemed to be a bit disinterested in me as a candidate. I had to know if this was all in my head or what...

"Is there something wrong with my resumé or portfolio?"

"No, no, actually your resumé and everything is fine," she replied. "I just expected you to be dressed better."

I was wearing the only "better" clothes I had then: a buttoned-up shirt, dress shoes, and pressed khakis with a leather belt—it was actually my Pier One uniform minus the nametag. (I couldn't afford anything nice that wasn't functional. I had a church suit but it was in the cleaners that week.)

"My clothes?"

"Well, yes. Our interns attend client meetings. And as the creative intern, you'd be working with our creative director—he wears 3-piece suits everyday."

As she rambled on about the creative director's $1,000 suits all I could think was, *This is a 20-hour-a-week unpaid internship... I gotta spend money on clothes just to sit in an office looking rich and staying broke...*

She wraps up her mini-lecture on professional attire with, "We do everything just like the white agencies do."

Just like the white agencies do... She seemed so proud of herself and her company when she said that. Just like the white agencies do. This was 1991—black companies were under so much stress to fit in. To be cleaner, more professional, more polished, less threatening, etc. Doing things just like the white companies do was a sign of excellence. In fact, like many black companies back in the day, DJ Rale didn't do *Casual Fridays.* Because most of their clients were white, they had to be on point at all times, including wardrobe. It was once explained to me like this: Black + casual = unprofessional.

For so long, whiteness has been the standard of quality and professionalism in every aspect of American society. For professionals like Mary and companies like hers living up to white America's ideals was just business as usual. Today things are different, in most industries at least. But for many black professionals and black-run companies there remains a fair amount of pressure to do just like the white companies do.

Roy, the 4-Color Separationist

"Roy" was classic. In 2001 he was a VP for Cingular Wireless, one of our clients. One day "Kyle," my boss, also a VP, goes down to Dallas (or was it ATL?) to present fresh creative work to Roy. When Kyle gets back a few days later, I find him sitting in his office smirking and shaking his head in apparent disbelief.

"Yo, how'd it go?"

"Juss round up the crew," he says. "We got changes to make."

I grab our team and we convene in Kyle's office. While Roy liked the headlines and copy (mine), Kyle notes that his real problem was our new campaign's visuals. Our concept was simple: *EVERYONE GETS ALONG WITH CINGULAR.* Each ad featured people from all walks of life bonding and having a good time. Some ads featured minorities, some had women, others had teens, and so on. We saw it as a simple, warm but effective way to push what was then a newly-launched wireless brand. But Roy saw things different.

"We have to change this picture," Kyle points to a poster featuring a black male and a white female. Why? "The client doesn't want to promote *interracial* relationships." Once Kyle clarified that this was a direct quote from the client, the whole room got stoned-cold silent. Then the fun began.

Kyle proceeds to run down every ad and why the pictures need to be changed. The ad with the two guys: *Gone*. Roy didn't want to promote homosexuality, even though there was nothing "homo" or "sexual" about the set-up. It was just two young white guys close together laughing. It came from a stock photo book—they could've been brothers for all we knew. Next, the ad with the group of black kids talking together: *Gone.* "We're not trying to *alienate* our *core audience*," was Roy's explanation. And the ad with the dark-skinned Mexican guy? "Too ethnic-looking." (This from a client in Texas.)

We had to change everything. As a joke, one of our art directors (who was Cuban) slugged in a pic of a Mexican guy in a big floppy sombrero-y straw hat hoping that if Roy saw something blatantly stereotypical he might lighten up and let us darken up. But Roy saw it and said, "Still too ethnic." So to stick it to him as much as possible without causing major trouble, they took the same pic and Photoshop'd it until all you could see was the big floppy hat on shoulders. It read like *Dr. Seuss Takes a Siesta*. Roy's response: "*Perfect. Run with it.*" In Roy's world, white was definitely not "negative space". (Of course, we never ran that ad.)

Roy was a fool with the balls and the wallet to back it up. If my company had any sense, they'd have told him that not only has society become one big melting pot (or at least one big salad bowl) but also in this increasingly multicultural era his stupidity would ultimately be a hindrance in marketing their brand. But this is The Hustle and remember the hustler's motto: *IT'S STRICTLY BUSINESS, NEVER PERSONAL.*

White Men (Still) Can't Jump

One day back in 2000, "Skip," another of my headhunters (I had a couple—I was cool like that) calls me up with, "I have a client who is specifically looking for *black* talent..." Skip was white, and on the PC side and didn't want to offend me. "I don't know if you're okay with this, but they're a really good company. They just won a basketball-related account and..." *(Basketball and black folks... How original.)*

I was told the only way this firm could work this $10-million account is if they had some black employees. Their plan was to stick every black person they had in front of the client and blow 'em away with street flava. Just one problem: Of the company's 150 employees only about 9 were black and half were support staffers. Adding me would've given them 5 blacks, a couple Latinos coming off the bench, plus a few "down white boys" in the mix.

If I took this gig, I knew I'd be getting pimped for quota fodder. (*Make your next move your best move—choose me...*) But I had an agenda, too: I was trying to get out for good as soon as possible and I needed to save up cash. I figured I'd need this freelance gig plus a half-dozen more like it before I'd have enough to run. Turning this one down would've been noble, but I was hustling and cash rules everything...

Anyway, after settling on a fee, I laced 'em up and went in. One morning "Bernie," one of the agency's higher-ups sits me down and runs thru the broad strokes:

The CBA has an estimated $10-million marketing budget, which is expected to grow annually. The CBA sees itself as the underdog league filled with talented unknowns with something to prove. Our solution is to target young blacks that love basketball with an edge. This way, the CBA would create a grimy underground coolness-a stark contrast to the NBA's mainstream-friendly image. The result would attract hiphoppers and anglo hipsters who regularly co-opt black culture-which equals big dollars. (We'll discuss this more in the "Universal Hustle" chapter.)

On paper, our team was suspect. "Craig," one of two black account execs in the entire shop, was an upper middle-class cat from Colorado. He was raised on tennis, snowboarding, and skiing. All he knew about Kobe was that it was Japanese beef and it went well with Merlot. But Craig was smart—he knew business and he knew people. He knew if he acted a "hard" and dropped a little slang, the client might buy it. Next was "Jaime," a seriously talented designer. She was smart, fast, worked hard. She also thought there were 4 innings in a basketball game. Jaime just didn't care about sports at all. But again, this is basketball and Jaime was black. (Jamie had a great attitude about race in business: she was good, she knew she was good and it was your loss if you didn't.)

Because the hoops' account got off to a slow start—a common occurrence with new accounts—I was asked to pitch in on other clients until things picked up. My gut reaction was to lame up until tip off. After all, they didn't think I was good for anything else anyway. Besides, there was $10 mill on the line and they didn't know any other black creatives. What were they gonna do, fire me? But I figured since I put on the jersey and took the money I might as well play. So I came to my senses and got to work.

My first assignment: A vodka project—smoked it. Next up: A telecom project. Nailed it. The next assignment: A cable provider—killed it. Project after project, I lit it up. Business-to-business ads, consumer ads, brochures, credit card stuff, soft drinks, you name it. I impressed everyone at every level and barely broke a sweat along the way.

About 2 months later, one of the VPs calls me into their office. "Look we owe you an apology. We bought you in to work on basketball stuff, but you're really good. You can work on anything we have. Wherever there's an opportunity, from now on, we'll give you a shot."

In mid-2000 the CBA went belly-up and our $10 million project vanished faster than Kobe Bryant's squeaky-clean image. Still, I stayed at the shop for another 12 months producing quality work for some big clients and made some nice change.

Funny part was I wasn't trying to impress I was just doing me. As a freelancer I get paid to produce no matter what. Plus, where I'm from if you don't work you don't eat so you learn to come thru even when you don't want to. But I don't think they ever quite got that. But what bothered me the most was that unlike all their white employees, if it weren't for the whole *blacks=basketball* stereotype they'd have never given me a shot in the first place.

At my arraignment screamin',
"All us blacks got is sports 'n' entertainment 'til we even"...
—Jay-Z [1]

A Funky, Funky Christmas

Later that year I attended that company's office party—a formal, black-tie optional affair: women in nice dresses, guys in nice suits...even a tuxedo or two rolled thru. But me being me I came in the door dipped head-to-toe in chocolate suede PARASUCO. Showed a black silky JORDAN 23 shirt with the stupid little JUMPMAN logo for the formal touch. I was Mr. Chocolate Chip in the cookie dough.

"Tim," one of our VPs caught me after a few drinks and said he was glad I showed up because I really "added some color to the scene." Of the 100-plus folks there I was one of maybe 4 blacks. Over a couple drinks we talked about the company's lack of diversity and how it was a problem throughout the industry. But all we did was talk. We both knew he wasn't about to hire anyone of color anytime soon.

Sideline activism's hilarious. We'll rock our colored ribbons and our pro-cause T-shirts. We do the charity events and photo-ops. We'll talk big game like James Worthy criticizing easy targets and then pat ourselves on the back like we've really changed something. But as for taking real action, Flav said it best: "I can't do nothin' for you man, I'm busy trying to do for me."

My Girl Friday

In 1999, I sent "Friday," an editor at *Adweek* magazine, an op-ed piece I'd written on the lack of diversity in the ad business. Friday responded that she couldn't run my piece because the magazine had just pressed-up a "minorities-in-business" issue. "Thanks, but we've already covered this topic." was how her handwritten letter read.

Still, I eagerly checked out the issue she referred me to. I was excited to know that someone with influence was willing to discuss this. And sure enough, there it was: a big "Special Edition" snipe across a cover filled with minority-flavored lead-ins. But as I thumbed thru the issue, I saw—and I couldn't make this up if I tried—page after page of white women of varying hair colors, ages, and backgrounds. There were salutes and profiles of innovation and excellence in the face of struggle... There were also white professionals from Europe, London, Greece, and France, etc. They squeezed in a couple stories on Asian professionals plus a condescendingly small nod to Hispanic consumers. But no blacks. No stories on black companies, black consumers, or black professionals. Not one word. Nothing. Not even a black and white photo. It read like an issue of Martha Stewart's *Living*.

I promptly sent her a sarcastic follow-up note. Since February was approaching I facetiously suggested that she profile Spike Lee or review a

Michael Jordan commercial. While I never heard back, during Black History Month they did run a couple stories on Black athletes and singers in marketing campaigns. In Friday's mind "minority" really seemed to mean blonde, brunette, redhead, and pale faces with foreign accents.

In mid-2003 *Adweek* ran a multi-page insert featuring several black business professionals discussing the role of hiphop and urban culture in marketing and business. My gut screamed "progress," until I noticed the words "Special Advertising Insert" atop each page. It was an *advertorial,* or paid insert.

As of June 2005, Friday is the mag's national editor. And admittedly, their coverage has gotten more inclusive. In fact, in late-2004 they launched a new magazine dedicated to minority consumers and industry professionals called *Marketing Y Medios*—for the Hispanic market. (Como se dice, "Still at the back of the bus" en español?)

"...and Women."

When discussing civil rights and affirmative action, people often refer to "minorities and women." But the corporate world taught me an important lesson: "...and women" is usually code for *white women.* Throughout my career I not only monitored the hiring practices of the companies I worked for but also those of companies where I had friends and contacts. The one consistency I found was this: Not only did white women count as minorities, but they also counted as white and usually got more opportunities as a result.

Over the years, I've worked at companies ranging from 5–5,000 people. I've dealt with mom-'n'-pop clients and global conglomerates. And in terms of diversity, women were commonplace at every level: CEO. President. Vice-president. Secretaries. Managers. Account directors. Supervisors. Clients. Media planners. Brand managers... However, they were always white. Minus my time at a couple of black-owned companies, I only worked with one Black female VP in 12 years; my remaining black female colleagues were mainly support staffers.

But this was never a concern to any of my white female coworkers or bosses. They'd regularly rail against the infamous "glass ceiling" and "old boys clubs" while sanctimoniously invoking "civil rights" and "women's issues." But unless it had to do with Oprah Winfrey, Halle Berry, or their favorite soul singer, Black women were never part of their discussion. In their world "women" only had white skin.

That time of the month...

One prime example of this came while I was at BBDO Chicago when we pitched the Tampax account. As I remember it, the account was an estimated $10 million to $20 million in billings, possibly more. The client wanted to do a national campaign—some real out-of-the-box work targeting younger women. Once we got the call, we went to work—at least some of us did.

LADIES ONLY, NO MEN ALLOWED was the agency decree. It was estrogen at every position: Female account execs. Female creatives. Female producers. Female media execs and researchers. They even brought in extra female free-lance talent. Our bosses said they wanted to "do it right," "get the proper insights" and "respect the consumer"...Whatever.

Regardless, the guys understood. We didn't like it, but we understood. People are different, so be it. However one guy didn't get it and complained—out loud. In front of everyone. His argument was that the male creatives were pros, too and were paid to sell products we don't necessarily use. He thought it was a great opportunity to do some cool work for a notoriously boring category and he was being denied simply because he was a man. He was promptly told, out loud in front of everyone, to shut up, and get over it.

Oddly (though not surprising), save for one black woman, every woman involved was white. Apparently black, Hispanic, and Asian women don't have feminine hygiene concerns and if they do, white women are more than woman enough to speak for them, too. (Besides, who wants hygiene advice from women who don't even shave their armpits?)

Note: The 1964 Civil Rights Act banned discrimination "against persons without regard to their race, creed, color, or national origin..." Many southerners promptly became republicans in protest, and have been ever since. In fact, upon signing the Civil Rights Act, LBJ told associates, "I am afraid we have lost The South for a hundred years."

So while minority women were already covered under the Act, in 1967 President Johnson, hoping to win back anti-Civil Rights voters, amended the Act via Executive Orders 11375 and 11246 to, in effect, classify white women as a minority group. LBJ intentionally created a legal loophole for subverting equality for minorities of color. Consequently, the one group that has most benefited from Affirmative Action initiatives and EEOC requirements across the board has been Caucasian women along with European whites.

Combine that with centuries of Euro-centric ideals of beauty, a feminist movement rooted in racism and selective memory, plus some good old-fashioned greed and arrogance at various levels and you get *"...and women."*

Trendspotting

Back in 1997, one of our clients, Wrigley's gum, was exploring a "youthful-more-urban" image. One of our account folks sets up a meeting where an expert on black youth culture would tell us what's hot and relevant in the black community. I thought this was a waste of time for obvious reasons, but it was a mandatory meeting so I went. When I hit conference room, it's me, one other black exec, plus a dozen or so white media, account, and creative folks, plus a young black teenager named LeAlan Jones.

LeAlan, his friend Lloyd Newman plus then-NPR producer David Isay had recently dropped *Our America*, a stunning Peabody Award-winning audio documentary, which also became a book and a movie of the same name. It chronicled LeAlan and Lloyd's lives in the Cabrini Green housing project plus the murder of this kid named "Yummy."

In the early-1990s Yummy, an 8-year-old who's real name was Eric Morse, was thrown out of a project window by two kids not much older than him. Eric's murder made national news. Every pundit and politician came out of the woodwork spouting theories and moral outrage. Conservatives blamed black music and failed liberal social programs. Liberals blamed conservatives for cutting social programs... It was a circus. Anyway, one of our account execs heard about LeAlan from someone who knew someone who knew someone at NPR who brought him in.

So we tune in as LeAlan starts telling us about his life and what he and his friends like to do. Listening to him talk, I think LeAlan felt his big reason for being there was so businessfolks could learn about his community. But we were on cultural safari and just playing him for angles to push product. As he spoke, we feverishly took notes hoping to disseminate what he was saying into some sort of psychographic consumer profile (TV viewing habits, spending habits, what "they" wear...).

Eventually, one of our researchers asks him to focus on music. In a weird way I remember feeling ignored and irritated so I jumped in and asked him if he liked Boogie Down Productions or whoever I was into at the time. He said, "Nah, that's old stuff. We into Wu-Tang now."

Wu-Tang?!

Faces frown. *What's a Wu-Ta—?* You could hear the room swell with smirks and creaks from old necks craning to relate. By then, Wu were living legends and still riding high on 36 Chambers, Meth's *Tical*, Raekwon's "*...Only Built 4 Cuban Linx*," plus Ghost's *Ironman*. But as far as hiphop went, my coworkers were still waiting for the next Beastie Boys joint to drop. So LeAlan explains Wu-Tang, plus a few other artists. They start fawning over him like Stockard Channing did Will Smith in *Six Degrees of Separation*. After another hour or so of picking his brain, LeAlan leaves.

For days on end, everyone who was in the meeting acts like they'd just returned from the Peace Corps. They start opining about the state of black youth and parroting LeAlan, which meant everyone saying "raw" and "real" 25 times a day, 5 days a week. And of course, everyone was coming up with their own honorary Wu-Tang names such as *Old Dirty Diapers* and *Masta ClapOff Beat*. (Ah, the joys of white liberal enlightenment...)

Also, over the next couple weeks, we held several brainstorming sessions to target the Yurban (young urban) audience. The most annoying part of the sessions was that whenever I threw out an idea or offered my perspective, someone would cut in with, "Well that's not what LeAlan said," or "Didn't he say they wouldn't respond to that kind of stuff?"

It was then I realized that I was more than just a little jealous of LeAlan. All my ideas were being held up to what they believed his standards were. Ironically I'd worked really hard at this place to ensure that my color had as little as possible with my ability to do with my job. Yet, this time it had everything to do with it; and now I wasn't *black enough*. (Plus, I was too old—I was around 24 then and LeAlan must've been 15, maybe 16 then.)

Out of our 150-plus employees fewer than 10 were black; few had kids. "Mary," one of 2 black VPs—had a couple sons, both around LeAlan's age. But they didn't count because they came from pretty stable homes and therefore weren't typical enough. "Grant," our Chief Creative Officer, had a couple daughters around LeAlan's age but he lived in the suburbs so his kids didn't count, either. None of us fit into our white colleagues' little box of what blackness was. Only LeAlan did. Plus, LeAlan was *theirs*—they discovered him; they could take credit for anything he brought to the table, therefore his opinion mattered most.

The funny thing was that outside of LeAlan, most of my coworkers had no black friends. Thru business and family they all knew plenty of teens and young folks, just not any black ones. Sure, some of our females execs had their occasional jungle fever trysts, but that was just sex. As for real black friends, like the ones you tell your parents about (or that you're not just using for sex), they had none.

It almost goes without saying that when it came to reaching any other group, we did more research. We had focus groups and talked to as many people as we could to at least get a rough sketch of that particular consumer group. But not in this case. This time it was just black kids. And if you know one black kid, you know 'em all.

The truth is that there is nothing noble in being superior to somebody else.
The only real nobility is in being superior to your former self.
—Whitney M. Young Jr., Civil Rights Leader (1921–1971)

Bait 'n' Switch

Most modern diversity initiatives are fueled by political correctness, liberal guilt, greed, and fear of lawsuits. Enter one of the hottest crop circles going, the Bait 'n' Switch.

A classic BS tactic is tokenism: Hire a couple minorities. Stick 'em in key visible positions. Keep the rest of your staff as white as sack of cotton balls. Get folks hyped about your new "minority initiatives." Then when you want those minority set-asides, earmarked loans, and contracts, and other financial/political goodies, put on your minority-face, step 'n' fetch for the camera and get that paper. And when no one's looking, simply shelve your select colored folks and get back to business as usual.

By 1997 I was at a company that, at its height, had over 175 employees, around 165 of whom were white. What few minorities we had were mainly support staffers. But because over half the staff, including the CEO and the top 3 VPs, were white females, the company was listed as a "minority company," and thus eligible for all sorts of minority goodies. It was smooth. And the best part of it was witnessing the self-denial that came with it. In 2001 I worked for a firm that had "minority status" even though most everyone there was white. Why? Many of the staffers including the president were openly gay. I've seen this hustle run at dozens of companies in the ad industry and have heard of it being run at countless more.

Today, many businesses have added a twist to the bait 'n' switch and it goes a little something like this: Let's say Mainstream Company Y wants their cut of the "koombya dollar" (minority contracts, ethnic marketing budgets, etc.). They do what's called a minority joint venture: Offer a minority person or group a stake in what will be a highly publicized strategic alliance or minority joint venture. The minority gets a little juice plus some public shine. The (white) silent partner supplies the (white) labor and infrastructure in exchange for an ungodly share of the revenues. It's like a vanilla sundae—a little chocolate up top but white everywhere else.

Many looking to help minorities support these ventures thinking they're doing the right thing. Government agencies hand 'em minority contracts thinking they're a minority company. And of course many consumers buy in thinking they're helping a minority business. But while the money and mostly artificial goodwill flows, black professionals by and large, stay shut out of true equity and opportunities. Plus, there's little, if any, investment in those communities. It's called having your cake and eating it, too. But on the low, most industry and regulatory agencies have been hip to this hustle for years. They're just rolling with it for the good PR (and probably some well-placed kickbacks).

So where is this hustle run most? From what I've seen firsthand and heard from professionals I've talked to, the marketing, advertising, and PR industries are infested with it. Most so-called minority firms have become fronts for general market firms looking to fatten their bottom-lines with minority revenues. Bait 'n' Switch is also commonplace in the music and entertainment game. Most all of the top "Black-owned" record labels are actually boutiques fronting for larger mainstream conglomerates who control the music and reap most of the profits. Oh, let's not forget the Native American gaming industry: It's an estimated $13-billion industry[2] yet it's "outside investors," management companies, and tribal elites that are benefiting most, leaving the average Native out in the cold.[3] It's bait 'n' switch run to perfection.

Baby, I Got Your Money...

One of the most popular crop circles/alarm clocks going in business is pay discrimination. When I started in the early 1990s I spent 3 years at a company where I regularly produced more work at a higher quality with greater returns than my colleagues, yet everyone around me had higher salaries. But like most, I didn't realize what was going on until it was too late.

Later in my career I learned that one major benefit to having friends in HR is that if you promise to keep your mouth shut, they'll hook you up with (among other things) salary information. Eventually, I got slick enough to find out who made what just about everywhere I worked. And over the years I've been able to do some semi-informal salary comparisons across my industry.

The results? Even today, black advertising and marketing professionals seldom make what their white counterparts make for doing the same job at the same or even higher performance levels. Overall, women seldom make what men make. Yet most never complain. Why?

First off, most white-collar employees don't know who makes what. People often assume that everyone's being paid fairly. And the chances of bosses sharing payroll info with employees are slim 'n' none. There's also the fear factor: No one wants to be a troublemaker; the squeaky wheel gets oiled right into the unemployment line. And if you're a minority, you're often on a shorter leash, so you tend to keep quiet about your suspicions. Meanwhile, them that's got (white skin privilege) keep getting over on them that's not.

[FYI: By 2003, for every dollar earned by white men, black women earned approximately 64 cents; which was less than white women (74 cents), and less than black men (78 cents).][4]

Pay us like you owe us for all the years that you hoed us...
—Jay-Z[5]

Breads & Circuses

In boxing, we vilify promoters like Don King, Bob Arum, etc., as fight pimps, but as I learned the hard way, the real Macks are in the office suites...

It's 1999 and I'm freelancing for a targeted agency in NYC. It's a morning conference call with NY; I'm on speakerphone in Chicago. Of the 10 people in the room, 9 are black and from the agency. Our client "Heather," a 30-something network VP, is the only white person there. She's a hip Jewish chick. Loves sports. Has a loud, raspy voice, and on was that "I'm-a-ballsy-broad-playing-a-man's-game-so-deal-with-it" tip. After a round of polite introductions, Heather runs down the assignment:

Our Client: A world-famous cable channel. *The Product*: A series of upcoming heavyweight fights featuring a famously troubled but still-immensely talented former heavyweight champ. *Our target*: African-Americans. *The Problem*: Blacks don't watch boxing, at least not in the numbers that whites do. The gap is even greater on pay-per-view. The core boxing fan—the one that goes to the fights *en masse,* drops $40–$50 on PPV events and bets a few bucks to spice things up—is the 25–45 white male making around 40K-plus...

The Solution: Short-term, Heather wants more blacks to buy The Ex-Champ's upcoming fights, which he still owes the network per his contract. Black viewers bring an added "cool" cache to the event, which will in turn bring more casual fans. The long-term goal is to build hype for a pending battle with then-undisputed heavyweight champ, a tall, built seemingly unbeatable brother with locks, Canadian ties, and a British accent.

She adds that The Ex-Champ is in seclusion training hard and can't be bothered with photo shoots and commercials so we'll have to piece together footage of his older fights with music and cleverly written promo info. We start quizzing Heather on the pros and cons of each fighter to see what angles we can work for the advertising. This is when things start to get interesting...

Heather launches into a big rant about The Champ who's under contract with HBO. She claims his camp held things up for months haggling over purse size, which side deserves more money from rebroadcast rights, etc. According to Heather, all involved knew that not only was The Ex-Champ the most bankable fighter since Ali, but HBO either loses money or barely makes money on The Champ's fights. When one of us asks why The Champ is such a bad draw, Heather lets loose:

For starters, The Champ just ain't black enough. He doesn't fit America's mold of what a black boxer should be: He's calm and focused inside the ring, articulate and personable outside the ring. He stays out of trouble. And while he's physically imposing, his fighting style is highly strategic and intellectual. (He often refers to himself as a "pugilist who's mastered the *sweet science.*") Many view him as a snob and soft because he'd rather tattoo a guy for 12 rounds than beat him to death in one. Combine that with his dual citizenship and British accent and the average fan just doesn't connect with him enough to care whether he wins or loses. So, unless they've got money on the line, they don't watch his fights.

Second word: *Style.* Like the old baseball commercial says, *CHICKS DIG THE LONG BALL.* Hoops fans love the dunk. We dig 80-yard bombs. And everyone loves the knockout punch. We love KOs so much we use KO as a metaphor to describe almost any action that's powerful, decisive, or victorious. There's just something about a grown man putting another grown man into a temporary coma with a single punch that turns casual observers into paying customers. But again, The Champ is no knockout artist; he's a "pugilist."

Next, Heather inexplicably swerves off on some crazy "Stella-gets-her-groove-back" tangent: She starts rhapsodizing about how The Champ is this "big, black African warrior god" and how she'd love to "get a piece of him." (Her words, not mine.) Next, she adds that since women find him extremely sexy, it might be possible to scoop a few casual female fans by playing up his "African warrior" appeal. (Keep in mind that dude is from the UK.) It was ridiculous. At one point I swore I heard tribal drums in the background.

After composing herself, Heather runs down why The Ex-Champ is a perennial cash cow, regardless of record: White people accept him. He's animalistic, in and outside the ring... He's a convicted felon with a dysfunctional background... He never comes off as terribly articulate or intelligent... He doesn't seem to care about anything, including himself. He's everything the average white person accepts, and in many cases, still expects a black fighter to be. He's the quintessential "crazy nigger" America loves to be disgusted by and entertained by. All of that combined with the fact that he still has one-punch knockout power drives folks to pay top-dollar to watch him fight no matter who he fights.

Heather's solution is to, in part, play the skin game. Even though there are still a couple tune-up fights for each man prior to this big showdown, our charge is to play up the black male stereotypes wherever possible: highlight The Ex-Champ's brutality, "animalism," and "street energy" while the other camp works the "civilized boxer" and "mainstream friendly" angle. It's all about contrasting styles. And as the old boxing saying goes, *STYLES MAKE FIGHTS*. It was like Chris Rock's old *BLACK PEOPLE* VS. *NIGGERS* bit and guess which corner we were in?

By now Heather's babbling a mile a minute and doesn't care who thinks what. And since she's holding the purse strings on this project and the key to more lucrative assignments, everyone else politely listens. Next thing you know, she reveals that The Ex-Champ <u>will</u> be available for commercials after all. In fact, he'll do whatever they tell him to, because, well, let's just say they have some serious financial leverage on him. She also discusses an eventual fight involving one of the Klitchko brothers because "people still want to see a white guy knock out a black guy," she reminds. So if we could sell the casual black fan, get the casual and core white fans all geeked up, it could be *Cooney/Holmes II*. (1981's Gerry Cooney vs. Larry Holmes still ranks as among the most profitable fights in boxing history.)

At one point she deads the conversation with, "Look, you guys know this is all a 'circus,' right?" By "circus" she was admitting that...well... I'll let you figure out what she was admitting to. Everyone always knew many boxing matches were suspect, but to hear an insider cop to it was rare. She spilled so much dirt about the fight game it's a miracle her body hasn't turned up in a river somewhere.

It was also clear by the chunks of dead silence and mumbled responses that Heather had either offended or scared everyone in the room. Twice. Near the end, Heather reminded us that she was a Jewish woman, which was just like being black so she should get a ghetto pass on any insults and misunderstandings that may have transpired. "We're all on the same team, you know," she claimed. I felt like I was stuck somewhere between *Bamboozled* and *The Skin Game*.

Once the meeting wraps, "Del," my partner who was also there, calls me back. It was like we were discussing a car wreck. We almost immediately agree we couldn't work on this project and we definitely couldn't work with Heather on anything else. Ever. We also decided to keep quiet about this for a few years fearing lawsuits and whatnot. But I figure it's safe to speak on it now.

The post-fight:
Once The Champ abused The Ex-Champ in their fight, he fought and barely beat Vitaly Klitchko in June 2003. The fight's ratings proved Heather right on one account: People still wanted to see a white guy beat a black guy. (It was one of the top-rated fights that year.) But the still lower-than-hoped-for ratings and general lack of buzz also reinforced another point: People were still indifferent to The Champ.

On Feb. 6, 2004, The Champ officially retired as the reigning heavyweight champ of the world; only the third man to ever do so. His mainstream popularity and endorsements are still lacking. Critics blame his lack of accolades on his generation's "low caliber" of opponents and his "aloofness." He'll go down as one of the greatest fighters no one ever really cared about.

Conversely, The Ex-Champ has gone the route of most aging black athletes: He's become a walking tabloid headline, a court jester of sorts. Sure, he had issues before, but before he was iron, he had skills and "bad intentions." He had value, but now he's just another nigga doing what niggas love to do—waste money: In August 2003, he filed for bankruptcy after blowing an estimated $200 million in career earnings. Self-destruct: He was arrested twice in 2003 and once in 2004. (That's in addition to countless run-ins with themedia.) He retired in 2005 after quitting in the middle of a fight. These days we laugh at him and his failures and take potshots from our soapboxes until the next hard-hitting nigga shows up to entertain us.

As for the Klitchkos: Vitaly took the WBC heavyweight crown in April 2004. But because he's a Euro of questionable talent and that whole "Ivan Drago" angle fell with the Berlin Wall, no one cares. Americans are still looking for a great white hope to call their own.

Reversed Affirmative Action

Working for black-owned companies is interesting. I remember interviewing for one job thinking, "Oh, I'm black, I got this." Wrong. Pull that "hook-a-brutha-up" crap on black businesses and they'll spit you out like bad sushi. In each case, they made it clear to me that I was hired because I was the best qualified for the job, period. They also let me know that most black execs and black-run companies are under so much extra pressure to produce they can't afford to hire "Ray-Ray's brother and 'nem." They have to hire the most qualified top-shelf black candidates possible because if that black person screws up, out come the haters.

And in what I found to be a slightly odd twist, several black execs have admitted to me that they often feel pressure to hire white and non-black candidates just to prove they're not too pro-black for their mainstream colleagues. It's sad to say, but when you're black in business, at some point, most of your decisions become political whether you like it or not.

On the flipside, over the years whenever my white friends coworkers got laid off or were considering switching jobs, I'd tell them about black companies or execs who I knew were hiring. They'd always give me the same responses: "Yeah, right. They won't hire me," or "Don't you have to be black to work there?" It was like listening to a guy who cheats on his wife assuming that just because he's cheating she must be cheating, too. They just assumed they'd get screwed by blacks in power simply because they knew blacks usually get screwed in similar situations.

Even after I'd tell 'em "No, they'll hire whoever's good and if anything, being white works in your favor," they still resisted. My offering to vouch for them didn't help either. Eventually they'd tell me it came down to one of three concerns: (1) For some reason many white professionals view working for a black company as a step-down career-wise. (2) Many fear being discriminated against in minority-run companies because they're white. (3) Many just aren't "comfortable enough" to work around a lot of black people.

And why did so many folks tell me this stuff? Because a few of them admitted that they saw me as one of the "good" black people. (After all, I am an Oreo, you know.)

Crazy, huh?

Taking a Flyer

A good 30% of marketing industry professionals I've met or have worked with over the years lack marketing or advertising degrees. And a few either didn't go at all or attended but didn't finish college but that seldom stopped them from working in the industry. Marketing and advertising is often about creativity and people and sometimes you really don't need a 4-year degree to understand either.

In fact, many companies often take a flyer on candidates who lack the textbook credentials but show great upside and ability to learn on the go. I've worked with numerous account execs whose only training was in sales or retail. I've worked with media buyers and planners who were hired strictly because they were good at math and loved pop culture and watching TV.

I also met my share of creatives that were hired based on the "A-great-ad-is-a-great-ad-even-if-it's-written-on-a-cocktail-napkin" philosophy: In lieu of the standard copywriter/art director's portfolio, they were hired based on portfolios filled with non-advertising stuff such as poetry, film scripts, short stories and op-ed columns or paintings, crazy designs, and illustrations.

Now there's nothing wrong with any of that as many of them went on to become successful professionals. But in 15 years I only met one minority with such a background. Every other minority professional I knew had industry-specific backgrounds and degrees. Why? Because companies warned them that they wouldn't get hired any other way.

In recent years, a few marketing companies have taken flyers on minorities whose sole marketing experience is their connections to hiphop, sports, or entertainment—most notably Spike Lee, who was able to start his own ad agency (Spike/DDB) primarily because several DDB Needham clients wanted him to direct their commercials. So have P. Diddy, Russell Simmons, Steve Stout, and others in hiphop. But save for the occasional minority with cultural cache that can be co-opted, professionals of color seldom benefit from "take-a-flyer" hiring.

They Call Me "Mr. Beachhead"

Once I was established in the industry, I decided to give back. I wrote a proposal for a minority-targeted summer internship program and presented it to my superiors. They went for it on one condition: it couldn't interfere with my workload. After promising that it wouldn't I checked with the department heads to see who wanted interns. Next, I hit up colleges for candidates. It was a ton of work but I figured somebody did it for me, so: *EACH ONE, TEACH MANY.*

But they changed the game on me: First the higher-ups told me that the program couldn't be exclusive to minorities. "Reverse discrimination," they warned. *Reverse discrimination*...this from a company whose 180-person staff was whiter than a Colorado blizzard. Anyway, I had to interview white candidates and guarantee that at least a couple whites would get in... Just be fair. I agreed and proceeded accordingly.

What followed was a good-old fashioned coup: My bosses decided that the program, while noble, was interfering with my work. And since running an internship program was deemed an "executive initiative," my boss offered to "help oversee it," as he put it. By then I'd interviewed a handful of candidates and had dozens more hungry and waiting. To make a long story short, he took over the internship program and picked the interns himself. That summer our department had five interns—3 male, 2 female, all white. Two even had ties to clients or high-level company execs.

The following year the internship program went down the same route: All white college kids, some with insider connects. When I complained, I was politely told I should be more concerned with keeping my own job.

Dawn of the Dimes

It's 2001; I'm in a creative strategy meeting one afternoon. It's me, "Sarah," my boss and VP group creative director, plus "Becky," our account exec. Becky starts walking us thru a creative brief for Mello Yello, who was looking to add some "urban sensibilities" to their latest promotional campaign. As we're discussing all things urban Becky throws a curveball:

"Hadji, what's a 'dime'?"

"Excuse me?"

Becky explains that while she was in the club over the weekend a black male approached her and said, "You're a dime." He then tried to buy her a drink, get a dance, etc. But she didn't know what he was talking about and she basically ignored him.

"So, c'mon, Hadji, tell me..."

Lemme explain Becky: She's your stereotypical mid-20s account exec: She's a cute (by most accounts) white, with dirty-blonde hair. She mixes businesswear with lots of tight jeans, low-cut blouses, short skirts, etc. She bar-hops, loves *Cosmo* and MTV and is as liberal as a sheltered Michigan party girl with a Big Ten degree can be. (Rumor had it there was some *Girls Gone Wild* footage of her floating around online.)

"...what's a 'dime'?"

So I tell. "Becky, a dime is a compliment. It means that he thought you were very attractive." Becky and Sarah look back at me all confused; and now, seemingly annoyed.

"But why a 'dime'?!" (At some point, every black professional gets shoved into the "On-behalf-of-black-folks-everywhere" corner...)

"See, a dime is being so attractive that you're addictive—like a 'dime sack of weed.' " They stare back blankly. So I try a movie reference...

"Ever see Bo Derek in *10?* Being called a 'dime' is like saying you're a perfect 10." Slowly, the understanding washes over their faces. I should've run.

"That's so offensive!" Suddenly, Becky and now Sarah decide that their womanhood has been insulted. "That's so disgusting!" Sarah adds, noting that she would've smacked the guy had she been there. They go on about how crude and misogynistic urban language is—aiming it all at me. Then Sarah—my boss and the one least involved in this—throws a pen at me to emphasize her disgust.

"A <u>dime</u>..." She ends with a smirk, "How stupid."

It was like being stuck in a *Gilmore Girls'* episode. I was heated. Not only was I getting bashed over someone else calls Little Ms. Last Call attractive, but my boss was in on it. And worse still, the original purpose of this meeting was to bring some urban flavor—which they clearly had no respect for—to one our clients.

But I quickly calmed down by reminding myself of three things. (1) I didn't insult anybody—all I did was translate. (2) This was just another alarm clock, and as a wise ruler once noted, *THIS TYPE OF THING HAPPENS EVERY DAY*. (3) Based on what I saw of their behavior outside of work, neither was above being a dime for the right brother, especially after a couple rounds. And lastly, Laura was known to talk about our company's "soup-to-nuts" capabilities; anyone who talks like that shouldn't get too upset by anyone else's choice of words about anything.

Shawn & Corey

From 2000–2001 I worked for "BlastOff Marketing," then the hottest integrated marketing firm in the country. They'd racked up some $100 million in annual billings doing promotional work for some of the most recognizable brands in America. At their height they were darlings of such trades as *PROMO, Brandweek,* and *Advertising Age.* They were rebels, risk-takers, and out-of-the-box thinkers who knew how to get results on small budgets. But that was just the outside.

On the inside the joint was nuts. Big airy spaces... Odd-length walls and curvy corridors... Weird-shaped furniture on every floor... Everything washed in bright primary colors... It was like working at IKEA. Top 40, Techno, and Alt. Rock CDs were piped thru the PA system daily; I wore headphones a good 6 hours a day just to keep my own musical tastes intact. Our lunchroom comfortably seated 70...100 if you lost the full-size pinball machine and ping-pong table. Maybe 110 once you toss that huge home entertainment system: a 60-inch TV with Direct TV, VCR, and DVD players, satellite radio, and floor-model speakers...

And if that wasn't enough, we had beer on tap. Lemme say that again: We had actual kegs of beer tapped up in the kitchen for random consumption. Plus, Krispy Kremes and bagels were on the kitchen counter every Friday morning. If that wasn't enough, Corner Bakery usually catered most every meeting that ran over an hour.

Socially, it was one big *Will & Grace-Queer Eye-L Word* marathon: Over 160 folks. Damn near everyone was gay and white, bi and white, or white and straight-but-really-liked-gay people. Most of the guys reeked of Banana Republic and Hugo Boss with a little International Male flavor thrown in.

Half the women dressed like TRL extras. The rest were overgrown alt. Punk-rocker clones—way too sheltered and soft to be rebels or outsiders, but worked real hard to come off as such.

"Shawn" was one of the first cats I met there and still among the best account execs I've ever worked with. He was smart. Clients dug him. He always tried to find the big picture. He asked questions. (Nothing worse than a know-it-all.) He was a point guard—tried to make everyone around him better. He also knew how to get in where he fit in.

He came to BlastOff practically fresh out of college. Over the years he built his rep, racked up some nice stats, and garnered numerous opportunities to go onto bigger, more prestigious companies. But he stayed put believing BlastOff had more upside (not to mention profit-sharing opportunities). Plus, he liked being the underdog and when BlastOff first opened, it was *the* industry underdog. Shawn was employee number 20-something. By the time I got there, they'd grown to over 230 employees with offices in Chicago, New York, and Canada. It was raining cash and they had new clients lined up like frat boys outside of Wrigley Field. The joint was hot and Shawn was a young gun who'd gotten in on the ground floor.

Out of the roughly 160 in our office, maybe 10 were black: myself, Shawn, "Corey" (who I'll get to in a sec), and a couple support staffers and entry-levelers. My problem wasn't numbers or anyone's sexuality; it was that at every opportunity BlastOff blew its horn to clients, press, and prospective employees about how inclusive and diverse it was. Their idea of diversity was blondes, brunettes, and redheads. But whatever. And Shawn, having been there since day one, was even more over it than I was.

Shawn had a simple philosophy: *LEAVE A HOLE WHEREVER YOU GO*. When you leave a hole, you leave such an imprint on your department, on your clients, bosses, and co-workers that people never want you to leave. Leave a hole meant that when an assignment came up with his name attached to it, everyone immediately thought, *Good, Shawn's handling it. We're okay.* But *l*eaving holes was hard.

At first, Shawn got stuck with small accounts—projects no one else wanted or had time to work on. But he took 'em. He gained clients' trust, pushed through quality marketing plans, and grew their business. His reward? More small stuff. His response? Leave a hole. He kept growing and excelling, showing and improving despite the occasional misstep here and there. But as BlastOff grew and gained bigger clients, Shawn kept getting passed over while other white, often less-qualified account execs got bigger, higher-profile accounts.

Shawn saw the game. Still he kept his mouth shut and kept leaving holes. Eventually his game got so tight he couldn't be denied. They made him a VP in 2003. Today he's a respected industry exec who calls his own shots and still leaves holes wherever he goes.

And then there's "Corey," another BlastOff account exec. For every Shawn, there's around 50 or 60 Coreys. Corey was smart, educated, talented, and hardworking. Corey was also a black gay male—one of the hardest things to be in America, and probably harder to be in Corporate America. Between America's idea of what "black" is and its idea of what "gay" is, being black, gay, and male is just too deep for most to handle. (I mean, how can you be the thugged-out, hypersexual animal prone to crime and violence America defines as black masculinity then go down on another man and sing show tunes?)

Corey's path was similar to Shawn's; both started at roughly the same time, both with small accounts. But as slow as Shawn's rise was, Corey's was stuck in park. Their bosses' mentality seemed to be *PROMOTING ONE IS ENOUGH.* They promoted recent college grads ahead of Corey. They fast-tracked outsiders ahead of him, too. But Corey kept working hard and never complained. In the year I worked with him, I learned something else about him: people liked him.

Now when I say people liked him, I don't mean we thought Corey was a nice guy. I mean clients were often so relaxed around Corey that they trusted his judgment and took his advice. To this day, Corey's the only account exec, male or female, I ever worked with who could consistently get coherent answers out of clients and get clients to push dates back. I watched him do it time and time again. They wouldn't listen to us, but they listened to him. People really liked him.

You can't teach height, you can't teach speed, and you can't teach, "Like me enough to let me help you." You either have that or you don't. And when you try to learn it or buy it, it usually comes off as fake. When you get a player with skills like that, you draft 'em. (I swear, you give me a couple people like that plus a few quality role players to do some heavy-lifting behind the scenes and I'll be on the cover of *Adweek* in five years.)

But instead they kept Corey on the bench and setting picks for everyone else to get the good shots. Corey kept doing the little things while others got the glamorous stuff. Again, I watched people (all white) with nowhere near his potential lap him: college grads, people he helped train, etc. And like Shawn, Corey kept quiet and kept working. Every once in a while when no one was looking, we'd talk about it. It bothered him but he just saw it for what it was. Plus, the whole company knew what was going on; to verbalize it would've just been redundant.

I also think Corey felt that this was one of the few places in town that he felt in professionally. I doubt there was any company of BlastOff's size and profile in a market the size of Chicago where Corey could openly be Corey and be fully accepted. But the funny part was that for all their boasts of inclusiveness, Corey was still an outsider. He was like them, but he wasn't one of them. (Over the years I've learned that "gay and white" isn't nearly the same as "gay and black." It's like gay blacks are the GLBT community's pet fetishes or mascots. The only time they seem to get attention is in sex, music, or when gay activists want to equate gay rights with racism and Black civil rights.)

Anyway, Corey stayed. In fact, I ran into him recently. He's still there, still fitting in.

Roz, the IT Ogre

A while back I met "Roz," a heavy-set, dark-skinned black woman. She smoked a lot. She was had *attitude*—meaner than a junkyard dog. At least, that's what people said. Actually what they said was: "Be careful, Roz will bite your head off... I hate asking Roz to look at my computer—she's so mean about it... Roz acts like she's doing you a favor by fixing your computer... Roz never smiles, ever! Roz is sooo mean."

I was young and still considered the company's "new guy" and people thought I was nice, so they'd tell me what/who to look out for. Roz was at the top of most everyone's "beware" list. Come to think of it, I think she was the list and I was dumb enough to listen. So for weeks, whenever I saw Roz in the hallway, we didn't really speak; I'd just say hi and run to the nearest well-lit area.

One day I asked "Dawn," an older black executive why Roz was so mean. She said Roz never struck her as mean and I should talk to her instead of riding with everyone else's opinion. So I sucked it up and walked by Roz's office, and there she was—surrounded by coffee cups, busted motherboards, crumpled cigarette packs, busted mouses, stacks of invoices, hard drives, cables, and computer catalogs... It was IT right out of Central Casting. There was this odd silence. Then I took a deep breath and politely asked her why she was so mean.

"Who says I'm mean?!"

"Uh, just about everyone I talk to."

She half-nods her head and says, "C'mere..."

So I sit down on her couch, which is littered with monitors, and we talk. Turns out that Roz doesn't run the IT department—she is the IT department. Over 100 computers and she's the only person there to fix 'em. And they were dinosaurs, too. We're talking 60 or 70 Classics, a few high-end Mac 7100s, some 3400 series PowerBooks for the VPs, plus a few standard PCs—juiced-up word processors, mostly.

Roz had a handful of rules: (1) Don't download files you don't recognize. (2) Don't use disks from home unless she scans them for viruses first. (3) Shut down your computer before you turn it off. (4) Don't leave your computer on overnight or over the weekend. (5) Don't hit, kick or attempt to "fix" your computer in any way.

We (myself included) ignored or forgot all of her rules. She sent out weekly memos and emails with *Do*s and *Don't*s. It didn't matter. We did it our way. As a result, every other computer had a glitch, a virus, or ran like a turtle on codeine. When Roz recommended getting new computers the higher-ups said no. When she asked for fresh IT employees she could oversee they said no. She was surrounded by folks who ignored her and told her no all day long. No, Roz wasn't happy.

Then one year Roz gets diagnosed with cancer, don't remember what kind. She goes in and out of chemo and eventually takes time off to recoup. Some folks send cards and whatnot, but for the most part, people kinda block it out. While she's gone, the company brings in a temp—this white guy named "Dale." He's a native Midwesterner, wife, 2.5 kids, friendly, smart, professional, etc. All in all he's cool people.

Dale comes in, sees there's only one person to do everything and requests help. Next thing you know Dale gets a budget to hire 2 extra people. He recommends new computers—we start getting them within a few weeks. Dale gets money for supplies, training, and everything he needs to get things rolling properly. For some reason they help Dale, not Roz, develop a decent IT department.

Next, the masses decide they like Dale. He's seen as a nice guy (which he was). When Dale brings a mini-cooler in his office loaded with beer and Jack Daniels people view it as "cool." Plus, given how hard Dale is working, it's overlooked by the higher-ups. Dale also makes it clear to everyone that he's just holding down the fort until Roz returns. But once that bit of news gets out, several employees make it clear they'd rather have Dale than Roz because Dale's "nice" and Roz isn't.

A few months later, around mid-December, I spot Roz standing alone in the building's mezzanine. I walk up to her ask her how she's doing and when she'll be strong enough to return full-time.

"I'm not. They fired me."

They fired her. It was the day of our company's Christmas party, less than two weeks before Christmas and they fired Roz. Dale took over full-time a few days later. A short memo was circulated regarding Roz's "choice to move on" and that was it. Roz's name was rarely mentioned there again.

There were rumors of legal action pending, plus Roz didn't know me that well, so she never gave me the complete lowdown. But from what I heard it had something to do with her illness. Cancer treatment is expensive and firing Roz meant our company and its insurance carrier could stop paying for her treatment. I also think it had a little bit to do with her race.

Roz was just one of a handful of blacks on staff, which seemed to be by design. Over the years, I saw plenty of black women at various levels of business and society catch Roz-type heat for being seen as "not nice." Unless they're always laughing, smiling, or playing the cheerleader role and regularly deferring to others, black women always get slapped with the "mean" label. The idea of black women as inherently mean or overly aggressive has been embedded into America's psyche since slavery days.

But the most ironic part is that most of this type of prejudice I saw directed at black women came not from men but from their white female colleagues. They would regularly reach into their feministic bag of tricks to pull out their "Aggressive-businessmen-are-strong-aggressive-women-are-bitches" cards all while treating black women like crap or clowns.

A couple years later "Carol," another woman at the company gets diagnosed with cancer. The company sends her flowers, cards, makes phones calls, hospital visits, etc. The company supports Carol 100%. People like Carol, even those who don't fully know her, which is most of the company. And once she gets out of the hospital, the company lets her work as long as she wants whenever she feels able to. She's allowed to keep her job and there's never any talk of replacing her.

Then after a few months of a seemingly full recovery, Carol suffers a nasty relapse. The cancer comes back and spreads. Carol passes away a short while later. It shocks everyone. As you could imagine, company morale tanks. Lots of sad days filled with awkward silences and good memories follow. The company is well represented at Carol's funeral. Though I was in NYC by then, I got a call about her passing plus an invitation to her funeral. To this day people talk fondly of her.

Carol was white.

"Left Us for the White Folks..."

When I was about 20, I started a spring internship at Brainstorm Communications, a small black-owned ad agency in Chicago. Our biggest client was SoftSheen, a multimillion-dollar black hair care company founded by the Gardner family, who also owned the agency. The joint was small, quiet, and the people were unbelievably nice to each other. After a few weeks, the president turned my internship into a full-time job and offered to work around my school schedule come fall.

A short time later, I was offered an internship at DDB Needham Worldwide, still among the biggest agencies in the world. Fortune 500 clients up the yin-yang. Award-winning talent. Big fancy office digs. Growth opportunities galore. This was like going from BET to NBC. But of the 500-plus employees in their Chicago office few if any were black. And this was precisely where I came in. I was offered a spot in a special minority internship program. "Jeanne," the internship coordinator, thought this was a great opportunity for someone like me to learn the business. And of course, it made them look good, too.

On the one hand, I was at a small place surrounded by good people willing to teach me the ropes and help me grow. And as a black-owned company they knew what it meant to give young black talent a chance. But as a black-owned agency, resources were limited, and there were lots of barriers. On the other hand, I had a huge company with potentially unlimited opportunities saying, "C'mon over." But their motives were a little suspect. So what's a young brother to do?

Every black industry professional I talked to said that with my age and talent, I'd be a fool to turn this one down. "Go get that general market experience—you can always come back later," was how they put it. So I bit the bullet and rolled with the big boys.

I did a whole summer at Needham. They were nice—that is when they weren't being condescending. I got a lot of "You'll-be-good-someday-just-not-here" pep talks. I got more than a few, "He's pretty good—for a black kid" reactions to my work. I was mistaken for the delivery guy on way too many occasions for it to be a simple misunderstanding. And despite the growing talk of my being hired on full-time at the end of my internship, they ended up hiring two white copywriters over me, both of them with portfolios and abilities so inferior to mine that when they saw my portfolio they both asked me the same question: "Why won't they hire you?" Still, I probably learned more at Needham than I would've learned at anywhere else—save for Brainstorm.

Over the years, I ran into my old boss at a couple industry functions. I remember the first time she greeted me at one. I'd been working steady for about 3 years by then and was doing okay. In fact, it was at an industry awards show when I walked up to her to say hi figuring I'd have to remind her of who I was. Instead she took one look at me and said, "Ah, there he is... Left us and ran off to the white folks."

She smiled when she said it. She clearly meant it as more of a light-hearted jab than anything. But the underlying message was serious and clear. She was acknowledging the stigma that many mainstream businesses hang on black professionals. At the same time, she said she understood why I left and that there were no hard feelings. Still I wonder how my career and my life would've turned out had I stayed.

Looking back, I can honestly say that my biggest professional regret was leaving Brainstorm when I did. Looking back, they were the only place I ever worked that truly respected and embraced me as a black creative. I wasn't a charity case or a quota-filler to them. I didn't have to play the just-happens-to-be-black card like I've had to do at other joints. And they weren't on that white-liberal-look-how-hip-and-inclusive-we-are BS so many other companies are still on. Nope. There, I was a black ad man—and the terms weren't mutually exclusive nor did they make me inferior.

Too bad I was too young to realize what I was walking away from.

"These Are *Real* Ads!"

Back in the day, I snagged an interview with "Lyor Silver," VP Chief Creative Officer of JL & Associates. They were a solid independent shop doing about $100 million in billings. Lyor was friends with "Keith," this art director at a smaller agency that I'd interviewed with earlier; he really liked my book but just couldn't afford to hire me so he gave me the names of some major shot-callers to help me out. (Very cool.)

So after a few calls, Lyor and I meet. He looks like Magnum PI (if he were about 5'5"): Bushy hair, bushy mustache, stocky build, bright-colored suits with shoulder pads, etc. He lets me know upfront that he's only meeting with me as a favor to Keith then starts up with a generic pep talk about what's it like in the real world. He sounds so disinterested that it feels like I'm back in high school on Career Day or something. So to speed things up I mention that Keith liked my portfolio and thought he should see it.

"You have a portfolio?"

Why he's surprised that a copywriter candidate has a copywriter's portfolio I had no idea so I just pull out my book and give it to him. He opens it up and looks at the first page. He pauses. He looks up at me eyes wide open, then back at my book then up at me then back at my book and turns the page.

"These are ads! These are actual ads!"

He says it again like he's cheering on a circus act. I calmly note that I'd put together my first portfolio as a freshman and that my writing influences were industry legends like Howard Gossage and Bill Bernbach and that I'd been reading *CA* annuals and *Archives* for years; and while I was only 21 I was hungry, willing to work cheap and felt I had lot to offer an agency. That's when I realized something important:

"These are actual ads... This is the kind of work that we do!"

He wasn't listening to a single word I said. He just kept looking at my book and at me and kept trying to figure out how the two got together...and of course, he kept saying stupid things like:

"So where did you learn how to do this stuff?"

Part of me wanted to tell Lyor that I was actually a crack dealer and one of my clients was a strung-out copywriter who traded me their portfolio for another hit. But instead I told him the truth.

"Wow. That's great that someone like you wants to get into this industry," he responds. "Now I know you probably can't tell to look at me, but I'm Scandinavian. I'm an outsider, too." (Sometimes people say things that make you squint because you can't believe you actually saw the words come out of their mouths. Businesspeople have made me squint a lot over the years. A lot.)

Lyor then proceeds to equate the struggles of being a below-average height, second-generation Scandinavian-American with a slightly unusual first name with being a black male in America. And just as he overcame those obstacles, I shouldn't let prejudice stop me from succeeding; and while he didn't hire me and wouldn't recommend me to anyone else, he was definitely "on my side."

Blacklisted

Just as black kids often take comfort in huddling together in school cafeterias, many black professionals do the same over lunch, online, at house parties, etc. We often swap stories and observations, some of which become lists—like this one:

You know you're black in Corporate America if:

1. On casual dress days you're mistaken for the secretary, the mailroom guy or a bike messenger.
2. Colleagues randomly note, "We don't see color with you. We don't think of you as black."
3. Coworkers regularly compare their suntans to your skin tone, often with comments like, "Hey, I'm finally darker than you!"
4. When coworkers see you talking to other black colleagues they ask, "What was that meeting all about?"

5. While talking to each other in a professional manner, they'll flex their hipness by occasionally talking to you in a blackcent and/or by using urban slang.
6. After swapping casual greetings with one or more black people, coworkers observe that you know "an awful lot of people."
7. White colleagues often remind you that they too are "outsiders" and have also overcome "certain social barriers."
8. They explain your exclusion from certain projects with, "Now, you know we think you're great, but The Client is old and..."
9. With no proof to the contrary, coworkers assume that you're a perfect fit for the company's sports teams, have had or currently have gang/drug ties, or know people in the music biz.
10. No matter what, your colleagues have passion for their jobs while you (often because you *seem mean*) have an attitude problem.
11. Regardless of your track record and credentials, colleagues are consistently pleasantly surprised by your successes, but seldom surprised by your failures.
12. Your colleagues can't help but point out your obvious resemblance to random black athletes or entertainers.
13. "It's because I'm white, right?"
14. You regularly have to explain why the concepts of *White History Month* and *White Entertainment Television* are redundant.
15. Three words: Perennial O.J. Outrage.
16. You are often trotted out as proof that your company's transparently weak diversity initiatives work or proof that your company still doesn't need one, even though you're the only minority there.
17. "We swear your race has nothing to do with you making less than everyone else that you're outperforming."
18. Female coworkers politely remind you that when they say, "tall, dark, and handsome" they don't always mean "tall, black, and handsome."
19. Three more words: Reverse Discrimination Complaints.
20. Your white liberal colleagues often try to score points with you by randomly noting that sometimes they hate white people, too.

S'up, nigga—I mean, "nizzle"!?

Times are changing, but "nigger" remains the ultimate alarm clock. When someone drops that one on you, you immediately wake up and remember that you're Black in America. Sometimes it's followed by hand-wringing and the typical, "Whoops, I didn't mean it; you know I'm not like '*that*,'" or "I didn't mean *you* I meant *them* (other blacks)." Other times, it's followed by more defiant, *"You (blacks) use it, why can't we?"* or, *"Get over it; it's just a word!"* qualifiers. But the funny part about "nigger" and prejudice in general is how creative people can be in expressing it.

For example: Back when Snoop Dogg was at his peek, just about every white person I worked with made a point of working "nizzle" into their speech knowing full well it was short for nigger. And whether they were citing rap lyrics or some comedy bit, they'd throw around "nigger" as often as possible. And if a black person challenged them on it, they immediately hid behind the "I'm-just-repeating-what-they-said" defense.

Pops saw more than his fair share of prejudice. Growing up he told me that he'd rather be called a nigger to his face than treated like one behind his back. ("If you're a bigot, just be upfront about," he added.) My experiences taught me that corporate folks in particular are quite skilled at doing both.

Concrete Jungle Fever

Not long ago I worked with two black male professionals; both worked at the same 99%-white marketing firm. Both got involved with white female colleagues. Unbeknownst to either man, the women were playing a game of "picnic": Both women, either having never been with a black man or simply enjoying interracial sex, bet each other to see who could seduce a black man first. So they schemed until they got the guys in bed. Once they had sex with them and determined who won the bet, they promptly dumped each guy. The guys, one of whom was actually a virgin, never knew what happened until months later.

Over the years, I've met numerous minority professionals who've learned—often the hard way—that interracial dating among coworkers can get especially ugly. (The corporate world is filled with "Sarahs" and "Beckys," some more conniving than others.) And while most didn't involve bets, there was usually a lot of trading on degrading sexual stereotypes of blacks by the colleagues they slept with. But few ever talk openly about this. In their world, interracial dating based on racial and sexual stereotypes only happens in Spike Lee flicks.

"On Behalf of Black Folks Everywhere..."

When the media marked the 10-year anniversary of the Trial of the Century, I was reminded that one of the worst parts of the O.J. Simpson trial was the number of blacks in mainstream companies who became verbal punching bags for their white colleagues' outrage. At my company it was a full year of:

You better not defend him because he's black! Why don't black people denounce him?! Anyone who thinks he's innocent is a "reverse racist"! What is it with black guys and domestic abuse?! No white person could ever get away with this! It was one dart after another. But it wasn't just O.J., it wasn't just me, and it wasn't just at this company.

From Michael Jackson to R. Kelly to Kobe Bryant, any time a black person gets in trouble or embarrassed themselves the alarm clocks went off. Every black professional I know at mainstream companies goes thru this. They dodge endless jokes and backhanded compliments (i.e., "I'm glad you're not like *them*,") or worse just because a black person does something white colleagues didn't approve of. But the biggest alarm clock gets sounded by the deafening silence when the shoe is on the other foot...

While we joke about *Girls Gone Wild* and take shots at individual gold-diggers on Reality TV, no one's ever dared suggest that all or even most white women are sluts based on what we see in the media, Hollywood or in the adult entertainment industry. And despite headliners from Susan Smith[6], Andrea Yates[7], and Dianne Odell[8], to Deanna LeJune Laney[9], Marilyn Lemak[10], Andrea Williams[0], etc., we never wonder if all or most white women are natural born killers or inherently unfit mothers.

For years, we defended Cher, Madonna, etc. as "provocateurs" or "strong women challenging male-dominated industries," while dismissing Britney Spears, Christina Aguilera, Paris Hilton, etc., as harmless copycats. We're consistent apologists for white male knuckleheads (*Jackass, Punk'd, WildBoyz,* etc.). And as rock bands and white pop acts produced some of the most misogynistic, anti-social music and antics around, we were always quick to note that "times change" and they were just *being rock stars.*

We gave passes to popular perverts ranging from Pete Townsend and Jerry Lee Lewis to Woody Allen and Roman Polanski. And despite the likes of Charlie Bishop[12], Charles McCoy, Jr.[13], Adam Ghadan and John Walker Lindh[14], Ted Kaczynski[15], Luke Helder[16], Eric Rudolph[17], Tim McVeigh and Terry Nichols[18], Lee Harvey Oswald[19], John Hinckley, Jr.[20], etc. or the KKK, skinheads, eco-terrorists/PETA-nuts, and abortion clinic bombers, we'll never view white people as terrorists. And no matter how many white males go on killing sprees, serial rapes, bank heists, etc., and no matter how often FBI profilers and police criminologists begin their profiles with *"white male, age..."* the idea that whites are just as prone to crime as blacks remains almost laughable.

Why? Because to indict all or even most whites based on the actions or words of a few would be, well, *racist*. And as we know, racism simply doesn't exist in business or society.

Dinner and a Show

"If you don't like it you can suck my big black titties!" I first heard that challenge as a TWC staffer cursed out a white customer during my first visit there a couple years back. And given my numerous visits since, that was sweet talk. Imagine the *Queens of Comedy*, the *Soul Plane* crew and just about every degrading stereotype you've ever seen or heard of about black women. Now imagine them serving you hotdogs, burgers, and fries. *That's* TWC for you.

TWC is a small shack of a hot dog place in Chicago's upscale Lincoln Park community. It's owned and run a by an older white couple who encourage their all-black female staff to not only curse each other out but to serve up ghettofied Black woman stereotypes to patrons. The joint plays to constant laughter and approval of Lincoln Park's 90%-white community which packs the place 8-days-a-week.

Some days, I find myself visiting TWC just to rubberneck because it is truly a car wreck...I'll sit and watch all the white customers laughing at the black women and encouraging them to do their "black minstrel thing" as they give what amounts to their spare change for a meal. I watch all the white people go in and do their *blackcents* as they mimic the black employees. I watch the looks of horror from random black folks who occasionally stumble into TWC. I also watch as the white couple who owns TWC smiles approvingly and quietly collects their profits in the background. But mostly, I go there to watch the "I've-got-to-be-black-on-someone-else's-terms-just-to-make-a-living" hustle; the same one I saw and lived thru in the advertising world.

The odd thing is that whenever I go to TWC, the employees are pretty nice to me. They throw around words like "ho" and "nigga," but never toward me. They curse, but never at me. They're rude, *talking-out-of-their-necks* "sistahs" to everyone else except me. No matter when I go there, they talk to me the same way many black folks do each other when whites aren't around—as human beings. It's not that they know me, recognize me, or like me... I think it's that they know that it's a hustle and by treating me reasonably well they're letting me know that they're somehow in on the joke.

But still, no matter how often I go there I always leave asking myself the same question: "Does being in on a crime make you any less criminal?"

Shock the Monkey...

Most all accounts in this chapter have one thing common: The minorities involved never saw 'em coming. I was shocked to discover that getting black college students internships at a 98%-white company was reverse discrimination. I was shocked that black professionals didn't get paid as much as whites and that black women are forced to struggle the way they do. I was shocked to learn that white professionals were the standard for all professionals.

I was also shocked by the number of white females who, despite having college degrees and living in big cities, still saw black men as sex toys or athletic savants or criminals-in-waiting. I was shocked that most of my coworkers saw me as "one of the good blacks." I was shocked by the day-to-day slurs, jabs, and ignorance that passed for humor. I was constantly shocked when older blacks told me stories of what they went thru in the 1980s and 1970s. I was shocked that none of my white colleagues wanted to openly address this. And after a while, I was shocked that I began accepting all this as just part of the business.

But in the end, I finally got shocked over not being shocked anymore.

And no matter how many minority professionals I meet who share similar stories with me, I'm not shocked to learn that the saga continues. I'm also not shocked by the fact that despite it all, like Vaseline on the faces of black children, we still manage to shine.

(Also I realized that no matter how many times people shock you, you have to love and forgive just as Christ loves and forgives us all.)

Why did one straw break the camel's back?

Here's the secret: There's a million more straws underneath it. Even in 2005, prejudice and discrimination are still rites of passage for many businesspeople of color: Glass ceilings. Double standards. Unequal pay. Narrow-mindedness. White-skin privilege. Clueless assumptions sandwiched between callous just-get-over-it pleas... It's still there, straw atop straw, brick atop brick. After a while, you start to believe that the biggest difference between being black and prosperous and being black and not, is who can call you a nigger and get away with it.

Again, this chapter wasn't about complaining or nitpicking. It was about painting a picture of what's going on in Corporate America then and now in all its increasingly subtle shades. I specifically focused on accounts where bigotry and prejudice often directly translated into tangible actions such as hirings and firings, pay, policy and treatment, budget, etc. And as you can see from these and other accounts, most of hurdles minorities face are more under-the-radar than in generations past. For the most part, folks are either savvy enough to avoid obvious slurs and over-the-top bigotry. And while the "Whites Only" signs are gone, many of the attitudes that once made those signs acceptable still exist, in some industries worse than others.

Also, as I learned thru "Rob" and others, many Hispanics and Asians have had and are still having some similar struggles. One could easily get professionals from different ethnic backgrounds to write their own chapters chronicling workplace bias and prejudice. Also, in today's global economy, whether it's sweatshops, outsourcing, or emerging markets, you'll find that people of color around the world are experiencing similar indignities based on ethnicity and gender.

And let's be clear here: I don't blame any one group for this. Prejudice, bigotry, and disenfranchisement are not crop circles; every professional and every company and every industry is responsible for solving these problems. These problems won't ever get solved until everyone commits to solving them. Together.

One wonders whether the majority still believes that race discrimination or, more accurately, race discrimination against non-whites— is a problem in our society, or even remembers that it ever was.
—Harry Blackmun, former U.S. Supreme Court Justice[21]

Get in Where You Fit in.

Some men see things the way they are and say "why"?
I see things that never was and say "why not"?
—AZ

Okay, now that we've talked problems, let's talk solutions. First to minority professionals:

If we want to make it in business as individuals and as communities, we have to be about the business of not only self-help but collective help. We can complain all we want about who's not doing what and who owes whom. And while some complaints are legit, "So what?" If someone punches you in the eye, you don't wait for them to heal your eye. You take steps to heal yourself and get help from those willing to help you.

Here are 17 keys for self-help and collective help for success:

1. No More Excuses.

The Hustle's greatest ally is the excuse-maker. There's nothing easier than making excuses for why you fail or haven't fulfilled your dreams. This book isn't about blaming "them"; it's about arming you with insight and ammo to overcome. So if you haven't already, commit to no more excuses and commit to overcoming no matter what. Otherwise, the info in this book will only become another excuse for why you can't make it.

Racism is not an excuse to not do the best you can.
—Arthur Ashe, Tennis Champion 1943–1993

2. Get Your Weight Up.

Skills. Regardless of industry, city, or company, you better bring skills to the party. Don't complain about prejudice if you don't have the skills to do the job in the first place. Companies are laying off MBAs, BAs, whites, their cousins, paraplegics, their mommas, hard-luck stories, cancer patients, AIDS patients, you name it. The business world cares about one thing: Can you help me get paid? If not, you're outta there. Gone.

As a professional, particularly one of color, you must constantly expand and polish your skills. Every year you should learn something you didn't know the year before. Learn different computer programs. Build your mouthpiece. Learn different languages. Stay current on what's in demand in your industry and learn about different industries. Plus, go different places and meet different faces—success will always be about who understands people best.

When you're on point with your skills, it's that much harder for anyone to use your race or gender to hold you back. It's also that much easier to overcome if they try to.

Without education, you're not going anywhere in this world.
—Malcolm X[1]

3. Lose the ABM/AM Chip.

Ah, the Angry Black Man/Angry Minority chip...folks are still bringing those things to work. Well in case you haven't noticed lately: It doesn't work. You might scare a couple of TRLers and soccermoms, but you won't scare many businessfolks—they just don't care enough to be afraid anymore.

You won't bully or guilt businesses into giving you anything. You're going to have to outwork folks. And in today's global economy qualified folks of color are actually a dime a dozen. If you mouth off or cop an attitude, they'll just replace you with a minority professional who's just as talented, works just as hard, and smiles more than you.

I understand the frustration of double standards, etc. But the best way to win is to outwork and outshine 'em. Then when they're not looking change the game on 'em. But you won't get the chance to do so if you show up mad. Being mad just makes you an easy target. So ignore the head-games. Lose the chip, get focused and get to work.

Just keep on pushin'. We're a winner!
—Curtis Mayfield[3]

4. Pick Your Battles.

I've learned that you can't snap every time someone offends you. You can't sue over every off-color remark or joke, even those that are clearly rooted in bigotry. (The previous chapter could've easily been 100 pages long, but instead of complaining and holding grudges, I chose very specific incidents that served a greater purpose and just let the rest of it go.)

But that doesn't mean you let people walk all over you. It simply means that there are better ways to handle it. Sometimes the "warning shot" works—let folks know that as a professional, their bigotry may be fine with their friends, but you won't tolerate it and neither will the bosses once you tell them about it. Kindness is also a weapon. So is ignoring petty small-minded people. So is education—believe it or not, some folks may not know that what they're saying/doing is offensive and/or prejudiced. So is prayer—pray for your enemies, pray for the stupid.

You can fight back, but be smart about it. And remember: you are not fighting alone.

You gotta get that dirt off your shoulders...
—Jay-Z[3]

5. No Whining.

The only thing worse than the *angry minority* is the *whiny minority*. You know the ones...they're always complaining and looking for sympathy. One who sticks out in my head is a colleague I knew named "Kate." Kate was a white female exec, extremely talented and hardworking and always got the job done. But she swore she was oppressed 24/7. "When a man is aggressive at work he's praised, when a woman is aggressive she's a 'bitch'..." She'd go on and on like April rain in Seattle. I can't say that it ever cost her a promotion, but this much I know: people truly hated working with her. Her constant complaining drove people nuts.

Whining just doesn't help, even when you're right. No problem ever got solved by complaining. No war has ever been won by whining soldiers and no disease has ever been cured by whining doctors. There's no crying in baseball and there's no whining in business—unless you're going bankrupt.

Change is about action. Be angry. Be upset. Be outraged. But at some point you have to shut up and refocus that energy into constructive action.

The thing women must do to rise to power is to redefine their femininity.
Once, power was considered a masculine attribute.
In fact, power has no sex.
—Katharine Graham[4]

6. Forgive.

Business is filled with people doing ugly and hateful things in the name of success. If you want to succeed you'll have to learn to forgive folks when they hurt you. For all the crap I experienced, I forgave all, not because I'm special, but because I had to. Staying angry was hurting me more than it would've ever hurt the folks I was mad at.

Some folks don't know any better; some know better and just don't care. Forgive them all equally. If not, you may end up too bitter to succeed; or worse, too bitter to enjoy your success. Whether on the block or in business I never met a successful angry person that didn't leave a trail of bodies, hurt feelings, or burned bridges in their wake. Don't be that person.

So if someone screws you, forgive and move on. Again, when I say, forgive, I don't mean, grab your ankles. I just mean make peace with it and leave the vengeance to God—you've got bigger fish to fry. Besides, success is still the best revenge of all.

If any man have a quarrel against any;
even as Christ forgave you, so also do ye.
—Colossians 3:13

7. Get In Where You Fit In.

For every door slammed in your face there's an opportunity to succeed somewhere else. The opportunity may be small, far away, or require harder work, but it's there. You just have to be diligent and find it. Why? Because business loves money. It lives for cream. Show 'em you can put money in their pockets and you'll find work.

Every successful black professional I know works hard, and not just "hard" but harder than most everyone around them. They have to. Their game has to be tighter than everyone else's. Their success depends on it. But they know that going in, so they suck it up and do it. Old black folks have a saying, "You have to work twice as hard to get just as far." It's still true in many cases, so roll up your sleeves and do it.

Flip your challenges into opportunities and assets. Get in where you fit in and own the space you're in. And as you flip those assets and opportunities into success, expand, build, and help others do the same. Get in where you fit in; leave holes and blaze trails.

No race can prosper till it learns
there is as much dignity in tilling a field
as there is in writing a poem.
—Booker T. Washington[5]

8. You Are Not the "Chosen Minority."

Some black Americans still believe that because of our history and struggle we're the only minorities in America that deserve to be respected. Well I got news for you: Pain is pain and everybody's got their something.

Just as we want America to respect us, we have to be more respectful of other communities, not just in business but also in society. And for what it's worth, most mainstream folks would rather hire/work with non-black minority professionals, for various reasons, most of which are less than noble. But the way to overcome all of this is to be the change you want to see. Be as inclusive of others as you want them to be of you.

Empower yourself with honesty.
—Cora Daniels, author[6]

9. Find Allies.

No one succeeds alone. No one. For everyone who wants you to fail, there's someone who wants you to succeed. Build with those folks and ignore the rest. You don't have to brown-nose; just show that you're a good investment and allies will find you.

Also, allies come in all forms so don't discriminate. Yours may be a CEO, a secretary, a teacher, a mentor, or someone outside your company or industry. And don't assume or expect people to help you simply because you're both minorities. (Ironically, some of my strongest allies and mentors were white; which just shows that nothing's as simple as 'black and white' and the Lord wants us all to work together.)

We get together like a choir
to acquire what we desire.
—Jay-Z[7]

10. Where You Go, the Whole Race Still Goes.

Don't sleep on this one because it's still true. Whether it's said to your face or behind your back, a lot of folks and companies still measure whole groups by the actions of a few. You do indeed represent your community when you're outside of it. You can view that as a burden or as a healthy responsibility. And again, it's not as hectic as it was back in the day, but it's still very real, so recognize and represent.

U–N–I–T–Y
—Queen Latifah[8]

11. Don't "Happen to Be."

Over the years, I met numerous black professionals who played the happen-to-be-black card. Everything they did was about treating their ethnicity like it was an embarrassing accident just to climb the ladder. And as I said earlier, I played Mr. Potato Head to appease my not-as-inclusive-as-they-claimed colleagues until I realized one thing: It was never going to be enough.

Individuality is your greatest strength in business, especially in the marketing and creative fields; nobody else can be you but you. Don't try to hide what you are just because someone else might be uncomfortable with it. Doing so adds unnecessary stress to your job and your life. Besides, the folks that will judge negatively because of your race/ethnicity, etc., will keep doing so no matter how much you change for them. So just do you. You don't have to rub it in anyone's face or be over-the-top with it, just be yourself.

12. Don't Talk About It, Be About It.

Over the years, I've heard everyone from street hustlers to MCs to VPs talk about changing the game and shocking the system. But whenever the time came to make those power moves, most were all talk.

No more sideline activism and bougie outrage from the only-going-for-mine seats. If you can open doors for other qualified people of color, do it. If you have influence over budgets and appointments, you use it. If you can help those who are getting screwed, help. Otherwise you're no better than the corrupt politician or multi-platinum rapper hiding in their gated community claiming to rep the people.

It's time to put up or shut up. No more speeches. No more meetings or marches. It's time for some action. Hire qualified minorities. Support quality minority businesses. Change is action. Action is muscle—start flexing.

You and I have been sitting long enough;
it's time to do some standing and fighting.
—Malcolm X

13. Lose the "Minor-Leagues" Mindset.

Too many folks, particularly successful/privileged blacks treat the black community like it's the minor leagues of American society. We don't live around blacks any longer than we have to. We don't want our money in black-owned banks. We won't support black retailers. Most won't use black vendors or black contractors. Most black executives only see *Black Enterprise* as a stepping-stone to *Forbes.* We still measure our success by the degree to which white institutions and consumers accept and support us.

For all of the talk I hear at black business conferences, I know very few Black executives who make any real efforts to recruit and/or train Black candidates. And just like mainstream professionals, they make the same excuses for why. Willie Lynch is dead. The paper bag test is dead; all this soft self-hating, crabs-in-a-barrel crap needs to die, too.

As individuals, as professionals and as people, we need to love ourselves. We need to believe that we are just as talented, just as worthy, and most importantly, when given a fair chance just as capable as everyone else. Success is not white. There's nothing inferior or minor-league about black professionals, black consumers, or black businesses. We are major not minor. But until we believe in ourselves no one else will.

Us must discuss us trusting us.
—KRS-ONE[9]

14. Get Out More.

From now on the people with the broadest minds, broadest experiences, and broadest sense of possibilities will have the most opportunities to succeed. But in order to be one of those people, you gotta get out more. Meet people from different parts of your city and state and different cities and states and different countries. Meet folks in different industries. Soak up as much knowledge and experience in as many areas as possible. Get off the block.

There's still a lot of segregation in America. Lots of folks at various levels are circling the wagons to perpetuate it. Still, we all have to expand our minds and get out more. I had to learn to meet different folk in different cities as well as from different countries. I had to learn to be more open-minded about people and my partnerships. It was necessary in order for me to grow. And guess what? I'm still growing, still learning. And I've still got a ways to go. We all do.

Again, this isn't about going mainstream or turning your back on your community; this is about growth, and empowerment. Don't accept staying within the same 5- or 10-mile area as living. Don't think that being at one company or having one set of skills is enough because it's not. Not anymore. This world is too big for that type of thinking. The possibilities are too great and more importantly, there's way too much at stake.

It pains God's heart that He gave you a whole house and you only use a closet.
—Bishop TD Jakes[10]

15. Bridge the Gap.

We have to close the generation gap between old and young black professionals. Too many young businessfolks are trying to reinvent the wheel each time out because older folks aren't passing down their knowledge and connections and younger folks aren't seeking 'em out.

Secondly, black parents must do a better job of exposing our kids to the business world. Whether you're in business or not, let your kids know that business is a viable, realistic option. Like culture and heritage, business opportunities are often passed down thru generations. One reason so many doors have been closed to blacks in the past is because those in charge kept things "in the family," thus making it even harder for outsiders to get in.

A child's future is largely based on their experiences—they're only as good as their options. So broaden their options. By age 10 every black child should know that business is as real of an option as sports or entertainment. By 14, they should believe that owning stock in a sneaker company is cooler than owning sneakers. If we do that, each generation will be able to build on the successes and advances of the last, thus create more opportunities, more equity and ultimately, more equality, and self-determination.

I for one believe that if you give people a thorough understanding of what confronts them and the basic causes that produce it, they'll create their own program, and when the people create a program, you get action.
—Malcolm X[11]

16. Do 4 Self.

Independence and self-determination are seldom if ever, achieved by working for someone else. So if your company is "doing you wrong," you should consider going the independent route. Start your own business. Freelance. Do for self. When you run things, you set policy, you help who you want to help, you can branch out and manifest your own ideas and go as far as your talents will take you. (See "Do 4 Self" chapter.)

Ain't no stoppin' us now...
—McFadden & Whitehead[12]

17. Pray.

I'm not preaching but I have to say this: I have never done anything worth doing in my life without knowing that God was working it. God's in the "overcoming business." You want to do big things, talk to the Big Man. Again, I'm not preaching, but as my pops says, "I'm not telling you what I heard, I'm telling you what I know."

"Ask, and it shall be given you; seek, and ye shall find; knock and it shall be opened unto you."
—St. Matthew 7:7

Well, them's my sweet seventeen. And please, use these strategies plus whatever position or influence you have to help others. Let's plant these seeds and grow together.

Some say this country will never stop being racist.
Well that doesn't mean you throw up your hands.
You acquire your own power, taking away other people's power over you.
That's just taking back what should have been yours anyway.
—Spike Lee[13]

Dear Gatekeepers...
Redefining "where you fit in"

There are two ways of exerting one's strength:
one is pushing down, the other is pulling up.
—Booker T. Washington

First off, the term "gatekeepers" applies all in power, specifically those who have the influence to change but aren't sure where to start or how to take things to the next level. Secondly, let's clear up one popular myth:

Whether many like it or not, extra elbow grease, added perseverance, and greater commitment to education by minorities is only part of the solution. Corporate folks and America as a whole must be equally committed to equality or it simply won't happen. And I'm not talking about tokenism, lip service or ad-hoc programs, but true, systemic diversity and opportunity that reflects America and the values we claim America represents and holds dear.

As many have noted, the American consumer has gotten darker and more diverse with each passing year. Hispanics, already our largest ethnic minority group, are expected to be spending almost $1 trillion annually by 2009 with blacks spending near $965 billion by the same time.[1] Our Asian and Middle Eastern communities have grown almost exponentially in size and affluence as well; plus, other ethnic immigrants of color, who continue to come by the boatloads, are gaining affluence. Before we know it, American will be full-blown autumn—a wealth of red, brown, yellow, and earth-toned faces as far as the eye can see. And once our booming sub-segments of multi-racial and multi-ethnic kids mature and have kids of their own, America will be one big pair of Khakis—beige. Now why should any of these consumers be diverse and open-minded in their purchases when so many businesses still refuse to do the same as it relates to hiring, marketing, comunity investment, etc.?

From now on, the businesses that survive and thrive will be those diverse enough to build with people. The rest will just fail. With all that said, I now offer 16 keys on creating real corporate diversity and equal opportunity for all once and for all:

1. Change of Heart

If you believe in your heart that everything is okay as relates to race and business, nothing you read from this point on will matter. No action or strategy outlined in this book will manifest without a change of mind and heart. So as you read on, look within your heart and challenge yourself to be an agent of change.

For every dollar of white income per capita, African-Americans had 55 cents in 1968 and only 57 cents in 2001. At this rate, it will take blacks another 581 years to catch up.[2]

1a. Want-to.

Winning in sports often comes down to who wants it more. Diversity is no different. The big reason most companies struggle with diversity is simple: *They really don't want it.* What too many companies are doing is trying to avoid lawsuits, get good PR, and benefit from the increased revenues minority consumers bring. But deep down inside, they don't believe in diversity and usually don't practice it in their personal lives, nevermind their professional ones. Consequently, their diversity initiatives sputter and their systemic flaws remain.

Equality doesn't happen without "want-to." Diversity requires want-to at every level, especially the top, or it degenerates into the kind of nonsense that we'll be discussing in numbers 4, 5, 7, 8, 9, and 12. In order to want diversity, people have to truly believe in it, not for the sake of profit or PR, but for the sake of right and wrong. So the big question isn't How do we achieve diversity? but, Do you believe in it?

Ah, do consider well this thing, you who do it.
—Germantown Mennonites, Feb. 18, 1688[3]

2. Get uncomfortable

Growth is uncomfortable. Progress is uncomfortable. Challenging racism and promoting diversity is uncomfortable, particularly for those who see no obvious benefit in changing the status quo. But we must move beyond convincing minorities that disenfranchisement is all in their heads or that "Life is hard for everyone and you just need to suck it up." If we truly want to move forward as businesses and a country, everyone must change. Not just minorities, but everyone. We need to have uncomfortable discussions at every level in every company. We need to have uncomfortable discussions in our homes. We need to make uncomfortable decisions and take uncomfortable risks. Nothing will change until we do.

Replacing direct language with "safe" words signals
a lack of clarity or a lack of commitment to the world of diversity.
Issues must be clearly defined and articulated before they can be changed.
—HR Focus *magazine*[4]

3. "Don't Talk About It, Be About It" Goes For You, Too

Any business can brag about how pro-diversity it is. Anyone can rip David Duke or George W. Bush's status as a legacy baby or spit Chris Rock punchlines. God knows it makes us sound cool at the business conferences and around our friends. But talk is cheap.

We must decide once and for all whether we're part of a continuing problem or part of the solution. Either we will recruit minorities or we won't. Either we will partner with minority businesses or we won't. Either we will respect minority consumers or we won't. We'll either work for change or we'll work against change. There is no middle ground.

In 2000, there were over 20.9 million businesses in America.
Only 1.2 million are owned by Hispanics while blacks own only about
890,000 businesses. This leaves nearly 18 million American businesses
owned mostly by whites.[5]

4. Spin Control is Not Change

Also known as the "Some-of-my-best-friends-are-black" approach. This is where companies use PR campaigns, token hires, and relationships to prove their diversity. Throughout my career I was called on by numerous companies whose diversity initiatives consisted of doing Black History Month ads and hyping minority charity donations or suspect partnerships they'd haphazardly thrown together.

Real action goes deeper than MLK, Jr. PSAs and checks to the NAACP. Real change is 24/7/365 at every level. So stop frontin' and be about it.

As of 2003, more than 890,000, or 81.3%
of the nation's 1.1 million self-identified
chief executive officers are white males.[6]

5. No More Colorblindness

Dogs are colorblind. Colorblind is what you put on your insurance form under "pre-existing conditions." Colorblind is just a politically correct way of saying: "I have so little respect for your ethnicity that the only way I can see you as equal is to ignore it." Ignoring melanin and heritage doesn't make you enlightened, it makes you a moron. People aren't crayons—you don't pick the colors you like and ignore the rest. Open your eyes and see everyone for everything that makes them human and valuable, including their ethnicity.

In order to get beyond racism, we must first take account of race.
There is no other way. And in order to treat some persons
equally, we must treat them differently.
—Harry A. Blackmun, U.S. Supreme Court Justice[7]

6. Hire Them

In early 2003, Tyrone Willingham, Notre Dame University's first black head football coach, was asked what could be done to get more blacks in the NCAA's still near lily-white Div. 1 coaching ranks. His response: "Hire them. There's plenty of qualified black candidates out there. Just hire them, it's that simple."

The oft-repeated notion that there aren't enough qualified black business candidates out there is a big pile of crap. I've seen 'em pounding the pavement in every industry and every city looking for a fair shot at every level. Don't talk about quotas or reverse discrimination. Enough with the excuses; just hire them. Hire blacks the same way we hire white candidates: We "just have a good feeling about."

And if your plan is to simply interview black candidates knowing full well that you're going to hire a white person anyway (like the 2003 San Francisco 49ers and 2004 Detroit Lions did with their respective head coach searches) save the drama and post a "Whites Only" sign out front.

Hire them already. Shut up and hire them. Period.

I've always felt diversity is the most important part of a writing staff.
—Jon Stewart, accepting his 2003 Emmy
with his all-white writing team[8]

(FYI: The irony in Willingham's quote was that despite his undeniable ability and track record, he wasn't hired until after ND was turned down by all the white coaches on their wish list and after their last-resort hire George O'Leary (from Georgia Tech) resigned after being caught lying about his credentials. In 2004 Willingham was fired after just three years and a 21-15 record. As of July 2005, of the 117 Div.1 coaches, only 3 were black.)

7. White Women, Anglo-Europeans, and Gay Whites are Not Black

Diversity is not blondes, brunettes, redheads, plus gay, fat, skinny, or short versions thereof. Over the years, several execs and HR folks let me in on a little secret, which I've confirmed thru research: Many businesses and colleges (public and private) have and continue to use white women and white-skinned ethnic groups as "diversity smokescreens" to continue discriminating against blacks and Hispanics. Overall, white women are the biggest winners of affirmative action programs, claiming more than 40% of all managerial or professional jobs in the late 1990s, this according to Catalyst, a NY-based research firm that promotes the interests of women in business.

Also, according to many HR and corporate insiders, when it comes to balancing EEOC requirements with a company's true feelings, white females are considered the most desirable hires, followed by white ethnic males and gay whites with blacks usually bring up the rear in preference.

7a. Who ordered the double cheese & sausage?

Modern diversity is like Spiccoli's pizza from *Fast Times at Ridgemont High*: The teacher, Ray Walston, didn't take Spiccoli's pizza and divide it up amongst the class out of fairness, he did so because he didn't like Spiccoli. Many have followed suit, using diversity as a "If-helping-all-groups-minimizes-helping-those-we-dislike-most-we-still-win" buffer. At best it's subtraction by addition; at worst, it's cutting off your nose to spite your face.

In the end, hire the best person for the job. But if you're marginalizing blacks in favor of other groups, stop it.

Race was the sacrificial lamb to launch "diversity" and make it palatable to Corporate America.
—Lisa Willis Johnson, diversity chair
Society for Human Resource Management[9]

7b. Lose the "Double-Minority" trick, too.

Women face glass ceilings; women of color, specifically black women, face the concrete ceiling of sexism plus racism. However some companies hire women of color because it counts as 2 minority hires under EEOC specs while physically they've only hired one person. It's a clever way to curtail rampant diversity.

In 2002, of the 10,092 women corporate officers at Fortune 500 companies about 605 were Asian females. Just 106 were black; only 24 were Latina. The remaining 9,350-plus female execs were white.[10]

8. Equal Pay

It's inexcusable for minorities to be paid less than their white counterparts for doing the same job at the same level. It's discriminatory, patently racist, and too many companies are still doing it. Pay people fairly. Period.

In 2003, the average weekly income for black men was $555 while black women made $491. The average weekly income for white men was $715 while white women made $567.[11]

9. Stop "Last Hired, First Fired"

Many employment studies are now backing up what most have known for decades: Whenever there's a recession, black employees tend to be cut first and most; when there's a boom, blacks are usually the last to benefit. Last hired, first fired is old news in the black community; but it goes on. It's time to stop.

Our fathers had to fight "Jim Crow"...
Now we have to fight "James Crow, Jr. Esq."
—Rev. Al Sharpton[12]

10. Diversify Your Partnerships

It's quite okay to partner with qualified minority vendors, contractors, banks, etc. They're just as professional, talented, and hardworking as any. And they're helping businesses grow everyday. So give 'em a shot—you won't be disappointed.

As of 2005, the top 100 richest white Americans have more money and assets than all estimated 40 million plus black Americans combined.[13]

11. Exceptions are Not "the Rule"

Don't make decisions about minorities based on the actions, good or bad, of a few. In 13 years I worked with screw-ups from all walks of life, but not once did I ever see a company negatively judge its white employees or white candidates based on the screw-ups of other whites. We forget that for every "Omarosa" or "Jayson Blair" there are countless Stephen Glasses[14], Jack Kelleys[15], Mike Barnicles[16], Elizabeth Wurtzels[17], etc. And for every minority firm that we're uncomfortable doing business with, there are numerous mainstream institutions deserving of similar criticism. Simply put, stop looking for proof to validate prejudice. Give everyone a chance.

Only 32% of whites report that their workplaces include different races and ethnic groups. While, 72% of blacks and 59% of Latinos work in places where employees are from a variety of races and ethnic groups.
—Gallup poll (2004)

12. Get Out More

As America continues to re-segregate, more whites are sticking with only whites; more blacks are sticking with just blacks, etc. (In fact, according to the U.S. Census Bureau, as of 2004, 80% of whites live in neighborhoods that are at least 95% white.) Most of us regardless of color won't leave our block, our neighborhood, or expand our circle of friends. Consequently, our misconceptions and prejudices about each other continue.

We think a week on a Maui beach is Hawaiian culture. We think wearing Yankees gear connects us to New York while our Bob Marley CDs and Red Stripe beers connect us to Jamaica. We confuse brief experiences and purchases and media images with genuine knowledge and understanding...

How can any business succeed if its workforce is sheltered by misconceptions and prejudices about potential customers and colleagues? You can't, so get out more. Get out of your neighborhood. Expand your experiences. The world doesn't end with our limited perceptions of it.

It pains God's heart that He gave you a whole house
and you only use a closet.
—Bishop TD Jakes[18]

13. Look In the Mirror.

In 13 years-plus of corporate life, 4 years of college, and years of travel, I realized that I have never met a single white person with any prejudice whatsoever. No, not one. No matter who I met, some of their best friends were always black. They slept with black people. (And we all know you can't be racist and horny at the same time.) They love black music and they can quote black celebrities. Nope, not one white person I ever worked with or went to school with harbored even the slightest bit of prejudice.

To them, America's race problem is at best, just some misunderstandings on the part of overly sensitive minorities. At worst, prejudice is a crop circle reserved for rednecks, southerners, and republicans.

Look folks: Relegating prejudice to extremists or generations past may be cute and comforting, but it's also a lie. It's time to look in the mirror and question our own hearts and actions. (And we can stop blaming white males for everything? I've seen just as much bigotry in business from white women and other ethnic groups as from white males.)

There are many humorous things in the world,
among them the White man's notion that
he is less savage than other savages.
—Mark Twain[19]

14. Stop Bragging

One thing that stuns me about Corporate America is its willingness to brag about its all-too-rare hiring of qualified minorities and working towards an even playing field. What kind of trifling backwards-thinking is this? You're not doing anything extra. Creating diverse work environments and fair hiring practices is like showing up for your 9-to-5 at 9A.M.—you're supposed to do that. Bragging about slow changes only proves that you're not serious about doing the hard work necessary to create real diversity and equity.

15. Talk to Your Kids

I'd have to say that 90% of the bias, prejudice that I've witnessed and/or continue to hear about in Corporate America has come at the hands of 18– 45 year-olds, most of whom are college-educated, city-dwelling, self-proclaimed "liberals". So where are they learning this pathology?

My guess? Home.

I'd say 80% of white professionals I met over the years told me they never seriously discussed race at home or with any adult growing up. I think it was because for the most part, their lives and livelihoods never depended on understanding or relating to anyone who wasn't white. Anyway, they had a lot of misconceptions about minorities and it affected their choice of friends, neighborhoods, and of course, coworkers and employees.

As parents don't assume that just because your kids love hiphop or quote Bob Marley and Maya Angelou that they're incapable of bias. And having black friends/dating black people does not inoculate one from prejudice. Talk to your kids about culture, stereotypes, and prejudice. Because kids take the lessons they learn (or don't learn) as children into adulthood—and into the workplace.

(Remember: Americans of color haven't seen centuries of oppression and marginalization because a select handful of really, really old white men willed it into eternity. Racism and prejudice existed then for the same reason they exist now: Each generation makes decisions to perpetuate it benefit from its existence. Each generation passes it onto their kids like a last name or a will. Each generation decides not to teach the next generation better.)

Racism is the only disease we try to cure thru denial.[20]

16. Pray

Racism and discrimination are sins. God overcomes sin. Pray.

We got to pray just to make it today.
—MC Hammer[21]

(By the Way...We Know)

No matter how well people hide it, gays know homophobia when they see it. Women know sexism when they see it. People of color know racism when they see it. No matter how well people think they're hiding or masking their bias and prejudice, they're seldom if ever fooling anyone. People know when they're not accepted or respected or seen as equal. People know when double standards and inequality exist. And what's worse, hoping or assuming that they're too stupid to realize what's going on only makes things worse. We have to stop this.

We have to stop making excuses for inequity. We have to stop pretending that just because we ignore it, everyone else will or should, too. Like it or not, everyone knows.

Forty years ago, Martin Luther King, Jr. wrote: "In this vast interdependent nation no racial group can retreat to an island entire of itself."[22] No business and no segment of society can thrive in a vacuum. Diversity and equal opportunity are not strategies to be implemented when it's profitable or cool to do so. They are self-evident truths and human rights; and to deprive folks of them or to stand by while others do is simply inhumane.

Now, we can go on pretending that nothing's wrong or that things will simply work themselves out. Or we can take a good hard look at what we do and how we live and make the changes we need to make for the betterment of all.

You may dispose of me very easily. I am nearly disposed of now.
But the question is still to be settled—this Negro question,
I mean; the end of that is not yet.
—John Brown, white abolitionist[23]

The Universal Hustle: The Business of Blackness & Multiculturalism

So what kind of power have you got, as a man,
if the very way you define yourself
comes from outside your environment,
your domain, your soul?
—Kevin Powell

I'm not sure exactly when, but at some point being black became my full-time job, my career. Being a good copywriter became secondary to being a good black copywriter. Being a smart marketer became secondary to being an *urban* marketer. At some point, my insights into the Black community and hiphop became my most valued assets; and after a while nothing else mattered. It wasn't because I didn't have value in any other capacity or role. And it wasn't because I was looking for an easy way out (or in). It was because that's all they wanted from me: Bosses...Clients...Coworkers... Consumers...Women... They wanted blackness; or at least a marketable, ownable version of it. Most days I felt like the token brother on SNL—*Give 'em Blackness.* On their terms. For their purpose. For their profit.

Some days I forgot that my experiences were simply par for the course. After all, black folks have always been big business here: Our labor. Our speech. Our styles. Our stories. Our humor. Our music. Our hair. Our skin. Our struggle. Our soul... There's always been profit in selling and consuming blackness; it still ranks as one of America's greatest industries and probably its most lucrative export. My career, especially my time spent in urban marketing, forced me to remember this. It also reminded me that we profit from it the least, if ever at all.

Show 'Em My Motto!

Backspin to Summer Y2K...

I'm in this brainstorming session for a major soft-drink client: There's me, a couple VPs, account execs, creative directors, etc., all sitting around a conference table staring at cans and bottles of product. The soda's image is flat; its market share is slipping. *Our assignment:* Re-energize the brand; make it hip. Make our core audiences of 12–17 year-old and 18–24 year-old mainstream kids already thirsty for coolness drink it by the caseload.

Our solution? Black folk. *The gist:* While our core audience is white, our client knows what most in the beverage, music, fashion, and entertainment industries have known and utilized for decades: black people are cool, trendsetters. And if you get black people to do it, most everyone else, in the great American tradition of co-opting black culture, will probably do it, too. So the plan is essentially to surround the product with black people, black music, and boom—sold to America. In business terms, it's the O.J. Principle reloaded:

Back in 1968 at the height of the Civil Rights Era, as top black sports figures like Jim Brown, Dr. Harry Edwards, Muhammad Ali, Kareem Abdul Jabbar, et al., are championing civil rights, a rising RB named Orenthal James Simpson who's just won the Heisman Award publicly distances himself from the movement by claiming it (black civil rights) "isn't his problem."[1] This public declaration makes him an instant folk hero among many mainstreamers and a cash cow for everyone from ABC and the NFL to Hertz to Hollywood.

Over the next 25 years, O.J. Simpson built a multimillion-dollar career of product-endorsing, motivational speaking, sports-commentating, and even acting, based almost exclusively on being universal—black but accepted by mainstream marketers and consumers. He protected his crossover appeal by consistently avoiding all things controversial or black (women, civil rights, race, etc.). And until his big trial, he was consistently ranked as one of the most beloved black people in America. Companies have been spinning the O.J. Principle ever since. (Many have cited Michael Jordan, Tiger Woods, and Will Smith as the O.J. Principle's most successful offspring.)

Now, back to the lab...

We start batting around ways to seed this soft drink into the Black community. Giveaways. Churches. Community events. Eventually someone suggests celebrity endorser. (The client has deep pockets and if we offered the right one, they'd bite.) Names start flying: Jordan. Janet Jackson. Chris Tucker. Chris Rock. Tiger. Sir Charles... Quickly, some begin expressing concerns over how black is too black for this brand. After all, the core audience is white soft-drink consumers; we need to attract blacks, but not if it means alienating whites.

As the celebrity prospects are discussed, a mild off-color comment pops up. Then a couple light-hearted but derogatory jokes... Criticisms of various aspects of black culture that they "just don't understand" follow... Next thing you know, a wholesale discussion breaks out over what "type" of black person our client should be associated with. Many champion Will Smith. He's "nice," "articulate," and not breaking the law "like the rest," as they put it. Other counter that Will isn't "real enough" and "too boring," or something to that effect. He's "too O.J." for them—pre-Bronco chase, of course.

As an apparent wildcard, someone offers up Allen Iverson. Quickly the room agrees AI is "a little too much" for the client. (Remember this is 2000—Iverson was still too street for most of America; even some NBA execs thought so.) Someone else suggests trying a black endorser who isn't an athlete or an actor "to avoid the obvious." But after a minute or two of dead silence, they realize they can't think of anyone. In between lots of hand-wringing all decide that it might not be interesting enough and possibly a disconnect to show a black person in that context. So it's back to athletes, entertainers, and who/what is "too black."

By now I'm so frustrated that I storm out of the room. I don't know what bothered me more—the discussion or the fact that I was in on it. I went back to my desk and began writing my resignation letter. While typing, I realized that I still needed money, and this whole "blackness" thing was lucrative. So I stopped and hit one of our big comfy bathrooms, splashed some water on my face and sat in a stall to chill out.

About 20 minutes later I went back into the meeting. Judging from the reactions, I don't think anyone noticed I was gone. In my absence 5 black endorser options had been scrawled onto one of those gigantic Post-It pads. They were noted as "final selects." I read the names... Will Smith was number one. The others left me shaking my head in masked disgust and counting the days until my next paycheck. (The client ended up going with a patchwork of messages until their L'il Penny rip-off took off.)

But that day got to me. There was something about being in a room full of whites with more power and influence than even they probably realized or would ever admit to having literally deciding what is too black. They were actually imposing their values on black culture and black people, not just in the name of commerce, but also in the name of America. But what got to me even more was that I helped them do it.

Looking back, that soda meeting was typical and actually quite mild compared to the rest of my marketing experiences and those of most black marketing professionals. Overall, the schemes are usually way more manipulative and exploitive. The clients and coworkers are usually more callous, clueless, condescending, biased, indifferent, *insert-descriptor-here...*

The images we created were often destructively stereotypical and fetishizing, even when we were being subtle. The ideas and ideals we attached brands to were often marginalizing and dehumanizing. The brands we pushed were often as disposable and empty as our perceptions of our ethnic target audiences. The money we made seldom if ever saw the pockets of minority professionals or vendors. (Most of the companies involved had few if any minority professionals on staff and spent as little money as possible with black vendors and companies. Such is still the case today.)

Funny thing, it never felt like some secret cabal or Illuminati-type stuff; it was just business as usual. And of course, it was ethical. Maybe that's why we seldom if ever cared about the repercussions.

When it comes to style and flavor America always had to love black people. Not only did we not need their love, we appeared not to be damaged by their spiritual abuse and violence. We were beautiful without them. We were more beautiful without them. That was dangerous.

—Michela Angela Davis[2]

The Rebirth of Slick

Remember our "cut" discussion? Well, the most effective cut is "cool." We all want it; more importantly, we want everyone else to know we have it. Business loves cool because it can be cut into anything with a price tag. Consumers love cool because it's the ultimate form of validation and acceptance. And if they don't have it, it gives them something to aspire to, a sense of purpose. Being cool ranks among the noblest of American pursuits.

As I've learned from many a business meeting, focus group, and music video: Black folks is cool. Just ask most anyone age 12 to about 35 and they'll tell you the same. Black athletes are cool. Black entertainers are cool. Black preachers are cool. Black music is cool. Black slang is cool. Black folks is just plain ol' cool.

But when we say cool, we don't mean it in a timeless, James Dean/Rat Pack/cowboy sort of way. We don't mean, cool in an individualistic-idealist-Jack Kerouac sort of way, either. No. We mean black people are cool as in "screw-authority-scare-Middle-America" cool. Cool as in "jungle-fever" cool. Cool as in "societal-boogie-monster" cool. Cool as in "it's-one-big-costume-party-amusement-park" cool. Cool as in "when-I-get-bored-or-outgrow-this-I-can-trash-it-with-no-real-consequences" cool. Blackness, by mainstream America's standards at least, has always been cool like that.

Consequently, blackness is the new cut. American business and society at large marginalizes blackness into a natural resource then mines it and commoditizes it as needed. When it suits us, business mixes it into whatever we're selling: TV Shows. Movies. Music. Sports. Fashion. Food. Cars. Jewelry. Liquor. Sex. Pick a brand, pick a service, pick a celebrity, pick a cause, even...chances are you'll find that at least a little flava has been mixed into it. Why? Because black is cool and cool sells, therefore black sells.

I'm so...Cool!
—The Time[3]

Bamboozling 4 Dollars

The marketing industry hustle is often divided up into 2 camps: General Markets and Targeted Markets. To clarify, general market is to White or Mainstream as targeted is to Urban, Black, or Minority.

At my general-market gigs, which I did for about 5 years, it was all about reaching mainstream consumers. From a business perspective, general market has more to do with race than income. For example: if you're rich and black, most marketers still classify you as urban; but if you're poor and white, you're still considered general market. Secondly, when a white-owned company or brand targets white consumers, it's called a general-market campaign. But if that same company goes after minority consumers, as many do today, they're still general-market clients but now they're targeting emerging markets. Conversely, black-owned businesses are urban no matter who they target. (Harpo, Inc. being the most obvious exception to this.) It's all about labels, and the general-market label still has the most cache (and money) in business.

Again, marketing is basically 50% educated guesswork, 25% making that guesswork look like hard science, and 25% dealing with the results of the guesswork. Success is well-timed correct guesses based on common ground; and common ground starts with race. The majority American consumer is still white. The clients are usually white. The media outlets we use to reach consumers are either run by/filled with white professionals, targeting white and mainstream consumers, or both. Consequently, we always understood that our most important job was to stick to the whiteness script: Understand white/mainstream clients and consumers inside and out. Or else.

Working on general-market clients was always odd. Like most people of color, I spent years trying to understand pub-crawls, Elvis, suburbia, grunge, jambands, and hair bands... I had to figure out why women like Julia Roberts and Cindy Crawford and Pamela Anderson were the sole standards of beauty; why Beck, Quentin Tarantino, and Seinfeld were geniuses, and why phrases like "All-American" and "boy/girl next door" had the connotations they had... From school to entertainment to everyday life, my academic and corporate survival was based on understanding people who looked nothing like me, had nothing to do with my life experiences. Most days I often felt like I was speaking 2 different languages and living in two different worlds. But when it came to selling gum or phones or soda, I could block a lot of that stuff out and just do my job. And as long as I kept it simple like that, I did okay. But working for targeted agencies was a different animal.

First off, they say, "targeted" (or urban) because it sounds more mainstream-friendly and inclusive than African-American or Hispanic or Asian, hence the label. They're also known as emerging (or emerged) markets, which is so condescending because minority consumers really didn't emerge as much as marketers finally stopped ignoring them. Anyway, we also target by sex, as is the case with the ever-exploding GLBT (gay, lesbian, bisexual, transgender) market; but it's also segmented by race. GLBT marketing, entertainment, and political and social trends are built almost exclusively around appeasing white GLBTers. (And quiet as kept, it's all a reflection of the entrenched racism, sexism, and hypocrisy within the GLBT community.) Anyway...

Traditionally, black advertising and marketing professionals, especially creatives, either work for general market agencies or they work at targeted agencies but few do both, mainly for reasons I've already explained. I'm one of the few who've not only done both but who can go back and forth at will. It's really moving between different worlds, different mindsets, different cultures every single day... It's a gift and a curse, really.

The prejudice exists everywhere. With targeted agencies, the clients don't respect you enough to pay you right or give you the opportunities to do great work that they give white agencies. And the white agencies either don't hire you at all or they do hire you then treat you like a token or a mascot or worse. Lemme explain:

Down By Law

Companies usually hire targeted firms for one of three reasons: (a) They've saturated the general market and are reluctantly turning to minority consumers as revenue boosters. (b) They have "image concerns" and hiring a minority firm is a nice way to avoid EEOC lawsuits, boycotts, or bad PR. (c) Their brand needs to be cool and aligning it with urban culture is often a quick superficial fix.

But regardless of the motive, there are always strings attached to targeting black consumers. First off, most targeted work is usually black versions of strategies and campaigns designed for mainstream consumers. Usually, a client comes with, "Here's what we're doing for our core (white) audience;

we need a black version." The black version often means *"THROW A BLACK FACE UPFRONT, ADD SOME SLANG AND FUNKY MUSIC-BUT KEEP EVERYTHING ELSE THE SAME."* Some called it synergy; most called it *blackface*. Secondly, Black consumers are seldom if ever a business's sole target—at some point the goal is to reach white consumers. So even if you're targeting minorities, you can't offend or alienate whites. So by default whites remain the judge of what is "black" or "too black," even for black people.

Consequently, from the debasing minstrel imagery of 1890s' advertising right on thru today, most marketing campaigns targeting blacks are based on a version of blackness that whites and non-blacks are comfortable with. So for years every other commercial folks saw had blacks playing basketball. Wearing Kenti-cloth or backwards baseball caps. Or playing saxophone or tap-dancing. Or sepia-toned, impossibly good-looking buppies. Or MLK, Jr. references, mostly in February. And of course, overtly grateful black folks singing and dancing about how much they love a certain product. In short: *stereotypes.*

Today the basketball construct has been resurrected as "streetball," a theme that's been hugely successful since 2000 with everyone from Reebok, Nike, and AND-1 to Frito-Lays, Mountain Dew, McDonald's, Sprite, etc. The saxophones and random-singing black folks have been replaced by (mostly buffoonish) emcees, deejays, and "street" dancers. And of course every industry from liquor to cars to fashion to sports to food continues to milk hiphop, further reducing it to a global circus of stereotypes and caricatures. Despite the progress, most days I didn't know if I was marketing brands or producing new millennium minstrel skits.

"What Makes This 'Black'?"

On most every assignment black marketing professionals have to answer the same degrading question: What makes your work "targeted" or "inherently black"? You see, as a black advertising professional or marketing firm, your biggest bargaining chip isn't ability but race; but it's also your biggest crutch.

You see, if you can't do work that's inherently black, most marketers and clients won't hire you to do anything else. Conversely, it's an unspoken but widely enforced industry rule that targeted-marketing firms aren't allowed to bid on general market accounts. Most companies have the mentality of, *Why should I hire a black marketing firm to reach white consumers when my general-market firm does that?* Many also wonder, *Why should I hire a black firm to reach black consumers if my general-market firm can crossover and reach black consumers, too?* It's the marketing industry's version of Jim Crow and it's been in effect ever since Aunt Jemima rocked 'do rags.

Over the years, when I worked on major brands such as Aleve, Cingular Wireless, Mello Yello, Procter & Gamble, SBC, Sprite, Wm. Wrigley, Jr. Co., etc., I did so thru general-market firms where white consumers were the focus. Occasionally they'd try to reach minority consumers, but they usually screwed it up. I lost count of the number of times I saw random white people running around screaming, "How do you say 'such-'n'-such' in Spanish?" or, "This won't offend anyone in Chinatown, will it?" But even today, there's still a "whites-only" mentality at most general market shops, which sucks because again, that's where most of the real money and opportunity is.

"Spoony Gee"

My first exposure to "Inherent Blackness" came back in 1999 when I worked on Kool-Aid thru Uniworld, a targeted agency in New York. As their targeted shop, our job was to help Kool-Aid reach black consumers. I think Ogilvy & Mather was the lead agency, which meant they handled all of the general-market work. (They may have launched the classic Kool-Aid Man campaign back in the day, but I'm not sure.) Anyway, as a Kraft Foods brand, Kool-Aid is a longtime staple in many black, 'scuse me, "urban" households. My role was to bring a younger urban perspective to the traditional "drink-it-and-smile-about-it" flavor Kool-Aid's targeted work had up until then.

My first TV spot was based on Walt Disney's *Fantasia* and my dad. Growing up, my dad always made Kool-Aid with the same large spoon. Since he rarely used that spoon for anything else, we called it The Kool-Aid Spoon. Turns out a lot of people who made Kool-Aid had their own special spoon—it was usually the only spoon they had that fit the big pitchers they used.

So I took that "magic spoon" memory and combined it with Fantasia to create "The Magic Spoon," an animated spot in which a packet of Kool-Aid brings a spoon to life, which in turn stirs up a kitchen full of fun including a pitcher of delicious Kool-Aid. When I presented the spot to my creative directors and superiors they all said the same thing:

"We love it, it's a great spot. But what makes it inherently black?"

The fact that everyone liked the spot and understood it was irrelevant. What mattered most was that the spot had no blacks, (no people at all, for that matter), and the music wasn't hiphop or R&B; there was nothing overtly black about it. And because of that it was argued that Kool-Aid's general-market agency could've done this ad. And if general-market agencies can reach black consumers, then clients don't need to hire black agencies. And if clients don't hire black agencies, then black professionals have to look to general-market agencies for employment. And since general-market agencies still won't hire black professionals in any reasonable numbers, you as a black marketer are out of work.

So I went back to the drawing board and developed another spot—one that would be clearly Inherently Black. It was a nice "family reunion" spot filled with happy, well-spoken, well-dressed, mainstream-friendly black people drinking Kool-Aid and smiling about how good it made them feel. There were even some black people singing about Kool-Aid at the end. The client loved it, bought it, shot it and it aired a few months later.

"It's Your World."

I saw the other end of the "Uniquely Black" spectrum while working on AT&T at the same shop. For years AT&T was king, but deregulation, competition, etc., caused them to fall off a bit. Now they were just big, old, and stodgy. So one of my first assignments was to convince young black consumers that AT&T's online services, then known as Att.net, were the perfect remedy for all their online shopping needs. Now when you're dealing with a highly commoditized category like ISPs, you go for the intimate, emotional connection with your audience, you want to get at the heart of what drives people. That's your best shot at setting yourself apart from the pack...

So I got inside the minds and hearts of our target consumer. What I discovered was at the time for a huge segment of black Internet users, the Internet's greatest appeal as a shopping vehicle (outside of convenience and access, which everyone offered) is that it offers a sense of equality. No one can discriminate against you in cyberspace because they don't know what you look like unless you tell them. Anonymity is power for a lot of Internet users, especially minorities. Now this was very different from the brick and mortar shopping experiences many minority consumers still have where they can face racial profiling, unfair pricing, inferior customer service, etc. So I developed a campaign based on empowerment and freedom—things that everyone wants, but is particularly relevant to black shoppers.

The first TV spot featured a group of young black teenagers trying to shop in an upscale store. The security guard follows them... The store workers give them second-class treatment, etc. So in a moment of inspired frustration, they decide to go home and shop online using att.net. They get the products they want, it's a safe and secure transaction that leaves them feeling empowered, and they live happily ever after.

Everyone loved the spot. But it died. Why? Because while the campaign appealed to black and ethnic consumers, it made whites (including the client), uncomfortable. And in the end, even when the audience is black, you have to be concerned with what white people think.

So again, to keep all of this from happening out came the inherently black advertising and marketing—work that appealed to whites as much if not more so than blacks. This is why you see so many marketing schemes and entertainment properties still feature suspect imagery and themes. For all of our significant strides, black people still have to "prove" their blackness to non-black people in order to succeed.

Our whole relationship to success has become how well we fit into a scheme we have no control over and we have not designed.
—Elaine Brown, author/former Black Panther on Blacks in America's consumer culture

10% Diss

The worst part of working at a targeted agency is when the client uses the targeted agency's work without paying for it. I've watched it happen for a few years. The program is simple:

The targeted agency shows its work. The client picks a campaign or creative direction. Next they bring in their targeted agencies (Asian, Hispanic, black, etc.) to essentially translate and tailor the lead agency's work for their respective audiences. But sometimes the targeted agency comes back with work that's hipper, stronger, and more relevant than the GM agency's. (This is often confirmed when the client focus groups everything and the targeted work tests higher or the general-market work tests poorly.)

Oftentimes when this happens, the client and/or general-market agency mysteriously puts off moving forward in lieu of further brainstorming sessions. This is where the client and/or lead agency take the work, including the targeted shops' ideas off to rethink directions, etc. A little time goes by and next thing you know the lead agency has a campaign that's remarkably similar to what the targeted agency showed weeks back. And if the idea explodes, the lead agency gets all the praise while the targeted agency is rewarded with a couple extra table scraps. (Beat biters, dope-style takers...)

Top Billin'?

As I said earlier, agencies are ranked according to their account revenues aka "billings." Agencies tend to fall into categories like: large, small, mid-sized and boutiques. "Large" agencies tend to have annual billings over $1 billion, with many claiming revenues upwards of $3 billion a year. (There's about 15 such companies, most notably: JWT, Grey, FCB, Leo Burnett, DDB, O&M, BBDO, Y&R, Saatchi, and Deutsch.) Typically, the "mid-sized" shops, which there are dozens of, tend to do between $600–$900mil a year and vary by market. (Think: Kirshenbaum & Bond, Fallon McElligott, C&K, W&K, etc.) "Small" is often anything under $400 million, while those with "boutique" status tend to specialize in project work for random clients as opposed to having a stable roster of accounts. And once you factor in major holding companies such as: Omnicom, Publicis, WPP, Interpublic, Euro RSCG, etc. who have squadrons of agencies under their respective umbrellas, the figures get even crazier.

Now to give you a taste of the entrenched inequities in the game, at their absolute zenith the three biggest black ad shops in the country—Burrell Communications, Carol H. Williams and Uniworld, NYC—never bill more than a decent small-sized shop in any year. At best they're seeing about 10% of what the general market agencies are doing. And most of the remaining black agencies are literally struggling to survive from year to year.

Why? Simply put, despite the ever-diversifying consumer bases and seemingly plentiful opportunities, mainstream clients (who hold the biggest purse strings) have engaged in economic collusion for the last 100 years. General market clients still aren't willing to work with black marketing and ad professionals or shops enough to support the existence of more than a relative handful of black agencies. And when clients do work with them, they get peanuts and table scraps for budgets. Such is the by-product of the often-incestuous relationships, bias and old boys' club mentality that remains rampant throughout the industry.

Now here's how these cancerous mentalities impact bottom lines and consumers:

More than ratings or subscribers, the media business revolves around ad revenue. Marketers are the engine and steering wheel for most all media vehicles. High ad sales and sponsorship dollars allow one to reinvest in infrastructure, pay for top media talent and hot entertainment properties, etc. But when clients allocate crap media budgets to reaching black consumers, black radio stations, black magazines, and black TV programs suffer. Professionals at black media outlets can't make the kind of money their white counterparts make. Black media talent can't make what their white counterparts make. Black entertainment properties (TV and radio shows, etc.) can't charge what white entertainment properties charge. And of course black media companies can't grow like their mainstream counterparts can.

And again, general-market brands reserve their account billings for general-market agencies, while targeted agencies, be they black, Hispanic, Asian, etc., are rarely if ever even allowed to compete for general-market money. In fact, experts such as New California Media group noted in that while advertisers spent over $145 billion reaching U.S. consumers in 2004, less than 4% was spent with ethnic media.[4] And by all accounts this represents a spending increase from previous years.) Now combine that with the fact that ethnic media reaches over 40 million ethnic-Americans—in addition to its ever-increasing crossover appeal, which translates into literally tens of millions of mainstream viewers, listeners and readers and the industry's greed, hypocrisy, and bias becomes painfully clear.[5]

So besides trying to pull urban consumers on their own, general market agencies will form alliances with targeted shops when needed; then they (with the client's support/help) proceed to give them crumbs for accomplishing what would never get done any other way. But this would actually be okay except for a couple key factors:

One: Annually, blacks spend anestimated $723 billion on products and services, the overwhelming majority of which are controlled by non-black-owned businesses; and by 2009, blacks are expected to spend $965 billion supporting these businesses.[6] *Two:* Because of mainstream America's appetite for ethnic culture, most black media outlets and programming reaches far more white and mainstream consumers than general-market analysts ever admit to. (Let's be real: If you just took the number of mainstreamers who watch BET, read urban mags, and consume black music, fashion, and entertainment properties, you could start your own small country; round up non-black folks who do the same on a global scale and you could colonize the moon.) So while profiting off the black community from all sides, mainstream businesses continue to screw their black counterparts out of billions of dollars in deserved revenues and opportunities, not to mention respect. (And of course it's all perfectly legal, even ethical.)

Anyway, I felt like I had no choice but to play the game. I walked the color line and gave clients what they wanted. And they bought it, either because they didn't care or because they only cared about profits. The media outlets always ran with it because they got paid. And consumers—black, white, brown, and every hue in between bought it because blackness is product, not humanity. Yet as professionals who made the pie bigger, we never got more than crumbs and slivers our troubles. And save for a couple fresh wrinkles, the saga continues, same as it ever was.

I'm not a prostitute but I can give you want you want.
—Missy Elliott[7]

E.L.E. (Extraction Level Event)

Culturally speaking, "blackness" no longer belongs to black people. Thanks in no small part to corporate forces, specifically those within the marketing and advertising industries, blackness has been extracted, harvested, distilled and repackaged into a product for mass consumption. And for the most part, it's being bought, sold, defined, and produced with little or no involvement from blacks. If blackness were a government, blacks would be its figureheads with the real power held by others.

From what I've seen, blackness (be it music, dance, style, language, etc.) goes thru 7 stages of extraction. (1) What's that? Outsider recognition. (2) Oh, that's just some thing "they" do/are. *It* and those connected to *It* are marginalized and devalued. (3) Hmmm, *It* looks interesting—bet I can do *It*/use *It*. They covet. (4) This could be profitable for us. Then comes greed. (5) This isn't yours, it's "ours"—it's "universal." Then it's taken and redefined. (6) What happened? *It* was so much better back when <u>we</u> started it... *It* loses its cool cache as revisionist history sets in. (7) What's next? Back to the 'hood to see what else the natives are cooking up.

By most accounts, blackness is now dangling somewhere between stages 5 and 6. Business' job is to maintain level 5 as long as possible, because once stage 6 hits, it's a wrap. Blackness will get flipped into a VH1 special. And maybe, say 10 years from now, it'll become kitschy or retro hip and the same forces that wrecked it out the gate will return to start the cycle all over again.

I take your culture and sell it back to you!
—Danny Hoch[8]

Hiphop is easily the most prominent case of cultural extraction in modern history. In 2004, hiphop generated an estimated $10 billion in music, fashion, entertainment (movies, videogames, etc.), and other cross-marketing ventures.[9] In 2003, hiphop, R&B, and urban genres accounted for nearly 40% of all albums sold[10], generating some $1 billion in revenue, lead mainly by Eminem and 50 Cent.[11] According to leading estimates there are 45 million hiphop consumers between ages 13 and 34, 80% of whom are white.[12] And this group is believed to have as much as $1 trillion in spending power.[13]

Now let's go to the supply side of the equation: Over 96% of America's major radio stations, national magazines and TV stations are white-owned, while 100% of the major chain retailers and distributors (Wal-Mart, Best Buy, Tower, FYE, Virgin, Circuit City, Amazon, etc.) that carry black music are owned by whites and non-blacks. Lastly, let's factor in the still near-systemic lack of diversity on Wall Street, in Hollywood, and on Madison Ave, all whom create the images, ideas, brands, and perspectives that shape America's pop culture and consumer landscape. What you're left with is an environment where blackness, from look to style to content, is shaped mainly by mainstream marketers, manufacturers, and retailers catering to the tastes of primarily mainstream consumers.

In the beginning, hiphop was born of Black American, African, Caribbean, Hispanic, and indigenous tribal expressions (Capoiera, Griots, black poetry movement of the 1960s, work songs and Negro spirituals, etc.) just as Blues, Funk, R&B, Soul, Gospel, House, Jazz, and Rock & Roll were. But just as with generations past, cultural extraction cut, scratched, and cross-faded those art forms into predominantly "white" (Rock & Roll, Alternative, Punk) or "universal" (Jazz, Funk, Techno, Blues, et al.) ones. Why? Because in each instance mainstream America decided it preferred a version of blackness it could own and control. And everyone from consumers to artists to manufacturers to marketers saw the value in engineering that extraction. And so it began...

In the case of hiphop, "certain" black artists were abandoned in favor of less-threatening ones. Music labels strategically sought out "universal" black artists. Video channels and radio stations followed suit. Magazines, craving mainstream advertising dollars and readers, joined in. The FCC puts the screws to urban artists via indecency hearings, fines, etc. Hollywood and Madison Ave joined in by reflecting and promoting what mainstream consumers wanted to see from black life. Mainstreamers began making their own "black" music and bringing their version of blackness to bear. (In fact, long before Eminem antagonizingly noted, "I use black music to get myself wealthy," five white rappers from dubbed themselves *Young Black Teenagers* and successfully declared "Blackness is just a state of mind.") Certain black artists and industry insiders join in. Hustlers, culture pimps, and corporate whores got into the game. And before you knew it, blackness had become a product for mass consumption.

And now that hiphop and by extension blackness has become global youth culture, my generation has extended the perennially marketable and comforting myth of blackness as something you can experience your way into and control thru co-option, purchases, and majority rules. (It's like lite beer: *"BLACKNESS—ALL OF BLACK PEOPLE'S FLAVOR BUT WITH NONE OF THE CALORIES OR CARBS OF BLACK MELANIN AND STRUGGLE."*)

Again, don't sleep on the consumer angle of this story because despite the growing number of high-powered minorities, all are ultimately beholden to the same consumers and corporate entities. Consequently, many end up perpetuating stereotypes just to grow their businesses and careers.

From the Negro we take only the magical-liturgical bits,
and only the antithesis makes them interesting to us.
—Hugo Ball[14]

Another problem with cultural extraction is the way in which devalues people. Now I agree with scientists who note that skin color is inherently little more than a random genetic trait like eye color, hair color, or height. However, for Black Americans, our culture and heritage and history *were* our skin color. We have no specific ancestral homeland, save for a continent that's too big and too distant to claim; and any specific tribal affiliations and ancestral family trees we may have are so intertwined in slaveships and plantation lullabies that they're long gone. Consequently black skin remained part and parcel of our arts, style, music, language, history, and everything that made us whole.

But now that blackness, or at least the most desirable aspects of it, have been extracted and co-opted worldwide...black skin is the only thing black folks can truly claim as our own without dispute (along with certain race-specific stereotypes and slurs). For better or worse, black skin is slowly going the way of the appendix—a once-valuable but now-irrelevant appendage. Now combine this with the continued inequities in our society, and it's as if blacks are being stuffed and mounted like social taxidermy.

And for all the spreading of cultural art forms, the most dehumanizing marginalizing portraits of Black Americans remain the most popular with mainstream America. We still love street flava and ghetto soul. We love the loud, cursing, blacker-than-thou comic. We love the *dawg/playa/why-must-I-chase-the-cat/sex-machine* brothas. We love the thug. We love pimps. We love the athletic savant. We love "the magical Negro" stereotype. We love the sistahs who talk out their necks and floss much attitude. We love the baby-mammas. And we still love our blaxploitation flicks. And before that we loved the coonish, foot-shuffling minstrel shows. And before that we loved the slave/wild savage stereotypes... And with the various stereotypes the various bits of discrimination and marginalization and disenfranchisement have, in one form or another, continued on.

> *They say after 500,000, you're selling to a whole different realm.*
> *Now you're selling to young white boys. I think once the corporations understood that, that was their time to come in and take control of it.*
> *Once the control was taken away, then came all of the nonsense.*
> —*MC Lyte*[15]

Winter of Our Dissed Content

A major example of inherent blackness and culture as product is BET. BET began about 20 years ago focused on black viewers, a group largely ignored and underserved by mainstream marketers and media alike. For a time BET was Black America's only TV outlet for black humanity, creativity, and commercially viable entertainment. But in a desire to expand, BET has adopted a more universal strategy.

As network execs touted in April 2005, their goal is to make BET a network for all ethnicities, particularly those in the coveted 18–34 demographic, not just the African-American community.[16] The most obvious manifestation of this is BET's tagline. In the late 1990s BET phased out its once proud *BLACK ENTERTAINMENT TELEVISION* theme in favor of a hipper *BLACK STAR POWER.* In 2005, Black Star Power got flipped into even more universal *IT'S MY THING.* And with these changes have come more mainstream-friendly fare, more slapstick urban comedies and movies, fewer heritage-driven shows, and the cancellation of news and public affairs programming such as *BET Nightly News* and *Lead Story*, and of course an increased emphasis on near X-rated music videos and hiphop-related programming.

Still black activists, politicians, educators, and viewers alike have decried the downward trend in BET's programming. But as a business BET is more answerable to its shareholders and marketing partners than anyone else. And despite those complaints, founder Bob Johnson and current owner Viacom continues to push black stereotypes around the world. Why? Because BET's ever-expanding audience and overwhelmingly mainstream marketing partners cosign it—the more they dumb down, the more their audience and ad revenues grow. Such is The Hustle.

But BET is not alone in this. Before black consumers see a movie, a TV show, hear a radio show, buy an album, or read the latest mag, those vehicles must be pre-sold to distributors, retailers, and advertisers. And if those decision makers don't like it or don't think it will sell, then those "properties" as they're called, won't see the light of day.

Consequently, so-called "black radio" walks the same path with cookie-cutter mainstream-friendly play lists, general-market savvy on-air personalities, and often-degrading antics. More and more, black magazines are tailoring their content to appeal to mainstream advertisers and distributors as well as be more sensitive to the tastes of mainstream readers. And of course Hollywood tailors even its most urban movie and television properties in hopes of achieving crossover success. And while this hustle generates income from advertisers like my former clients, it continually hurts minority artists and communities by putting us all in little black boxes. But as BET and others have learned, The Hustle is too profitable to be knocked regardless of the cultural costs.

Everyone wants to talk about the number of African-American viewers and their spending power. Now is the time to put up or shut up. Bring the blue-chip advertisers and the powerful programming that does us right!
—Oscar Joyner, president of Reach Media.[17]

Welcome to the Ghetto Show

The worst part is how this complex mess has impacted generations of Black Americans. It has us seeing ourselves as products and believing that our cultures and heritages should be products as well. Our children grow up embracing these ghettofied constructs as legit realities. Even our adults are buying into it.

We accept athletics and entertainment over education as primary escape routes. We see our neighborhoods as traps to escape from rather than as communities to build up and maintain. We accept assimilation as progress. We become the thugs that kids from Italy to Sweden to Toronto want to see. We live the hustler-and-pimp lifestyles so entertaining to the TRL crowd. We remain fetishized as postmodern Mandingo studs and roughneck sex-machines so many still fantasize about. We accept "drug dealer," "stripper," and "babymamma" as valid occupations. We call ourselves (and each other) "gangsta," "nigga," "nigger," "bitch," "ho," "tip-drill," "cut-up," etc., for all sorts of reasons, mainly because it's expected of us and we've embraced those expectations as much as those who've put them on us.

We accept the broken families and abandoned kids. We accept the continual degradation of black women and marginalization of black men. We see prison and gangs like Jews see bar mitzvahs—as legit coming-of-age rituals. We accept the lies and omissions from the history books, schools, and media. We accept failing schools and failing attitudes about school. We accept black-on-black crime and an unjust judicial system for the same reason most of America accepts the constructs hoisted upon us: Black people are more product than human; and it's okay to miseducate, marginalize, co-opt, and disenfranchise product. After all, product is disposable and replaceable. Human beings are not.

You can also see the blackness-as-product mentality in the products we buy: Over-hyped rotgut liquors like Alizé. Hennessey. Hypnotiq. Courvoisier. Tanqueray. Crown Royal. Remy Martin. Belvedere. Cristal... We empty our wallets and stuff our closets with $200 button-ups, $150 sneakers and other overpriced fashions destined to be played-out within months. (Want to buy a used $300 throwback?) We push Escalades, Hummers, and luxury sedans like ghetto chariots while struggling to keep the tanks full. We cop the latest cellphone. We smoke weed (because as you know, "real niggas" smoke weed). We get jewelry—first dookey gold chains, then silver, then platinum, then diamonds, then colored diamonds... Next it'll be whatever Harry Winston, Jacob and The Iceman, De Beers, Kellwood Co., Condé Nast, Viacom, Allied Domecq, Clear Channel, and the other culture pimps want us chasing.

And guess what? We'll buy it. No matter what it is or how much it costs, we'll just pull up our pants, lean back, and buy it. Why? Because everyone knows that we won't be "black" until we do.

Career-wise, most black folks weigh career options in terms of what aspect of ourselves can we exploit along with our ability to live down to society's expectations of us. We become social bridges, doing whatever gets us over. We cheerlead token hires and liberal lip service as progress, because deep down inside we believe that's all we are worth. Consciously or subconsciously, we buy into the constructs, we name our price, and we continually sell ourselves short.

Now to be sure, some of us raise hell about this. We discuss the destructiveness. We decry the constructs and schemes and those who profit off of them at will. We fight—but only for a few days like it's the National Guard & Reserves. Then we fall back in line and go back to our 24/7 grind of acceptance and indifference. In short, we accept our positions and embrace the constructs. We actively participate in our own destruction. Like the overeater or the drug addict, black folks have become our own worst enemy.

I think most of us do so because as much as the constructs and stereotypes hurt, it still beats being ignored all together. Every human being craves acceptance. (Any who claim different are delusional, stuck in self-denial, or sociopaths.) And when blacks put on our gear, our attitudes and stand in our constructs we're "accepted." We are acknowledged and tolerated. As long as we continue self-destructing... As long as we remain willing footballs for politicians and businesses to kick around... As long as we keep giving away our soul, letting others define it, define us; control it, control us. As long as we don't challenge The Hustle, we are accepted.

Walkin' talkin' dead though we think we're living (black zombies)...
We just copycats following the system (black zombies)...
—*Nas*[18]

One Love? Multicultural Marketing

Multiculturalism. It's been a business buzzword since the late 1980s. Socially, it's the new Americana: Diverse hues and communities building on common ground. For business, multiculturalism is about fulfilling the shared desires of all consumers while tailoring brands with enough cultural relevance to simultaneously reach multiple communities.

But in reality, multiculturalism doesn't exist in America, at least not yet. True multiculturalism requires two factors: integration and equal footing among communities. And besides certain parts of New York, Florida, Texas, Louisiana, and California, most of America remains deeply segregated with many areas currently re-segregating. People are divided even further by income, religion, politics, etc. Consequently, everything most Americans learn about communities outside their own comes from the media and entertainment industries, neither of which are interested in telling the truth.

Now a certain amount of multiculturalism has been created by interracial and intercultural relationships, friendships, and alliances of varying types. But I'd say less than a fifth of such experiences have been based on respect, love, understanding, and community. I believe that most of our multiculturalism has come from generations of consuming ethnic cultures in commoditized forms (music, fashion, entertainment, slang, sex, etc.).

Again, the mechanisms and infrastructures thru which culture are shared (music, fashion, entertainment, politics, etc.) are controlled and defined by one group; so there is no balance of power between those spreading culture and those whose culture gets spread. Consequently, blackness isn't dictated by blacks any more than "Indians-as-mascots" was dictated by Native Americans, any more than Ricky Martin's or J. Lo's success was dictated by latinos, any more than *Lost in Translation*/*American Idol's* William Hung, *Harold and Kumar go to White Castle*/Asians as innately-tech-savvy-no-driving-bell-curve-breaking-kung-fu-kickers, etc., was dictated by Asians, any more than hula dancing for tourists is dictated by Native Hawaiians. Just as the conquerors write the history books, mainstream America defines its culture along with everyone else's.

We also have to recognize the role of social blowback. Consider this 2004 gem from Maryland's Governor Robert Ehrlich: "I reject the idea of multiculturalism. Once you get into this multicultural crap, this bunk, you run into a problem."[19] The governor was speaking out against bilingual education for Hispanics and minorities for whom English is a second language. Today, millions of Americans echo Ehrlich's sentiments that multiculturalism equals everyone speaks English, while accepting mostly white America's view of history, aesthetics, etc. And you can find their views being championed by the RNC, NRA, Minutemen, FNC, and others.

Steal my culture; try to make it yours (there they go)...
—Mos Def[20]

We also need to check the role social, economic, and political inequities play in multiculturalism. Over the years I've kicked it with many an athlete, dealer, club dancer, artist, etc. Most all of them had one thing in common: They believed that their current paths were their only way out. They believed that their bodies, their athleticism, their criminal enterprises, etc., were their only means of survival and escaping their environment.

Conversely, I've met thousands of mainstream folk who took more traditional routes. They were doctors, politicians, lawyers, factory workers, businesspeople, waitresses, etc. For all their varied struggles, the idea of taking seedier routes to survival never seemed necessary to them. Regardless of their socio-economic backgrounds, they all had a sense of hope that comes being accepted as "American" without the added cultural barriers most minorities face in order to be accepted as such.

So much of culture gets exploited because the people of those cultures believe that doing so is their best, if not only, means of survival/success and/or acceptance. They sell their artistry, not out of love or opportunity but out of survival. They sell their expressions because traditional job opportunities aren't available to them. They allow their histories and identities to be manipulated because it seems to be only way they'll be accepted by the larger society. When people believe their options are limited, they will consider the inconsiderable. They will put a price on the priceless and sell the unsellable. They will sell their bodies. They will sell drugs. They will sell their cultures. They will sell their souls.

Culture in its purest form is a combination of birthright, heritage, and communal expression. On its own, culture is hustle-free; it's in the blood of people and the people are in it, and together they decide where it goes and what forms it takes. So in order for a culture to become a hustle it must be controlled and commoditized. And for that to happen, the culture must either be extracted from the people or the people must marginalized until they are no longer accepted as the keepers/authorities of the culture. As those things occur, that culture can be co-opted and consumed. And that is what modern American multiculturalism is: Cultures being sliced and diced and packaged into marketable, controllable commodities for mass consumption—at a healthy profit for industry.

True multiculturalism is art and we don't paint pictures anymore; we just trace co-opted templates and fill in color-by-numbers imagery. And as long as America accepts the construct that culture doesn't exist until America discovers it or defines it and culture has no value until America puts a price on it, the Culture-as-Product hustle, which modern American multiculturalism is a byproduct of, will continue.

A race of people is like an individual man; until it uses its own talent,
takes pride in its own history, expresses its own culture,
affirms its own selfhood, it can never fulfill itself.
—Malcolm X[21]

Comin' Straight Outta LoCash!

In an arena where culture is currency, commodity, and industry, fighting to make it anything else can be career suicide. When confronted by the machine, you either roll with it or get rolled on. You can defy clients and bosses and argue with consumers and coworkers, but in the end it's like bringing a garden hose to a forest blaze. Plus, no company will tolerate that behavior for very long. And beyond standing on corners with a bullhorn screaming about culture vultures, Willie Lynch-isms, etc., you won't have much of a social life, either.

Then again, you could just accept the game and get paid. I think that's why I stayed as long as I did. I know marketing. I can sell any product or service to any consumer. I can sell clouds to the sun, if need be. And like most every black professional that came before me I told myself, *Why not do what I'm good at? If I don't someone else will.*

And to be honest, having clients and coworkers come to me for insights into my heritage and culture was sort of an ego trip. No matter how much research they did, no matter how many "black friends" they had, I always knew more than them. I lived what they focus grouped. I brought added value. It made me feel important and respected. After a while, I even felt, ick, *validated.*

See, America makes you an opportunist and at
the same time they institutionalize you.
So the fact that niggas get big record deals,
big money and then go to jail shouldn't surprise you—
that's what lies do.
—Black Ice, 410 Days in The Life[22]

My journey often got me thinking about the marketing pioneers that inspired me, folks like: Madame CJ Walker, Oprah Winfrey, and Russell Simmons. In the 1920s Walker became America's first black female millionaire. But she built much of her cosmetics empire by reinforcing Anglo-European standards of beauty and sophistication to market hair-straightening products and bleaching creams to black women. (Yet despite her millions, her race left her with few if any, protected civil rights.)

Then there's the godfather of hiphop. "Hustle" Simmons (as he's known to some) has flipped the urban lifestyle into a gazillion-dollar global empire encompassing everything from music and fashion (Def Jam, Baby Phat/Phat Farm) to Broadway and movies (*Def Poetry, SLMG*) to credit cards (UniRush Financial). But as much as I admire Russell and other hiphop moguls (i.e., Shawn Carter, Sean Combs, etc.), I often ask myself, *Just what have we sold?*

Oprah Winfrey is of course our first black female billionaire and the only American female to achieve such without inheritance or marriage. She made hers thru hard work, innovation, and dedication. But she's become one of the most powerful brands in the world, by catering to the largest consumer group possible: white women. I'm not saying she sold out, but as thousands upon thousands of women of color have noted over the years, "Oprah doesn't talk to us (black women); she's for white women."

I've met countless black women who feel so disconnected from and more importantly alienated by Oprah. They talk about her show's focus on soccermoms, desperate housewives, etc. They talk about how out of touch she seems to be with average black women but seems so at home with average white women... As a male, her show isn't really marketed toward me, so I'm no authority on this one way or the other; but after watching my fair share of *Oprah* over the years, I can see their point.

Maybe it's progress. Then again Oprah could just be a hustler who sees the game so well that she's simply pimping soccermom narcissism and white liberal myopia/boredom, etc., to create a branded, mass-marketable illusion of postmodern Americana paradise. But whatever the case, Oprah's a grown woman; she be what she be. Besides, she has over a billion more opportunities to leave the world better than she found it.

Conversely, black power-hitters like Tom Burrell (founder Burrell Communications) Carol H. Williams (founder CHW Advertising), Stanley O'Neal (Merrill Lynch CEO), Dick Parsons (Time Warner CEO), Ann Fudge (former Young & Rubicam CEO), Ken Chenault (American Express CEO), Renetta McCann (Starcom North America CEO), Earl G. Graves, Sr. (Black Enterprise, Inc. Chairman/CEO), John Thompson (Symantec CEO), et al., have climbed their respective mountains without compromising a thing. So it would be foolish to say that the only way minorities can succeed in business is to sacrifice their soul.

Still, much of my career had me asking some admittedly stupid but plausible questions: *Should minorities only work for minority companies? Should minority companies only cater to minority consumers? Should black consumers "buy black" no matter what?* After all, if you have a dollar and lose 12 or 15 cents, you're not ruined; but if you lose 87 cents (the equivalent of non-Black America) you might as well get a whole new dollar. And who's to say you won't get clowned by your own folk? (God knows we've been as trifling as any.) Or do you just suck it up and work for whoever'll hire you and sell whatever's in demand to whoever wants it?

I dunno. Again, I know those are stupid questions, but what we've done so far hasn't been smart, either. If Debra Dickerson was right when she wrote about the mind being the last plantation, the marketing world has taught me one thing: As it relates to culture and business, black folks still haven't risen much above sharecropping.

I'm just trying to make a dollar out of what makes sense.
—Mos Def[23]

The Construct of Whiteness

Booker T. Washington once said, "You can't hold a man down without staying down with him." Therefore, it's impossible to discuss culture as product in America without looking at the impact it has white people. Business has taught me that the hardest thing to be in America is you and not even white people are immune to this struggle. The social cliques I mentioned upfront (Charmins, Potatoes, etc.) were folks who bought into the construct of whiteness. America's full of 'em. From birth they're taught to chase, embrace, and perpetuate this weirdly romanticized, almost-fetishized, ideal of Anglophile humanity.

Throughout my academic and corporate career, I knew tons of people who bought into it. It's like they were ashamed of being ethnically or culturally different. They did everything they could to fit in. I worked with folks who were Jewish or Irish, but never at the expense of being white. Others were Italian, Polish, or Greek, but never at the expense of being white. Others still were Arab, Chinese, Russian, French, Mexican, Korean, etc... No matter what their heritage, nationality, or ancestry was, it always took a backseat to embracing this ever-softening soul-draining cocoon of homogenized whiteness. It was their standard for all things good and human; and they worshipped it like a god. It was some type of self-imposed post-modern eugenics experiment.

And as is with most constructs, I realized that with whiteness comes stereotypes, self-hatred, narcissism and neurosis, fear 'n' loathing, and most importantly, the near-endless consumption opportunities businesses live for: The endless hair and makeup products for achieving that idealized look of "white" beauty. The fashions tailored to accentuate the perfectly "white" body. The foods, music, media, and entertainment properties developed to feed and nurture those perfectly "white" cultural sensibilities. And on a grander scale, there are the politics, histories, religions, and laws designed to protect, reward, foster, and spread the perfectly "white" set of values, beliefs, social paradigms, etc. And may a semi-Judeo, very-Anglo-Western-manifest-destiny-loving-God help you if you see things any differently.

The result has been generations of Americans constantly hustled into chasing this falsely constructed white reality. And since we're all connected, everyone—black, white, Asian, Hispanic, native, immigrant, indigenous, foreign, etc., is, to one degree or another, affected by it. Those who buy into whiteness reap the rewards of white-skin privilege. But the rest, who are too dark, too ethnic, or simply too stubborn to accept it, get criticized and marginalized. But for The Hustle, whiteness equals power, profit, opportunity, obedience, and control. It has since day one.

(And as I noted in "Gatekeepers," this construct has to be an inside job. The folks best equipped to solve it are those who've benefited the most from it. At some point, all those who see themselves as "white" need to lead the charge for solutions.)

...There were no "white" people in Europe until 1492.
With the transatlantic slave trade—first Indian,
then African—Europeans increasingly saw "white"
as a race and race as an important human characteristic.
—Prof. James W. Loewen[23]

All Soul'd Out: Blacklash

Every successful product launch or trend has consequences. And in today's global economy blackness has gone worldwide:

Chinese kids are trading in mandarin for E-40 slang. Japanese kids have locked and twisted their hair and become turntablists. French and Italian girls have traded their couture for BabyPhat, Sean John, Ecko, etc. White girls from Boston to Belgium to Borneo now have ghetto booties. Maori, Aborigine, and even Native American kids are embracing black street culture as their own leaving their ancestors' cultures to fade away. I've heard drunken Irish kids call themselves "The Blacks of Europe." Young Cuban, Portuguese, Brazilians, and Philippinos are B-boying and graf-writing while their indigenous traditions atrophy from neglect. African kids from Algeria to Kenya to Mozambique quote Tupac, BIG, Nas, and Jay-Z bar for bar while slowly forgetting their native tongues. Everyone from Paris Hilton and Prince William to the average suburbanite has rocked cornrows and dreadlocks, while most all black hair styles have been reduced to costume-party accessories and visual punchlines. Whole generations of UKers, Russians, and Germans have grown up crip-walking, twerking, jooking, Harlem-shaking, poppin' collars, and getting crunk. Middle-Eastern kids from Afghanistan to Israel to Jordan "rep their 'hoods." "Ghetto" and "thug" have become global euphemisms for all things Black American while "nigger" remains among the most popular words in the world. And regardless of culture or heritage, many under-35 speak in occasional blackcents just for fun... All around the world it's the same song.

But what happens when the party's over? What happens once these consumers get older, get bored, or start hungering for more substance, such as knowledge of the cultures their parents and grandparents tried to pass down? What happens once they realize everything they've sacrificed in order to consume blackness? What happens when they want to undo the damage? My guess:

Blacklash.

As many have noted, there is indeed a culture war brewing; and blackness is slowly joining terrorism, free speech, and family values as an important battleground. Much of our current culture war is being driven by a growing desire to protect what many see as "traditional Western values" against what is, in their minds, the corruptive influence of minority cultures.

Of course, few openly call themselves "anti-minority" as that would be overtly racist. But their actions and words are proving otherwise. In recent years, culture critics, both liberal and conservative, have begun blasting urban music, art, fashion, and political views like never before. And on a seemingly weekly basis, major media outlets run stories linking black music to violence, crime, misogyny, STDs, and general societal decay. Affirmative Action and Mexican immigration are attacked on an almost hourly basis... But things are just warming up.

I predict that by 2010 blacklash will drop minority celebrities to second-tier status in terms of marketability and perceived artistic merit. Brands and products traditionally recognized as urban will become significantly less popular with mainstream consumers. And slowly, blackness will cease to be cool among many mainstreamers.

Keep in mind, at some point markets usually get saturated, consumers get bored, annoyed or outraged, and backlash follows. Every wildly successful brand/phenomenon feels it. Barney the Dinosaur, Acid-wash jeans, J. Lo, boy bands, and '80s hair bands all felt it. Hit shows like *Beverly Hills 90210* felt it; Reality TV is feeling it. The fast-food and tobacco industries are feeling it. And as a product, black culture's turn is coming, too.

However, the difference will be the extent and severity of the backlash. First off, black culture has been consumed by the greater society like nothing before. For that reason alone, the impending reaction against it may be at least as widespread. Secondly, let's consider similar cultural phenomena of the past: grunge, the yuppie materialism of the 1980s, the psychedelic counter-culture of the '60s, the sexual revolution and the women's movement of the 1970s... The leaders and most vocal participants and supporters of those products were primarily white and mainstream. And not surprisingly, the backlash always had palpable undertones of paternal disappointment and "How-could-you-do-this-you're-one-of-us?" frustration. There were also consistent undertones of *IF YOU CHANGE BACK, WE'LL TAKE YOU BACK.*

But since the faces of hiphop, blackness, and immigration, are people of color or those mimicking people of color, the blowback may well be meaner, more visceral, and less compassionate. Also, the undertones previously present may not exist for obvious reasons.

For an already well-documented history of American blacklash, look no further than the music world: From the late 1890s thru the early 1930s much of Jazz, Blues and later Rhythm and Blues were marginalized as "race music" and "nigger music." The longstanding belief was the masses of white Americans needed protecting from the corruptive powers of black music and black culture. It wasn't until Jewish, Italian and other non-black musicians began playing Jazz and blues did those art forms become more acceptable and harder to marginalize.

Also, much of the backlash against early Rock & Roll was rooted in racism; the biggest often slurs levied against such artists as Elvis, Jerry Lee Lewis, The Beatles was that they were race-traitors for bringing a version of the blues and soul to white audiences.

And whether it was made by the Bee Gees, Donna Summers, or ABBA, historians agree that the crux of Disco music was "black dance music for the masses" and the backlash against disco in was rooted largely in racism and of course, homophobia given the rising AIDS epidemic of the early 1980s.

And then there was NippleGate 2004. Despite the fact that MTV produced the Super Bowl halftime show; despite the fact that fellow acts Kid Rock and Aerosmith had misogynistic lyrics and behavior, etc.; despite the fact that Mark Roberts jumped onto the field, stripped down to a G-string and danced an Irish jig and moonwalked in the 3rd-quarter stunt he promoted in advance on his website; and despite the fact that Justin Timberlake ripped Jackson's top off prior to singing the lyrics, "...Gonna have you naked by the end of this song"—only Janet Jackson and the black artists were blamed for the fiasco. The NFL responded in 2005's Super Bowl with a virtually all-white broadcast and halftime show featuring ex-Beatle Paul McCartney and his all-white band. That's what you call blacklash.

Here are a couple more recent examples of blacklash:

Blackwatch.

In recent years, millions have begun rising up against one of Black America's biggest allies—affirmative action—calling it "anti-white racism," "reverse discrimination," and "pandering to special interests."

Since 2002, college students such as those at Roger Williams University (RI) have protested affirmative action by offering "Whites-Only" scholarships.[24] On dozens of other campuses including USC, SMU, UC Berkley, University of Washington, Northwestern University, and UCLA, students and faculty have protested by holding bake sales in which black and Hispanic students receive cookies at deep discounts or for free (symbolizing AA) while white and Asian students are either wildly overcharged or turned away (to fund the minority discounts).[26] And in 2004, the student groups at Texas A&M offered $1,500–$5,000 scholarships to students for the best essays on "overcoming affirmative action."[27] Other campuses have seen more traditional protests such as boycotts and anti-AA op-eds in campus newspapers.

Then there's the flood of lawsuits such as 2003's precedent-setting "reverse discrimination" case against the U. of Michigan where plaintiffs claimed it was unconstitutional that black students were being admitted ahead of whites, despite having lower SATs and grades, simply because of their race. However they expressed no outrage over white students being given preference over other whites based on class, legacy, etc. And when over 1,400 white students were admitted ahead of the U. of M. plaintiffs, despite having lower scores and/or grades, there was zero outrage from the plaintiffs.[28] Also there has been little or no outrage over government and private-sector estimates that around 90% of all college scholarship money (public and private) actually goes to whites, not minorities of color.[29] There also is little outrage over the spiraling costs of higher learning, which comes courtesy of the mostly white elites who run the schools. This, as much as any preference programs, is why all students are struggling to afford a college education.

> *The emphasis is on the white skin... If you are white, you are entitled to privilege. The fact of the matter is people feel white skin makes you better and black skin*

makes you inferior... In the beginning, that was enforced by the state and the federal government... But 50 years after Brown, you'd think segregation would be a little less prevalent in education than it is... Black children aren't getting equal education in the cities...
—Judge Robert L. Carter, chief architect and litigator, Brown v. Board of Ed. (1954)[30]

"Blow it out your..."

Bill O'Reilly. *Fox News.* (Nuf said.)

"I'll be that..."

In late 2003 when songs featuring Eminem calling black women "black bitches," "gold diggers," and "niggers," were unearthed, Em's fans along with MTV, *Rolling Stone, Spin,* etc., supported him noting that blacks have used similar language for years therefore whites should get a pass. Despite outrage from many blacks, the story died. (This was a stark contrast in reaction to when Eminem's angry lyrics were perceived to have been aimed at white women. In those instances, his lyrics became the subject of national debate and was even boycotted such orgs as GLAAD, N.O.W., and the ADL.)

In another show of indifference, Fat Joe (who is Puerto Rican and Cuban) dropped 2004's summer jam "Lean Back," which featured the chorus: "My niggas don't dance, they just pull up they pants and do the Roc-A-Way..." The song made Mr. Cook Crack the second non-black artist in any genre to score a To-40 hit using any version of "nigger." (Jennifer Lopez was the first, having sung "nigga" on 2001's "I'm Real" remix.)

"Deep Cover."

Blacklash has long-infected our nation's law enforcement arena: In addition to the continuous racial profiling, inequitable sentencing laws, etc., various law enforcement groups have begun investigating urban artists based largely on their lyrics and images. In April 2004, the *Village Voice* revealed the existence of a hiphop intel and surveillance unit within the New York Police Department.[31] There have also been reports of similar units and investigations being conducted not only by police departments in Miami, L.A., and Atlanta, but also by the FBI. While officials claim that these groups solely investigate criminal organizations and activities, they've been roundly criticized as being fronts for racial profiling and government-sponsored Cointelpro operations.

Contrast this with the lack of profiling and investigations against mainstream artists for their countless violent lyrics and suspect affiliations, and the blacklash becomes crystal clear. And while prominent artists like G-Unit's Young Buck, Beanie Siegel, Mystikal, R. Kelly, C-Murder, etc., have indeed committed crimes these select individuals are being used as proof that Black music is a breeding ground for criminal and morally destructive behavior.

"Negroes Being Athletic"

There are 2 seldom-discussed truths about the NBA: (1) Like most all major American sports, the NBA's core audience—one who buys memorabilia, season tickets, fills skyboxes, satellite packages, etc. is 25–49 year-old white males. Has been for some time. (2) The NBA has struggled to maintain its core audience ever since stars like Bird, Magic, Jordan, and Barkley retired.

Why?

When asked for specifics fans, critics, and sportswriters cite bloated salaries, egos, and rampant unprofessionalism. Many complain about the streetball and hiphop "influences." Others have come right out and called the NBA "too-ghetto" and "too-street." And most importantly, their sentiments have been reflected in slumping ad revenues and TV ratings.

And like any business, the NBA owners have responded, mainly by outsourcing. Since the early 1990s, NBA teams have scoured the globe for more fan-friendly talent. And since 1992's Dream Team, the NBA has marketed itself as a universal brand (*Read:* more international, less urban). Besides creating generations of foreign talent who view the NBA as a career, foreign consumers now see the NBA as a global entertainment brand.

Today, the NBA is steadily being gentrified with foreign talent from China, Germany, Russia, Brazil, Canada, and all points in between. And while home-growns such as LeBron, Shaq, T-Mac, and KG are stars, the NBA is hyping its foreign players like never before. Players such as Yao Ming (China), Dirk Nowitzki (Germany), Peja Stojakovich (Yugoslavia), Tony Parker (France), Steve Nash (Canada), and others are being pushed not only as superstars but also as "league ambassadors" because of their "good character." And while the skills of the international players have mostly been undeniable, their paler skins and decidedly non-ghetto personalities haven't been lost on fans or marketers.

Besides their obvious talents, the foreign-import hype machine is driven in no small part by the NBA's failure to find domestic heirs to Bird's throne. And while Bird deservedly ranks as one of the top 3 players of all time, many insiders have admitted that a significant part of Bird's appeal was his skin color. As a result, Bird more so than Magic Johnson was hailed as having saved the NBA in the 1980s (apparently from its black players).

Over the years, the NBA has tried to manufacture a new Larry Legend by hyping the likes of Toni Kukoc, Christian Laettner, Sarunas Marciulionis, Vlade Divac, Danny Ferry, Keith Van Horn, Jason "White Chocolate" Williams, Wally Szczerbiak, Brent Barry, Detlef Schrempf, Tom Gugliotta, Bobby Hurley, etc. And before them, there was endless and completely unnecessary white-hype of legitimate NBA greats such as John Stockton, Chris Mullin, Jeff Hornacek, Tom Chambers, etc. Such is the nature of blacklash.

Still, David Stern and NBA execs consistently swear that race plays no role whatsoever in marketing or evolving Dr. Naismith's game. Noted cultural and sports psychologist, Dr. Harry Edwards agrees (sorta): "The race thing right now is incidental to economics... The game has always changed due to market forces. They brought in the Harlem Globetrotter style of play when the game got stagnant in the '50s and '60s. They did the same thing when they emphasized Magic Johnson and Larry Bird and Michael Jordan. Their (The NBA's) latest capitalistic ploy is globalization...the style of play has been changed to accommodate the market."[32]

However, in a 2004 ESPN interview, Larry Bird said the league needed more white superstars in order to maintain its white American fanbase.[33] And Bird's not the first to say this. In 2001, professor Mark Kanazawa (of Carleton College in Minnesota) and Jonas Funk, a financial analyst in San Francisco, published a study in the *Journal of Economic Inquiry* that examined what effect white players have on Nielsen ratings. Using a complicated formula and terms like "heteroskedasticity"—which took into account a team's record, number of all-stars playing, whether the white players were on the court or benchwarmers—Kanazawa and Funk came to the conclusion that each white player on a team increased ratings by 0.54 of a point. That would increase the number of households watching by 3,500 to 36,200 for each white player, depending on market size.[34]

Also consider that in 2002 the NBA switched its TV contract from NBC to Disney (ABC, ESPN, and TNT) meaning that very few regular-season or playoff games are shown on network TV. So what's the big deal? Well, according to most entertainment industry sources minority households still have significantly less access to cable than whites.[35]

NBA blacklash may be more about money than race but one thing's clear: With each draft, the NBA grows more international, paler, and less black. By 1995, NBA rosters were over 82% black. By 2001, that was down to 78%.[36] And with high schoolers flooding the draft each year, college programs are recruiting foreign players like never before, further lightening the college game and by default the pro game. As these trends continue (currently the NBA is 75% black and lightening), black NBA players (like black baseball players) will become, for lack of a better term, minorities, within the next 10–15 years. But as long as the cream flows, the NBA and others will spin it as "progress."

But according to Dr. Edwards, progress ain't cheap: "The NBA is a uniquely American institution, and a black institution as well. It's the equivalent of jazz. For many years, jazz tried to get away from its roots, to bring in a larger audience. As a result, jazz is now a marginalized music form. When you change the style of music, there are consequences, so I caution the NBA to think of what style they are changing the game into."[37]

In the end, data can be flipped and events can be spun to reflect whatever opinion or stance folks are comfortable with, but you can't hide the truth, especially when it's right there in (decreasingly) black and (increasingly) white.

The NBA's ratings and attendance are down.
The white audience doesn't like to see a bunch of guys
with tattoos and cornrows who get in trouble all the time.
Anyone who doesn't believe that, they're stupid.
—Charles Barkley[38]

Killa Cos from Outer Space.

Not since Dr. C. Dolores Tucker, Dionne Warwick, and friends ripped hiphop in the early 1990s has a black celebrity wilded out like Bill Cosby's *"Blame the Black Poor"* tour of '04–'05. Now in case you missed it, the legendary entertainer spent several months, starting with the 50th anniversary of *Brown v. Board of Ed.*, verbally swinging on lower-middle class and poorer blacks for embracing street slang over proper English, poor parenting, foolish consumerism, crime, etc. And not surprisingly, many mainstreamers are still using Cosby's remarks as "I-told-you-so" ammo in their own blacklash campaigns.

Truthfully, much of Cosby's comments boil down to personal responsibility and self-reliance—messages that everyone from Marcus Garvey to Farrakhan to Malcolm X to my parents have preached for generations. But once again, we only mention personal responsibility when it's someone else's. And this is precisely what puts Cosby's remarks in the blacklash category.

Watch for The Hook

As the blacklash reaches a tipping point, people may take sides. Companies may be asked to choose between urban and mainstream identities and consumers. Many companies may begin de-emphasizing diversity initiatives in favor of colorblindness. Ethnicity-based affirmative action may be eroded while anti-immigration sentiments will grow.

Musically, look for artists who've long trafficked in blue-eyed soul, hiphop, R&B, etc. to strategically embrace more mainstream sounds. (We've already seeing an explosion in rock, alternative, and Latin genres.) Expect Hollywood to focus more on middle-America and less on urban-America. Expect fashion designers to ditch street influences for haute couture and more traditional styles. Expect politicians to re-energize their base by targeting NASCAR Dads, Soccermoms, Heartlanders, Boomers and aging Gen-Xers...

Lastly, as I touched on earlier, blackness has reached a global scale. And in countries with high levels of anti-Americanism, many link much of what they hate/fear about America with black-American culture. American companies may face blacklash from foreign consumers and businesses looking to protect their own cultures and communities from negative Western influences" (i.e., blackness).

Now I'm not saying that global or even widespread domestic blacklash are 100% certainties, but don't bet against it.

People are always talking about the influence the Negroes had on me.
What about it? We all loved the fetishes.
Van Gogh said his generation had Japanese art—
we have the Negroes.
—Pablo Picasso[39]

Radio stations, you may begin your fade here...

To me, culture as Product remains the most compelling business case study in 50 years. To one degree or another it touches every industry imaginable. Combine that with our changing consumer base: By the year 2040, if not much sooner, there'll be about 420 million Americans, over half of whom will be non-white; however blacks will still only be about 15% of the population.[40] So we'll be looking at dozens, if not hundreds of ethnicities and cultures trying to coexist and consume within one country. And with business's desire for profit and competition rising, culture and commerce will be conjoined twins for life. Juju and Les said it best: "There's no escpain' this."

Folks, there is a fork in the road and I can hear The Hustle's stomach grumbling. Now we'll either end up with a nice cultural gumbo that'll feed everyone equally or we're headed for a major food fight. But in the meantime, the first company to find the balance will get rich enough to print their own money. They'll also become the keepers of American (and possibly global) culture for generations to come. I once saw this quote on a museum wall; it hung like a warning, felt like graffiti:

> "There is this scandalous allegation of peoples without culture. While it is true that those who were really responsible for colonization knowingly fabricated this myth, it is nonetheless surprising that generations of cultural and spiritual authorities have conceded that men could live in a community and have no culture. There is no people without culture. But what is often lost sight of is the quite natural link, which I am bound to mention for the sake of frankness, between the political and the cultural."
>
> —Alioune Diop[41]

Also, culture as product isn't just about black folks; it's about all people. I focused on the black community because I'm black and I know that experience. I'm not qualified to speak on any community other than my own; but I know that every ethnic group goes thru this on one level or another.

Culture as product runs deeper than this book or even hiphop. Culture as product is just one step removed from people as product. When we commoditize a people's culture, we commoditize their souls. When we devalue and marginalize people, we'll do anything to them including discriminate, terrorize, imprison, wage war against, etc. Culture as product goes hand-in-hand with discrimination, greed, hate, geo-political strife, etc.

Again, if you commoditize a people long enough, you stop seeing them as people and start seeing them as things. And again, commodities are disposable and replaceable.

Of course, culture as product isn't the sole cause of our social ills, but I believe it's a major player in the game. In our global village of technology, multinationals and everything's-a-marketing opportunity, culture as product helps box people into demographics and consumers and "we" into "us" vs. "them." It's all tied into humanity, or inhumanity as the case may be.

Point is, we better figure this out and soon; not for the sake of commerce but for the sake of people. All people.

There is no people without culture.

Youth Marketing
Who Sold Out Our Kids?

What's wrong with our future?
—Heavy D

I have a younger brother, some nieces and nephews, too. While spending nights and weekends warning them against materialism, I spent my days developing marketing campaigns to convince masses (often not much older than them) that a $70,000 German automobile (with American parts, Asian and Mexican labor) is the ultimate status symbol. Upfront I touched on the amount of weight I gained mainly due to my sedentary corporate lifestyle. Maybe it was deserved given that I spent some time convincing young adults that McWings were a valid in-between meal snack. I had no cavities up until I was about 22, but after the last few years you can just call me "Yuckmouth". And maybe it's poetic justice, given that I spent that same stretch attaching coolness to everything from Wrigley's Gum to Sprite. Looking back, I was quite the little pied piper.

Under the umbrella of Youth Marketing, I gave kids what they wanted while conditioning them to want, not what they needed, but to want what I needed to sell them. Through the images and ideas I crafted for cars, soft drinks, fast foods, etc., I encouraged behaviors in youth that I now criticize and despise. And now that I'm older, I'm starting to see the fruits of the seeds I helped sow.

It's hard for me to solely blame teens for seeing war and violence as a videogame when we've made war and violence X-Box-, SEGA-, and PS2-

compatible, not to mention the theme of countless summer blockbusters, music videos, TV shows, and CDs. I can't even complain about rampant teen sex, pregnancy, and STDs given that sex sells everything under the sun. It's hard to be surprised that so many young women are cock-teasers when my adult colleagues push misses thongs, low-rider jeans, and stripper-inspired fashions while touting ho-ish entertainers as role models. I can't complain about teenage alcoholism and binge-drinking when our liquor companies sponsor Spring Break, sporting events, and covertly target the under-age drinkers nationwide.

We bombard them with Reality TV, and then wonder why teens think humiliating themselves and/or each other is a fair trade-off for 15 minutes of fame. I'm not surprised that kids don't respect adults when most every movie and TV show on MTV, Nickelodeon, Disney, etc., pigeonholes those over-50 as un-hip, gullible fools who serve no purpose other than to give kids something to rebel against and outsmart. I can't complain about youth putting athletes and entertainers on pedestals when we as adults keep building pedestals and idols for them to worship. We covet the dollars and loyalty of the 13–17 and 18–34 crowds so much that we'll do whatever it takes to be their friend, regardless of the lessons our actions teach them.

Riddle me this: How many 12-year-old CEOs do you know? How many 14-year-old network or studio executives are pulling strings behind the scenes? How many 16-year-olds are running major record labels or serving as A&Rs? How many teenagers are running radio stations and video channels? How many 24-year-olds are running retail chains? How many 17-year-olds control multi-million dollar marketing budgets or develop ad campaigns? That's all us adults, folks.

Mommy may tell her little Lisa it's okay to be an A-cup with acne, but we sure as hell won't—not while we've got overpriced cosmetics, plastic surgeries, and disposable fashions to sell her on. We won't tell her she doesn't have to look like a model—not while we have *Seventeen, Marie Claire, Lucky! Jane, Cosmo*, etc., subscriptions to fill. We won't tell boys it's okay to be awkward and skinny or a little chubby as long as we've got steroids, diet pills, and workout gear to push. We won't teach our kids to value and respect culture, heritage, and individuality over mass-marketed styles as long as we have airtime to fill and product to push. It's called Youth Marketing. Not "youth development," but Youth Marketing. We're about selling stuff to kids. Period.

Adults are supposed to be society's leaders. But we're too busy chasing cream, brand loyalty, power, and satisfying our own selfish needs to lead properly. And don't tell me "It's the parents' responsibility." Marketing's ultimate goal is to shape consumers' values and judgment to induce purchase (ideally repeat purchase) and brand loyalty. And if it comes down to morality and values vs. brand loyalty and profits, marketing's mission is to kick values' teeth down morality's throat. We can't complain about what kids do, think, want, or become without looking in the mirror first. We are their pied pipers; we led them down the roads we despise. This is the truth of The Hustle.

Sure, I know every generation pushes and craves. But adults are supposed to push back, guide, and say "No." But we don't. Not anymore. And today's teens are so on to us that they don't care, either. They've seen the little man behind the curtain and they know it's us. About 30 years ago, marketing pioneer Bill Bernbach warned us it would happen when he noted: "There is indeed a 12-year-old mentality in this country—every 6-year-old has one."

I'm sick of adults throwing their hands up on this one like the root causes are some sort of cosmic mystery or glitch in our DNA. We can't do everything in our power to influence youth for-profit then claim we have no influence over them once something or someone goes wrong. Young consumers and consumers in general aren't blind sheep born to be fleeced, but adults are the shepherds. When they do get fleeced, we are responsible. (But again, we only talk about "personal responsibility" when it's someone else's.)

Until the rise of American advertising,
it never occurred to anyone anywhere in the world
that the teenager was a captive in a hostile world of adults.
—Gore Vidal[1]

In the end, the question remains: "If not me, then who?" Back in the day, Hilary Clinton bit an old African proverb—"*IT TAKES A VILLAGE TO RAISE A CHILD*"—for one of her goofy books. But in typical white liberal fashion, she missed the point. It's not that you need a village to raise a child as much as the fact that the village will raise your child, with or without you.

Kids don't grow up in vacuums. Maw 'n' Paw Kettle can teach Junior right and wrong, make him memorize the Bible, the Qu'ran, the Torah, and do life-affirming chants until the cows come home. But once he goes outside, junior belongs to the village. Soon as your little princess turns on the TV, radio, or logs-on, the village starts teaching. As far as the world is concerned, you must learn and class is always in session. So if the village is foul, your kid will be foul. And to all those "Oh-not-my-child" parents: *YES, YOUR KID, TOO.*

People do what they see, what they're told, what they're shown, and most of all, what they can get away with. That's just how human beings learn. If it was stupid when Charles Barkley said, "I am not a role model," then it's also stupid for every businessperson to pull the same card. (And don't forget, Mr. Round Mound was pushing Nikes when he said that.)

I think a big reason many kids still feel Tupac so many years after his death is because 'Pac knew most adults, especially those in business, government, and entertainment were full of crap. 'Pac once said (either while on his way to jail or on his way out) that he was America's child and America helped make him what he was. He even summarized this philosophy in a popular acronym: *THUG LIFE: "THE HATE U GAVE LITTLE INNOCENTS F***S EVERYBODY."* He was more honest about his flaws than his critics were about theirs. We felt that. And when kids see how most adults roll today, it's no wonder they still feel it.

Young people don't care much about politics because they see that most politicians don't care enough about government to run it honestly. Kids don't care much about school because they know that most of the adults running the schools keep running them into the ground. Youth listen to us condemn gang violence only to form bigger gangs so we can fight arbitrary wars and hunt down folks we don't like. They hear adults complain about rampant teen drug use, sex, and pregnancy only to rationalize the '60s and '70s as "I was just experimenting, everybody was doing it...things were different then." DL Hughley once said about raising boys, "You'll never learn to be a man until you see a man." If adults can't be the change we want our kids to be, how will they ever see the change they're supposed to become? How can adults spend our 9-to-5's promoting, accepting, condoning, and profiting off of all that we abhor, then come home and pull a "Do as I say, not as I do?"

Plus, nothing's free in The Hustle...

Wrinkles are ugly. Gray hair spells weakness. Birthdays magnify our annual decay. Actors over-30 must become "character actors" or risk not working at all, while most actresses over-40 get stuck playing mothers, grandmothers, or other asexual, comical roles. The average model is "washed up" by 27. Most musicians over-35 get locked out of the Viacom/Clear Channel/Condé Nast/Disney/WB pabulum machine. Ageism is rampant in the business world. Thru entertainment and even politics, we often paint old people as clueless often-comical servants of the young, sexless secondary characters or stubbornly uncool authority figures hell-bent on ruining the lives of everyone under 25... Thanks to Youth Marketing, youth is no longer wasted on the young; age is just the albatross of the old.

Blame Youth Marketing for helping turn growing old into a sin. As marketers and entertainers we've worshipped and coddled 12–34 year-olds so long that we've hustled ourselves into believing our own hype. And now, for all of Youth Marketing's loyal consumers, we've also created a nation of 20-, 30-, 40-, and 50-somethings hell-bent on *Nip/Tuck*ing, Rogaine'ing, GNC'ing, and trendspotting their way into happiness, relevance, and coolness. (And take it from me, it's no accident that just about every beauty, haircare, and fashion product talks about "looking and feeling younger" and "turning back the clock"...)

Also, despite the fetishized sex-symbol status of the cast of *Desperate Housewives,* Lauren Hutton, Sean Connery, Bill Clinton, The Rolling Stones, and MILFs (if you don't know, don't ask), when's the last time you saw someone over-40 hailed as a role model or a great athlete or a pop star? More importantly, think about how you view the average non-famous person over, say, 35...

Youth Marketing has also made culture and heritage a "young man's game," as Ice Cube once said. Youth Marketing continuously validates the rumor that older people have nothing teach, nothing to offer, and have no value in defining culture. Young white consumers, age 12–34 have more input in validating and defining black culture than black people over-40 do... People like Jon Stewart have more relevance than folks like Dr. Cornell West... For the most part, Youth Marketing has helped put culture, heritage and even to a certain degree, the responsibility for passing on history in the hands of the least qualified and least interested of us. But it's profitable and progress so, "Whatever dude."

Call it irony, call it poetic justice, call it coincidence...just know this: The Hustle always gets everyone in the end.

Pimps hoes hustlers, players, dealers, customers...
everybody's stuck in the "Oh-My-God"...
—Common and MC Lyte[2]

One More Thing:

If you want to know a society's level of compassion, look at how it treats its elderly and its mentally ill. If you want to know a society's heart, look at how it treats its women and its sick. If you want to see a society's character, look at how it runs its government and businesses. If you want to know a society's sense of justice and fairness, look how it treats its minorities, its poor, and its criminal. And if you want to know a society's morals and values, look at how it raises and teaches its children.

Yeah, they sacrificed their sons and daughters unto devils...
Thus were they defiled with their own works,
and went a whoring with their own inventions.
—Psalms 106:37–39

Tribes, Warlords and Merchantnaries:
The Future of Marketing and Branding

Welcome to the world we livin' in.
You ain't been here before? Well, come on in...
—Asheru & Blue Black

By the way, the Target Audience is dead.

Within 10 years or less, the traditional consumer base as is we've known it—the 18–34 year-old male, the 45–54 year-old female, the 13–17 year-old, the 10–12 year-old "tweener," etc.—will be gone; in most cities they're already being chopped and screwed like an old H-town mixtape. Of the roughly 295 million Americans, maybe half will remain homogenous enough, predictable enough and group-thinking enough to fill these old-world categories. For them, the labels will still apply, along with the traditional strategies for reaching them.

But the other half (and growing) is quickly becoming a collective of liquid coalitions—fluid, elusive consumers that're increasingly diverse, sophisticated, jaded, and unpredictable. And the one thing these emerging consumers have in common is their evolving ability to dodge and flow thru just about all our traditional demographic and psychographic boxes and boundaries.

Consider:

As recent as 2003 "metrosexual" was an accurate and still-trendy term for describing the then-growing number of overly fashion/hygiene conscious, arguably effeminate straight males. But today, there are so many metrosexuals that they've become mainstream thus making the term obsolete. And of course, categories like "mainstream," "alternative" and "underground" have 20 different definitions and examples depending on whom you ask, where you ask, and what you're asking about.

As we've seen with all things "urban," cultural co-option and integration continues to blur styles, tastes, and expressions to the point that it's harder than ever to tell the original from the bootleg from the remix. And with each passing year, ethnic labels are becoming at once more divisive and less divisive. An African-American from Detroit can no longer be grouped with the African-American born in Mozambique but now living in Atlanta. The Chinese kid in the 'burbs that only knows Mandarin as a style of cooking can't be marketed to the same way you would the Chinese kid in Chinatown for whom Mandarin is still spoken in the home. And when you say "Jewish," are you talking about the kid with the "Jewish"-sounding last name and lineage but who's also agnostic, or the Ethiopian-Jewish kid who speaks Hebrew and goes to Israel every year, or the Jewish kid in Memphis, TN who believes in Christ? And when it comes to GLB'Ters, are you talking about white gays and lesbians, etc., black ones, latino ones, the "down low" ones, the liberal ones, or conservative ones?

Yup, the walls are tumbling down. And it's precisely this kind of social shape-shifting that will ultimately kill the advertising hustle.

As I said upfront, a big part of the advertising hustle is based on convincing clients and consumers that ads and brands are the same thing. Most clients still believe in the shotgun blast of TV commercials, plus a little print and radio, is the best and some cases only way to build a brand. And as long as consumers were boxed into broad, predictable categories, that hustle worked. But again, hiphop, immigration, post-modern sexual and religious revolutions, the Internet, growing media outlets, changing geo-political dynamics, etc., have all scattered that homogenous, lock-step consumer base; and with it, every excuse agencies have ever had for pushing traditional advertising as their main branding tool. And as more clients figure this out, more will demand to know which half of their annual ad budget is being wasted again and why.

So what's next? What are the solutions?

Tribes

Tribes—that's as close as we'll ever get to a traditional consumer demo again. As America gets browner and more multi-ethnic, and more sexually and socially inclusive, people will get more tribal. There won't be one dominant group; instead you'll see lots of little tribes who'll bond and connect based on a whole combination of things: shared musical tastes, sexual orientation, faith, social activities, slanguague, etc. And it'll all be mixed up like never before.

These groups will be like little bowls of cultural gumbo. They'll have some commonalities, but they won't be obvious to anyone other than them. And for all their apparent bonds, theses tribes will be just independent enough and sophisticated enough that what works for reaching one group in one city or town or region, won't work in another. Think of it as a type of social Darwinism. Also, most tribes will never grow past a certain size—they're not meant to. Now you may see purchasing alliances—where tribes connect on certain brands and embrace them, but don't confuse that with tribal consolidation. Tribes are like extended families: the members will work to keep that family small enough to feel like family, not unlike, say a street gang. And it'll be that tangible sense of intimacy and familia more so than any hipness factor or status that will be a tribe's biggest strength and asset.

When it comes to reaching a tribe, shotguns are out, darts are in. All bets are off. There won't be one celebrity that they'll relate to; there won't be one activity they all have in common; there won't be one single media outlet that reaches them all or even most of them. No, you're going to have to be specific, more focused and intimate than ever before. You're going to have to build with them. (We'll discuss "building" in the next chapter.)

Warlords

One key to building with these new tribes will be going thru the cultural warlords. For tribes, the warlords won't the sole source of inspiration or movement or change, but the tribes will be so insular and independent that the warlords will become the gatekeepers and conduits for outsiders, like marketers, to get in.

So, I know what some of you are thinking: "Hadji, isn't a warlord just a fancy word for 'trendsetter'?" Nope, there's a colossal difference. *Consider this old joke:* You know the difference between the class clown and the class comedian? The class clown streaks across the golf course with a sign on his back reading, "19th hole," and an arrow pointing to his butt. The class comedian is the one who put him up to it. A trendsetter is simply the first one to announce what's next; the warlord manifests what's next. The trendsetter is the prophet; the warlord is the prophecy.

Consider:

One of my boys in NYC runs with Reebok, Int.—his agency does a lot of RBK work (S. Carter/G-Unit shoes, etc.). A couple years back, Reebok, like everyone else, was still trying to get in on the throwback and athletic gear craze (they needed a late pass, like most corporate entities trying to leverage cultural trends). Anyway, they spent mad loot developing fresh athletic styles to reach the cool kids who'd been up on this for a few seasons by then. But then the prophecy came:

> *"And I don't wear jerseys, I'm 30-plus.*
> *Gimme a crisp pair of jeans, n****, 'button-ups'*
> *S.Dots on my feet make my cipher complete..."*[1]

Five bars give or take, and it was done. One of hiphop's greatest warlords breathed and suddenly jerseys, which had been hot for several years were a wrap. Off came the Mitchell & Ness and NBA knock-offs and on flew the preppy shirts, cuff links, blazers and crisp jeans. Companies like Roc-a-wear, Sean John and Phat Farm followed by rolling out fresh lines. And as the tribes headed to the preppy stores, jersey sales tanked and folks at Reebok and other athletic gear pushers threw fits as they scrambled to change clothes. (But Reebok wasn't completely out of style; after all, their S. Carters rank as one of their best-selling shoe launches of all time; plus, their G-Unit shoes have been top-sellers.)

A trendsetter could've never done anything like that. For example: While P. Diddy and Russell Simmons aren't warlords, they're among the greatest trendsetters and businessmen in recent memory. They didn't create hiphop, but they helped take it mainstream and then global. And Michael Dell didn't invent laptops or home computing, but he was among its first prophets and became a billionaire as a result. Apple didn't invent the MP3 format, but Steve Jobs and crew saw the light; and while everyone else was suing college kids and grandstanding, Apple dropped iPods and became trendsetters. Again, warlords create; trendsetters cheerlead creations.

Conversely, it's not impossible for a trendsetter to evolve into a warlord. Nike's done it to a certain extent. Back in the day, Converse was the preeminent and seemingly invincible leader in basketball shoes, while Nike was just a small upstart relegated to outfitting the track and field set, mostly middle distance runners in the Pacific Northwest at that. But in addition to a couple of design advances, Phil Knight & Co. spotted a couple tribal trends (namely a certain baldhead-slick skywalker from Chi); the result pushed them so far out in front of everyone else that they became warlords for basketball, casual athletic gear, and for a time, urban streetwear.

Oprah Winfrey didn't invent soccermoms or talk shows, but while the rest were doing celebrity sycophant-fests and white-trash circuses, Oprah flipped the nation's you-go-girls and desperate-housewives-in-training-bras into an empire. Martha Stewart didn't invent that WASP-y, *American Beauty* aesthetic, but she saw the light and not even her 2004 prison stretch stopped her shine. NASCAR really didn't invent auto racing, but they rode it to warlord status.

Note: While certain celebrities can become warlords, most can't because most tribes will always dislike celebrities. Tribes, being the super savvy consumers that they are, are realizing that to become a celebrity you must have the support of entities outside your tribe—companies and consumers—who won't always have your tribe's interests at heart. Tribes are also realizing that because money and celebrity can change people, many celebrities often become too detached from the masses to be taken seriously as authorities or advocates, which is a big part of being a warlord. But some celebrities will become warlords because they were accepted into the tribe long before they got famous. (The Olsen Twins, who are a self-contained entertainment/fashion brand, are great examples—they literally grew up with the tribes that made them half-billionaires.)

Also, unlike traditional trendsetters and hipsters, warlords have power and influence beyond the trend or advent they've championed. For all of Hugh Hefner's success, he really has no real power or influence beyond Playboy; His realm is adult entertainment and even in that arena his influence only goes so far. For all of Howard Stern's dominance, he has no real influence beyond his radio show. But real warlords—Oprah, Bill Gates, Warren Buffet, TD Jakes, Creflo Dollar, the DNC/RNC, etc., can influence their tribes on issues beyond their accepted areas of expertise. Why? Their tribes trust their judgment and accept their gatekeeper status.

The Merchantnary

Part businessperson, part hustler, the "merchantnary" is the new marketing animal. As individual tribalists, they'll switch tribes if it improves their cool standing or status. As warlords, they'll ride with whoever pays most or promises them the most power. As brands and corporate entities, they'll say, sell, and do whatever it takes to align themselves with whichever consumer tribe seems most lucrative at the time.

(Think MTV, which for a time wouldn't play black artists, is now gatekeeper of all things urban; or NASCAR, who after generations of being the ultimate segregationist brand, is now courting multicultural fans.)

And what does this have to do with advertising?

Well for too many clients, traditional advertising is still 70% or more of their marketing mix. And for select behemoths like M&M Mars and IBM, that have the money/market share, they'll stay that lopsided with little blowback. But for maybe 85- or 90% of the other business out there, you're facing a world where TV commercials, radio, and print ads will be maybe 15–25 percent of the mix; and for most businesses, TV won't even be an option. Ever. For them, marketing and branding will be about building.

Branding Thru Building

As a business and as a brand, it's about intimate relationships. It's about doing you and letting them come to you. It's about becoming part of someone's life without forcing it. Sponsoring everything in a tribe's daily life isn't building, it's smothering and eventually the tribe will cast you out. You'll suffer backlash for no other reason than that you're clearly tying too hard and they know it.

And before you say 'em, terms like "Relationship Marketing" and "Integrated Marketing," while cute, are not building and won't work, not for long at least. And you can forget about that *g* word, because when it comes to building, guerilla marketing is like bringing a knife to a gunfight. (Yes, it's really that serious.)

We'll explain a little more in the next chapter.

Hey you, get off my cloud!
you don't know me, you don't know my style.
—Method Man[1]

Let's Build!

All for one...One for all, all for one!
—Brand Nubian

Everyone needs help. No matter what you do in this life, big or small, you're going to need help. Conventional wisdom says that this is where networking comes in.

But I don't believe in networking. I know, that's blasphemy, right? Well sorry, but I just don't believe in it. Networking is phony. Networking is about cattle-calling your way thru conferences and industry schmoozefests where waves of people who couldn't care less about each other armed with fake smiles, fresh resumés, and embossed business cards trying to get paid. Once they get you in their sights it's hours of feigned interest, lame small talk and awkward "So-can-you-get-me-a-job?" inquiries. (I went to a few of these events and usually did my best to play the background and fill up on the free liquor and food.) Networking is about using people; and truth be told, most people hate being used.

Networking is also about agendas. When you network, you're out for the quick score, trying to figure out who can fulfill your needs. When you network, the bond ends soon as the job ends. The handshakes and hugs stop once the checks stop clearing. The phone calls and lunches dry up soon as the opportunities stop panning out. On a business level, networking is simply about getting laid. (Not surprisingly most networking involves alcohol.)

But if you're not going to network, how do you get the help and connections you need in order to succeed?

Build.

Where networking is about quick fixes, building is about relationships. When you build, you bond with people who are about the same things you're about, even when there aren't any specific opportunities out there. When you build, you're connecting with people as you grow until you become supports for each other, even if you end up on different paths. Building is about bonds, lasting bonds.

Building is organic, fluid. When you build, you don't seek help as much as you make yourself worth helping. *It's like this:* Once you get past a certain age, you don't hang out with kids anymore. Why? Because you're not a child. Now that doesn't mean you don't have any younger friends, it just means that the younger friends are gravitating toward you and not the other way around. In short, networking is about chasing the game. Building is about living and letting the game come to you.

When you build, you don't worry about meeting the "right" people or even finding the "right" opportunities. You concern yourself with doing the right things and walking the right path. Meeting the right people becomes a by-product of doing the right things. *For example:*

Want to attract backers for a new business? Don't go networking for backers. The thing to do is build the best business model and best product possible. Next, stay true to who and what you are as a person. When you do that, you'll put yourself on the right path to meet backers. In business, people are always watching; and once they see what you're about, even if you're not a "finished product" yet, the right backers will come.

Early in my career, I did a lot of networking; met a lot of folks. I'm no longer in contact with 90% of those people and never really trusted them when I was. The foundation of those relationships was mainly job opportunities and clients. But once I stopped being of value to them, they jetted me for a better networking opportunity. Conversely, I've managed to build with a few folks in recent years. They're cool people. We met under the right circumstances, once I was done networking and decided to just do me and bond appropriately. Today, when the time comes, I have a small stable of people I can call on for support and vice versa because we're all on the same level. And business goals aside, we're actually friends.

Slow Down

Building takes time. It's definitely not "Hey, here's my business card" one minute and "I know him, tell him I sent you" the next. Building is a process. Give the tree a chance to grow and bear fruit. And be selective. Just as you can't sleep with everybody, you can't build with everybody. Some people, no matter how nice they are, are either just bad for business or simply aren't on your level. Just be patient and stay rooted in what you are and what you're about. If you do that, the right folks will come thru and the rest will fall by the side just like they're supposed to.

Building Blocks

By the way, not to air any more dirty laundry but: Black folks, we is terrible at building. We're so bad at it that only bad grammar can properly describe the problem. I don't know what it is but black folks, especially young, black folks, get caught up in these little subgroups: old, young, middle-class, neighborhood, underground, mainstream... It's like pulling teeth just to get many of us to stretch beyond our little circles and build.

We have to overcome this myopia. We have to stop being so cliquish and petty toward one another. We have to be willing to help someone else even if there's nothing obvious in it for us. Once again, we can't complain about what other folks won't do for us or are doing to us if we won't do anything for each other.

Maybe it's part of that minor-leagues mindset we discussed earlier. Maybe we're still harboring a fantasy that some knight in shining armor will come along and save us... I don't know. But if you're waiting for the cavalry, just remember: the cavalry always killed the Indians. My guess is whatever help we think we need won't come from anyone but us. There's a reason why you can't spell "community" or "opportunity" without "unity." No one climbs alone and divided communities never grow.

The first step for Black folks is realizing
that there is not going to be a leader and
there isn't any movement—unless you count economics.
—Shawn Baldwin, 36, founder and CEO
Capital Management Group Securities[2]

Get Out More (reprise)

Outsourcing and international partnerships and alliances have made most businesses and economies global. Plus, immigration, art, and media have made culture so fluid that everyone is from everywhere now. It's not about black or white or foreign and domestic anymore. It's about people everywhere expanding their opportunities along with their sense of community.

Black Americans have to "get off the block." We must realize that we are a global people and expand our sense of community to include folks of color in other states, countries, and industries. Worldwide, people of color are having similar struggles and fighting similar battles as us. And they're making similar progress and innovations. Alliances are being formed. Companies are being built. Countries are being rebuilt. Cultures are being spread. Opportunities are being created, shared, and multiplied. Money is being made. Destinies are being fulfilled.

There is no reason why all Black Americans and Americans of color can't be a part of this change. There's no reason why we can't lead this change. In fact, I believe that we must—our futures depend on it. No one is going to bring anything to us; we have to go get it ourselves. But in order to do so, we have to open our eyes and get out more so we can build, create, and accomplish.

Three Extra Keys to Building:

1. Humility.

There's a definitive line between self-confidence and arrogance. No one wants to help or work with arrogant folks. Be humble in all your pursuits. (Yea, all of you be subject one to another, and be clothed with humility: "for God resisteth the proud, and giveth grace to the humble." Peter 5:5)

2. Be open-minded.

The best relationships often start in unlikely places and situations. Don't always settle for the obvious connections and traditional opportunities. Help doesn't always look like help.

3.Follow-thru.

Stick to your word and fulfill your promises. Never stop working.

We grow from sea to tree...me and my people building!
—Blk Sonshine featuring Masauko Chipembre[3]

Ante Up!
Consumerism as Civil Disobedience

Do You Want A Revolution?!
—Kirk Franklin & Nu Nation

So how thorough is the marketing hustle?

We have so equated humanity with consumerism that we now look down on those who can't or won't spend as much as we do. *Think about it:* What's among the worst things a woman can call her boyfriend or husband? *Cheap.* Once again, we live in a society where "cheap" is an actual insult. (And what's more embarrassing than being told your credit card is maxed out while trying to buy something in a crowded restaurant or store?) I tell you, folks, we've put entirely too much value on spending. Too much.

It's been said the world is divided into two groups: buyers and sellers. While I don't know that I'd go quite that far but I will say this: In a capitalistic, free-market society such as ours, consumption is key to any evolution.

Politicians listen to businesses more than they listen to voters. Voters who shop definitely have more influence than voters who don't. Voters who own have more power than those who rent or lease. Politics is business; business is hustling, and hustling is about being opportunistic and income agnostic. Politicians say and do whatever gets them power. Companies do what sells and ditch what doesn't.

So if you want change, you have to show these entities that it's profitable to do so and suicidal to do otherwise.

Buying is more "American" than thinking
and I'm as American as they come.
—Andy Warhol

Paid In Full

The thing I miss most about the early days of hiphop was not only its complexity but also the daily acts of simple evolution it inspired. The foundation of hiphop was people of color rebelling against repressive constructs that dictated what they couldn't be and couldn't have. Acquiring any symbol of individuality and success was a fist in the face of those who felt they didn't deserve either.

A black male driving a Benz, BM, or a Pathfinder was indeed crass consumerism, but it was also about being antagonistic toward a system that said nice cars were only for whites. A black female shunning couture for her own flavor was a middle finger to every designer, runway model, and magazine on the newsstand. Rocking fat gold chains back when gold was the hottest metal was like saying, "You disenfranchised me, but still I rise." Dressing ridiculously fly on a shoestring budget was like telling the fashion industry, "You won't make clothes for me so I'll make my own." Turning common turntables into musical instruments and Krylon on brick walls into art challenged the NEA, the art world, and anyone else who said minorities had no creative voice. And again, this was done mostly thru conscious consumerism.

It also reminded us that while class is indeed a major divider, what allows people to flow from one class to the next is access to capital, opportunity, education, and social acceptance—all of which are often facilitated by *race.* Mos Def's 1999 classic, *Mr. Nigger,* eloquently illustrates this. The song follows a young rich black man trying to assimilate into the mainstream thru hard work and consumerism. He buys all the right clothes, buys the right house, gets the right car, travels first-class, has a great job, etc. He does everything he's been taught will make him "American" but it's never enough: "Who be riding up in the high-rise elevator/other tenants be prayin' he ain't the new neighbor? Mr. Nigger... Nigger, nigger..." It reminded us that while racism and classism may not be twins, they're at least kin.

Unfortunately, conscious consumerism has fallen off. Now we simply buy to be accepted and consume what's acceptable. Today we're trying harder keep up with the Joneses than we did when the phrase "keeping up with the

Joneses" was fresh. Meanwhile, the prejudices and disenfranchisement remain, along with our unwillingness to challenge the roots of it all. And not surprisingly, the "It's-not-race-it's-class" excuse like all the rest flows on, today stronger than ever.

We survivalists turned consumers just to get by.
—Talib Kweli[1]

For Us Buy Us

Back in 1995, activist, political commentator, and businessman, Tony Brown wrote: "The most successful economic boycott ever conducted in America is the boycott by blacks of their own businesses."[2] In 2004, blacks and Hispanics spent an estimated $723 billion and $686 billion, respectively, on consumer goods.[3] Yet, in the case of both communities, as much as 85 cents of every dollar (by most estimates) was spent with businesses owned by folks outside these communities. Something's gotta change.

We can't complain about what corporations and so-called "outsiders" are doing to us if we won't ban together and do for ourselves. The Wal-Marts, McDonald's, Starbucks, etc., of the world can't bumrush small businesses and exploit communities of color if those communities stand up and support the small businesses already within those communities. We flock to spend money on everyone else's businesses except ours, then complain about what we don't have, don't own, and what we still can't afford to do.

As I noted earlier, by 2009, blacks are expected to spend $965 billion annually, Hispanics around $992 trillion, with Asians spending $528 billion.[4] That's nearly $2.5 trillion annually combined. Once again, By 2009, blacks, latinos, and Asians alone will be spending an estimated <u>Two Trillion, Five-Hundred Billion Dollars</u> each year on toys, cars, shoes, clothes, electronics, and other consumer goods. Now I don't know much about a lot, but I do know that if you can drop 12 zeros *in front* of the decimal point annually, you have power to create changes.

But it's also worth noting that as of 2004, White Americans were spending an estimated $7 trillion (yes, that's trillion with a *"t"*) a year in consumer goods and will be approaching $9 trillion annually by 2009.[5] And make no mistake: Those communities are looking out for themselves, first and foremost, and will continue to do until they feel they have no choice but to do otherwise. This economic gap, and all the continuing inequities related to it, which are largely the result of generations and in some cases centuries of institutional prejudice and disenfranchisement, will continue until people of color band together and commit to collective economic growth.

Freedom is not given or taken. It is realized.
—Meshell Ndegeocello[6]

Today's Topic: Self-destruction . . .

The biggest threat to wealth-building for people of color is destructive priorities. Consider the huge gap between blacks and whites in terms of access to quality healthcare. Some of it is institutionalized disenfranchisement, most of it isn't. *Question:* "How many of us have health insurance?" *Answer:* "All of us." Some of us just choose to spend our premiums and deductibles on Sean John and X-Box Games. Health insurance is expensive, obscenely expensive; but we can't bargain shop for doctors then pay top dollar for cars and clothes. Let's cut back on the brand names then take that money and put it towards acquiring/upgrading our healthcare coverage.

Secondly, we need to invest more than we consume. So much of our money goes to building wealth for companies that we don't even own a piece of. For example: As much soda as we drink, doesn't it make sense to snatch up a couple shares of Coca-Cola or Pepsi? Upwards of 40% of Wrigley's Doublemint gum is chewed by blacks, yet how many black folks have been savvy enough to own stock in the company? On average, blacks smoke more than most any other group, yet how many of us own stock in Philip Morris? Nike and Adidas make billions off black consumers, yet how many black folks profit from owning their stock? We'll buy the latest cellphone but not invest in Cingular or Motorola. We'll buy nice furniture but won't invest in home ownership.

I say we commit to putting 10- to 20% of our annual income into stocks, mutual funds, and other investment options. (By the way, lottery tickets are not an investment; they're a donation.) And if you don't know anything about stocks, start reading. If we can spend thousands of dollars a year (which we do) on brain candy like VIBE, The Source, *Rolling Stone,* and music CDs that we'll just burn up and flip into coasters after a few spins, then we can take some of that wasted loot and subscribe to *Forbes, Black Enterprise, NV, Fast Company,* and other pubs that'll teach us more about what's good in what sector and where to put our dough short-term and long-term. Here are a few more thoughts on how we can invest in ourselves and each other:

21 Questions...And They All About Us

1. What if people of color fought gentrification by pulling their money out of banks with poor track records of loaning money to minorities, particularly those trying to invest in their own communities?

2. What if we only supported businesses owned by people who live in our communities and that employed people in our communities?

3. What if women stopped supporting fashion designers and magazines that don't offer realistic ideals and diverse images of women?

4. What if we start leveraging our purchasing power against companies that support politicians that work against our interests?

5. Since some 65% of all African diamonds are purchased by the U.S. & UK, what if consumers refused to support our jewelers until our government committed to ending Africa's civil wars and rebuilding the communities we helped rob of natural resources in the first place?

6. What if we turned off BET, MTV, MTV2, VH1, etc., until they: (1) Ban videos that degrade minorities, particularly women of color. (2) Promote more diverse and independent artists. (3) Offer news and non-music programming beneficial to the communities whose cultures they're exploiting?

7. What if all minorities committed to becoming debt-free before age 28?

8. Since only 2% of Native Americans get casino money, what if the public stopped patronizing casinos whose revenues don't benefit those tribes as intended? (Also, what if the government stepped in and regulated?)

9. What if consumers stopped supporting companies who use manipulative campaigns and false problem-solving theorems (i.e., "Be cool/accepted by consuming this...")?

10. What if consumers demanded that for every 5 black amateur athletes forced to wear Nike, Reebok, Adidas, or AND1 gear by their teams/schools that those companies must provide a full academic scholarship to one slow-running, no-jumping black kid who wants to go to college?

11. What if everyone with a net worth of at least $1 million gave their social security checks to a poor senior citizen or low-income person?

12. What if for every $5 million in annual revenue food companies like KFC, Taco Bell, McDonald's, General Mills, Nabisco, Krispy Kreme, etc., subsidized one family farmer and used that farmer's crops to feed poor people?

13. What if we spent just 50 cents of every earned dollar in our own communities (instead of the current estimates of less than 15 cents)?

14. Because one of the biggest factors in the wealth gap between whites and people of color is home ownership, what if every person of color committed to home ownership by age 35?

15. What if insurance companies refunded 25% of their annual premiums to insureds who stayed healthy enough to avoid medical care each year?

16. What if companies like Nestle, Waters North America, Inc., or Coca-Cola—who made 35% of its 2001 revenues from its Dasani brand and other global water-related interests[7] unded clean water and sanitation in countries where hundreds of thousands die annually from dirty water and poor sanitation-related diseases?

17. What if hiphop's core consumer-base admitted that they like seeing blacks portrayed as niggers, pimps, strippers, bitches, and whores and decided to change their views, which would in turn force the industry to change it's portrayal of blacks?

18. What if minorities began viewing our cultures as intellectual property and began protecting them accordingly?

19. What if we forced companies to divest from those involved in the Prison Industry Complex (*Wackenhut*, *Corrections Corporation of America*, etc.)?

20. What if we realized that a big step to fixing our failing schools is to end

the continual white-flight and redlining that began with 1954's *Brown vs. Board of Ed.* when whites fled to suburban, private and parochial schools to keep their tax dollars and kids out of inner-city schools?

21. What if consumers refused to support companies that profit off of wars (Bechtel, Lockheed Martin, Raytheon Corp., McDonell Douglass, General Dynamics, etc.) until we're assured that we're only fighting just wars and that civilians and soldiers worldwide are only dying for just causes?

Bonus Question: What if people shopped based on their respective faiths?

So whaddyathink?

What do we own? Not enough land, not enough homes,
not enough banks to give my brother a loan...
—Nas[8]

Shut 'Em Down?

I'm not a big fan of boycotts. Why? Because with few exceptions, modern boycotts don't work. Boycotts are inherently temporary: "I march until you listen... I do this until you do that..." Just as consumers have gotten smarter over the years, companies and governments are now savvy enough to call their bluff. They've realized that as long as they control whatever's being boycotted, boycotters eventually have to break bread with them. So more often than not, they just dig in and ride it out.

What scares companies and governments, and most people for that matter, is *permanent change*. Companies don't fear picket signs and bullhorns; they fear permanent loss of business. Companies don't fear bad quarters they fear bankruptcy. Marketers don't fear trends, they fear fundamental paradigm shifts. Politicians don't fear apathetic voters; they fear voters permanently switching parties or forming viable alternate parties. Governments don't fear protests they fear coups. Californians aren't afraid of earthquakes, they're afraid of the one that turns the City of Angels into the Lost City of Atlantis. New Yorkers aren't afraid of terrorism; they're afraid of Hiroshima II on Broadway & 5th. People fear permanent change. If people think you or your group is capable of causing permanent change in their world, they'll listen to you as if their lives depended on it. Because, figuratively, they just might.

Looking back, the last truly successful boycott I can remember—and by successful I mean that one that brought permanent change—was 1992's "Cop Killer" boycott. When Ice-T ripped crooked cops and police brutality in that song, police organizations and mainstream consumers and retailers became so outraged that they marched against *TimeWarner* demanding that the song be banned and Ice-T lose his record deal. For months media elites blasted Ice-T and other rap artists at every turn. Time Warner eventually pulled the song and ultimately sold its stake in Interscope and distanced itself from "controversial music." (For a while at least.)

As consumers, voters, and citizens, we have to start thinking in terms of permanent change. Whether your goals are lofty (e.g., true equality, world peace, universal education and healthcare) or small (e.g., less bad TV) you need to ask yourself 3 questions: Who is the biggest cause of this problem or biggest barrier to solving it? (2) Who/what scares them most? (3) How do I get a hold of or aligned with it/them? Answering those questions can put the possibility of permanent change on your side thereby giving you the influence you need. Love of change and hatred of complacency are our greatest weapons. Complacency is soft. Love of change means being willing to do what complacency won't. *Remember:* The Hustle was built by hard hearts feeding on softened minds and weakened souls.

Now this doesn't mean go out and buy a Ché Guevara T-shirt, load up on bottled water, Common or Talib CDs, and Michael Moore books and go vegan. That's just shopping and anyone can shop. And this doesn't mean violence. Again, violence solves nothing. This is about using your purchasing power, your position as employees and your voice as voters to change how you and your communities are treated. This is about sacrificing, pooling resources, and focusing energy in the name of independence. This is about change.

Capitalism might be the wicked game, but we're caught up in the middle of it. So we better make up our own rules...
The only way to change problems isn't necessarily a violent revolution, but a revolution in education at least.
—Chuck D.[9]

You're Only a Customer...

One of the first rules in the marketing hustle is to remind the consumer that the products they buy are more than just purchases. We have to convince folks that they're buying "an experience," that they're participants in a brand's growth. We have to convince them that being a consumer entitles them to judge, shape, and even destroy that which they pay to consume. If we don't, they won't buy as much stuff; and as marketers, we ain't havin' that.

This is a major reason why they're so many fights at sporting events. Sports fans have been hustled into believing that their ticket entitles them to be more important to the game than they really are. Sports fans are just observers who pay to observe an event. Their $100 tickets don't give them ownership over any player, team or venue. Truth is they're just renting a view until the game clock hits zero. Period.

But for the last 25 years or so The Hustle has hooked fans into believing their ticket/merchandise purchase entitles them to moon players, throw stuff at players, sling slurs and expletives at players, spread rumors about players, live out their dreams thru players, etc. And the players, who've long since been repackaged as entertainment product, should just shut up and take it. After all, it's the tickets, merchandising, cable packages and media coverage that pay player salaries. Sports fans are really minority owners (pun intended) and as such deserve to use their product purchases as they see fit. Right?

Again, if the game were just a game, throwbacks wouldn't have gone for $300 and new shoes wouldn't cost $150. If the game was just a game, advertisers wouldn't sponsor it, and 45-year-old white men wouldn't worship 22-year-old black boys with 40-inch verticals, .350 batting averages or 4.25 speed. If the game was just a game, it wouldn't sell. And sports is a business and business is all about doing what sells, no matter what sells.

You see this in hiphop where people buy a CD, some Lugz or DJ equipment, and suddenly decide that they're co-owners of the culture. This is why we hawk Hollywood stars... After all, we bought their movies, watched their TV shows, etc. They owe us the autograph and intimate details of their lives. We're consumers—we paid good money to star-worship; they owe us. And the luxury brand we just overpaid for makes us part of the upscale crowd, doesn't it? I buy the symbol, therefore I own what it symbolizes, right? Right.

In the end, it's all just sugar water, it was probably made in Taiwan or Indonesia, and it will eventually end up in a dollar store or on one of those tired "What-were-we-thinking?!" pop culture TV lists. The most revolutionary thing a consumer can do is to buy what you need first, question why you want what you want, and always recognize when you're being hustled.

You're only a customer—
you're walking in the presence of hustlers...
—LL Cool J[10]

Choose or Lose

Business is political and politics is such big business that it's impossible to discuss changing one without realizing you have to impact the other. We only have two viable political parties, and one thing the Democrats and Republicans agree on is that a viable third (or fourth or fifth) party will knock their hustle right off the tracks. They take comfort in knowing that every 4 years about 100 million Americans (or 50% of eligible voters) won't vote. They take comfort in the corrupt 527s and the truckloads of soft money that line their pockets every election. They take comfort in the compromised lobbyists and scheming special-interest groups that feed off of them and vice-versa... It's all about the few controlling the many, and most of them wouldn't have it any other way.

So if you want real change, we have to recognize that the ballot and the wallet are two sides of the same coin. Get educated about the brands you consume and the companies you support because they're choosing the politicians you vote for and the leaders you follow way more than you are. Be willing to use the power of fundamental permanent change to uplift your cause. And again, violence solves nothing; so focus on the constructive actions I mentioned earlier like voting, communal responsibility and collective works. The most frightening thing to a manipulator or a control freak (like the ones ruining government and big business) is to hear masses of people rise up at every turn and say, "You can leave now; we don't need you anymore." *Remember:* Business is nothing without consumers and politicians are just civil servants; make them work for you, not the other way around.

(Oh by the way, MTV's *Choose or Loose,* like most of its programming, is a colossal hustle built on lip service from trifling hypocritical liberals and mallrat-rebels, self-denying moderates, greedy entertainment companies, culture vultures, and clueless celebrities. And what's worse is everyone from the DNC to the RNC knows it and milks it for all it's worth.)

It's bigger than hiphop...
—Dead Prez[11]

Someday I'd like to see <u>all</u> communities recognize the power they already possess. Someday I'd like to see communities realize that we are not markets to be penetrated or saturated; that we are not target audiences to be owned and manipulated. But rather, we are people with money. We are human beings with power and no brand or product or comany can take away our power unless we let it. Change is not out of our hands. We don't have to buy everything they sell us and we don't have to remain subservient to politicians and leadership that doesn't represent us. We can empower ourselves. We can empower each other. We can change things. We can; and more importantly, we must. (But don't sleep: we can only change what we claim as our own.)

In order for us to get it like it's supposed to be...
we gotta get together and do it for ourselves.
—The Philadelphia International All-Stars[12]

Boss Up!
(Having a Job vs. Having Control)

Down the road that we call "eternity"—
where knowledge is formed and you'll learn to be
self-sufficient, independent, to teach to each...
—D-Nice

The Player/President

I guess in a perfect world, we'd all have a steady flow of loot and a plot of land to call our own, leaving us free to focus on love, equality, and peace. But this isn't Reality TV, so the next best thing is having independence. But the only way you can truly knock The Hustle is to not be a part of it. The first step to that is getting Christ in your life. The second step is bossing up, like Prince or Ani DiFranco, and controlling your own destiny.

But I have to say this: *If you go into business for yourself just to get rich or get even, then you've missed the point of the book and The Hustle's already beaten you.* Bossing up is about self-determination and self-reliance. It's about freedom. Freedom, at least in a spiritual sense, has no real price tag other than the blood of Christ, and that's already been delivered free of charge. On a more worldly level, the main reason I started ProdigalPen was so I could write what I believe without someone else hanging dollar signs and restrictions over my head. *That's* freedom.

But it's tough. When you're working for someone else, you have that automatic safety net, that built-in infrastructure. Even if your job sucks, you know that someone will still cut you a check every two weeks. If you work hard and keep quiet, barring layoffs, you can circle the last and the 15th on your calendar and get benefits. The routine of going to the office each day is comforting. Giving all that up seems nuts if you think about it.

As a freelancer, a temp, or an entrepreneur, there is no buffer; there is no safety net. It's just you and the marketplace, and the marketplace can be brutal. The marketplace doesn't care if you're a nice person with 3 kids to feed. All it wants to know is, "Do you have something I want to pay for?" The marketplace doesn't care if you spent 22 hours a day developing it. It doesn't care if you're passionate about it; all it wants to know is, "Can I afford it?" The marketplace doesn't care if you've got $47,850 in student loans, it just wants to know if it can use your skills. If the marketplace answers "No" to those questions then, if you're lucky, you can move back home and flip burgers until the marketplace feels like saying "yes."

Still, I believe if you want any real sense of freedom, you have to try to do something for yourself at least once. You don't want to be a 50-year-old housewife wishing you had patented that little thingy you made for your kids and their friends back when they were 6. You don't want to be 43 with an ulcer and a twice-refinanced home panicking every few months over layoff rumors. You don't want to spend year after year watching other people take risks and take control while you tell yourself, *I could've done that.*

Until you decide otherwise, you'll always be at the mercy of someone else: Your boss... The bus driver with the attitude... That moron doing 75 mph while on the cellphone who may or may not see you coming... The waitress who's about to spit in your pasta because her last customer left a 13-cent tip... The overworked doctor who may have misdiagnosed that itch in your crotch or that pain in your chest. You'll be always at someone else's mercy. The trick is to minimize the number of "someone elses" by taking charge yourself.

You're Fired!

It was back in August of 1998. After 3 and a half years at the same firm, which is like dog years in the ad world, I got fired. I'll never forget it. They waited until 4:30 P.M. on Monday. The VP of Human Resources called me into her office. When I got there, I'd walked into a tribunal of three white 40-something execs all with their game faces on and strategically aligned in feng-shui power positions.

One of the VPs, my immediate supervisor, mumbled through his "You're-not-producing-like-you-used-to...we're-going-in-another-direction" speech then promptly left the room like he'd just been caught cheating on his wife. He barely looked me in the eye. The other handed me a trumped-up resignation letter to sign noting that their lawyers had assured them they were perfectly within their legal rights to do this. As I looked it over, they added that I was welcome to have my lawyer look it over, but I'd simply be told the same thing. All I could do was stare blankly and think, *Lawyers? After 3 and a half years of hard work and good behavior they actually thought I'd sue them...* If I weren't so shocked, I would've laughed out loud.

But I really wasn't mad. I'd turned down other jobs to stay there and was as big a cheerleader for that place as any. I thought I was good at what I did and I always tried to make the job feel like a family or at least like a neighborhood. But when it was all said and done, all they saw were numbers and the numbers weren't adding up anymore; so, my number was up. I went from being the lone successful brother on *L.A. Law* to Jack Lemmon in *Glengarry, Glenn Ross*. The only thing missing was Alec Baldwin reminding me "Coffee is for closers." But even then, it was hard to be mad. It was just business and I knew it. Just business, nothing more nothing less.

Once I got fired, I realized that the only thing I really learned in college was how to work for someone else. College is great, but it often teaches you to follow more than lead, memorize more than think, and like it. In fact, resumés are all about highlighting how good you are at doing for others and following orders. I also realized that more often than not, no matter how much I do for "them," it'd never be enough. I'll always be overhead. If I was ever truly going to be free, I had to figure out how to go for self.

Mr. Microwave

Growing up, I was a Detroit Pistons fan, which was blasphemy given that I was a Chicagoan during Jordan's prime. Even when MJ was dropping 50 every night and Pippen was serving triple-doubles left 'n' right, I still checked for the Pistons. Why? To see The Microwave. Vinnie Johnson sorta looked like my dad—muscular, balding, and not real tall. (Even when Vinnie was young he looked old.) He was the consummate super-sub: always came ready to play even when he didn't get to play. He'd come off the bench, give you 20 on 7-for-11 with a couple treys and dimes for good measure. He got hot fast, cooked 'til they won, kept quiet and cashed his checks. By the time Vinnie hung 'em up, he'd driven most every defense nuts, made a few million, and earned a couple championship rings.

Watching Vinnie taught me something: If you want to be that hired gun people call when they need it hot and fast, you have to hone your craft. I was never a lazy full-timer, but at some point I got complacent. And once the frustration and typical corporate BS got to me, I started coasting. Had I settled for another full-time gig right away, I probably would have spent the next 25 years staying just good enough to collect a pension.

Getting canned woke me up quick. I took everything I'd learned, good and bad, and used it to step my game up. After a while, I got to a point where every single place I freelanced for offered me a full-time job—that's when I knew I was good. But the coolest thing about freelancing and consulting is even though someone else is signing your paychecks, you still work for yourself. You determine how long you want to work at a particular place. You determine your own salary. If you decide you won't work for less than 10G a week, then you don't. On the other hand if no one's offering 10G you have to lower your fee and possibly your standards. You also have to be willing to go wherever the money is, which for me often meant hitting other cities—that's what took me to NYC. As I said earlier, freelance is a risky proposition—depending on your city, your industry, and the economy, you work in spurts, but at least you're your own boss. And that's always a good thing.

Funny thing is, some companies respect freelance talent more than they respect their own employees. They know how stupid it is to hire somebody for hundreds or thousands of dollars a day and then not listen to them. But when you're on staff, it's like you're their property. They'll make you work overtime and weekends knowing it costs them the same amount no matter what. Plus they'll push you to produce more knowing they can threaten to fire you if you don't. But as a freelancer, you tell them what you can do and how much it'll cost them once they agree. It's as close as you can get to a partnership without starting a business.

And that's what it means to freelance. If you can get sharp and stay on point, you'll always get paid to help a team win. Companies will always pay for talent. And since most companies and industries are too shortsighted and greedy to train and retain talent, they will always pay for polished talent. And if you catch 'em at the right time, they'll overpay for it. The downside is that you don't always know when you'll work again or even how much you'll make from month to month. Plus, health insurance is usually up to you. Also, you have to work extra to maintain connections since business changes so much so quickly. But in a weird way, it's worth it. You have freedom as a freelancer that you'll never ever have as a permanent staffer.

As long as you work for someone else, there'll always be someone else to worry about. So I'm putting my faith in the biggest, strongest someone else I know—God—and just rolling wherever He takes me. Whether this book goes platinum or wood, it'll be my words, not a watered-down version of what a publisher that's only giving me 10% wants. I'm not writing for Hollywood or *The NYT's* bestseller list. I'm writing for God and regular people like you. And if that means I end up at UPS or flipping burgers, so be it. But rich or not, no one will ever tell me what to write or how to write again.

I don't think you can ever find truth if the only path you're on is the one somebody else is running. That's what The Hustle is: being suckered into following somebody else's path. If you don't like my route, fine. I just want you to know that you have more options than you think. Besides, if you want to eat—I mean truly eat to live—you can't wait for table scraps to fall off of somebody else's plate. And when you work for companies, especially big companies, all you're doing is waiting for them to finish eating and throw you some crumbs.

I've worked at companies where I helped clients boost their revenues by millions of dollars while helping my bosses make money hand over fist. But my reward was an annual salary of 20G, 40G, at best 100G. Give a company a few decades of yourself and maybe you've got 6 figures in your late 60s to play with. Nope, I can't go out like that anymore. Again I'm not greedy or looking to get rich. But if I'm baking the pie, I deserve a slice. We all do. So going solo, at least for me, is the best chance I have at achieving that.

Here are a few more things to consider...

12 Keys to a Successful Solo Career:

1. Don't just look for a job, look for work.

If you're just looking for a job, you might miss out on your chance to work. The chance to make your mark may come by working for someone else or it may come from recognizing a hole in the marketplace that no one else is filling. So be open to opportunities no matter what form they may come in.

2. Don't play yourself.

Don't undervalue your skills. Charge what you believe you're worth for your services or product. Starting out, I underbid my services a lot believing I wasn't worth more. But after a while, I realized that people respected my work and were willing to pay for what I brought to the table and I started charging them accordingly. I cost myself a lot upfront, but learned a valuable lesson in the long run. In short: never sell yourself short.

3. Don't hustle yourself.

Writing isn't work for me. It's what I love; it's how I grow, how I pray, how I breathe. I'm not chasing a paycheck. I'm not compromising my words for anyone; those who relate will pay for my words, those who don't, won't. Had I simply gone from one company to the next, I would've been hustling myself. I would've been trading one headache for another, old pimp for a new pimp.

Some people like working for someone else and just need to take an occasional break. Nothing wrong with that. Just be honest with yourself and know which move is best for you.

4. Don't pimp yourself.

Being your own boss is your chance to respect yourself and be a professional on your own terms. If your old boss/industry was pimping you, don't turn around and abuse yourself. Don't overwork and underpay yourself and give yourself ulcers chasing a fatter bottom line—that's what your old boss was for.

5. Do the little things.

Dot your *I*'s, cross all the *T*'s, and read between the lines because it's the little things that'll get you every time. For example I didn't realize how expensive health insurance was. I probably should've leased my first computer instead of buying one outright. Should've saved more money before striking out on my own, too. Should've set aside a little extra time early on for incorporating, etc. Those are just some of the little things that drove me nuts early on. Like a friend once told me, "Yeah, a knife can kill you but so will enough paper-cuts."

So before you make that move, think it through. Don't treat it like a vacation, treat it like moving day—pack everything you need the first time. Do the research and plan it out. Don't talk yourself out of taking that big leap of faith, just do your due diligence first. In the end, no one will handle the little things but you.

6. Wake up running.

There's an old African story about the gazelle and the lion—it goes like this:

Lions eat gazelles. But gazelles are always running and they're way too fast for a lion to just sneak up on. So in order to catch one, the lion has to wake up running; if he doesn't, he can't catch a gazelle and he won't eat. The gazelle wakes up running because that's the only way to dodge the lion. Both their survival is based on waking up running.

When you're on your own, you have to wake up running. If I don't get up and write, I have nothing to sell, then I can't pay rent. I have to wake up running or I don't eat. So wake up running and don't stop running until you reach your goal.

7. Know the ledge.

Know your limitations. Know your weaknesses. Know your flaws. When you know what you're missing, you'll understand what you need most to succeed.

8. Me, Myself & I, Inc.

If you're going solo you should incorporate. Whether you do an "S

Corp." or an "LLC." Incorporate yourself now. Call your company "Employee, Inc.," I don't care, just incorporate. You'll save a boatload on taxes, etc. If you're a freelancer, you're a business anyway—might as well make it official.

For what you've probably spent on fancy suits, you can get your business incorporated, registered, licensed, and get stationery and corporate identities designed. For the price of a pair of Air Force Ones you can copyright entire bodies of work: books, song lyrics, artwork, story ideas, screenplays, and all sorts of intellectual property. (I spent a whopping $35 plus postage to copyright this book.) Furthermore, all necessary info and forms are available online. The trademark, patent, and copyright forms are available thru the United States Patent and Trademark Office (www.uspto.gov) and Library of Congress' Copyright Office (www.loc.gov/copyright) respectively. Incorporation forms and info are also available thru your city's Small Business Administration office and websites, as well as at most local libraries.

Lastly, get yourself a website. Online services have become so commoditized that you should be able to get set up properly at a good price. Just do some research and find a reputable web designer and web host, develop a clear message and get out there.

Again, all of this requires extra planning upfront, but it's worth it on the back-end. Besides, it's a good feeling to know that you're in charge of what you do.

9. Call a Cochran.

Every businessperson needs some jurisprudence. Talk to a lawyer. And don't call your cousin who watches Court TV or reads Grisham novels; budget for an official juris doctorate-holding, contract-understanding, legalese-spitting attorney. Sure, I rip lawyers constantly, but I've seen many a man go broke or go to jail because they had a bad lawyer or no lawyer at all.

Lawyers can be pricey, but there are plenty of qualified affordable attorneys out there. And truthfully, as a freelancer you probably don't need one. But again, if you're starting a business you should at least consult with one. Just make sure they specialize in your area of need (i.e., start-ups, intellectual property, music industry, taxes, etc.)

10. The taxman cometh...

Also, get yourself a registered CPA. If you're freelancing, an accountant can save you a ton every April. And if you're a business, a good accountant can keep you out of prison.

11. Freestyle fellowship.

Besides shouting out a classic '90's Left Coast crew, this one's a reminder of the importance of building and vibing. I can't stress that enough. Just because you're striking out on your own doesn't mean you have to carry the load by yourself.

As you build your enterprise, maintain relationships no matter what. Call on folks from your old job, friends of friends, etc. Help is not a dirty word. In fact, you should keep a short-list of about 5 people you can call on for advice, connections, etc.

And if you leave your current gig on good terms (which you always should), don't be afraid to call on former bosses or clients for freelance work. Most companies don't mind supporting upstarts, especially ones that they already have established relationships with.

Share each other's troubles and problems,
and in this way obey the laws of Christ.
—Galatians 6:2

12. Make sure your crew is as tight as you.

Speaking of help, at some point every plan needs a crew: a group of people working together to flip that plan into a successful reality. So if your business idea falls into that category (as most all do), make sure your crew—your investors, your partners, employees, family, etc., are as committed to your vision as you are. Make sure they're as professional about manifesting it as you are. And most importantly, make sure they're qualified and capable of doing whatever tasks you're asking them to do. If they're not, they might slack off or sleep on something crucial. If their game isn't as tight as yours, you'll be finished before you start.

Well, those are the particulars. *Remember:* Don't talk about it, be about it. Between cyber cafes, the library, and Kinko's, the tools are right in front of you. Lots of first-time businesses fail, but a lot succeed. I guess it just depends on what you truly want out of life. There's nothing wrong with working for other people other than that you'll always be working for other people. Freedom starts and ends with what you allow to happen in your life. So roll up those sleeves and get free.

Now, I'll be the first to admit that I complain a lot about America; and there's a lot wrong here. But being able to start your own business with little more than some faith, planning, and elbow grease is definitely one of the right things about this joint. So take advantage of the good and you can change the bad or at least overcome it.

I'm a hustler, baby. I just want you to know,
It ain't "where I been", it's "where I'm about to go"...
—Pharrell & Jay-Z[1]

Validate Yourself

I see myself as a queen but it ain't for rank.
It's for all, not one, not for income.
It's for knowing who and where we descend from.
—*Queen Latifah*

One of my former companies used to give an annual award—they called it the *Pioneers' Day Award*. Basically, it was their MVP trophy. Most thought it was a joke because the only ones who ever won it were the CEO or higher-ups. But one year, Norman changed the game.

Every company in the world has at least one "Norman": Really super-quiet and humble. All he did was work. You never heard about him getting in any kind of trouble. You never ran into him at any of the local clubs or bars. He just worked his 10-plus hour days and punched out every night. He kept the same quiet smile and polite demeanor. He reminded me of Stuart Smalley from the old *SNL* shows only with darker hair and fewer sweaters. We used to joke that if anyone would ever show up armed, it'd be Norman because "It's always the quiet ones..." But in all his years as a company fixture, you never heard Norman complain about a thing. He just worked. Work seemed to be his life.

So one year in front of the whole company, our CEO announces the winner: It's Norman. The whole place—maybe 200-strong at the time—goes nuts; everyone's applauding and cheering him on. We're all hugging him as he makes his way up to the front. And it's not that smile-for-the-camera phony congratulatory stuff they do at the Oscars or Grammies; this was real love. We truly liked Norman. And as they handed him his little statuette-thingy, he spoke:

"I feel so validated."

Those were the first words out of his mouth as he broke down in tears of joy. I feel so validated. Norman went on and on, choking back tears and soaking in the validation. I feel so validated. Norman continued by confessing how important his job was to him and how important it was to be acknowledged for it. The award gave him purpose and a reason for being, he added.

In an odd way, I felt sorry for him. His job really seemed to be his life. His job was his validation. His job was his purpose. As far as I was concerned, Norman was a good man, but I never, ever wanted to grow up and be anything like that. I never wanted to be someone who needed validation from a company or a boss to feel whole or good about themselves. But Norman was that guy. And he wasn't alone.

I met a bunch of Normans over the years: People who, at various stages of their careers were driven by a need for validation. I bet you know people like that, too. Their boss criticizes them in the morning and they go home at night still all twisted up over it. Or they lose out on some type of workplace adulation or opportunity and it eats at them for days. It's sad. But companies love that crap because it keeps us working hard. And quiet as kept, there's a little bit of Norman in all of us. Everyone wants to be validated.

Don't clock anybody let 'em all clock you.
Don't be down with anybody let 'em all be down with you.
—Heavy D.[1]

Do me a favor and highlight this one: *No job can validate you.* No boss can validate you. Validation is not external it's internal. Before you punched a clock, you were a human being. Before you had paychecks, you had a soul. Your job does not make you. What validates you should be your relationship with God, your family, and yourself. You shouldn't need a fancy occupation, title, or award to feel more human or accepted. Besides, they already hired you—that should be validation enough.

America is funny like that. We constantly teach people, particularly men, that their jobs and possessions are what make them whole. We teach folks that being the breadwinner is what it's all about. The more money you have, the more successful you are, the better a person you are. When we see someone with a minimum wage job, we assume that they're less intelligent, less hardworking, and even less of a citizen than someone with a big salary or a cushy office position. The man with advanced degrees has more stature than the guy with the nametag. But don't sleep; it's all just another part of The Hustle.

Be your own man, don't be "borrowed" don't be "bought".
—Heavy D.[2]

No Validation Required...

I remember lunching in this one food court—it was in the concourse of a big fancy office high-rise that I worked in. It was one of those upscale food-spots that all the businesspeople regularly hit. I'm talking European cheeses...Couscous...Exotic stir-fries...Paninis...Ten-dollar salads...Imported beers and wines with really long names... Plus an array of designer pseudo-pure juices and smoothies—6 bones per baby-bottle's worth... I don't think I ever ate there for less than a 10 spot.

The joint was always packed with uppity corporate broads: they rolled in between noon and 2 in packs of 10–20 deep stinking of *Cliniqùe*, *Maybeline*, and L'ORÈAL. The profiles were always the same: Ann Taylor power suits. *Kate Spade* gear. *Liz Claiborne* specs. Plus *Filene's Basement* knock-offs. But hands down, the most stunning lady in the place every day was the cashier.

I went out of my way to end up in her checkout line. Watching her was like beholding lilies in a field. She was so real and regular...couldn't have been more than 5'4", but she was stunning: No make-up. Ever. She was blue-collar-girl thick, you could just tell there was a great body under her uniform, which always looked a little too big. Some days her apron bunched-up in weird places on her, but it didn't matter. Long thick black hair usually in a ponytail 'cuz of the dumb green company hat she had to wear, dark olive skin, these big warm, dark eyes, soft thick lips... She was a beautiful Chicana...incredible smile, too.

Plus she was cool. She didn't talk like a GMAT study guide. Didn't blab about shopping, office agendas, or weekend getaways like most of the crowd she served. And no matter how snotty they were toward her, she was nice to them. And you could tell that when her shift was over, she went home (wherever home was) and work didn't cross her mind again until she punched back in. Her customers worked for a living; she worked while she lived. No validation required.

Conversely the business world is filled with folks who are so workcentric they have no clue who or what they are outside the office. They are their title. Their company is their family. They live their industry. The only culture they know is the one they're immersed in for 60-plus hours a week. When they go on vacation—make that if they go on vacation, they take their cellphone and their laptop, because God forbid they're out of the loop for a day. Folks like that just can't see life thru the trees.

But again, I had stretches early on where I became my job, too. And when someone criticized my work, it was like they were criticizing me, taking shots at my sense of self. It would kill me some days. Shopping was a good distraction then. Spending money was proof I was making money, which was proof that I was somebody important. But of course, shopping validates nothing and having a career doesn't validate your humanity.

I am what I am and that's all I be.
—Lady of Rage[3]

BabyMamma Drama

In many ways the marketing/ad world is Hollywood's mini-me: wall-to-wall super-egos begging to be stroked rampant narcissism and neurotics starving for validation. (It's no accident that most top Tinsel Town-ers got their start doing commercials.) Each year the ad world hands out awards—OBIE's, One Show pencils, Clios, Cannes Lions, etc. They're basically our Oscars, Emmys, Tony's, and People's Choice awards, except 99-44/100% of the world couldn't care less about these awards or who wins them. But for industry heads, (especially creatives) "award-winning" is the ultimate validation. And truth be told, I cosigned that until . . .

One day, I was doing what most copywriters seeking inspiration do: thumbing thru my agency's One Show annuals and dreaming about the day I'd claim my spon in one. ("Annuals" are catalogs of the year's best ads. One Show has long been considered the cream of the awards crop.) And while searching for a muse, one ad did what every great ad does: stop me cold:

A black male, mid-teens. He stood proudly in a tracksuit, holding up trophies with several track medals around his neck. Above him was this headline: *"If you want to see how fast he can really run, wait until his girlfriend tells him she's pregnant."* The ad was for a Planned Parenthood-type client. it was awarded a Gold pencil—the highest prize in its category.

I stared at it for what seemed like hours. At the time, I wasn't much older than the kid in the pic and all I'd heard most of my life was how irresponsible and worthless black men are; and now I was seeing it in print, and it was being celebrated.

I think that was the day I gave up on winning industry awards and being upset when I didn't. Over the years, I've learned that awards are just someone else's opinion of you; and quite often their opinion isn't worth having. The downside of not chasing or openly championing the edgy-for-edgy's-sake work that the awards shows love is that you're not seen as a "good creative." The upside of just focusing on work that respects consumers as much as clients is this: Every company I've ever freelanced for has tried to hire me fulltime, while just about every client I've ever worked for has grown their business because my work. (I'm good with that.)

(FYI: If folks knew some of what the ad world has celebrated and occasionally still celebrates as "award-winning" or "creative" Madison Ave would get boycotted and/or sued for hate speech every other week.)

Employees are Consumers, too

A big part of validating yourself is realizing that your bosses need you as much as you need them. As an employee, you are also a consumer. Your job is the product. Your boss and your company are the manufacturers. Your industry and your career are the brands. You buy into all of this thru your your presence.

So become an educated consumer; know what job/company is right for you. If you're not getting the quality you deserve where you're at right now, shop around. Business always needs quality workers. The only way a business or an industry can provide quality workers is to offer a quality product (good work environment, decent pay, benefits, etc.). So when it comes to your job, remember to shop smart and never forget, *"Buyer Beware."*

A job ain't nuthin' but work!
—Marlon Wayans[4]

It's Just a Job

A job is a tool, a tool for income and paying bills, a tool for providing for your family. But a job is not you. It shouldn't validate or define you. The moment you let your job define you, the moment you look for personal validation from your boss or your job is the moment The Hustle controls you. It doesn't matter whether you work for yourself or someone else, what you do for income shouldn't determine your self-worth. Handle your business; don't let your business handle you.

In the end, there's nothing wrong with enjoying your job or your career; there's nothing wrong with enjoying your success or possessions. In fact, you should enjoy 'em all. But when it comes to seeking validation you should look within and above and never lose focus.

Validation is Free

For generations "consumption" was the common term for tuberculosis (TB) because of how the illness consumed or wasted away its victims. Today we suffer from a different type of consumption—mass consumption.

Like the female professionals I saw in that food court, too many of us go into debt trying to validate ourselves with things, purchases, and brand names. We floss the hottest, the trendiest, or the most expensive whatever just to feel validated, just to feel part of something bigger or to feel better than the next person.

Just remember: *NO MATTER WHAT YOU BUY REAL VALIDATION IS ALWAYS FREE.*

Marvel not, my brethren if the world hate you...
—I John 3:13

Word: Life

I returned, and saw under the sun,
that the race is not to the swift,
nor the battle to the strong, neither yet bread to the wise,
nor yet riches to men of understanding,
nor yet favour to men of skill;
but time and chance happeneth to them all.
—Ecclesiastes 9:11

Once I saw an ad: A man in his 40s, holding a baby, obviously his son. The headline read: "When you're 80 years old, you won't look back and say, 'I wish I'd worked more weekends'..." I forgot what they were selling but I remembered what they were saying. You don't need a job to live. Things like rent, clothes, and food require a job, but living doesn't. You can and should live outside of work. And here are 5 tips to help you do just that:

1. Be Out By 5.

Most companies expect folks to work past 5 P.M. in order to be taken seriously for promotions and raises. People equate working late with caring about your job and being a team player. Well, screw these people, too. Working late is overrated. Work late only when you absolutely have to. Otherwise, put in your 8 hours and go home.

A couple extra hours a day can make all the difference between having a life and not having one.

2. No More Weekends

I once knew this exec, she was Jewish. Every Friday afternoon she had the same debate with herself: Saturday synagogue or Saturday in the office. She almost always chose work because of the pressure to excel and impress the higher-ups. One Friday afternoon somebody said to her, "God will get you another job, but your job can't get you another God." She went to synagogue that Saturday and most every Saturday afterwards...for a while, at least. It didn't hurt her career. Much. But she was much happier when she kept her weekends to herself.

Take back your weekends. Weekends are yours. Weekends are when you remember that you're human. People recharge on weekends. People party on weekends. People worship on weekends. People reconnect with their families on weekends. When you let a boss or a job own your weekends, you're letting them own you. So screw folks who say your weekends aren't yours—they're just saying it because they have no life outside of work and don't want you to have one, either. Weekends belong to people, not companies.

White folks have wonderful weekends.
All we have is "a couple days off"!
—Steve Harvey[1]

3. I'm On Vacation!

American workers are terrible at taking vacations; we average just 10.2 days off a year. Yet in Western Europe, law mandates four weeks of vacation while six weeks off is not uncommon.[2] But in America, employee vacation time is optional. That's right. America is the only Western industrialized country that doesn't legally require employee vacation time. And why aren't most bosses losing sleep over this is? Gee, I wonder... Could The Hustle have something to do with this?

In all my years, I saw only two bosses tell any employee, "Why don't you take a couple days off, it's okay." It's not that the other bosses were evil; it's just that they were more concerned with the company's wellbeing than their employees'. If it were up to them, employees would work 365.

So weekends aside, everyone should take off at least once every 2 months. One, maybe 2 days...Flip a Friday into a 3-day weekend. Even if you can't afford to travel, take time off. Sleep in. See a movie. Hit the beach. Catch up with family or friends. Just take some time off.

Also, when you go on vacation, don't tell anyone where you're going or how to reach you. Lose the celly. Ignore the email. Don't check in. The whole point of time off is to have time off, not to be at the beach fielding "We-need-some-files-off-your-computer" and "Hey-can-you-stop-in-for-a-sec," calls. No. Vacation means: *LEAVE ME ALONE UNTIL I COME BACK TO WORK.*

And don't worry about losing your job or a promotion while you're out. If your job's in jeopardy, it'll be in jeopardy whether you're there or not, so you might as well get some rest out of the deal. In fact, if you have to work 24/7/365 just to keep it or to succeed, then your job sucks and you're getting pimped. A vacation is the least of your problems.

Looking back, I would've sacrificed extra salary for an extra 2 weeks of paid vacation time. That's how important I believe vacations are to healthy living. In fact that's part of why I freelance—I feel better now than I ever felt when I was clocking 70-hour weeks for some company. So if you can, next time you're up for a promotion or a raise, trade some money for some extra paid time off.

Eddie Gaylord (Oklahoma Publishing founder) died
at his desk at the age of 101. I should be so lucky.
—L. Lowry Mays, Clear Channel Founder/Chairman[3]

4. S.H.A.P.E. Your Future

Most of us spend our whole lives trying to figure out what we're meant to do, where we're meant to work, etc. One reason so many of us put our careers ahead of our lives is because we don't know what to replace it with. We often stay at the same job simply because we don't know where else to go or what else to do. I'm no different. What helped me sort thru things was the realization that at some point, we all need to sit down with ourselves and look at our shape.

In *The Purpose Driven Life*, author Rick Warren talks about S.H.A.P.E. It's an acronym for *Spiritual gifts, Heart, Abilities, Personality*, and *Experiences*. It's based on the belief that God gives each of us the tools we need to accomplish, overcome, and find our place in the world largely thru these 5 avenues. If you're struggling to find out what you should be doing, where you should be going, etc. I highly recommend *The Purpose Driven Life.*

There is nothing quite as potent as a focused life, one lived on purpose.
—Rick Warren, author

5. Service

The Hustle teaches selfishness. It teaches us that the world revolves around us and the only reason we're here is to take, take, take...make money, get fat, live for self, and everyone else is either competition or an angle to be worked. And many of us live that lesson to the fullest until we drop. Besides being the wrong way to go, it's a big reason why so many folks in the business world struggle to have a life outside of work. Truth be told, this life is about service—service to God and service to each other.

In fact, the loneliest, unhappiest (and meanest) people I've ever met also happened to be among the most selfish and shortsighted ones. They took more than they gave and they asked for help more often than they ever offered it. At some point, we all have to commit to service. At some point, we all have to commit to using our gifts and blessings to help others. Now you may not have to quit your job or give away all your worldly possessions, but at some point, you'll be called on to use those things to serve God and others. For me personally, *Knock The Hustle* is just one small part of what I hope to be a long life of service.

So if you're looking to reclaim your life, find a greater sense of peace, purpose, etc., pray. Find out how you can be of service to God and others.

For brethren, ye have been called unto liberty;
only use not liberty for an occasion of the flesh,
but by love serve one another.
—Galatians 5:13

Well that's it for this one. Malik Yusef, a really nice poet from Chicago put it best on Com's *Someday it'll All Make Sense*: "They asked me what I do for a living. I said, 'I breathe oxygen'." Sometimes perspective is as simple as an exhale. So take a good look in the mirror then breathe in...don't let work define you, breathe out...define yourself beyond work and the material. The most important job you'll ever have is being the best human being possible. Don't let business and materialistic nonsense get in the way of that.

Live joyfully with the wife whom thou loves
all the days of the life
of thy vanity, which he hath given thee under
the sun, all the days of thy vanity:
for that is thy portion in this life, and in thy labour
which thou takest under the sun. Whatsoever thy
hand findeth to do, do it with thy might;
for there is no work, nor device, nor knowledge,
nor wisdom, in the grave, wither thou goest...
—Ecclesiastes 9:9-1

The Outro
(Conclusion)

Thank y'all for comin' out.
God Bless and goodnight.
—Russell Simmons

Well, it's time to rest my pen...carpal tunnel's setting in. Again, I want to thank you for reading and supporting me. I just wanted you to have at least one honest, straight-from-the-heart look at business that offered the kind of thinking that's risky enough (and proven enough) to actually work. Hopefully, I've done that.

But this was a tough write. Most of the time I kept thinking about how easy I had it. I mean, for all the hustlers, stupid people, pimps, etc., the truth was, I met a lot of good people and had more than a few good days. But more than anything, when things were good, I felt like I had some of that American Dream stuff: the job, the comfort, the security, the possibilities, etc...Short of being an athlete or an entertainer, how many people get paid well to do what they're good at and enjoy? It's hard to walk away from that, even after you stop believing in it.

The hardest thing about leaving was the money. When the money was good, I made more than both of my parents combined and I know for a fact I never worked as hard as either of them, not even once. But I never got rich, not even close. Still, with the exception of my first year or 2, I wasn't hurting, either. A colleague once said, "Ain't no heavy lifting and we ain't curing cancer." He was right. The only injuries I ever got came from playing company softball and maybe doing one too many 12-oz. curls.

In the end, business is just folks in offices saying, "Think this'll sell? Don't know; let's find out." Whether you're a lawyer, an accountant, a marketing exec, or a secretary, all you're really doing is figuring out what will sell, who'll buy it, and what's it worth to find out. The Hustle comes when they make you believe that it's any more serious or complicated than that.

The last thing business wants is for the average person to realize they don't have to be subservient to all these stupid constructs. They want sheep to sheer for profit. They want to "validate" you. They want you rat-racing and paper-chasing your life away. They want you to think "hard" is an office without air-conditioning. They want you to believe that you can't live without their brands or their images. Pimps need hoes. Hustlers need agendas and suckers. They need their soylent green. But don't let 'em get you. It's just a job. It's just sugar water. Don't believe the hype.

The Hustle is not a mythical machine or even some faceless cabal. The Hustle is made of people—good people, greedy people, smart people, stupid people...it's all people. And people can change.

So Who's Really Who?

I'm not saying. While *Knock The Hustle* is 100% and features real people, it's really a book about issues and solutions, not embarrassing folks or starting witch-hunts. I believe that's our only hope for change. (Besides, everyone involved already knows who they are.)

Swinging at Windmills...

As a shorty, I had this doctor—this cool Muslim cat my parents always took me to right off 79th & Stoney Island in Chicago. He used to give out suckers—the ones with the little curvy loopy stick so you could wear them like rings as you licked them. Looking back, outside of Cliff Huxtable, I didn't really know any black doctors. Anyway, maybe when I was about 8 or 9 I asked him why he was a doctor and he said something like, "I want to become irrelevant... I want to get so good at helping people and I want to see medicine get so good that everyone will get healthy enough to not need us anymore." I thought it was a weird thing to say so I never forgot it. But I didn't actually remember it again until I started writing this book.

The poet Saul Williams once spoke, "We are waiting for the past to die." Maybe Saul was on to something. Maybe that's what true progress is; maybe that's how The Hustle will finally get knocked out in the end. Maybe the older generation of businessfolks will just have to go before business gets it right. Maybe it'll take everyone like me to die off before racism, classism, and other societal ills get solved.

Maybe, right now, somewhere there's a bunch of 20-somethings doing business on nothing but cash, handshakes, and possibilities. Maybe there's a bunch of 18-year-olds, foreign and domestic, doing their thing together while respecting each other's cultures and communities. And maybe the reason we can't see any of 'em is because they're all hiding in the shadows just waiting for us to die. I'd like to believe all of that... Then again, I'd like to believe in Santa Claus, too.

Upfront I called Corporate America a housing project. Well there's one obvious difference: We're not bulldozing Wall Street or Madison Avenue and shipping our shirt-'n'-tie types out to the boonies. Business is here to stay. And for the most part, it is what it is. But every thing man made, man can change. And whether I'm in an office, on the streets, or on a desert island, Corporate America affects everything I see, hear, buy, use, or ingest. So I have to stay and fight. We all do.

We have an obligation to change, to fight for something greater than a paycheck or coolness. We are not what we buy. We are not our bank accounts. We are not our jobs. We are not each other's definition of ourselves. Culture isn't a commodity. Ethnicity shouldn't be a construct. Nationality is not a brand. Life is not logos and programming. We are not the illusions and delusions that bind us. We were all born to be more. We are all destined to be more. We just have to want this more than The Hustle wants to keep us from it.

Knock The Hustle isn't a destination. It isn't the means to an end. It's just one leg of a really long journey and ain't no half-steppin'. Don't be afraid to take that first step.

Peace,
Hadji Jon Steven Williams, author/founder
ProdigalPen, Inc.

Then I looked on all the works that my hand hath wrought,
and on the labour that I had laboured to do: and,
behold, all was vanity and vexation of spirit,
and there was no profit under the sun...
—Ecclesiastes 2:4-11

Peace To...
(Thank Yous)

Yo, what happened to "peace"?
—Eric B.

My Lord and Savior Jesus Christ, thank you for everything before, after, and in-between. Hope I did good by you on this one. Help me to do better next time. ***Dad,*** much of the knowledge in this book came from your blood, sweat, and wisdom. If I can see further than you did it's only because I'm standing on your shoulders. Thank you for raising me to be a man. ***Mom,*** you birthed me, earthed me, and raised me. You also helped me see that God is real and good. Thank you for all of that and so much more. Always. ***My fam in Chi, Gary, East St. Louis, and Miss:*** I write so that our stories won't die with us. ***My Brown Angel,*** you are a truly wonderful woman and one of the most genuine blessings my life has ever received. Thank you for everything. ***Sherman,*** for proving that business and friendship can mix. (CG will be great.) ***CMT,*** I'm glad you and 'nita are my friends. ***Candace and Trace,*** for being such good friends. (Hey Candi: "Another day, another day-rate!") ***Every man, woman and child of color in America:*** The Streets and The Suites aren't that different. Fight the good fight and never give up. ***Paulette, Herb, Sherlene, and CC,*** I wouldn't have made it without you. Thank you all. ***Sandy, Breda, Jen, Sissy:*** Thanks for getting me my first good gig. You guys were always wonderfully supportive folks. ***Vanessa and Carrie,*** for being great lawyers. Thank you both. ***Chi-town,*** from Southside to Westside to North, I love every segregated, corrupt, hustling, beautiful struggling part of you. ***The Guys @ BoJono's,*** for always being real (and of course, the good grub). ***NYC*** and ***California***: I love every minute I'm there. ***Gwynne Forster***, for hooking me up with 2 bookstore owners at the '04 BEA. (Also, I love your books!) ***Langston Hughes, Nikki Giovanni, Rakim, Gil-Scott Heron, Paul Robeson, Ralph Ellison, Cornell West, Rick Warren, Saul Williams...*** Hope I have a little bit of your ink in my pen someday. ***Apostolic Church of God,*** for bringing the good news nonstop. ***Dan Poynter,*** your self-publishing manuals helped turn a grueling marathon into a walk in the park. ***Tavis Smiley:*** I wanna be juss like you when I grow up! ***Davey D., Big CED,*** **Playahata.com**, ***Yaminah, Isoul, Kym, Farai C.*** and ***Jean C.***, ***Audie V.***, ***Cpt. Rex, Wayne MT, B. Entertainment, MG***, and everyone else who's supported me. I truly appreciate it. ***Janice Phelps and Joan Phelps,*** thank you for all your technical support, input, and advice. You guys are wonderful (www.janicephelps.com). ***Everyone I met in Corporate America;***, in some way you all influenced, inspired, or touched me. May you all knock The Hustle for life. ***Everyone who reads this book:*** Once again, whether you did so out of curiosity, loyalty, boredom, or hunger, I wrote it for you. Thanks for your support. Let the journey begin.

Quotables
(References & Sources)

I take a phrase that's rarely heard,
flip it—now it's the daily word.
—Rakim

This is my intentionally unorthodox bibliography. The goal here is to share my recipe of *where's*, *from's*, and *why's* I used to cook up this book. First off, my two core ingredients for info and inspiration were the Bible and black culture. The Bible was an obvious choice. Best book ever—no book has more lasting wisdom or truth.

Get yourself a thick Bible so there's no words missing.
—Bill Cosby, (Bill Cosby: Himself, 1983)

Before *Knock The Hustle,* I'd written a different business book. It was safe, cheerleaderish, and very radio-friendly...it would've been a bestseller. Even started promoting it back in 2002... But it wasn't real; it wasn't true. So I scrapped it and started over. I grabbed a pen and a pad and started digging and rebuilding. I wrote the truth and built on what those who came before me did. I chose voices and perspectives forged from adversity, common sense, real insights, ingenuity, and soul.

I encourage you to review the sources my sources and wherever possible, purchase the artists' works I've cited. I did so under the auspices of scholarly research and adding literary/intellectual value to you the reader. Once you listen to the larger bodies of their respective works, I think you'll be surprised by how much insight many of these men and women have to offer us all. With that said, here are my quotables:

2. *The Education of Gore Vidal*, PBS documentary (2003)
3. *The Miseducation of the Negro* by Dr. Carter G. Woodson. (Africa World Press 1990)
4. "Grindin'" (song) The Clipse (2002)
5. "You Don't Know" (song) Jay-Z (2001)
6. "The Bridge Is Over" (song) KRS-ONE (1987)
7. "Sound of Da Police" (song) KRS-ONE (1993)
8. "Ode to the Pro" (poem) Hadji Williams (2002)
9. "Career Opportunities!" (song) The Clash (1977)

CHAPTER 5: Less Bosses "Slow down, let the leader lead."
Leadership 101 from Rakim's seminal *Follow the Leader* song/album of same name. (1988)
1. "Runnin' Thangs" (song) Busy Bee (1988)
2. *Working Mothers* Magazine (Dec. 2002)
3. Fortune.com archives
4. Abraham Lincoln (bio) by Carl Sandburg (1954)
5. Jennifer Reingold, "Rush Hour: The Godfather of Hiphop" *Fast Company* (Nov. 2003)

CHAPTER 6: Role Call! "For as we have..."
Romans 12:4...It's a blessing to know you role.

CHAPTER 7: Support Your Support Staff "I love my posse!"
Disco Dave was a legendary underground hiphop DJ from 1980s Chicago. He ended every show with his trademark verse, including this quote. He understood that his community was the foundation of his success. Businessfolks should do the same.
1. "Worst Comes To Worst" (song) Dilated Peoples (2001)

CHAPTER 8: No More CYA "Funny how some things change..."
A Week Ago, a classic Hov' 'n' Short collab (1998) Real businessfolks don't CYA.
1. Hadji Williams.

CHAPTER 9: Shook Ones "Scared to death scared to look..."
Classic Mobb Deep (*Shook Ones Pt. 2*) (1995). Fear is a bad leader, and worse follower.

CHAPTER 10: Word is Bond "There is no 'maybe'..."
From *Amistad* (1997), Steven Spielberg's slave-revolt saga. In a key scene, a defense lawyer meets people who don't understand "maybe," only "yes" or "no"; that's "word is bond."

CHAPTER 11: Less Communicating..."Seeing that we have such hope..."
II Corinthians 3:12. Speak plain English. Let your message do the talking for you.
1. "Manifest" (song) Gang Starr (1989)

CHAPTER 12: Do You. "I'mo do me..."
"Do You" (song, 1998) from Heather B. (former BDP/Real World alum). Be yourself.
1. "We Got Our Own Thang" (song) Heavy D. & The Boyz (1989) Bun. Diddley.

Diddley. Dee.
2. "10% Diss" (song) MC Lyte, 1989. Lyte as a rock (or should I say a boulder?)

CHAPTER 13: Kill the Dogs 'n' Ponies "Got me working..."
Classic MJ (1979's *Off The Wall*). He sang of working hard to impress a woman. Companies and employees do the same just to get a rep. And it's usually counterproductive.
1. The former Chicago Cub first baseman on the then-loveable losers' suspect roster moves.
2. "Clients, Agencies react to ONDCP guilty verdicts" by Jim Edwards Adweek 2/28/2005
3. "I Get The Job Done" (song), Big Daddy Kane. (1989)
4. "Automatic" (song), E-40. (2003)

CHAPTER 14: People Trying To Give..."Until you do right by me..."
From 1985's *Color Purple* (movie). Treat people fair. Okay?
1. "Respect" (song), Otis Redding 1964. (The originator, FYI.)

CHAPTER 15: Company Cancers "Everybody works with someone..."
Classic Kings of Comedy (2000). Self-explanatory.
1. *Bebe's Kids* (comedy album), the legendary Robin Harris. (1990)

CHAPTER 16: Caste Warfare "For the love of money..."
For The Love of Money (1978). Classic O'Jays. Nothing divides people quite like money.

CHAPTER 17: Equally Yoked "Be ye not unequally yoked..."
II Corinthians. Mad, mad, mad wisdom.
1. *Forrest Gump* 1994 (movie)

CHAPTER 18: Friends vs. Coworkers "Friends, how many of us have them?"
Friends (song) Classic Whodini (1986). Can friendship and money mix?

CHAPTER 19: For My Seeds..."Be a father..."
Be A Father (1991) An Edo G. classic. Family first.
1. "Poppa Was A Rolling Stone" (song) The Temptations (1972)
2. "Grown Folks" (song) Raphael Saadiq (2004)

CHAPTER 20: Do The Knowledge "Teacher, teacher..." Genius from *"The Greatest Adventures of Slick Rick"* (album) by Slick Rick (1988)
1. Jennifer Merritt, "B-Schools: A Failing Grade on Minorities," *BusinessWeek Online,* 5/12/03.
2. "My Philosophy" (song) KRS-One *By All Means Necessary* (album 1987)
3. "Teach the Children" (song) Eric B. & Rakim *Don't Sweat The Technique* (album 1992).

CHAPTER 21: Movin' On "Gotta go, gotta go, gotta go!"

More from Mr. Robin Harris, one of the funniest cats ever.
1. "Movin' On" (song) Mya (1997)
2. "Should I Stay or Should I Go?" (song) The Clash (1982)

SIDE B: THE TAKEOVER "Get Free or Die Trying." From Dead Prez's 2002 mixtape of the same name. KTH's B-side focuses on big picture issues facing business and society.

CHAPTER 1: Honor Among Thieves? "Better is a little..."
Proverbs. Lite on verbage. Heavy on wisdom.
1. Dan Russell. "The Racist Roots of The Drug War" *PARANOIA Magazine* Spring 2001.
2. *New York Times, Feb. 8, 1914*
3. "Yum! Restaurants International Opens 1000th KFC In China" (Business Wire) 1/16/2004.
4. "Yum! Restaurants International Opens 300th Pizza Hut Restaurant in South Korea" (Business Wire) 1/15/2004.
5. "Yum! Charges in China: KFC Colonel leads way as company grows, aims at Tibet." By Ted Anthony (Associated Press) 1/20/2004.
6. Industry Data, *NPD Funworld* (www.gamemarketwatch.com) Jan. 2004.
7. Retirement speech from Jerome Kohlberg, Jr. founder of Kohlberg, Kravis, Roberts & Co., May 5, 1987.
8. *Civil Disobedience* (essay) Henry David Thoreau. (1846)

CHAPTER 2: The Great American Paper Chase "All hail the almighty dollar..."
From *New Jack City* soundtrack (1992), Latifah rhapsodizes on money's dark side.
1. "D'evils" (song) Jay-Z (1996)
2. *The World Is Yours*, Nas (1994)
3. "Gimme The Loot" (song) Notorious BIG (1994)
4. "Country Grammar" (song) Nelly (2000)

CHAPTER 3: Crop Circles & Alarm Clocks "A lot of 'nigger' callin'..."
From Nas' *Lost Tapes* 2003. The great self-contradictor analyzes modern race-relations in business.
1. "Can't Knock The Hustle" (song) Jay-Z (1996)
2. "Casino Cash Fuels Rash of Tribal Feuds" Brian Grow and Douglas Harbrecht BusinessWeek Online, 5/2/2003
3. "Special Report Indian Casinos: Wheel of Misfortune," Donald L. Barlett and James B. Steele, *TIME* 12/16/2002
4. National Committee on Pay Equity. (2003)
5. "H to the Izzo" (song), Jay-Z (2001)
6. In 1994 Susan Smith drowned her two kids in a lake then claimed "a black man with a gun" stole her children. Serving life.
7. In 2001 Andrea Yates systematically drowned her 5 children in a bathtub in 2001 while her husband was at work. Her life sentence was overturned in 2005.

8. In December 2003 Dianne Odell was sentenced to concurrent terms of 15, 20, and 25 years for murdering 3 of her children in the late 1980s and carrying their mummified bodies around until 2002. Trial ongoing.
9. On May 10, 2003 Deanna Lejune Laney beat two of her 3 kids to death with a brick while her husband slept.
10. In 1999 Marilyn Morrissey Lemak drugged and suffocated her 3 children, apparently to get even with her estranged husband. Now serving life.
11. In 2004 Andrea Williams killed her 3 kids in 2004. Trial ongoing.
12. On January 5, 2002 Charles Bishop, then 15, stole a single engine plane and crashed it into the Bank of America building in Tampa, FL. His suicide note (in part): "*Osama Bin Laden is absolutely justified in the terror he has caused on 9-11. God blesses him and the others who helped make September 11th happen.*"
13. Charles McCoy, Jr. Committed 24 shootings on Ohio freeways between May 2003 and March 2004. Convicted 2005.
14. Adam Ghadan and "John Taliban" Walker Lindh. Lindh was caught in Afghanistan fighting for the Taliban in 2001. Now serving 20 years. An American-turned-Al-Qeda-soldier, Ghadan is still loose and believed to be plotting attacks against the UK and US.
15. Theodore "Ted" Kaczynski, ("The Unabomber") sent out an estimated 16 mail bombs from 1979 to 1995 injuring and killing several. Serving life.
16. In 2002, 21-year-old Luke Helder terrorized America's heartland with a multi-state pipe bomb bombing spree, injuring several and killing one. The bombs were sent along with anti-U.S. rhetoric-filled letters. Trial pending.
17. In 2005 Eric Robert Rudolph confessed to bombing the 1996 Olympics in Atlanta, plus an abortion clinic and a gay nightclub.
18. In 1995 Tim McVeigh and Terry Nichols bomb the Oklahoma City Federal Building killing 168 Americans. McVeigh is executed in 2002. Nichols is serving life without parole.
19. Lee Harvey Oswald. Assassinated President John F. Kennedy on 11/22/63. Killed before trial by Jack Ruby.
20. John Hinckley, Jr. Shot president Ronald Reagan on March 30, 1981. Now serving life in a mental hospital.
21. Observation from former Supreme Court justice Harry Blackmun on business's growing anti-diversity sentiments and the increasing difficulty of suing for workplace bias.

CHAPTER 4: Get in Where..."Some men see things..."

From 2002's Aziatic, AZ was speaking on turning barriers into opportunities. Peace to AZ one of the smoothest flows ever.

1. Excerpt from Malcolm X's speech at Militant Labor Forum, NY. (May 29, 1964)
2. "We're A Winner" (song), Curtis Mayfield (1968)
3. "Dirt Off Your Shoulder" (song) Jay-Z. (The Black Album 2004)
4. Katharine Graham, Pulitzer Prize winner/longtime publisher of the Washington Post.
5. Excerpt from Booker T. Washington's speech given Sept. 18, 1895 at the Atlanta Cotton States & International Exposition in Atlanta, Georgia.

6. Cora Daniels, author *(Black Power Inc.: The New Voice of Success.)* She wrote this quote in my book at a book signing.
7. "Can't Knock The Hustle" (song) Jay-Z (*Reasonable Doubt* 1996)
8. "U.N.I.T.Y." (song) Queen Latifah (*Black Reign* 1994)
9. "Over Ya Head" (song), KRS-ONE (1997)
10. Excerpt from a T.D. Jakes's Sunday sermon (2003)
11. From Patricia Robinson's essay, "Malcolm X, Our Revolutionary Son & Brother."
12. "Ain't No Stoppin' Us Now" (song) John McFadden & Gene Whitehead (1979)
13. *Move the Crowd,* p. 118 Gregor and Dimitri Ehrlich, (Pocket Books 1999)

CHAPTER 5: Dear Gatekeepers "There two ways..."
Booker T. Washington...We're all in the same gang.

1. "The Multicultural Economy 2003, America's Minority Buying Power" (study) by Jeffrey M. Humphreys, Selig Center for Economic Growth, Terry College of Business, U. of Georgia, 2003.
2. "State of The Dream 2004: Enduring Disparities in Black and White" study. (ufenet.org)
3. German Mennonites' Anti-Slavery Proclamation, Germantown, Pennsylvania, 1688.
4. Delyte D. Frost, "Review Worst Diversity Practices to Learn from Others' Mistakes," HR Focus, 4/1/99.
5. U.S. Census Bureau data, 2000.
6. U.S. Census Bureau study, 2003.
7. From Justice Blackmun's decision in 1978 Regents of the *University of California vs. Bakke.*
8. "The Daily Show With Jon Stewart" at 2003 Emmy Awards (The E! Channel 9/21/03)
9. Study from Catalyst, Inc. Feb. 2004 (Catalyst.com)
10. *Black Power, Inc.: The New Voice of Success* by Cora Daniels. P. 80 (Wiley 2004)
11. Department of Labor study: Gender and salary differences, 2003.
12. Rev. Sharpton, on workplace diversity during a Democratic presidential debate, 2003.
13. FORBES' 400 Richest Americans list. (FORBES.com, Feb. '05.)
14. Stephen Glass. Fired for plagiarizing/fabricating 29 of the 41 stories he wrote for the New Republic. His story was flipped into a movie (Shattered Glass) and a major book (The Fabulist). He's since written for Rolling Stone magazine.
15. Jack Kelley. Resigned from USA TODAY in 2004 after plagiarizing several pieces.
16. Mike Barnicle. Former top *Boston Globe* columnist. Fired in 1998 for fabricating quotes. Now a popular on-air personality and pundit for MSNBC.
17. Elizabeth Wurtzel. Fired by the *Dallas Morning News* for plagiarism. Later wrote for the *New Yorker* and the *New York Magazine;* also penned the bestseller *Prozac Nation.*
18. Excerpt from a TD Jakes' Sunday sermon (2003)
19. *Following The Equator* (book) Mark Twain, 1897.
20. Hadji Williams (2002)
21. "Pray" (song) MC Hammer (1990) (Why? Because we dogged him for being "soft".)

22. Dr. Martin Luther King, Jr., "Black Power" (essay) 1967.
23. From John Brown's final interview after his failed raid on Harper's Ferry in 1859. (New York Herald, Oct. 21, 1895.)

CHAPTER 6: The "Universal" Hustle "So what kind of power...?"
From Kevin Powell's book *Who's Gonna Take The Weight?* (Real world insights.)
1. "O.J. Simpson: A Study in Black and White." HBO Documentary (Nov. 2002)
2. *Everything But The Burden* (book of essays), Greg Tate, ed., p. 132 (2003)
3. "Cool" (song), The Time (1983).
4. Stepp, Katherine. "Black-Owned Media Miss on Advertising," International Press Service 6/22/05.
5. Ibid.
6. *The Multicultural Economy 2004, (*a report) by The Selig Center for Economic Growth.
7. "Work It" (song) Missy Elliot (2003)
8. *Jails, Hospitals, and Hiphop* (spoken word show) Danny Hoch. (1999)
9. "Billion-Dollar Bling: Hip-Hop Industry Stretches to Include Specialized Cars, Water and Music." Julie Watson, Forbes.com 2/24/04.
10. Nielsen Soundscan and Nielsen BDS 2003: Year End Music Industry Report (12/31/2003)
11. "Billion-Dollar Bling: Hip-Hop Industry Stretches to Include Specialized Cars, Water and Music." Julie Watson, Forbes.com 2/24/04.
12. Ibid.
13. Ibid.
14. *Everything But The Burden* (essays) Greg Tate, ed., p. 15 (2003)
15. "Blacks debating negative images of hiphop" by Vanessa E. Jones, The Boston Globe 3/31/2005
16. "Game on for 'ultimate hustler!'" by Julie Keller E! Online 4/5/2005
17. Mediaweek, April 4, 2005
18. "Black Zombies" (song) Nas (2002)
19. Darragh Johnson, Matthew Mosk, "Immigrant Remark Still Burns," HispanicBusiness.com, 5/14/2004
20. "I am Rock & Roll" (song) Mos Def (2000)
21. "Malcolm X, Our Revolutionary Son & Brother." (essay) by Patricia Robinson (1965)
22. *410 Days in The Life* (spoken word piece), Black Ice (2002)
23. "Know That" (song), Mos Def (2000)
24. *Lies My Teacher Told Me: Everything Your American History Book Got Wrong,* James W. Loewen, pp. 67–68 (Touchstone/Simon & Schuster 1995)
25. "New scholarship created for whites only." Associated Press/cnn.com, 2/16/2004.
26. "Bake sales used to protest affirmative action." Associated Press/cnn.com, 12/24/2003.
27. A. J. Bauer "A&M YCT creates new scholarship" *The Daily Texan,* 2/18/2004 (online ed.)
28. "Reflections on the Brain-Rotting Properties of Privilege" by Tim Wise (zmag.org)
29. Ibid.

30. Excerpt from *New York Times* interview, May 5, 2004
31. "The Hiphop Cop: A Tale of NYPD's Rap Intelligence Unit," by Dasun Allah, *Village Voice*. 4/6/2004
32."The Foreign Invasion of The American Game." Dan McGraw. VillageVoice.com,
33. "2-on-2 with Jim Gray" on ESPN. Originally aired 6/10/04.
34. "The Foreign Invasion of The American Game." Dan McGraw. VillageVoice.com, 5/28–6/3/2003
35. Ibid.
36. Ibid.
37. Ibid.
38. Excerpt from ESPN's Sunday Conversation with Charles Barkley, 2002
39. *Everything But The Burden* (essays) Greg Tate, ed. P. 245 (2003)
40. U.S. Census Bureau, 2003 study
41. Museum exhibit "The Short Century: Independence and Liberation Movements in Africa, 1945–1994" MCA in Chicago, 2000.

CHAPTER 7: Youth Marketing "What's wrong..."
Heavy D. was deeper than party and bull. Off 1994's underrated Peaceful Journey, Hev contemplates the problems of young America.
1. *Rocking The Boat* (novel), Gore Vidal (1962)
2. "A Film Called Pimp" (song) by Common & MC Lyte from Com's *Like Water for Chocolate* (MCA 2000)

CHAPTER 8: Tribes, Warlords, and Merchantnaries...
"Welcome to the world we livin' in..." Asheru & BB...Seven Heads, baby!
1. "What more can I say?" (song) Jay-Z Black Album 2003.
2. "M.E.T.H.O.D.M.A.N." (song) Method Man 1993

CHAPTER 9: Let's Build! "One for all..."
From Brand Nubian's 1990 classic LP *All For One*. Unity. Love. Power.
1. Cora Daniels, *Black Power Inc.: The New Voice of Success* (Wiley 2004)
2. Ibid.
3. "Building!" (song), Blk Sonshine featuring Masauko Chipembre (1999)

CHAPTER 10: Ante Up! "Do You Want A Revolution?!"
2000's Revolution (song) Kirk Franklin & The Nu Nation Project. (GP, are you wit me?)
1. "Get By" (song), Talib Kweli (*Quality*, 2003)
2. *Black Lies, White Lies: The Truth According to Tony Brown by Tony Brown,* p. 267 (Quill 1995)
3. *The Multicultural Economy 2004,* (a report) by The Selig Center for Economic Growth.
4. Ibid.
5. Ibid.

6. "Dead Nigga Blvd Pt. 2" liner notes, *Cookie: The Anthropological Mixtape,* Meshell Ndegeocello (2002)
   "Black Consumer Spending 2004" (study) from Target Market News: The Black Consumer
7. Internal sales data when I worked on Coca-Cola projects in 2001.
8. "Black Zombies" (song), Nas (2002)
9. *Move the Crowd,* p. 21 Gregor and Dimitri Ehrlich, (Pocket Books 1999)
10. "Mary Jane" (Remix), Mary J. Blige & LL Cool J (2000)
11. "Hiphop (It's bigger than)" (song), Dead Prez (1999)
12. "Let's Clean Up The Ghetto" (song) by The Philadelphia International All-Stars (1977)

CHAPTER 11: Boss Up "Self-sufficient, independent..."
From D-Nice (the TR-808) & the Stop The Violence Movement's 1989 classic "Self-destruction," Take control or else.
1. "I Just Wanna Love You" (song), Jay-Z w/Pharrell (2000)

CHAPTER 12: Validate Yourself "I see myself as a queen..."
From *Nature of a Sistah* (1990). Queen was about self-empowerment long before Dr. Phil.
1. "We Got Our Own Thang" (song) Heavy D. (1988)
2. Ibid.
3. "Afro Puffs" (song) Lady of Rage (1994)
4. *Mo' Money* (movie). Damon Wayans (dir.) (1992)

CHAPTER 13: Word: Life "I returned and saw..."
Ecclesiastes, the preacher was a baaad man. Life doesn't wait for business, etc.; it goes on.
1. *Steve Harvey Live...down south somewhere.* Harvey's classic comedy album (1997)
2. "The MacKenzies: Our Frazzled Family." *Ladies' Home Journal,* March 2004.
3. "The Radio Titan everyone loves to hate," by Brett Pulley, *Forbes*, Oct. 18, 2004.

Outro "Thank y'all for comin' out..."
Big Rush's HBO Def Poetry Jam sign-off. Mr. Hustler Supreme.

Peace To (Thank You's)... From Ra's partner in rhyme, Eric B. on 1987's *Paid in Full.* (Still trying to answer this one.)

Quotables "Take a phrase that's rarely heard..."
Off 1988's *Follow The Leader*. All hail the honorable microphone phenomenal. (Anyone studying 'Pac should study Rakim first.)

BONUS CHAPTERS "I will arise..."
Just getting back to the essence...

B1. Attack of the Attacking Things "As long as the differences and diversities..."
"Black Power" (essay) Dr. MLK, Jr. (1967) Prophetic.
1. *Batman* (movie) w/Jack Nicholson as The Joker (1989)
2. *Nocturnal* (album) Heltah Skeltah (1992)
B2. Back to life..."Steady, are you ready?"
From 1989's "Back To Life" (song), Soul II Soul and ProdigalPen's future.
1. "Keep On Movin'" (song) Soul II Soul (1989)

OTHER SOURCES/RECOMMENDED READING:

<u>Internet:</u>

• adage.com, adweek.com, associatedpress.com, blackelectorate.com, brandweek.com, census.gov, diversityinc.com, dol.gov (Dept. of Labor), forbes.com, fortune.com, mbnet.com, targetmearketnews.com, workplacediversity.com.

<u>Periodicals:</u>

• *Advertising Age, Adweek, Black Enterprise, Brandweek, Chicago Sun-Times, Chicago Tribune, Crain's Business, Ebony, Essence, Savoy, The Source, The Wall Street Journal, XXL.*

<u>Books:</u>

- *Black Lies, White Lies: The Truth according to Tony Brown.* By Tony Brown (Quill 1995)
- *Black Power, Inc.: The New Voice of Success* by Cora Daniels (Wiley 2004)
- *Who's Gonna Take The Weight?* By Kevin Powell (Three Rivers 2003)
- *Credit Card Nation* by Dr. Robert Manning (2002)
- *Everything But The Burden: What White People are Taking from Black Culture* edited by Greg Tate (Harlem Moon 2003)
- *Lies My Teacher Told Me: Everything Your American History Book Got Wrong* by James W. Loewen (Touchstone/Simon & Schuster 1995)
- *Move The Crowd: Voices & Faces of the Hiphop Nation* by Gregor and Dimitri Ehrlich (MTV Books 1999)
- *New York Ricans From the Hiphop Zone* by Raquel Rivera (Palgrave/Macmillian 2003)
- *The Purpose Driven Life by Rick Warren* (Zondervan 2002)
- *Soul On Ice* by Eldridge Cleaver (Delta/Random House 1964)
- *Stupid White Men* by Michael Moore (Regan Books 2001)

<u>TV:</u>

• *60 Minutes,* NBC, Fox News, C-SPAN, CNN, MSNBC broadcasts, 2000–2004.

Made You Look!
(KTH Index)

You's a slave to a page in my rhyme book.
—Nas

Bring that beat back!
Bring that beat back!
(KTH Bonus Chapters)

I will arise and go to my father...
—St. Luke 15:18

Dear Reader,

Welcome back; or in the timeless words of Teddy Riley & Guy: *Hold up, it ain't over... The party ain't over...* Anyway, just so you get a little more bang for your buck, I'm giving you three bonus chapters. (You almost have to go back to those "Choose-Your-Own-Adventure" joints to get this kind of love from a writer.)

The first, "Attack of The Attacking Things," is an ode to the future of American society. The second chapter, "A Happy Face..." explains more of what ProdigalPen is about and what I hope it will become. The third, "Workplace Mixtape," is about the lighter side of white-collar life.

Thanks again for all your support. Enjoy the bonus stuff. Until then, God bless and see you at the crossroads.

Peace,
Hadji
www.knockthehustle.com

August 2005

Attack of the Attacking Things

This is a multiracial nation where all groups are dependent on each other, whether they want to recognize it or not.
—Dr. Martin Luther King, Jr.

Originally, this chapter was called "Fear of a Black Planet" in honor of, among other things, Public Enemy's last good album. But I realized it wasn't encompassing enough. So I rolled with Ms. Jean (I'll kick a mean 16) Grae's beautifully vicious *Attack of the Attacking Things* because this chapter is about the rise of something many of us are afraid of acknowledging, nevermind embracing. (By the way, "bootleg of the bootleg" is pure jeanius.)

One day while still in my teens, my frustrated pops turned to me and said, "Son, someday you're gonna have to listen to somebody. You're going to have to consider somebody besides yourself. You'll have to follow somebody's rules; if not my rules, then *somebody's* rules..."

Right about now, America is officially as white as it'll ever get. Ever. Our current 70% Caucasian/Anglo population is shrinking. Once again, by about 2040—probably sooner—half the country will be non-white, with blacks still making up only about 15% of the new America. That means the population explosion is coming from all those shades, ethnicities, and heritages in-between. So, as little Carol Ann once warned:

Theyyyy're here.

Before you know it, every other employee, every other neighbor, every other voter, every other soldier and every other consumer will be darker than a suntan. Seasons change and autumn's just days away. And once the colors change and the leaves fall, we'll all have to listen to somebody else. In business, in society, in politics, entertainment, a people who are not white will be in charge. (It's Lou Dobbs' and Michael Savage's worst nightmare.)

No. They will talk different...dress different...think different...be different. And no matter how different they are, and no matter how uncomfortable it will make us, we will have to listen to them. We will have to follow their rules: Consider their views. Live in their neighborhoods. Adjust our perspectives and institutions for them. Measure ourselves by their ideals and their standards. We'll have to learn their language. Yep, one day we will have to listen to them.

They won't fawn over the Celebrity Couple Of The Moment. (Long live *Bennifer* and *Bradifer!)* They won't bend it like David Beckham, scream for Jude Law or Johnny Depp. Their kids won't care about TRL or WB; and they won't scream for Lindsay Lohan, Hilary Duff or Raven, or any of Disney's child-star machinations. They won't wish they had Nicole Kidman's porcelain skin, Jennifer Aniston's hair, or J. Lo's booty. They won't jock Sarah Jessica Parker's shoe game. They won't care about Beyonce's legs or Usher's abs. They won't look to Milan or Paris or NYC or LA for fashion trends. And most of *People's 50 Most Beautiful People* won't be all that cute in their eyes.

They won't be mindless SNL sycophants. They won't parrot Bill O'Reilly or Al Franken or Michael Moore or Ann Coulter. They won't be lockstep Republicrats. They'll realize that watching Jon Stewart isn't helping, either. They won't tan or Botox. They won't be sheep for Starbucks, and Pottery Barn. They won't guzzle Bud Lights while inhaling chicken fingers and Krispy Kremes. And they won't pimp their rides; in fact, they won't want anything to do with pimps, hoes 'n' such. They won't be fascinated by *The Sopranos* or *Curb Your Enthusiasm*. They won't watch *King of Queens* or any of the crap on ABC. They won't have *Scarface* or *Goodfellas* memorized. Viacom won't dictate their culture; neither will *The Source, Rolling Stone* or *Vogue.* They won't hang on Oprah or Dr. Phil's every word. They won't be glued to *Regis & Kelly*, the E! Channel or *The View.* They won't waste their days on soap operas and Reality TV. They just won't care about that stuff.

What they will care about is what matters to them, whatever that ends up being. And they'll be so entrenched in our society that we will have no choice but to care about what matters to them. Whether by plane, boat, train, foot or birth they'll come here with their culture in tact. They'll come knowing their history and heritage. We won't be able to marginalize or disenfranchise them. We'll try to, because we wouldn't be America if we didn't. But it won't work; not this time. They'll be so secure in their own skin and have such a healthy sense of self that we won't be able to break them. And they'll stand up to us, probably wave the Constitution or the Declaration in our faces and say, "Remember this? Live up to it."

So who will they be? Maybe they'll be our exploding Hispanic communities. Or Asians. Or our growing Arab and East-Indian communities. Or our growing multiracial population. For all I know "them" may simply be "us" all mature and evolved. Maybe they will be a cross-section of folks from different backgrounds and cultures who finally decide that being an American doesn't mean having to sacrifice one's cultural heritage and identity in order to be an American. I don't know. But whoever they are, one thing's for sure: they will be so fundamentally different from us that they'll scare most of us, just as "they" have scared "us" in generations past. But this time, there won't be a thing we can do about it.

Wait 'til they get a load of me.
—Jack Nicholson[1]

So what does any of this have to do with business? Everything. For starters, they'll make up the bulk of the workforce. We'll have to hire these folks whether we want to or not. They'll be qualified and educated. They'll be our coworkers. And furthermore, they'll be our bosses; they'll own businesses that will thrive when most of ours fail. They will also be our educators and doctors. They will be our neighbors. They will be our biggest target audience. And as businesses and marketers we won't get away with ignoring them, offending them or "misunderstanding" them. There'll be too many of them with too much spending power and too much "I'd-rather-do-without-than-be-done-wrong" attitude, for that. And if we don't adapt to them, our businesses won't struggle, they will die.

Additionally, my guess is whoever this new group ends up being, they will demand that marketers speak to them as human beings and respect them as collectives without co-opting their culture. The only thing they'll let us take from them is their money; and that will only be in exchange for quality products and services. Yep, business will have to listen. And for that matter, so will our government. And when I say, "listen" I mean *a-president-who-isn't-white-or-a-puppet-for-the-elite* listen.

Yep, I've said it once, I'll say it again: Business is first and foremost about people. And the one thing I've learned in business is this: Corporate America still don't know snot about people. But lucky for us, the new people know. And soon as they get here, they'll show us; they will show us all.

And this time, we will listen.

Here we come...Here we come...
—*Heltah Skeltah*[2]

Back To Life...

Steady, are you ready?
—Soul II Soul

Overall, the publishing industry is hustle. The big boys lock down the major bookstore retailers, tie-up the distribution lines, and keep most critics and reviewers in their back-pockets. That way, when an author wants to play ball, it's on their turf, on their terms.

Example: The typical author deal is around 8–15%, depending on genre and name recognition. Why so low? Because the publishers say so. And since they're holding all the cards, they lean on authors even more: *Rewrite this... Change that... Make the ending "happier"... Just follow our lead and we'll make you the new Clancy or Grisham or Sedaris...* Before you know it, you're stuck with a book that's nothing like what you wrote and a publisher patting you on the head and putting you on a plane to sell it to America—for your cut of around 11 cents on the dollar.

And just as music artists owe labels, you, the author, owe your publisher all sorts of "recoupables": writer's advances, travel expenses, promo/reviewer copies, editor fees, marketing/PR, etc. But if the book sucks, the critics and readers won't blame your publisher, they'll blame you. But I'm supposed to give some pulp-pimp 90 cents of my dollar? Nah. Game recognizes game, and I saw 'em all coming...

So What Exactly is ProdigalPen?

The foundation of ProdigalPen is St. Luke 15. In part, it tells of the Prodigal Son—this kid who got greedy enough, selfish enough, and shortsighted enough to lose his way in the world. After some wild and reckless living, he realizes he's lost. He's broke. He's alone. And worse yet, he's empty. He realizes he's been living for all the wrong things. All he has left in him was the desire to find his way back home where he hoped that maybe he could be forgiven. And so his journey begins...

So what exactly is ProdigalPen?

The foundation of ProdigalPen is St. Luke 15. In part, it tells of the Prodigal Son—this kid who got greedy enough, selfish enough, and shortsighted enough to lose his way in the world. After some wild and reckless living, he realizes he's lost. He's broke. He's alone. And worse yet, he's empty. He realizes he's been living for all the wrong things. All he has left in him was the desire to find his way back home where he hoped that maybe he could be forgiven. And so his journey begins...

For the longest time, I only wrote for things: Clients. Media. Profit. I basically pimped my pen for whatever and whoever seemed good at the time. Even when I was giving my ink away, I still felt like it wasn't right. I felt like I was missing something. A while back I realized what it was.

Before now, I'd never really written anything for God. I don't mean like trying to so some crazy religious stuff. I just mean that everything I ever wrote was about putting money in somebody's pocket or stroking my own ego. I just wasn't using my pen right. Now I'm trying to change that.

ProdigalPen is about trying to get right, reflection and exploration, all sorts of good stuff...Nothing's off limits.

The Future? The Future of ProdigalPen...

ProdigalPen will be busy these next few miles—mostly non-fiction: essays, anthologies, and poetry, plus a spoken-word album or two. We also plan on flipping the occasional T-shirt and poster.

But regardless of the form, every drop of blood, sweat, and ink will be dedicated to The Journey: finding good in this world and getting back home. We'll walk thru the fun parts, the hard parts, and the ugly parts. The "real-life" parts. The "real-soul" parts. The "honest-struggle" parts. The "dilemma-and-drama" parts. The forks in roads and which road will get you back home parts.

Now relax; you won't catch me dipped in bougie'd-up linens and sandals, playing some urbanized Dr. Phil or some neo-soulified business guru. I am not the black Tony Robbins or some bootleg Creflo Dollar. There will be no "build-a-better-employee" seminars. No team-building retreats. No "finding-your-spirit" speeches. Nope, I refuse to go out like that.

The last thing folks need is another speechmaker. Between Reality TV and all the talk shows, everyone's flapping their gums. And most are talking loud but sayin' nothing. *Knock The Hustle* is about each individual taking action and responsibility for themselves, their careers, and their communities. You can do that without me.

Personally, I'm focusing on my journey and helping folks along the way. And as you can see from this book, I plan on raising some hell in the process. The areas I grew up in are still falling apart. Our schools still ain't teaching. People like me are still dying over nothing and living like their tomorrow has already come and gone. Businessfolks and people in general just aren't cool toward each other about much of anything anymore. The way I see it, we're all in need of a journey.

So far as I'm concerned, it's time to stop and find the way home. It's time to find ourselves, reclaim our souls, reclaim our lives, and find Christ. That's the journey I'm talking about. Hopefully we can keep each other company along the way. And like I said earlier, whether I sell a million books or end up slinging packages for UPS, The Journey is officially on. And I'm going to write until my pen runs dry and walk until I can't go any further.

Until then, hit me at: publisher@prodigalpen.com. See you at the crossroads.

Keep on movin'... don't stop, no!
—Soul II Soul[1]

The Workplace Mixtape

Bonus Cuts for the People

Lemme clear my throat!
—DJ Kool

Welcome to the Workplace Mixtape. Again, I want to thank you for making it this far, figuratively and literally. This was a hard journey for me and I'm glad you took it with me. Hopefully you'll put this book down feeling inspired, focused, and empowered to knock the hustle. Thanks again.

Now For this chapter, I dug through the crates of my lighter business experiences. This is a collection of miscellaneous observations, rants, and suggestions for better corporate living. It's a little funny, a little rude, but it's all true and worth sharing. So press play and nod your head to the beat:

33 1/3rd

Back in college I knew this cat—a part-time fireman. After graduation, he went into marketing. He told me that while his occupation had changed, his job stayed the same-putting out fires. A third of his day, he figured was wasted on non-emergencies, office politics, panicky clients, computer glitches, and other nonsense.

"A third of every day," he'd sigh.

For years I saw it firsthand: 33$^1/_3$ of the average corporate workday is wasted. Now some of your day is spent on actual work. Some of it is spent prepping to do actual work. But I don't care if you're an accountant, a sales rep, an ad exec, a lawyer, or an insert-occupation here, I can all but guarantee you that a good 33% of the average corporate worker's day is wasted on nonsense. Sometimes it's self-inflicted; sometimes it's colleague-driven; sometimes it's boss/client-caused. But a third of most every workday is nonsense.

VPs are not Mardi-Gras beads

So what's the deal, if you flash a boss, you get a VP title? Remember when being "vice-president" meant something? Yep, me neither. VP used to mean you were a heart attack or two away from becoming CEO. But these days most VP titles are like a tattoo—everybody's got one; and depending on where you get yours, you'll regret it later.

Bosses:

If everyone's a VP, then being a VP is worthless. Here's a rule: If you can field a softball team with your VPs, you have too many. Extra titles mean extra attitudes, extra layers, and extra drama. If one VP is good enough for Uncle Sam, then one (three at most) should be good enough for your company.

Workers:

If your company offers you a VP slot because they can't afford to give you a raise (or won't give you a raise without it) then you can't afford to be a VP there. Throw a "veep" on your resume too soon and you're looking at downward and lateral moves for years to come.

Stoopid people hate laces.

Now I'm not sure when I noticed the correlation, but I did and it's real. Stoopid people don't like shoelaces. Next time a colleague/client says or does something stupid check their shoes. Chances are they're wearing loafers, slip-ons, flats, etc. Stoopid folks just don't wear laces very often.

Tying your shoe is a simple task but if you don't do it, you'll slip. Listening and thinking before you speak are also simple tasks, but if you don't do 'em you'll slip. Stoopid people always sleep on the simple things.

Strictly Business, Never Personal

Besides EPMD, I never heard the phrase, "it's just business" until I hit the business world; then I heard it at least once a day. And it always felt like it was a prayer for forgiveness or a rationale for sin. Whenever someone got screwed out of a promotion, sold harmful products, lied, or did any dirt under the sun "it's just business" was the official cause. After a few years, I realized, "it's just business," was really just hustler/pimp talk for "Everyone for themselves, no holds barred."

Word is life. We manifest what we speak. Tell lies and you'll start to live them-or at least live with their consequences. Call something ugly and soon you'll treat it as if it is. If you say it's just business long enough you'll believe it and everything you do will become just business. And in business nothing matters but money. (It's no accident that businesspeople tend to have the worst personal relationships and lead some of the most stressed out lives.) So next time you say, "it's just business," recognize what you're actually saying and understand what it really means.

Less ego-trippin'

I used to hit a lot of corporate parties; some were built around industry awards, emerging trends, celebrity speakers, etc. Others were just social functions and networking ops. But they all had one thing in common: *Big. Huge. Egos.*

After a few years of conferences, parties, and industry watering holes, I just couldn't take it anymore. It always cracked me up to see businesspeople, 99.5% of whom the average person has never heard of and couldn't pick out of a lineup, prance around like off-brand superstars. Some strutted around like they were waiting for VH-1's *Best Week Ever* crew to critique their outfits. (And it didn't help that there was usually trade press on hand to stroke their mini-me egos.)

We know Jack Welch, Donald Trump, Warren Buffett, etc., but the other 99.9% of these legend-in-their-own-minds really need to get over themselves. Most folks don't understand Corporate America enough to worship those in it, especially those of us in the marketing and advertising industries. If you told the average person Donny Deutsch was a standup comic and Omnicom was a pharmaceutical company or that Crispin &

Porter was a brokerage firm, they'd believe you. At the end of the day, we're all just working stiffs-some of us are a little stiffer, some of us work a little harder, some make a little more loot.

I say, until you cure AIDS or catch Bin Laden show some humility. Okay?

Lose the ho's uniform

I'd like to take this time to thank 85% of my female colleagues for giving me 15 years of intentionally overexposed cleavage. I'd like to thank you for the countless too-perky-for-work nipple shows courtesy of your too-sheer-for-work tops. Thanks for the endless thong-teases from your shake-whatcha-momma-gave-you slacks and jeans. Thank you attending client meetings in your stripper/"last call" skirts. And lastly, thank you for the weekly camel-toe parades, often courtesy of Casual Fridays. Thanks, ladies; thank you one and all.

Over the years I've heard every excuse under the sun for the crap women wear to work: *"It's my body... How I dress has nothing to do with my ability..."* Yap-yap-yap. Ladies: Spit out the feminist kool-aid. If you flash your headlights hitchhikers will want a ride. Whoa, not so fast, fellas: I know you've been lifting all winter and you're just dying to flex your BowFlex bodies, but save the muscle-shirts, etc. for the nightclubs. Now you don't necessarily need a closet full of button-ups, but business is for adults—dress like one.

You may not be a ho,
but you are wearing the "ho's uniform."
—Dave Chappelle

Polishing Turds

Polishing turds... One of many phrases I never heard until I hit Corporate America. First time I heard it was from some older execs decompressing from a bad client meeting. Polishing turds. It's what folks say when they have to make a bad idea or a bad product look good. Business, especially marketing, is filled with turd-polishing. And believe me, I've spit-shined my fair share.

There are two kinds of turds: the Baby Turd and the Caterpillar Turd. The Baby Turd is a bad idea that was bad right out the gate; and no matter how much it gets tweaked and refined it never gets any better. But for some reason, a boss or a client likes it, so it lives. Conversely, the Caterpillar Turd always starts out good, sometimes brilliant. But somewhere along the way it gets mobbed by meddlers, CYAers, and folks who have no business being in business. And before you know it, the Caterpillar morphs into a turd.

So how do you avoid polishing turds? Upfront honesty. When a turd comes your way say, *"No, this idea is so bad I refuse to be a part of it."* And once you say no, offer something better. Otherwise, get out your rag and start polishing.

If there's one thing great advertising can do
it's help bad products fail faster.
—Bill Bernbach

What's your 6:20?

Remember "Monty"? Monty's daily goal was to catch the 6:20 p.m. train. That train represented his life outside of work. He always wanted to get home to his family, especially his wife, whom I believe was pregnant at the time. His 6:20 train helped him maintain his perspective.

What's your 6:20? What's your life outside of work? What truly makes you happy? Whatever it is find it and never let it go. And again, don't work for anyone who says work is more important than your 6:20. Because the only reason they'll ever say that is because they don't have one and they just want you to be a soft workaholic right along with them.

Angel Investors

I can remember leaving J. Walter Thompson Chicago one day... I was heading home completely dejected-I didn't get the job. It was interview number lost-count-after-63 and now I was alone on an elevator going down. I was broke; flat-out, all-I-had-came-from-my-folks broke. My bank account was literally in the negatives. Credit card companies were calling daily. And I was tired of writing cover letters, tired of running to Kinko's for fresh resumes, tired of putting on suits and smiles just to be told "no" by someone who somebody else had said "yes" to. Yup, I was beyond tired.

Then this non-descript lady in a business suit gets on. We'd never seen each other in life and I really wasn't in a talking mood. I don't even think I acknowledged her presence. Then out of nowhere, for no good reason at all, she looks over at me and says, "Don't give up. I know it's hard but keep trying; you'll make it." She didn't say another word after that, not a peep. Then she got off the elevator like two floors later and vanished.

I was shocked. I swear I didn't know her, she didn't know me. *Don't give up.* When she said that, I just felt like, I dunno… It just hit me. I felt like God was sending me some encouragement. I really felt like He sent an angel to keep me going.

I got a job a few months later, mainly because I didn't quit looking and she was a big reason why I kept looking. *Don't give up…* To this day I can't tell you what she looked like, but I'll never forget her.

Don't Be Blinded By Your Blessings

We are all connected-every community, every culture, every country, every business, every person. The problems of one eventually become the problems of all. If the folks in the cubicles are mad, the execs are next. If one area is suffering, other areas will follow. If one group is struggling, eventually every group will suffer.

Don't assume that because all is well in one department or for one fiscal year that all is well everywhere or will continue to be well. Be humble, be grateful, but always be about constant improvement and collective growth. Have vision.

As a man once said, *There but for the grace of God go I.*

Sorry, I already gave at the office.

About the Author

A Chicago native, Hadji J.S. Williams is a 15-year veteran of Corporate America. He produced his first ad when he was 19—it was a billboard honoring MLK, Jr. for *Chicago Tribune,* which ran during Black History Month back in 1990. Since then, as a copywriter then as a brand consultant, Hadji has helped shape some of America's top brands including: Aleve, Bank of America, Cingular Wireless, Coca-Cola, Ford Motors, Mercedes Benz, Radio Shack, SBC, and the William Wrigley Co., just to name a few. But his business career couldn't have been more opposite from his upbringing.

Born to hardworking parents, Hadji was raised on the South and West sides of Chicago in what is commonly known as "the 'hood." While his family was stable, his neighborhoods were anything but. Typical inner-city pitfalls such as drugs, gangs, police, and random violence were common. But it was precisely this rich yet precarious environment tempered by his deep Christian faith that helped Hadji develop his unique business acumen, creativity, and powers of observation and problem-solving.

Once he made it to Corporate America, Hadji began to recognize striking parallels between the streets and the suites. "I saw pimps and hustlers in the streets just about every day. Once I began working with Fortune 500 clients and blue-chip brands, it was more of the same—only at work the rules and the players were a little more sophisticated." It was Hadji's ability to balance urban and mainstream life plus his faith that gave birth to *Knock The Hustle.*

Now, officially "out the game—this time for good," Hadji is an author, poet, teacher, and contributing writer to a variety of urban publications and hiphop websites. And as founder of ProdigalPen, Inc., he continues to dodge what he calls, "the long arm of The Hustle." On occasion, he shares his expertise and insights with select companies, professionals, and students looking to get out from under and live more prosperous, hustle-free lives.

You can reach him at: author@knockthehustle.com.

ProdigalPen, Inc. Quick Order Form

Online Orders: www.knockthehustle.com
Mail Orders: ProdigalPen, Inc.
PO Box 236
3023 North Clark St.
Chicago Illinois 60657

Payment Options (select one)
VISA ___MasterCard___AMEX_____Discover_____
Check:____ Money Order:_____
(Please make all checks/money orders payable to ProdigalPen, Inc.)

Card No: ____

Name (as appears on card): ______________________Exp: __________

Signature: ____________________________Date: ______________

Qty: ______ Sub Total: ______________________________
($24.95 per book)
Add $4.95 per book for Shipping/Handling): __________
(All orders shipped UPS/USPS)
Sales Tax: __________
(Illinois residents please add $2.85 per book)
Total: __________

[Corporate and Academic discounts available. See website for details.]

Billing Address Information:

Name: ____
Address: ____
City/State/Zip: ____________________________________
Email address: _____________________________________

Shipping Address (if different from billing address):

Name: ____
Address: ____
City/State/Zip: ____________________________________
Mail address: ______________________________________

Please send FREE information on:
❒ Future ProdigalPen Releases ❒ PP/KTH Merchandise ❒ KTH Consulting

Strange game…
The only winning move is not to play.
—Joshua

For God sent not his Son into the world to condemn the world,
but that the world, through Him, might be saved.
—John 3:17